PENGUIN BUSINESS

MANAGEMENT AND MOTIVATION

Victor H. Vroom is John G. Searle Professor of Organization and Management at Yale University. Considered an international expert on leadership and decision-making, he came to Yale in 1972 as Chairman of the Department of Administrative Sciences and Associate Director of the Institution for Social and Policy Studies. When the School of Management was founded in 1976, Professor Vroom was named to its original board of permanent officers. As a teacher and researcher, he has focused on the psychological analysis of behaviour in organizations. He is the author of several books and over fifty articles. His 1964 book *Work and Motivation* is regarded as a landmark in that field and his 1973 volume *Leadership and Decision Making* is widely cited as a breakthrough in the study of leadership in formal organizations. His latest book is *The New Leadership*, published in 1988.

A native of Canada, Professor Vroom received his BS and MA degrees in psychology from McGill University in 1953 and 1955. After receiving his Ph.D. in psychology from the University of Michigan in 1958, he was named Study Director in Michigan's Institute for Social Research and lecturer in psychology. He later served as Assistant Professor of Psychology at the University of Pennsylvania and Associate Professor of Psychology at the Carnegie Institute of Technology. In 1966, he was named Professor of Psychology and Industrial Administration at Carnegie–Mellon's Graduate School of Administration. Professor Vroom has been elected president of the Society of Industrial and Organizational Psychology and is a Fellow of the American Psychological Society. He has been a consultant to several major corporations, including General Electric, Bell Labs, GTE and American Express.

Edward L. Deci is Professor of Psychology and Director of the Human Motivation Program at the University of Rochester, New York. He holds a Ph.D. in psychology from the Carnegie–Mellon University and has also studied at the University of Pennsylvania, University of London, Hamilton College and Stanford University, where he was an interdisciplinary post-doctoral fellow.

Professor Deci has done research on many aspects of human motivation and is author of the following books: *Intrinsic Motivation* (1975), *The Psychology of Self-Determination* (1980), *Intrinsic Motivation and Self-Determination in Human Behaviour* (1985) and *Why We Do What We Do* (1995). He is a fellow of the American Psychological Association and a member of many other professional associations, and has lectured and consulted for universities, public school systems, corporations and mental health agencies throughout the world. He also has a private practice in psychotherapy.

MANAGEMENT AND MOTIVATION
Selected Readings

SECOND EDITION

EDITED BY
VICTOR H. VROOM AND
EDWARD L. DECI

PENGUIN BOOKS

PENGUIN BOOKS

Published by the Penguin Group
Penguin Books Ltd, 27 Wrights Lane, London W8 5TZ, England
Penguin Books USA Inc., 375 Hudson Street, New York, New York 10014, USA
Penguin Books Australia Ltd, Ringwood, Victoria, Australia
Penguin Books Canada Ltd, 10 Alcorn Avenue, Toronto, Ontario, Canada M4V 3B2
Penguin Books (NZ) Ltd, 182–190 Wairau Road, Auckland 10, New Zealand

Penguin Books Ltd, Registered Offices: Harmondsworth, Middlesex, England

First published in Penguin Education 1970
Reprinted in Penguin Books 1989
Second edition 1992
3 5 7 9 10 8 6 4

The acknowledgements on pp. 482–3 constitute an extension of this copyright page

The moral right of the editors has been asserted

Filmset in 9/11 pt Monophoto Times New Roman
Printed in England by Clays Ltd, St Ives plc

Contents

PART B: MOTIVATION IN WORK SETTINGS

Section IV: Motivation, Satisfaction, and Performance: Persons and Contexts

Section V: Making the Job More Motivating

Section IX: Organization Change and Development

Introduction to the Second Edition

More than twenty years have passed since Penguin published the first edition of this book. During that time the field of human motivation in the workplace has matured as an area of academic inquiry and has continued to be informed both by basic research on human motivation and by the exploration of complex interpersonal dynamics in organizational settings. This increase in scientific knowledge, while impressive in its own right, is dwarfed by the explosion of managerial interest in the topic. Spurred by global competition and the consequent quest for ever more efficient utilization of organizations' human resources, managers have turned to motivational concepts for ideas on how to increase productivity. Books and journals on management abound with terms such as quality circles, self-managing work groups, high-performance work teams, and high-involvement management, all of which have important motivational components or consequences. The current volume, like its predecessor, seeks to put those ideas into perspective for the serious student or manager.

First, let us attempt to clarify the elusive concept of motivation as it applies to work performance. Imagine observing a group of persons performing the same job. You would undoubtedly note that some do it better than others, whether the group consists of secretaries, clerks, assemblers, salespersons, middle managers, or corporate executives. If you had some quantitative measure of their contribution to the organization, you would probably find that the best person in each group is contributing two, five, or perhaps ten times what the poorest is contributing. Such observations raise two interrelated questions of both psychological and managerial interest; namely, what are the causes of these differences in performance, and how can these causes be influenced by people in positions of responsibility?

One approach to answering the questions suggests that the performance differences reflect varying abilities or skills on the part of individual workers. People have different innate potentials, and they also vary in the degree to which they possess the necessary endowments for learning from their varied experiences. This approach to understanding the issue of performance differences underscores the importance of ensuring a high level of appropriate skills within the organization. There are three different types of organizational strategies for ensuring appropriate skill level. First, one can *select* people who have the abilities or skills that are necessary for effective performance on a particular job. Second, one can *train* people in the skills that are requisite for their jobs. Finally, one can *design jobs* to make them consistent with the existing skill levels of their incumbents or of the labor force more generally.

There is, however, another approach to answering the questions about performance differentials among people doing the same kind of work, and this approach le ds to somewhat different organizational strategies for improving job performance. The approach of which we now speak suggests that differences in performance among people doing the same kind of work reflect differences in their motivation. At any given point in time, people vary in the extent to which they are willing to direct their energies toward the attainment of organizational objectives. There have been varied views on how best to affect people's motivation, and these have led to different management strategies for improving employees' performance. Among the strategies have been incentive pay structures, changes in other aspects of the work context (e.g., benefit plans), the redesign of jobs to make them more motivating, and leadership training programs aimed at teaching managers to facilitate the motivation of their subordinates.

It is now quite clear that each of these approaches – the abilities approach and the motivation approach – captures a piece of the truth. The performance of a person on a job has been shown repeatedly to be a function of both the person's abilities and his or her motivation to use those abilities in the effective performance of the job.

In a similar vein, let us consider not individuals but rather work groups, or even organizations, that differ in their effectiveness and productivity. Depending on the size and nature of the groups or organizations, one might seek explanations for performance differences in technology, organizational structure, or access to raw materials and distribution channels. Such factors are undoubtedly important, but they should not cause us to overlook differences in the abilities and talents of the people in those groups or organizations or, even more importantly for our present discussion, differences in the degree to which managers of the groups or organizations have been successful in motivating the members.

It is the variables related to motivation that are the basic concern of this book. The problem of motivating employees is as old as organized activity itself, but only within the last half century has the scientific method been brought to bear on its solution. In this relatively short period of time we have witnessed attempts to apply the conceptual and methodological tools of the behavioral sciences, particularly psychology, to the relation between people's motivation and performance and to the managerial issues involved with that relationship.

Awareness of the importance of motivational factors in the workplace was greatly influenced by a set of classic experiments performed in the Hawthorne Plant of the Western Electric Company during the 1930s (cf. Roethlisberger & Dickson, 1939). Conducted under the leadership of the Australian psychologist Elton Mayo, then a professor at the Harvard Business School, these famous 'Hawthorne experiments' are regarded by most scholars as the first systematic effort to understand work motivation and to search for effective ways of managing it.

At about the same time that Mayo was directing the Hawthorne experiments from his office at 'the B School', another important research operation was underway on the other side of the Charles River. Using an elaborate interview procedure, Henry Murray, a psychology professor at Harvard, was exploring the dimensions of human motivation and summarizing that work in a landmark book on personality (Murray, 1938). His work and that of his successors, like McClelland (e.g., McClelland & Burnham, 1976, Reading 19) and White (1959, Reading 3), have also had a tremendous influence on our understanding of motivation in the workplace, even though Murray and Mayo represented two very different traditions. The former was an academic psychologist interested in the basic motivational processes of individual behavior, while the latter was an applied psychologist whose primary concern was the process of management.

Working in the same tradition as Murray, also in the 1930s and 1940s, people like Maslow (1943) and Lewin (1938) also focused attention on explicating the nature of human needs and goal-setting processes. Although these and other academic psychologists carried out some of their work in industrial settings, their principal purpose was to clarify motivational concepts and test hypothesized relations among those concepts.

Upholding the tradition of Mayo, on the other hand, have been scholars such as Argyris (1964; see also Reading 41), McGregor (1960; see also Reading 32), Likert (1961; see also Reading 33), and Bennis (1966), each of whom was dedicated to improving the practice of management and therefore employed the concepts and findings of academic psychologists, to the extent they were useful, toward that end.

In the early days of the quest to understand motivation in the workplace, there was little exchange between these two traditions. If Mayo knew about the work of Murray, or of Lewin, who was only a couple of miles away at MIT, it is not clear from his writings. Similarly, there is no evidence that Murray or Lewin was influenced by the work of Mayo. It was therefore quite noteworthy that in 1960 McGregor, in his now classic book *The Human Side of Enterprise*, brought the two traditions together by basing his theories of management very heavily on the motivational theory of Maslow (1943, Reading 2).

Now, half a century after Murray and Mayo published their influential findings, and three decades after McGregor's book, there is substantially greater interchange between the motivation theorist and the management theorist. Academic disciplines like organizational behavior and fields of professional practice like organization development have arisen out of this interchange, and they have blurred the boundaries that separated their intellectual forefathers. The present volume reflects this strengthening partnership and the changing nature of the field. Still, one can see representative contributions from the tradition of academic psychology and the tradition of management theory, as well as those that have emerged from the melding of traditions.

This book is divided into three parts, in line with the above discussion. The first part emphasizes contributions that have come from areas of basic psychology – personality, learning, and social psychology. The introductory essay to that part describes and organizes the history of psychologists' efforts to understand basic processes of human motivation. The perspectives of pioneering theorists such as Skinner (1953; see also Reading 1), Hull (1943), Lewin (1938), Freud (1923/1962), and Murray (1938) are compared and contrasted, and the relevance of their ideas for understanding management issues is discussed. It is concluded that the theories which emphasize either psychological needs or goal-directed behavior are most directly relevant, so the readings of Part A emphasize these viewpoints. However, the operant, reinforcement perspective has also been applicable to organizational behavior, so it too is represented in the readings of that part. Finally, the effects of group and social influences on the motivation of behavior, effects that have been explicated by experimental social psychologists, are judged to be important for understanding work behavior, so the third section of Part A comprises representative readings from this tradition within academic psychology.

Part B of the book consists primarily of the work of industrial and organizational psychologists who have done motivation research within work settings. This work represents a clear melding of academic psychology and management, for it utilizes the methods of research psychologists to explore motivational processes in work environments. These writings could be characterized either as the study of social-personality psychology within organizational settings, or, alternatively, as the study of human behavior in organizations using a motivational perspective.

In the final part of this volume, Part C, we follow the tradition of scholars like Mayo by adopting a perspective that is even more clearly managerial. Part C focuses on general management theories and on the implicit motivational underpinnings of these approaches. However, instead of beginning with motivational concepts and looking to organizations as proving grounds for the theories, as an academic psychologist would do, we begin with the theories of management and ask about their motivational components. It should become clear from the readings that each theorist had a clear viewpoint about human behavior (whether explicit or implicit), for the motivational assumptions are quite easily discernible.

The introductory essay of Part C compares and contrasts the important historical works of people such as Taylor (1911, Reading 30), Mayo (1945), and McGregor (1960; see also Reading 32). It also considers the theories and applications that have become central to the field in the last few years. Concepts such as contingency theories of leadership (e.g., Vroom & Jago, 1988; see also Reading 38) and Japanese management (e.g., Ouchi, 1981; Marsland & Beer, 1983, Reading 35) are considered, as is the field of organization change and development (Section IX).

Many of the readings in this edition have been published since the first edition appeared in 1970, although we have retained several of the classics that appeared in the first edition. It is important to recognize while considering these earlier works that they are not only of historical significance but also represent viewpoints that continue to be pertinent today.

Readers of this collection should not expect to find a single perspective represented here, or even an integrated set of concepts and ideas. The perspectives represented in the various readings are quite diverse, and they present different sides of important controversies. None the less, there are at least two themes that do emerge. The first pertains to the view that human behavior is goal-directed (e.g., Vroom, 1964; see also Latham & Locke, 1979, Reading 16) and that work settings will be more motivating when they are instrumental for goal attainment and need satisfaction. The second concerns the implications for job design and management practices of the fact that human behavior can be intrinsically as well as extrinsically motivated (e.g., Deci, 1975; see also White, 1959, Reading 3).

It is our hope that readers of this volume will gain important insights into the central issues in the broad field of motivation and management from these writings by many leading figures in the field. More importantly, though, we hope that the volume will stimulate you to participate in the lively debates represented by the readings we have selected.

REFERENCES

Argyris, C. (1964), *Integrating the Individual and the Organization*, New York: Wiley.

Bennis, W. G. (1966), *Changing Organizations*, New York: McGraw-Hill.

Deci, E. L. (1975), *Intrinsic Motivation*, New York: Plenum.

Freud, S. (1962), *The Ego and the Id*, New York: Norton. (Originally published 1923.)

Hull, C. L. (1943), *Principles of Behavior: An Introduction to Behavior Theory*, New York: Appleton-Century-Crofts.

Lewin, K. (1938), *The Conceptual Representation and the Measurement of Psychological Forces*, Durham NC: Duke University Press.

Likert, R. (1961), *New Patterns of Management*, New York: McGraw-Hill.

McClelland, D. C., & Burnham, D. H. (1976), 'Power is the great motivator', *Harvard Business Review*, *54*, 100–110.

McGregor, D. (1960), *The Human Side of Enterprise*, New York: McGraw-Hill.

Marsland, S., & Beer, M. (1983), 'The evolution of Japanese management: Lessons for US managers', *Organizational Dynamics*, *11* (3), 49–67.

Maslow, A. H. (1943), 'A theory of human motivation', *Psychological Review*, *50*, 370–96.

Mayo, E. (1945), *The Social Problems of an Industrial Civilization*, Cambridge, Mass.: Harvard University Press.

Murray, H. A. (1938), *Explorations in Personality*, New York: Oxford University Press.

Ouchi, W. G. (1981), *Theory Z*, Reading, Mass.: Addison-Wesley.

Roethlisberger, F. J., & Dickson, W. J. (1939), *Management and the Worker*, Cambridge, Mass.: Harvard University Press.

Skinner, B. F. (1953), *Science and Human Behavior*, New York: Macmillan.

Taylor, F. W. (1911), *Principles of Scientific Management*, New York: Harper.

Vroom, V. H. (1964), *Work and Motivation*, New York: Wiley.

Vroom, V. H., & Jago, A. G. (1988), *The New Leadership: Managing Participation in Organizations*, Englewood Cliffs, NJ: Prentice Hall.

White, R. W. (1959), 'Motivation reconsidered: The concept of competence', *Psychological Review*, *66*, 297–333.

PART A

Understanding Human Motivation

EDWARD L. DECI

The History of Motivation in Psychology and Its Relevance for Management

The word motivation is ubiquitous in the conversations of people such as managers who are in positions of authority. It seems to be used most often in reference to subordinates when they do not live up to their managers' expectations, and it typically conveys the manager's desire to change the subordinate's behavior.

For psychologists, the term motivation is concerned with three fundamental questions related to behavior regulation: what energizes action; how action is directed; and to what extent action is under voluntary control. Thus, although the field of motivation is concerned with the regulation and change of behavior, it goes deeper to consider the very nature of human beings. By exploring people's basic motivational processes, we can gain a fuller understanding of human beings while accumulating information that is relevant both to changing their behavior and to creating the circumstances within which they will change their own behavior if it is advantageous for them to do so.

This essay will consider the issues of behavior regulation and change by reviewing the history of relevant theories from the diverse areas of learning, social psychology, and personality and by assessing the applicability of these theories to organizational practices and prescriptions.

Five different clusters of theories will be addressed, and the work of the pioneering psychological theorists within each cluster will be highlighted. The first four clusters have been organized around the type of concept that is at the core of the theories. The four organizing concepts are: responses, physiological needs, goals, and psychological needs. The fifth cluster is defined by the idea that behavior is influenced by social forces. Although most of the 'mini-theories' that comprise the fifth group are not explicitly motivational, they are directly relevant to an understanding of human motivation in organizations. We now consider each of the five clusters in turn.

RESPONSES

Some theories have focused on responses (i.e., specific behaviors) that occur in the presence of some stimulus or contingency of reinforcement and whose rate of emission can be observed and recorded. Skinner (1953; see Reading 1) has been the most prominent spokesman for this approach, which has its roots in the work of Watson (1913) and Thorndike (1913). Derived from Thorndike's Law of Effect, the central principle in Skinner's operant theory states that when responses are reinforced their rate of occurrence will increase and when they are punished their rate of occurrence will decrease.

The concept of reinforcement is defined in terms of operationally separable consequences of a response which, if administered immediately after the response, will increase its strength (or rate) of occurrence. In practice, the concept of reinforcement is commonly interpreted to mean material rewards and praise (i.e., verbal reinforcements), so these are advocated for increasing desired behaviors. Although it is widely recognized that punishments decrease the rate of a responding, Skinner has demonstrated that punishments are less reliable than rewards for achieving desired behavior change and that they often have disruptive emotional side-effects.

Skinner's theory, which is the prototypic theory of behavior control, does not have an explicit motivational (or energizing) component. The concept of reinforcement is implicitly motivational, though Skinner did not relate reinforcements, as functionally defined, to any internal condition of the organism. Thus, he did not address *why* something reinforces, only *that* it reinforces. In operant experiments, with rats, monkeys and pigeons, food and water have frequently been used as reinforcers, and the researchers have ensured that these substances would reinforce by depriving the animals for several hours prior to the experiments. Still, the reinforcement value of a substance was never theoretically tied to an underlying drive such as hunger or thirst; indeed, operant theorists continually asserted that it is not necessary to resort to the use of these internal variables to predict or control behavior.

In operant theory, the issue of how behavior is directed, and thus the issue of how behavior is controlled, is addressed in terms of reinforcements. People are said to engage in behaviors because they were reinforced in the *past* (*not* because they expect to be reinforced in the *future*) and because some stimulus (properly called a contingency of reinforcement) is currently present. From this, one can readily see that in operant theory behaviors are not considered to be voluntarily regulated.

Instead they are controlled by reinforcement histories and contingencies – both of which are in (or derived from) the environment.

Operant theory, which is the theoretical basis for work in behavior modification, has been very prominent in psychology and has been frequently applied in organizational settings (see Hamner, 1974, Reading 4). This is undoubtedly because it provides a simple and straightforward prescription for changing behavior – namely, change the reinforcement contingencies. Although the theory is often misinterpreted and poorly employed, it has made two significant contributions to applied psychology that are important for the practice of management. The first is that behavior can be much more effectively controlled by reinforcing desired behaviors than by punishing undesired ones: praise works better than criticism. And, second, if reinforcements (rewards) are to work effectively, they need to be given for specific behaviors in such a way that the reinforcements are tied directly to the behaviors (for example, by giving them immediately after the behaviors are emitted). Giving rewards prior to a response or independent of the response is not effective as a reinforcement strategy.

Scientific Management (Taylor, 1911, Reading 30), which is closely related to the idea of Theory X Management (McGregor, 1960, Reading 32), has been extremely influential in American organizations during most of this century. It is based on the notion that the planning and doing of a job should be separated – that managers should make the decisions and subordinates should carry them out. In this approach, piece-rate payments, where one's pay is a direct function of one's output, are used to control the subordinates' behavior (i.e., to ensure that they carry out the managers' plans and decisions). Thus the motivational underpinnings of Scientific Management are quite consistent with operant theory: rewards (i.e., reinforcements) are administered to strengthen the desired responses.

Although operant theory, and its application through practices such as piece-rate payments, has had an enormous impact on both experimental and applied psychology, there are at least three considerations that question its validity and limit its utility: first, to the extent that reinforcements do control behavior, it is not clear whether it is past reinforcements or expectations about future reinforcements that are determinative (e.g., Rotter, 1954); second, the theory fails altogether to recognize a class of potent motivators referred to as intrinsic motivators (e.g., Deci, 1975); and, third, people sometimes resent being controlled and may even rebel against it (e.g., Brehm, 1966). These considerations will be discussed later.

PHYSIOLOGICAL NEEDS: DRIVES AND INSTINCTS

The motivation theories that received the greatest attention in psychology prior to 1960 are typically referred to as drive theories. Although the terminology has varied, drives can be thought of as strong, cyclically recurring urges that are based in biological disequilibria and persist as energizers of behavior until equilibrium has been restored (i.e., until the drives have been reduced). Interestingly, there have been two very different types of drive theories, each of which has been quite prominent in its own realm. The two types are best represented by Hull's (1943) drive theory and Freud's (1925) instinct theory, the former derived primarily from laboratory experiments with non-human species and the latter primarily from clinical interviews with psychiatric patients.

Experimental drive theories
Hull (1943) proposed that all behavior can be explained in terms of the learning that occurs from the reduction of four basic tissue needs (that set up drive states): hunger, thirst, sex, and the avoidance of pain. Like Skinner's operant theory, Hull's drive-reduction theory is considered a behavioral, stimulus–response (or associationist) theory because it asserts that responses are strengthened by reinforcements. However, for Hull, a stimulus may be an internal, physiological cue that signals disequilibrium (called a drive-stimulus) as well as an external object or event, and, further, a reinforcement is defined in terms of returning one's internal biological condition to equilibrium rather than in terms of behavior change (as was the case for Skinner). According to drive theory, learning results from reinforcement; in other words, organisms will engage in those behaviors that have previously led to drive reduction.

In Hull's theory, behavior is energized by the drive state that results from basic tissue needs, and the direction of behavior is a function of the associative bonds that have linked responses to drive-stimuli through previous reinforcements. Thus, since behavior is said to be controlled by drives and associative bonds, volition is not relevant – in fact, cognitions more generally have no place in the theory.

Of all notable theories relevant to motivation, the empirical drive theories have had the least influence on management theory and practice, presumably because the conditioning of behavior through primary drive reduction would be unwieldy and impractical in applied settings. Even though the drive-theory approach has been adapted and extended to the areas of personality (Dollard & Miller, 1950) and attitude change, (e.g., Hovland, Janis, & Kelley, 1953), this work has not been utilized in discussions of management and thus is not represented in the readings of this volume.

Even within psychology, the drive-theory approach is now receiving very little attention, both because cognitive concepts make it easier to explain many forms of learning and because the premise that all behavior is derivative of physiological needs has not held up under empirical scrutiny (e.g. Berlyne, 1950; Harlow, 1953).

Psychoanalytic instinct theory

Freud's motivation theory (1925) asserted that all behavior can be reduced to two basic instincts: sex and aggression. These instincts, which are largely unconscious aspects of the id, become cathected to (or associated with) objects in the environment, primarily as a result of early interactions with parents.

The two basic drives are said to provide the energy for all human behavior, which is directed toward cathected objects (including other people). Thus, much of our motivated behavior is theorized to be a function of unconscious internal processes and so not under volitional control. However, in Freud's theory (1962/1923), there are also ego processes which develop out of conflicts between the id and the environment and which regulate behavior in more rational ways using energy that has been neutralized from the id. Regulatory processes of the ego can be under volitional control, functioning in part to keep the instincts in check.

Freud's psychoanalytic theory, unlike the theories of Skinner and Hull, was not formulated to predict and control specific behaviors but rather to provide explanations for psychic processes and patterns of maladaptive behaviors. As such, it has had relatively little influence on managerial psychology, although Levinson (e.g., 1981) has provided interesting discussions of organizational behavior using psychoanalytic concepts (see Reading 25 for an example), and psychoanalytic theory is central to the Tavistock group-process approach to organization development (Rice, 1965). Still, most descriptions and prescriptions related to motivation in organizations have not utilized psychoanalytic drive theory, just as they have not utilized Hull's drive theory, presumably for the same types of pragmatic reasons.

It is noteworthy that in psychoanalytic psychology, as in experimental psychology, it became increasingly clear, on the basis of observations of children (Hartmann, 1958), that much human behavior is motivated by non-drive-based energy sources. This led White (1959, Reading 3), in a landmark paper reviewing the evidence pertinent to both experimental and psychoanalytic drive theories, to postulate an independent energy source called effectance motivation that we shall discuss in the section on psychological needs.

GOALS

Two German *émigrés* who had been influenced by Gestalt psychology argued forcefully that focusing on cognitive processes is important for understanding social relations and learning. Specifically, Lewin (1936) proposed a motivational analysis of social behavior that has had widespread influence on psychological and management theories, and Tolman (1932) applied a similar model of motivation to the area of learning. Both were important forces in shifting the emphasis from associative bonds between stimuli and responses to cognitions as explanatory concepts; however, because Lewin's work is more germane to the topic of this book, we will restrict our discussion to Lewin.

Lewinian theory

In Lewin's theory, the energy for behavior comes from tensions, which can be based in drives or created by thoughts. The influence of the concept of 'Gestalt', which refers to a tendency to create unified wholes in one's perceptions and actions, is very evident in this aspect of the theory, because Lewin (1951) proposed that when one does not meet some standard or finish some business a tension forms and persists as a motivator until the standard has been met or the business finished (i.e., until the Gestalt has been completed). Tensions, said Lewin, lead people to set goals (i.e., desired future states) that they believe will decrease the tensions.

Although the concept of tension as the energy source for behavior was not an influential aspect of Lewin's theory (see Deci, 1980, for a discussion of this), the concept of goals as the directional concept has had a substantial impact on many subsequent theories. Since goals require decisional processes, volition was central to the theory. Thus, unlike the other motivational theories discussed so far, Lewin's theory emphasized that behavior is intentional. Change, he said, occurs when one attends to one's behavior patterns, thus unfreezing them and allowing new directions for voluntary action.

More recent theories utilizing the element of 'goal' – or the closely related concepts of 'anticipated outcome', 'expected reinforcement', or 'desired future state' – have been numerous and varied. Most of these theories have abandoned the notion of tension and have not utilized any comparable energizing force. In this regard, the theories share with Skinner's theory the characteristic of defining their core motivational concept from a functional perspective rather than grounding it in some energizing aspect of the organism. Stated differently, the theories explain that, when people set goals or expect to attain reinforcements, they will be motivated to engage in instrumental behavior, but the theories fail to explain *why* goals or reinforcements are valued. They neglect to relate the future event to some physiological drive, psychological need, or emotional process in the individual. Accordingly, most theories of goal-directed behavior are said to describe the *processes* of motivation (i.e., how it is directed) rather than the *content* of motivation (i.e., the specification of what it is that people want).

Control-of-reinforcement theories

In all the cognitive (i.e., goal-directed) theories, expectancy is a key idea. People are said to engage in behaviors because they *expect* those behaviors to lead to their goals. The line of theory that most clearly represents a melding of the Skinnerian and Lewinian perspectives is represented by the work of Rotter (1966), Seligman (1975), and Bandura (1977, Reading 5). The necessary condition for a person to be motivated, these authors assert, is the expectation that his or her action will lead to a desired reinforcement. Without that expectation, the person will not be motivated. Furthermore, if the expectation of behavior-reinforcement independence persists through time, the person will develop an external locus of control (Rotter, 1966) and learn to be helpless (Seligman, 1975).

Rotter (1966) used the term 'locus of control' to refer to a generalized expectancy either that one's behavior is reliably linked to reinforcements (internal control) or is not reliably linked to reinforcements (external control). It is an individual difference or personality variable that can be assessed with a scale that he developed. It asks, for example, whether or not people believe they can have an influence on the political process. Believing that one can indicates an internal locus of control. The scale has been used in hundreds of studies, dozens of which have been conducted in work organizations, and a recent review by Spector (1982, Reading 8) concluded that an external locus of control is associated with low work motivation, poor performance, and job dissatisfaction.

While the research on locus of control is interesting and consistent with the general idea that motivation requires outcome expectancies, the locus-of-control concept does not have direct applicability for management (except perhaps as a selection device) because it is formulated in terms of individual differences rather than environmental factors over which managers have direct control. Of greater utility for managers is a general understanding of the concept of reinforcement expectancy. The idea quite simply is that people will be motivated to behave if they expect the behavior to lead to a reinforcement. Recent expectancy theories (Abramson, Seligman, & Teasdale, 1978; Bandura, 1977) specify two situational conditions, which managers can control, that promote reinforcement expectancies and thus motivation: the situation must be structured so that performance will lead to desired outcomes, and the task must be one at which the workers will feel competent. Bandura in particular used the term 'self-efficacy' to refer to a person's belief that he or she is competent to perform the behaviors that are necessary to achieve desired reinforcements.

Expectancy–valence theories
A second line in theorizing that derived from the Lewinian perspective was actually formulated within the area of work motivation. It has been extensively researched in organizations and has been widely taught to managers and trainees. Represented by the work of Georgopoulos, Mahoney, and Jones (1957), Vroom (1964), and Porter and Lawler (1968), this approach is sometimes referred to as path–goal theory because motivation is believed to be a function of a behavior's being the path to workers' goals. More generally it is called expectancy–valence theory because, in the same vein, motivation is believed to be a function of workers' expectancies that a behavior will lead to outcomes that have valence (i.e., psychological value) for them. These theories have the clear implication for managers that work should be structured so that effective performance will lead to desired outcomes.

Vroom's theory, which is stated as a set of algebraic equations, is the most precise, and thus has been researched the most, though Porter and Lawler's theory is outlined in a way that is more readily interpretable by practicing managers. The concepts in these theories can also be found as central elements in leadership theories such as the path–goal leadership theory of House (1971).

Goal-setting theories
The final line of work that derives from Lewin's theory concerns the goal-setting process. Discussions of goal setting in terms of individual

behavior can be found in the research and prescriptions recently presented by Locke and Latham (1984; see also Reading 16), based on the goal theory of Ryan (1970) and others. This work emphasizes that specific goals are more motivating than general ones (Locke, 1968) and that proximal goals are more motivating than distal ones (Bandura & Schunk, 1981). In terms of general management practices, goal setting is central to the approach called 'management by objectives' or MBO (Drucker, 1974; Tosi & Carroll, 1970, Reading 34), which suggests that managers should focus on *whether* goals are achieved rather than *how* they are achieved. More generally, goal-setting theorists assert that by setting clear, specific goals, by specifying the time frame for achieving the goals and the process for determining whether they have been met, and by allowing employees latitude in how to achieve the goals, one can maximize the employees' motivation.

PSYCHOLOGICAL NEEDS

The final concept that has been at the heart of many motivation theories is that of psychological needs, commonly referred to simply as *needs*. Needs, which can be either innate or learned, differ from drives in that they are tied to aspects of the person's psychological makeup rather than physiological condition. Furthermore, the concept of need is typically used in 'pull' theories (i.e., theories in which the person is said to be pulled toward desired outcomes), whereas the concept of drive is typically used in 'push' theories (i.e., theories in which the person is said to be pushed by a drive and directed by an associative bond or cathexis).

The work of Murray (1938) presents the earliest comprehensive theory of human needs. From the analysis of very extensive interviews and tests with adult subjects who visited his psychology clinic at Harvard, Murray derived a set of more than twenty needs that could consistently be inferred from the subjects' responses and discussion. These included such things as the need for affiliation, the need for autonomy, and the need for achievement.

Need hierarchy theories
Shortly after the publication of Murray's theory, Maslow (1943, Reading 2) used the term needs to refer to both physiological and psychological needs, proposing that there are five sets of human needs: physiological needs (i.e., the basic drives), safety needs, love needs,

esteem needs, and the need for self-actualization. Maslow further proposed that these sets of needs are arranged hierarchically, from lower-order to higher-order needs, in the order presented above. In other words, he asserted that physiological needs are the most basic and will be the central motivators until they are well satisfied, at which point the safety needs will be prepotent until they are satisfied, and so on. A subsequent theory of work motivation by Alderfer (1972) posited a three-level need hierarchy consisting of existence, relatedness, and growth needs.

It is worth noting that the concept of self-actualization – which first appeared in the writings of Goldstein (1939), is central in Rogers' (1963) personality theory, and is complementary to Murray's theory – was something of a revolutionary concept for psychology at that time because it emphasized the individual's inherent growth tendencies. According to this view, people's nature is to grow, to develop, to mature, to accept responsibility, and to relate positively to others. This represented a more positive view of human nature than was conveyed in most previous theories, particularly the operant and drive theories in the behavioral tradition and the early psychoanalytic instinct theory.

Most theories that emphasize psychological needs tend to employ a more growth-oriented view of humans. Accordingly, the need theories view people as volitional, as do the goal-oriented theories, though the need theories provide an answer to why certain outcomes are valued: outcomes are valued because they satisfy needs.

The need theories, with their growth-oriented view of the person and their emphasis on the 'higher-order needs', represented an important impetus for the development of the newer management theories presented in Sections VII and VIII. These include the general approach represented by Theory Y Management (McGregor, 1960, see Reading 32), participative management (Marrow, Bowers, and Seashore, 1967), System 4 Management (Likert, 1967, Reading 33), Theory Z Management (Ouchi, 1981), and high-involvement management (Lawler, 1986, Reading 37), as well as the contingency theories of management that detail the appropriate conditions for using participation (Vroom & Jago, 1988; see also Reading 38).

McGregor (1960) for example, when initially proposing Theory Y, used Maslow's theory as a foundation. He argued that people have inherent higher-order needs that would motivate effective performance in organizations if people were provided with appropriate conditions. Those conditions, of course, are ones that are created by participative managers.

McGregor made the further point that in our society the lower-order needs of many people are reasonably well satisfied, so the high-order needs for esteem and self-actualization tend to be salient for these people. Hackman and Lawler (1971) assessed the salient needs (both lower- and higher-order) of a large sample of workers and found considerable variability. They also found that participative methods led to better performance only for those people with strong higher-order needs. Still, numerous authors have argued that a commitment to employee development (through participative methods) can help all workers to flourish in contingently participative settings (e.g., Vroom & Jago, 1988).

Currently there are two lines of research in motivational psychology that can be traced back to the work of Murray (1938) and his colleagues, such as Allport (1937). The first is typically thought of in terms of achievement motivation and the second in terms of intrinsic motivation.

Achievement motivation theories

McClelland and his colleagues (McClelland, Atkinson, Clark, & Lowell, 1953; McClelland, 1961) have carried out a vigorous research program on achievement motivation. The need for achievement, which refers to the motivation to try to match some internal standard of excellence, is a personality variable that is typically measured with the projective Thematic Apperception Test (see Atkinson, 1958). A high level of this motivation has been associated with the tendency to take moderate risks, to set specific goals, and to persist at achievement tasks. It, along with power motivation, has also been found to be related to organization success (McClelland & Boyatzis, 1982; see also Reading 19).

Like the concept of locus of control, the concept of achievement motivation has been well researched but is not readily useful for most managers because of its focus on individual differences rather than situational determinants of action. None the less, McClelland has suggested that the need for achievement is a learned rather than innate need, and as such it should be possible to increase one's achievement motivation. McClelland and Winter (1969) undertook an extensive training program with entrepreneurs in India and documented that the need for achievement can be increased and will result in increased productivity. The relevance of these findings is that management training programs could be designed to include achievement motivation training.

Atkinson (1964) expanded on McClelland's work by including the need for achievement in an expectancy (i.e., goal-oriented) formulation of achievement behavior. Taking into account the two personality variables of need for achievement and anxiety about failure, plus the variables of probability of success and incentive value of success, Atkinson derived an algebraic representation of the likelihood of people's taking on a particular achievement challenge. His formulation has been much researched, though again the only variable in the equation that is amenable to managers' control is the task difficulty, so the theory has had relatively little impact on management practices.

Intrinsic motivation theories

In White's (1959, Reading 3) critique of drive theories, he concluded that the concept of a psychological need for effectance or competence could complement the concept of physiological drives to provide a fuller explanation of motivated behavior. White argued that a great deal of human activity, ranging from young children's learning to adults' leisure pursuits, is energized by an innate propensity to be effective in one's interactions with the social and physical environment.

deCharms (1968) echoed White's assertion, though he used the concept of personal causation, asserting that the basic motivational propensity is the desire to be an 'origin' or initiator of one's own behavior rather than a 'pawn' to external forces. In the tradition of Murray (1938) and McClelland (e.g., McClelland et al., 1953), deCharms (1976) used projective methods to assess this motivational tendency and successfully conducted motivation training programs aimed at helping teachers and students of inner-city school systems feel more like origins, be more internally motivated, and achieve at a higher level.

The ideas of effectance and personal causation are typically encompassed by the concept of intrinsic motivation (Deci, 1975). This concept has been used in two different, though related, ways, and each way can be seen to represent a counterpoint to one of the two prevailing behavioral associationist theories of the 1940s and 1950s. First, in line with White's discussion, intrinsic motivation has referred to the specific, innate psychological needs for competence and self-determination, thus contradicting Hull's assertion that all behavior is based in four physiological drives. Second, in opposition to Skinner's definition of reinforcements as operationally separable, external events, intrinsic motivation has referred to the fact that the task itself can be rewarding – in other words, that people can experience gratification from doing certain activities independent of any separable consequences that might accrue.

When used in this latter sense, the focus of research and discussion has tended to be on characteristics of the task that make it interesting, whereas, when used in the former sense, the focus of research and discussion has tended to be on the person's experience of competence and self-determination and on how factors in the environment can either diminish or enhance intrinsic motivation by either allowing or thwarting the satisfaction of the person's needs for competence and self-determination (Deci & Ryan, 1985). These two approaches to conceptualizing intrinsic motivation can be seen to be complementary in the sense that the characteristics that make the task intrinsically interesting – for example, being optimally challenging or permitting one to make choices – have their motivating effect because they are instrumental for the person's satisfying his or her intrinsic needs for competence and self-determination.

A substantial amount of research has shown that external factors that either diminish a person's self-determination or signify the person's incompetence tend to undermine intrinsic motivation. These include extrinsic reward structures, threats of punishment, the imposition of goals, and zero-sum competitions. In contrast, external factors that support self-determination and promote competence – things like the opportunity for choice and the provision of non-evaluative feedback – tend to enhance intrinsic motivation.

A further line of research has shown that the general ambience or social context within which the above-mentioned, external factors are administered will have an important influence on the effects of those factors. For example, Ryan (1982) showed that positive feedback can be administered in a way that tends to be experienced by the recipient either as controlling and demanding (in which case it will decrease intrinsic motivation) or as signifying competence and personal initiative (in which case it will maintain or enhance intrinsic motivation). Ryan, Mims, and Koestner (1983, Reading 27) found the same to be true for external rewards. Further, Deci, Connell, and Ryan (1989, Reading 23) found that in work organizations, a manager's personal orientation, which can either be toward *supporting the autonomy* or toward *controlling the behavior* of subordinates, is a critical factor in determining the work climate for those subordinates.

In Deci and Ryan's (1985) self-determination theory, human needs are said to provide the energy for behavior; people value goals because the goals are expected to provide satisfaction of their needs. These authors have asserted that the direction of behavior is volitional, but that regulation can be either through choice (i.e., self-determined) or through control (i.e., pressured by some interpersonal or intrapersonal force). The mode of regulation, whether through choice or control, can be analyzed either in terms of personality or in terms of the autonomy supportive versus controlling aspects of the situation. The important point about this is that considerable research has shown that when regulation is through choice (i.e., is self-determined) people are not only more intrinsically motivated but they are more creative, display greater cognitive flexibility and conceptual understanding, have a more positive emotional tone, are healthier, and are more likely to support the autonomy of others (Deci & Ryan, 1985).

Intrinsic motivation and management

The work on intrinsic motivation has a number of important implications for management theory and practice. For example, a number of writers, working in the tradition of goal-directed theories, have asserted that optimal motivating conditions are those that combine extrinsic motivators and intrinsic motivators (e.g., Porter & Lawler, 1968). By making work challenging (an intrinsic motivator) and by making monetary rewards directly contingent on completion of the task (i.e., a task-contingent, extrinsic motivator), the two types of motivation will sum to yield a high level of total motivation. The problem with this, of course, is that the task-contingent rewards can undermine the intrinsic motivation, and if the rewards are structured so that peers must compete against each other to obtain them, these rewards will certainly have negative consequences. It is only when the social context, as influenced by the manager's orientation, is clearly supportive of self-determination and the extrinsic rewards are used to signify self-initiated competence that the two types of motivation are likely to be additive or positively synergistic.

A similarly important point can be made regarding the goal-setting method (e.g., Locke & Latham, 1984). Studies have shown, for example, that goals can have a negative effect on intrinsic motivation if they are experienced as restrictive, imposed, or pressuring (e.g., Manderlink & Harackiewicz, 1984). Such studies emphasize the importance of managers' encouraging subordinates to set their own goals and evaluate their own performance, a point that can be found in Reading 24 by McGregor (1957). When managers support the self-determination of their subordinates by encouraging them to set their own goals, decide how to achieve these goals, and evaluate their own performance, then goal setting can be an extremely effective motivational process, at least for some employees.

Research on intrinsic motivation has increasingly provided motivational justification for participative decision making (e.g., Vroom &

Jago, 1988; see Reading 38), for job enlargement (Herzberg, 1966; see also Reading 21), and for an autonomy-supportive management orientation (Deci, Connell, & Ryan, 1989, Reading 23). Such an approach does not mean, of course, that all decisions should be made by work groups. Rather, it means: that the attitude of managers should be one of respect for their employees while at the same time providing structures and expectations (Bowers & Seashore, 1966), that the managers should be committed to the development of their subordinates as professionals, and that they should provide as much latitude for behavior and as much involvement in the planning and deciding as is appropriate given the characteristics of the situation.

Management approaches involving participative elements have become quite popular not only in the academic literature on management (e.g., Lawler, 1986, Reading 37) but also in the popular management literature (e.g., Peters & Waterman, 1982), and many major corporations have been experimenting with the utility of participative methods. It is clear that such methods work best when a whole organization is fully committed to employee involvement and job enlargement, though some remarkable managers are able to maintain a highly effective, participative approach even when others around them are very controlling. The problem all too often is that organizations adopt these newer, participative approaches in a relatively superficial way, espousing them when things are going well, but falling back on more traditional, authoritarian approaches when things get tough. This inevitably creates problems of mistrust and resentment, thus undoing any advantages that were obtained. The general participative approach (to the extent that it is situationally appropriate) must be fully accepted by top management and used conscientiously in bad times as well as good if it is to work effectively. When it is, the approach can have remarkable effects on employee attitudes and work effectiveness (e.g., Likert, 1967, Reading 33).

SOCIAL AND GROUP INFLUENCES

The motivational theory of the person–situation interaction proposed by Lewin (e.g., 1936) has been very important not only because of the expectancy and goal theories that have derived from it, but also because it played an important role in the development of experimental social psychology as a field of inquiry.

Over the past forty years, social psychology has been characterized by what are termed 'mini-theories'. These theories, such as social comparison theory (Festinger, 1954), pertain to specific phenomena or sets of phenomena and are stated with terms and propositions that can be relatively easily tested. Whereas the personality and learning theories that have been discussed in the first four sections of this essay have tended to be macro-theories – pertaining to a much broader range of behavior – the theories discussed in this final section are more narrow in scope and relate to the influence of social forces on human behavior. Some of these theories have been stated using motivational terminology, though many have not. Still, since the theories deal with the influences of groups and social environments on people's behavior, they are directly relevant to the study of motivation and to the study of work behavior.

Among the findings of this area of investigation are: that people often conform to the way others are behaving even when the people themselves think the behavior is inappropriate (Asch, 1958); and that people often comply with the demands of an authority figure even when the demands go against their own values (Milgram, 1974). It is clear from such studies that social forces can be extremely strong in shaping a person's behavior, and the underlying implication seems to be that people have a very powerful desire to be accepted or approved of by others.

In motivational terms, this suggests, first, that people have an innate need to relate to (Alderfer, 1972) or affiliate with (McClelland, 1985) others. Further, it suggests that even though the need for autonomy and the need for relatedness can be complementary in fostering achievement and adjustment, the two can be pitted against each other in such a way that people will relinquish their own self-determination in order to feel accepted.

Some research has explicated a positive motivating effect of others' presence on one's performance. Referred to as social facilitation (Zajonc, 1965, Reading 11), this work suggests that the presence of others tends to enhance performance on well-learned tasks but to interfere with learning of new tasks. In a way, this work complements the work of McGraw (1978) showing that rewards facilitate performance of overlearned (algorithmic) tasks but impair performance of heuristic tasks, such as problem solving. Together, the work suggests that the presence of others tends to have a salient controlling element which will facilitate performance if the task requires little or no intrinsic motivation but will impair performance if intrinsic motivation is necessary for effective performance. According to work on the effects of social contexts on motivation by Ryan, Mims, and Koestner (1983, Reading 27), the negative effects of others' presence can be overcome when those others evidence an autonomy supportive orientation or attitude. When, however, for whatever reason, the actor experiences the others as controlling, he or she may either comply (French & Raven, 1959, Reading 13) or rebel (Brehm, 1966) but in either case there are likely to be negative consequences for the person's performance and internal states (Deci & Ryan, 1985).

People's need for social approval also has interesting ramifications in work organizations through what is often referred to as the 'informal organization'. This can be seen in one of the more intriguing findings from the so-called Hawthorne studies (Roethlisberger & Dickson, 1939), namely that people will restrict their own productivity to comply with the norms of their reference group. In other words, the informal organization of their peers can be more influential than the formal hierarchy within the organization. Such knowledge would seem to be particularly important for practicing managers whose job it is to facilitate greater productivity within their work units.

Another central finding in the social psychological studies is that people seek balance (Heider, 1958) or consonance (Festinger, 1957) in their cognitive structures. Thus, many studies have shown that people will deceive themselves and rationalize their own behavior because of the strong need to reduce the discomfort of dissonant cognitions. For example, studies have shown that when people are induced, without force, to engage in a counter-attitudinal behavior, they will change their attitude to make it consistent with the behavior (e.g., Cohen, 1962). Although there has been a small amount of discussion about cognitive dissonance reduction in work settings, the idea of balance applied to work situations is perhaps most evident in the equity theories (e.g., Adams, 1965, Reading 10). Essentially, the theories suggest that people will be most satisfied and work most effectively when they believe that their rewards or outcomes are in balance with their inputs. Although this would at first appear to be a wholly intrapersonal process, the basis for determining what are equitable rewards is often derived from social norms and social comparative processes.

It is interesting to note that, according to equity theories, people will be uncomfortable when they are over-rewarded as well as when they are under-rewarded, and there is some experimental support for this hypothesis (e.g., Pritchard, Dunnette, & Jorgenson, 1972). However, anecdotal evidence from recent developments in leveraged buyouts and various securities and exchange activities seems to indicate that people are quite willing to accept rewards that are far greater than would be considered equitable by any logical standard. Presumably, there is social support among their peer group for exorbitant incomes, and perhaps the dissonance that may have been caused by such incomes was reduced by the people's convincing themselves they deserve these rewards.

SUMMARY

This essay has reviewed five clusters of theories, from the areas of learning, personality, and social psychology, that relate to motivation. A general overview of each type of theory was presented and the relevance of that approach for understanding management practice was considered. The first three sections of this book, which comprise Part A, present a set of basic psychological readings that deal with these motivational concepts and that we believe are most relevant for management practice. In the first section, the readings deal with the nature of human needs (the so-called *content of motivation*) and with the question of whether such concepts are useful for predicting behavior. In the second section, focus shifts to the so-called *processes of motivation*. Here, two positions are represented – the reinforcement perspective of operant theory and the goal-directed perspective of expectancy theories. Emphasis is place on the latter. Finally, in the third section, we present readings that attest to the impact of social influences on individual behavior. These three sets of readings provide a sound motivational foundation upon which to consider research on work motivation (presented in Part B of this book) as well as the motivational basis of various management theories (presented in Part C).

REFERENCES

Abramson, L. Y., Seligman, M. E. P., & Teasdale, J. D. (1978), 'Learned helplessness in humans: Critique and reformulation', *Journal of Abnormal Psychology*, 87, 49–74.

Adams, J. S. (1965), 'Inequity in social exchange', in L. Berkowitz (ed.), *Advances in Experimental Social Psychology* (Vol. 2, pp. 267–99), New York: Academic Press.

Alderfer, C. P. (1972), *Existence, Relatedness, and Growth*, New York: Free Press.

Allport, G. W. (1937), *Personality: A Psychological Interpretation*, New York: Holt.

Asch, S. E. (1958), 'The effects of group pressure upon the modification and distortion of judgments', in E. E. Maccoby, T. E. Newcomb, & E. L. Hartley (eds.), *Readings in Social Psychology* (pp. 174–83), New York: Holt.

Atkinson, J. W. (1958), *Motives in Fantasy, Action and Society*, Princeton, NJ: Van Nostrand.

Atkinson, J. W. (1964), *An Introduction to Motivation*, Princeton, NJ: Van Nostrand.

Bandura, A. (1977), 'Self-efficacy: Toward a unifying theory of behavioral change', *Psychological Review*, *84*, 191–215.

Bandura, A., & Schunk, D. H. (1981), 'Cultivating competence, self-efficacy, and intrinsic interest through proximal self-motivation', *Journal of Personality and Social Psychology*, *41*, 586–98.

Berlyne, D. E. (1950), 'Novelty and curiosity as determinants of exploratory behavior', *British Journal of Psychology*, *41*, 68–80.

Bowers, D. G., & Seashore, S. E. (1966), 'Predicting organizational effectiveness with a four-factor theory of leadership', *Administrative Science Quarterly*, *11*, 238–63.

Brehm, J. W. (1966), *A Theory of Psychological Reactance*, New York: Academic Press.

Cohen, A. R. (1962), 'An experiment on small rewards for discrepant compliance and attitude change', in J. W. Brehm & A. R. Cohen (eds.), *Explorations in Cognitive Dissonance* (pp. 73–8), New York: Wiley.

deCharms, R. (1968), *Personal Causation: The Internal Affective Determinants of Behavior*, New York: Academic Press.

deCharms, R. (1976), *Enhancing Motivation: Change in the Classroom*, New York: Irvington.

Deci, E. L. (1975), *Intrinsic Motivation*, New York: Plenum.

Deci, E. L. (1980), *The Psychology of Self-Determination*, Lexington, Mass.: D. C. Heath (Lexington Books).

Deci, E. L., Connell, J. P., & Ryan, R. M. (1989), 'Self-determination in a work organization', *Journal of Applied Psychology*, *74*, 580–90.

Deci, E. L., & Ryan, R. M. (1985), *Intrinsic Motivation and Self-Determination in Human Behavior*, New York: Plenum.

Dollard, J., & Miller, N. E. (1950), *Personality and Psychotherapy: An Analysis in Terms of Learning, Thinking, and Culture*, New York: McGraw-Hill.

Drucker, P. F. (1974), *Management: Tasks, Responsibilities, Practices*, New York: Harper & Row.

Festinger, L. (1954), 'A theory of social comparison processes', *Human Relations*, *7*, 117–40.

Festinger, L. (1957), *A Theory of Cognitive Dissonance*, Evanston, Ill.: Row, Peterson.

French, J. R. P., & Raven, B. (1959), 'The bases of social power', in D. Cartwright (ed.), *Studies in Social Power*, Ann Arbor, Mich.: Institute for Social Research, University of Michigan.

Freud, S. (1925), 'Instincts and their vicissitudes', in *Collected Papers* (Vol. 4, pp. 60–83), London: Hogarth. (Originally published 1915.)

Freud, S. (1962), *The Ego and the Id*, New York: Norton. (Originally published 1923.)

Georgopoulos, B. S., Mahoney, G. M., & Jones, N. W. (1957), 'A path–goal approach to productivity', *Journal of Applied Psychology*, *41*, 345–53.

Goldstein, K. (1939), *The Organism*, New York: American Book Co.

Hackman, J. R., & Lawler, E. E., III (1971), 'Employee reactions to job characteristics', *Journal of Applied Psychology*, *55*, 259–86.

Harlow, H. F. (1953), 'Motivation as a factor in the acquisition of new responses', in *Current Theory and Research in Motivation* (pp. 24–49), Lincoln, Nebr.: University of Nebraska Press.

Hartmann, H. (1958), *Ego Psychology and the Problem of Adaptation*, New York: International Universities Press. (Originally published 1939.)

Heider, F. (1958), *The Psychology of Interpersonal Relations*, New York: Wiley.

Herzberg, F. (1966), *Work and the Nature of Man*, Cleveland, Ohio: World.

House, R. J. (1971), 'A path–goal theory of leader effectiveness', *Administrative Science Quarterly*, *16*, 321–38.

Hovland, C. I., Janis, I. L., & Kelley, H. H. (1953), *Communication and Persuasion: Psychological Studies of Opinion Change*, New Haven, Conn.: Yale University Press.

Hull, C. L. (1943), *Principles of Behavior: An Introduction to Behavior Theory*, New York: Appleton-Century-Crofts.

Lawler, E. E., III (1986), *High-Involvement Management*, San Francisco: Jossey-Bass.

Levinson, H. (1981), *Executive*, Cambridge, Mass.: Harvard University Press.

Lewin, K. (1936), *Principles of Topological Psychology*, New York: McGraw-Hill.

Lewin, K. (1951), 'Intention, will, and need', in D. Rapaport (ed.), *Organization and Pathology of Thought* (pp. 95–153), New York: Columbia University Press.

Likert, R. (1967), *The Human Organization*, New York: McGraw-Hill.

Locke, E. A. (1968), 'Toward a theory of task motivation and incentives', *Organizational Behavior and Human Performance*, 3, 157–89.

Locke, E. A., & Latham, G. P. (1984), *Goal Setting: A Motivational Technique That Works*, Englewood Cliffs, NJ: Prentice Hall.

McClelland, D. C. (1961), *The Achieving Society*, Princeton, NJ: Van Nostrand.

McClelland, D. C. (1985), *Human Motivation*, Glenview, Ill.: Scott, Foresman.

McClelland, D. C., Atkinson, J. W., Clark, R. W., & Lowell, E. L. (1953), *The Achievement Motive*, New York: Appleton-Century-Crofts.

McClelland, D. C., & Boyatzis, R. E. (1982), 'The leadership motive pattern and long term success in management', *Journal of Applied Psychology*, 67, 737–43.

McClelland, D. C., & Winter, D. G. (1969), *Motivating Economic Achievement*, New York: Free Press.

McGraw, K. O. (1978), 'The detrimental effects of reward on performance: A literature review and a prediction model', in M. R. Lepper & D. Greene (eds.), *The Hidden Costs of Reward* (pp. 33–60), Hillsdale, NJ: Erlbaum.

McGregor, D. (1957), 'An uneasy look at performance appraisal', *Harvard Business Review*, 35 (3), 89–94.

McGregor, D. (1960), *The Human Side of Enterprise*, New York: McGraw-Hill.

Manderlink, G., & Harackiewicz, J. M. (1984), 'Proximal vs distal goal setting and intrinsic motivation', *Journal of Personality and Social Psychology*, 47, 918–28.

Marrow, A. J., Bowers, D. G., & Seashore, S. E. (1967), *Management by Participation*, New York: Harper and Row.

Maslow, A. H. (1943), 'A theory of human motivation', *Psychological Review*, 50, 370–96.

Milgram, S. (1974), *Obedience to Authority*, New York: Harper & Row.

Murray, H. A. (1938), *Explorations in Personality*, New York: Oxford University Press.

Ouchi, W. G. (1981), *Theory Z*, Reading, Mass.: Addison-Wesley.

Peters, T. J., & Waterman, R. H. (1982), *In Search of Excellence*, New York: Harper & Row.

Porter, L. W., & Lawler, E. E., III (1968), *Managerial Attitudes and Performance*, Homewood, Ill.: Irwin-Dorsey.

Pritchard, R. D., Dunnette, M. D., & Jorgenson, D. O. (1972), 'Effects of perceptions of equity and inequity on workers' performance and satisfaction', *Journal of Applied Psychology Monograph*, 56 (1), 75–94.

Rice, A. K. (1965), *Learning for Leadership: Interpersonal and Intergroup Relations*, London: Tavistock Publications.

Roethlisberger, F. J., & Dickson, W. J. (1939), *Management and the Worker*, Cambridge, Mass.: Harvard University Press.

Rogers, C. (1963), 'The actualizing tendency in relation to "motives" and to consciousness', in M. R. Jones (ed.), *Nebraska Symposium on Motivation* (Vol. 11, pp. 1–24), Lincoln, Nebr.: University of Nebraska Press.

Rotter, J. B. (1954), *Social Learning and Clinical Psychology*, Englewood Cliffs, NJ: Prentice Hall.

Rotter, J. B. (1966), 'Generalized expectancies for internal versus external control of reinforcement', *Psychological Monographs, 80* (1, Whole No. 609), 1–28.

Ryan, R. M. (1982), 'Control and information in the intrapersonal sphere: An extension of cognitive evaluation theory', *Journal of Personality and Social Psychology, 43*, 450–61.

Ryan, R. M., Mims, V., & Koestner, R. (1983), 'Relation of reward contingency and interpersonal context to intrinsic motivation: A review and test using cognitive evaluation theory', *Journal of Personality and Social Psychology, 45*, 736–50.

Ryan, T. A. (1970), *Intentional Behavior*, New York: Ronald Press.

Seligman, M. E. P. (1975), *Helplessness: On Depression, Development, and Death*, San Francisco: Freeman.

Skinner, B. F. (1953), *Science and Human Behavior*, New York: Macmillan.

Spector, P. E. (1982), 'Behavior in organizations as a function of employee's locus of control', *Psychological Bulletin, 91*, 482–97.

Taylor, F. W. (1911), *Principles of Scientific Management*, New York: Harper.

Thorndike, E. L. (1913), *The Psychology of Learning*, New York: Teacher's College, Columbia University.

Tolman, E. C. (1932), *Purposive Behavior in Animals and Men*, New York: Century.

Tosi, H. L., & Carroll, S. J. (1970), *Management by Objectives*, New York: Macmillan.

Vroom, V. H. (1964), *Work and Motivation*, New York: Wiley.

Vroom, V. H., & Jago, A. G. (1988), *The New Leadership: Managing Participation in Organizations*, Englewood Cliffs, NJ: Prentice Hall.

Watson, J. B. (1913), 'Psychology as the behaviorist views it', *Psychological Review, 20*, 158–77.

White, R. W. (1959), 'Motivation reconsidered: The concept of competence', *Psychological Review, 66*, 297–333.

Zajonc, R. B. (1965), 'Social facilitation', *Science, 149*, 269–74.

Basic Needs and Human Nature: The Content of Motivation

1

B. F. SKINNER

The Causes of Behavior

Abridged from B. F. Skinner, *About Behaviorism*, Chapter 1, New York: Knopf, 1974.

Why do people behave as they do? It was probably first a practical question: How could a person anticipate and hence prepare for what another person would do? Later it would become practical in another sense: How could another person be induced to behave in a given way? Eventually it became a matter of understanding and explaining behavior. It could always be reduced to a question about causes.

We tend to say, often rashly, that if one thing follows another, it was probably caused by it – following the ancient principle of *post hoc, ergo propter hoc* (after this, therefore because of this). Of many examples to be found in the explanation of human behavior, one is especially important here. The person with whom we are most familiar is ourself; many of the things we observe just before we behave occur within our body, and it is easy to take them as the causes of our behavior. If we are asked why we have spoken sharply to a friend, we may reply, 'Because I felt angry.' It is true that we felt angry before, or as, we spoke, and so we take our anger to be the cause of our remark. Asked why we are not eating our dinner, we may say, 'Because I do not feel hungry.' We often feel hungry when we eat and hence conclude that we eat because we feel hungry. Asked why we are going swimming, we may reply, 'Because I feel like swimming.' We seem to be saying, 'When I have felt like this before, I have behaved in such and such a way.' Feelings occur at just the right time to serve as causes of behavior, and they have been cited as such for centuries. We assume that other people feel as we feel when they behave as we behave.

But where are these feelings and states of mind? Of what stuff are they made? The traditional answer is that they are located in a world of non-physical dimensions called the mind and that they are mental. But another question then arises: How can a mental event cause or be caused by a physical one? If we want to predict what a person will do, how can we discover the mental causes of his behavior, and how can we produce the feelings and states of mind which will induce him to behave in a given way? Suppose, for example, that we want to get a child to eat a nutritious but not very palatable food. We simply make sure that no other food is available, and eventually he eats. It appears that in depriving him of food (a physical event) we have made him feel hungry (a mental event), and that because he has felt hungry, he has eaten the nutritious food (a physical event). But how did the physical act of deprivation lead to the feeling of hunger, and how did the feeling move the muscles involved in ingestion? There are many other puzzling questions of this sort. What is to be done about them?

The commonest practice is, I think, simply to ignore them. It is possible to believe that behavior expresses feelings, to anticipate what a person will do by guessing or asking him how he feels, and to change the environment in the hope of changing feelings while paying little if any attention to theoretical problems. Those who are not quite comfortable about such a strategy sometimes take refuge in physiology. Mind, it is said, will eventually be found to have a physical basis. As one neurologist recently put it, 'Everyone now accepts the fact that the brain provides the physical basis of human thought.' Freud believed that his very complicated mental apparatus would eventually be found to be physiological, and early introspective psychologists called their discipline Physiological Psychology. The theory of knowledge called Physicalism holds that when we introspect or have feelings we are looking at states or activities of our brains. But the major difficulties are practical: we cannot anticipate what a person will do by looking directly at his feelings *or* his nervous system, nor can we change his behavior by changing his mind *or* his brain. But in any case we seem to be no worse off for ignoring philosophical problems.

METHODOLOGICAL BEHAVIORISM

The mentalistic problem can be avoided by going directly to the prior physical causes while bypassing intermediate feelings or states of mind. The quickest way to do this is to confine oneself to what an early behaviorist, Max Meyer, called the 'psychology of the other one': consider only those facts which can be objectively observed in the behavior of one person in its relation to his prior environmental history. If all linkages are lawful, nothing is lost by neglecting a supposed non-physical link. Thus, if we know that a child has not eaten for a long time, and if we know that he therefore feels hungry and that because he feels hungry he then eats, then we know that if he has not eaten for a long time, he will eat. And if by making other food inaccessible, we make him feel hungry, and if because he feels hungry he then eats a special food, then it must follow that by making other food inaccessible, we induce him to eat the special food.

Similarly, if certain ways of teaching a person lead him to notice very small differences in his 'sensations', and if because he sees these differences he can classify colored objects correctly, then it should follow that we can use these ways of teaching him to classify objects correctly. Or, to take still another example, if circumstances in a white person's history generate feelings of aggression toward blacks, and if those feelings make him behave aggressively, then we may deal simply with the relation between the circumstances in his history and his aggressive behavior.

There is, of course, nothing new in trying to predict or control behavior by observing or manipulating prior public events. Structuralists and developmentalists have not entirely ignored the histories of their subjects, and historians and biographers have explored the influences of climate, culture, persons, and incidents. People have used practical techniques of predicting and controlling behavior with little thought to mental states. Nevertheless, for many centuries there was very little systematic inquiry into the role of the physical environment, although hundreds of highly technical volumes were written about human understanding and the life of the mind. A program of methodological behaviorism became plausible only when progress began to be made in the scientific observation of behavior, because only then was it possible to override the powerful effect of mentalism in diverting inquiry away from the role of the environment.

Mentalistic explanations allay curiosity and bring inquiry to a stop. It is so easy to observe feelings and states of mind at a time and in a place which make them seem like causes that we are not inclined to inquire further. Once the environment begins to be studied, however, its significance cannot be denied.

Methodological behaviorism might be thought of as a psychological version of logical positivism or operationism, but they are concerned with different issues. Logical positivism or operationism holds that since no two observers can agree on what happens in the world of the mind, then from the point of view of physical science mental events are 'unobservables'; there can be no truth by agreement, and we must abandon the examination of mental events and turn instead to how they are studied. We cannot measure sensations and perceptions as such, but we can measure a person's capacity to discriminate among stimuli, and the *concept* of sensation or perception can then be reduced to the *operation* of discrimination.

The logical positivists had their version of 'the other one'. They argued that a robot which behaved precisely like a person, responding in the same way to stimuli, changing its behavior as a result of the same operations, would be indistinguishable from a real person, even though it would not have feelings, sensations, or ideas. If such a robot could be built, it would prove that none of the supposed manifestations of mental life demanded a mentalistic explanation.

With respect to its own goals, methodological behaviorism was successful. It disposed of many of the problems raised by mentalism and freed itself to work on its own projects without philosophical digressions. By directing attention to genetic and environmental antecedents, it offset an unwarranted concentration on an inner life. It freed us to study the behavior of lower species, where introspection (then regarded as exclusively human) was not feasible, and to explore similarities and differences between man and other species. Some concepts previously associated with private events were formulated in other ways.

But problems remained. Most methodological behaviorists granted the existence of mental events while ruling them out of consideration. Did they really mean to say that they did not matter, that the middle stage in that three-stage sequence of physical–mental–physical contributed nothing – in other words, that feelings and states of mind were merely epiphenomena? It was not the first time that anyone had said so. The view that a purely physical world could be self-sufficient had been suggested centuries before, in the doctrine of psychophysical parallelism, which held that there were two worlds – one of mind and one of matter – and that neither had any effect on the other. Freud's demonstration of the unconscious, in which an awareness of feelings or states of mind seemed unnecessary, pointed in the same direction.

But what about other evidence? Is the traditional *post hoc, ergo propter hoc* argument entirely wrong? Are the feelings we experience just before we behave wholly unrelated to our behavior? What about the power of mind over matter in psychosomatic medicine? What about psychophysics and the mathematical relation between the magnitudes of stimuli and sensations? What about the stream of consciousness? What about the intrapsychic processes of psychiatry, in which feelings produce or suppress other feelings and memories evoke or mask other memories? What about the cognitive processes said to explain perception, thinking, the construction of sentences, and artistic creation? Must all this be ignored because it cannot be studied objectively?

RADICAL BEHAVIORISM

The statement that behaviorists deny the existence of feelings, sensations, ideas, and other features of mental life needs a good deal of clarification. Methodological behaviorism and some versions of logical positivism ruled private events out of bounds because there could be no public agreement about their validity. Introspection could not be accepted as a scientific practice, and the psychology of people like Wilhelm Wundt and Edward B. Titchener was attacked accordingly. Radical behaviorism, however, takes a different line. It does not deny the possibility of self-observation or self-knowledge or its possible usefulness, but it questions the nature of what is felt or observed and hence known. It restores introspection but not what philosophers and introspective psychologists had believed they were 'specting', and it raises the question of how much of one's body one can actually observe.

Mentalism kept attention away from the external antecedent events which might have explained behavior, by seeming to supply an alternative explanation. Methodological behaviorism did just the reverse: by dealing exclusively with external antecedent events it turned attention away from self-observation and self-knowledge. Radical behaviorism restores some kind of balance. It does not insist upon truth by agreement and can therefore consider events taking place in the private world within the skin. It does not call these events unobservable, and it does not dismiss them as subjective. It simply questions the nature of the object observed and the reliability of the observations.

The position can be stated as follows: what is felt or introspectively observed is not some non-physical world of consciousness, mind, or mental life but the observer's own body. This does not mean, as I shall show later, that introspection is a kind of physiological research, nor does it mean (and this is the heart of the argument) that what are felt or introspectively observed are the causes of behavior. An organism behaves as it does because of its current structure, but most of this is out of reach of introspection. At the moment we must content ourselves, as the methodological behaviorist insists, with a person's genetic and environmental histories. What are introspectively observed are certain collateral products of those histories.

The environment made its first great contribution during the evolution of the species, but it exerts a different kind of effect during the lifetime of the individual, and the combination of the two effects is the behavior we observe at any given time. Any available information about either contribution helps in the prediction and control of human behavior and in its interpretation in daily life. To the extent that either can be changed, behavior can be changed.

Our increasing knowledge of the control exerted by the environment makes it possible to examine the effect of the world within the skin and the nature of self-knowledge. It also makes it possible to interpret a wide range of mentalistic expressions. For example, we can look at those features of behavior which have led people to speak of an act of will, of a sense of purpose, of experience as distinct from reality, of innate or acquired ideas, of memories, meanings, and the personal knowledge of the scientist, and of hundreds of other mentalistic things or events. Some can be 'translated into behavior', others discarded as unnecessary or meaningless.

In this way we repair the major damage wrought by mentalism. When what a person does is attributed to what is going on inside him, investigation is brought to an end. Why explain the explanation? For twenty-five hundred years people have been preoccupied with feelings and mental life, but only recently has any interest been shown in a more precise analysis of the role of the environment. Ignorance of that role led in the first place to mental fictions, and it has been perpetuated by the explanatory practices to which they gave rise.

2

A. H. MASLOW

A Theory of Human Motivation

Abridged from A. H. Maslow, 'A theory of human motivation', *Psychological Review*, Vol. 50, 1943, pp. 370–96.

THE BASIC NEEDS

The 'physiological' needs. – The needs that are usually taken as the starting point for motivation theory are the so-called physiological drives. Two recent lines of research make it necessary to revise our customary notions about these needs, first, the development of the concept of homeostasis, and second, the finding that appetites (preferential choices among foods) are a fairly efficient indication of actual needs or lacks in the body.

Homeostasis refers to the body's automatic efforts to maintain a constant, normal state of the blood stream. Cannon (1932) has described this process for the water content of the blood, salt content, sugar content, protein content, fat content, calcium content, oxygen content, constant hydrogen-ion level (acid–base balance) and constant temperature of the blood. Obviously this list can be extended to include other minerals, the hormones, vitamins, etc.

We cannot identify all physiological needs as homeostatic. That sexual desire, sleepiness, sheer activity and maternal behavior in animals are homeostatic has not yet been demonstrated. Furthermore, this list would not include the various sensory pleasures (tastes, smells, tickling, stroking) which are probably physiological and which may become the goals of motivated behavior.

In a previous paper (Maslow, 1943) it has been pointed out that these physiological drives or needs are to be considered unusual rather than typical because they are isolable, and because they are localizable somatically. That is to say, they are relatively independent of each other, of other motivations and of the organism as a whole, and secondly, in many cases, it is possible to demonstrate a localized, underlying somatic base for the drive. This is true less generally than has been thought (exceptions are fatigue, sleepiness, maternal responses) but it is still true in the classic instances of hunger, sex, and thirst.

It should be pointed out again that any of the physiological needs and the consummatory behavior involved with them serve as channels for all sorts of other needs as well. That is to say, the person who thinks he is hungry may actually be seeking more for comfort, or dependence, than for vitamins or proteins. Conversely, it is possible to satisfy the hunger need in part by other activities such as drinking water or smoking cigarettes. In other words, relatively isolable as these physiological needs are, they are not completely so.

Undoubtedly these physiological needs are the most prepotent of all needs. What this means specifically is that in the human being who is missing everything in life in an extreme fashion, it is most likely that the major motivation would be the physiological needs rather than any others. A person who is lacking food, safety, love, and esteem would most probably hunger for food more strongly than for anything else.

If all the needs are unsatisfied, and the organism is then dominated by the physiological needs, all other needs may become simply non-existent or be pushed into the background.

It is quite true that man lives by bread alone – when there is no bread. But what happens to man's desires when there *is* plenty of bread and when his belly is chronically filled?

At once other (and 'higher') needs emerge and these, rather than physiological hungers, dominate the organism. And when these in turn are satisfied, again new (and still 'higher') needs emerge and so on. This is what we mean by saying that the basic human needs are organized into a hierarchy of relative prepotency.

One main implication of this phrasing is that gratification becomes as important a concept as deprivation in motivation theory, for it releases the organism from the domination of a relatively more physiological need, permitting thereby the emergence of other more social goals. The physiological needs, along with their partial goals, when chronically gratified cease to exist as active determinants or organizers of behavior. They now exist only in a potential fashion in the sense that they may emerge again to dominate the organism if they are thwarted. But a want that is satisfied is no longer a want. The organism is dominated and its behavior organized only by unsatisfied needs. If hunger is satisfied, it becomes unimportant in the current dynamics of the individual.

This statement is somewhat qualified by a hypothesis to be discussed more fully later, namely that it is precisely those individuals in whom a certain need has always been satisfied who are best equipped to tolerate deprivation of that need in the future, and that furthermore, those who have been deprived in the past will react differently to current satisfactions than the one who has never been deprived.

The safety needs. – If the physiological needs are relatively well gratified, there then emerges a new set of needs, which we may categorize roughly as the safety needs. All that has been said of the physiological needs is equally true, although in lesser degree, of these desires. The organism may equally well be wholly dominated by them. They may serve as the almost exclusive organizers of behavior, recruiting all the capacities of the organism in their service, and we may then fairly describe the whole organism as a safety-seeking mechanism.

Although in this paper we are interested primarily in the needs of the adult, we can approach an understanding of his safety needs perhaps more efficiently by observation of infants and children, in whom these needs are much more simple and obvious. One reason for the clearer appearance of the threat or danger reaction in infants is that they do not inhibit this reaction at all, whereas adults in our society have been taught to inhibit it at all costs. Thus even when adults do feel their safety to be threatened we may not be able to see this on the surface.

The average child in our society generally prefers a safe, orderly, predictable, organized world, which he can count on, and in which unexpected, unmanageable or other dangerous things do not happen, and in which, in any case, he has all-powerful parents who protect and shield him from harm.

The healthy, normal, fortunate adult in our culture is largely satisfied in his safety needs. The peaceful, smoothly running, 'good' society ordinarily makes its members feel safe enough from wild animals, extremes of temperature, criminals, assault and murder, tyranny, etc. Therefore, in a very real sense, he no longer has any safety needs as active motivators. Just as a sated man no longer feels hungry, a safe man no longer feels endangered.

Other broader aspects of the attempt to seek safety and stability in the world are seen in the very common preference for familiar rather than unfamiliar things, or for the known rather than the unknown. The tendency to have some religion or world-philosophy that organizes the universe and the men in it into some sort of satisfactorily coherent, meaningful whole is also in part motivated by safety-seeking. Here too we may list science and philosophy in general as partially motivated by the safety needs (we shall see later that there are also other motivations to scientific, philosophical or religious endeavor).

Otherwise the need for safety is seen as an active and dominant mobilizer of the organism's resources only in emergencies, e.g., war, disease, natural catastrophes, crime waves, societal disorganization, neurosis, brain injury, chronically bad situation.

Some neurotic adults in our society are, in many ways, like the unsafe child in their desire for safety, although in the former it takes on a somewhat special appearance. Their reaction is often to unknown, psychological dangers in a world that is perceived to be hostile, overwhelming and threatening.

The neurosis in which the search for safety takes its clearest form is in the compulsive–obsessive neurosis. Compulsive–obsessives try frantically to order and stabilize the world so that no unmanageable, unexpected or unfamiliar dangers ever appear (see Maslow and Mittelmann, 1941). They hedge themselves about with all sorts of ceremonials, rules and formulas so that every possible contingency may be provided for and so that no new contingencies may appear. They are much like the brain-injured cases, described by Goldstein (1939), who manage to maintain their equilibrium by avoiding everything unfamiliar and strange and by ordering their restricted world in such a neat, disciplined, orderly fashion that everything in the world can be counted upon. They try to arrange the world so that anything unexpected (dangers) cannot possibly occur. If, through no fault of their own, something unexpected does occur, they go into a panic reaction as if this unexpected occurrence constituted a grave danger. What we can see only as a none-too-strong preference in the healthy person, e.g., preference for the familiar, becomes a life-and-death necessity in abnormal cases.

The love needs. – If both the physiological and the safety needs are fairly well gratified, then there will emerge the love and affection and belongingness needs, and the whole cycle already described will repeat itself with this new center. Now the person will feel keenly, as never before, the absence of friends, or a sweetheart, or a wife, or children. He will hunger for affectionate relations with people in general, namely, for a place in his group, and he will strive with great intensity to achieve this goal. He will want to attain such a place more than anything else in the world and may even forget that once, when he was hungry, he sneered at love.

In our society the thwarting of these needs is the most commonly found core in cases of maladjustment and more severe psychopathology.

Love and affection, as well as their possible expression in sexuality, are generally looked upon with ambivalence and are customarily hedged about with many restrictions and inhibitions. Practically all theorists of psychopathology have stressed thwarting of the love needs as basic in the picture of maladjustment. Many clinical studies have therefore been made of this need and we know more about it perhaps than any of the other needs except the physiological ones (see Maslow and Mittelmann, 1941).

One thing that must be stressed at this point is that love is not synonymous with sex. Sex may be studied as a purely physiological need. Ordinarily sexual behavior is multi-determined, that is to say, determined not only by sexual but also by other needs, chief among which are the love and affection needs. Also not to be overlooked is the fact that the love needs involve both giving *and* receiving love (see Maslow, 1942; and Plant, 1937, Chapter V).

The esteem needs. – All people in our society (with a few pathological exceptions) have a need or desire for a stable, firmly based, (usually) high evaluation of themselves, for self-respect, or self-esteem, and for the esteem of others. By firmly based self-esteem, we mean that which is soundly based upon real capacity, achievement and respect from others. These needs may be classified into two subsidiary sets. These are, first, the desire for strength, for achievement, for adequacy, for confidence in the face of the world, and for independence and freedom.[1] Secondly, we have what we may call the desire for reputation or prestige (defining it as respect or esteem from other people), recognition, attention, importance or appreciation.[2] These needs have been relatively stressed by Alfred Adler and his followers, and have been relatively neglected by Freud and the psychoanalysts. More and more today however there is appearing widespread appreciation of their central importance.

---

[1] Whether or not this particular desire is universal we do not know. The crucial question, especially important today, is 'Will men who are enslaved and dominated inevitably feel dissatisfied and rebellious?' We may assume on the basis of commonly known clinical data that a man who has known true freedom (not paid for by giving up safety and security but rather built on the basis of adequate safety and security) will not willingly or easily allow his freedom to be taken away from him. But we do not know that this is true for the person born into slavery. The events of the next decade should give us our answer. See discussion of this problem in Fromm (1941).

[2] Perhaps the desire for prestige and respect from others is subsidiary to the desire for self-esteem or confidence in oneself. Observation of children seems to indicate that this is so, but clinical data give no clear support for such a conclusion.

Satisfaction of the self-esteem need leads to feelings of self-confidence, worth, strength, capability and adequacy of being useful and necessary in the world. But thwarting of these needs produces feelings of inferiority, of weakness and of helplessness. These feelings in turn give rise to either basic discouragement or else compensatory or neurotic trends. An appreciation of the necessity of basic self-confidence and an understanding of how helpless people are without it can be easily gained from a study of severe traumatic neurosis.[3]

The need for self-actualization. – Even if all these needs are satisfied, we may still often (if not always) expect that a new discontent and restlessness will soon develop, unless the individual is doing what he is fitted for. A musician must make music, an artist must paint, a poet must write, if he is to be ultimately happy. What a man *can* be, he *must* be. This need we may call self-actualization.

This term, first coined by Kurt Goldstein, is being used in this paper in a much more specific and limited fashion. It refers to the desire for self-fulfillment, namely, to the tendency for him to become actualized in what he is potentially. This tendency might be phrased as the desire to become more and more what one is, to become everything that one is capable of becoming.

The specific form that these needs will take will of course vary greatly from person to person. In one individual it may take the form of the desire to be an ideal mother, in another it may be expressed athletically, and in still another it may be expressed in painting pictures or in inventions. It is not necessarily a creative urge although in people who have any capacities for creation it will take this form.

The clear emergence of these needs rests upon prior satisfaction of the physiological, safety, love and esteem needs. We shall call people who are satisfied in these needs, basically satisfied people, and it is from these that we may expect the fullest (and healthiest) creativeness.[4] Since, in our society, basically satisfied people are the exception, we do not

---

[3]See Kardiner (1941). For more extensive discussion of normal self-esteem, as well as for reports of various researches, see Maslow (1939).

[4]Clearly creative behavior, like painting, is like any other behavior in having multiple determinants. It may be seen in 'innately creative' people whether they are satisfied or not, happy or unhappy, hungry or sated. Also it is clear that creative activity may be compensatory, ameliorative or purely economic. It is my impression (as yet unconfirmed) that it is possible to distinguish the artistic and intellectual products of basically satisfied people from those of basically unsatisfied people by inspection alone. In any case, here too we must distinguish, in a dynamic fashion, the overt behavior itself from its various motivations or purposes.

know much about self-actualization, either experimentally or clinically. It remains a challenging problem for research.

The preconditions for the basic need satisfactions. – There are certain conditions which are immediate prerequisites for the basic need satisfactions. Danger to these is reacted to almost as if it were a direct danger to the basic needs themselves. Such conditions as freedom to speak, freedom to do what one wishes so long as no harm is done to others, freedom to express oneself, freedom to investigate and seek for information, freedom to defend oneself, justice, fairness, honesty, orderliness in the group are examples of such preconditions for basic need satisfactions. Thwarting in these freedoms will be reacted to with a threat or emergency response. These conditions are not ends in themselves but they are *almost* so since they are so closely related to the basic needs, which are apparently the only ends in themselves. These conditions are defended because without them the basic satisfactions are quite impossible, or at least, very severely endangered.

If we remember that the cognitive capacities (perceptual, intellectual, learning) are a set of adjustive tools, which have, among other functions, that of satisfaction of our basic needs, then it is clear that any danger to them, any deprivation or blocking of their free use, must also be indirectly threatening to the basic needs themselves. Such a statement is a partial solution of the general problems of curiosity, the search for knowledge, truth and wisdom, and the ever-persistent urge to solve the cosmic mysteries.

An act is psychologically important if it contributes directly to satisfaction of basic needs. The less directly it so contributes, or the weaker this contribution is, the less important this act must be conceived to be from the point of view of dynamic psychology.

The desires to know and to understand. – So far, we have mentioned the cognitive needs only in passing. Acquiring knowledge and systematizing the universe have been considered as, in part, techniques for the achievement of basic safety in the world, or, for the intelligent man, expressions of self-actualization. Also freedom of inquiry and expression have been discussed as preconditions of satisfactions of the basic needs. True though these formulations may be, they do not constitute definitive answers to the question as to the motivation role of curiosity, learning, philosophizing, experimenting, etc. They are, at best, no more than partial answers.

This question is especially difficult because we know so little about the facts. Curiosity, exploration, desire for the facts, desire to know may certainly be observed easily enough. The fact that they often are pursued even at great cost to the individual's safety is an earnest of the partial character of our previous discussion. In addition, the writer must admit that, though he has sufficient clinical evidence to postulate the desire to know as a very strong drive in intelligent people, no data are available for unintelligent people. It may then be largely a function of relatively high intelligence. Rather tentatively, then, and largely in the hope of stimulating discussion and research, we shall postulate a basic desire to know, to be aware of reality, to get the facts, to satisfy curiosity, or as Wertheimer phrases it, to see rather than to be blind.

This postulation, however, is not enough. Even after we know, we are impelled to know more and more minutely and microscopically on the one hand, and on the other, more and more extensively in the direction of a world philosophy, religion, etc. The facts that we acquire, if they are isolated or atomistic, inevitably get theorized about, and either analyzed or organized or both. This process has been phrased by some as the search for 'meaning'. We shall then postulate a desire to understand, to systematize, to organize, to analyze, to look for relations and meanings.

Once these desires are accepted for discussion, we see that they too form themselves into a small hierarchy in which the desire to know is prepotent over the desire to understand. All the characteristics of a hierarchy of prepotency that we have described above seem to hold for this one as well.

We must guard ourselves against the too easy tendency to separate these desires from the basic needs we have discussed above, i.e., to make a sharp dichotomy between 'cognitive' and 'conative' needs. The desire to know and to understand are themselves conative, i.e., have a striving character, and are as much personality needs as the 'basic needs' we have already discussed.

FURTHER CHARACTERISTICS OF THE BASIC NEEDS

The degree of fixity of the hierarchy of basic needs. – We have spoken so far as if this hierarchy were a fixed order but actually it is not nearly as rigid as we may have implied. It is true that most of the people with whom we have worked have seemed to have these basic needs in about the order that has been indicated. However, there have been a number of exceptions.

(1) There are some people in whom, for instance, self-esteem seems

to be more important than love. This most common reversal in the hierarchy is usually due to the development of the notion that the person who is most likely to be loved is a strong or powerful person, one who inspires respect or fear, and who is self-confident or aggressive. Therefore such people who lack love and seek it may try hard to put on a front of aggressive, confident behavior. But essentially they seek high self-esteem and its behavior expressions more as a means-to-an-end than for its own sake; they seek self-assertion for the sake of love rather than for self-esteem itself.

(2) There are other, apparently innately creative people in whom the drive to creativeness seems to be more important than any other counter-determinant. Their creativeness might appear not as self-actualization released by basic satisfaction, but in spite of lack of basic satisfaction.

(3) In certain people the level of aspiration may be permanently deadened or lowered. That is to say, the less prepotent goals may simply be lost, and may disappear forever, so that the person who has experienced life at a very low level, e.g., chronic unemployment, may continue to be satisfied for the rest of his life if only he can get enough food.

(4) The so-called 'psychopathic personality' is another example of permanent loss of the love needs. These are people who, according to the best data available (Levy, 1937), have been starved for love in the earliest months of their lives and have simply lost forever the desire and the ability to give and to receive affection (as animals lose sucking or pecking reflexes that are not exercised soon enough after birth).

(5) Another cause of reversal of the hierarchy is that when a need has been satisfied for a long time, this need may be underevaluated. People who have never experienced chronic hunger are apt to under-estimate its effects and to look upon food as a rather unimportant thing. If they are dominated by a higher need, this higher need will seem to be the most important of all. It then becomes possible, and indeed does actually happen, that they may, for the sake of this higher need, put themselves into the position of being deprived in a more basic need. We may expect that after a long-time deprivation of the more basic need there will be a tendency to re-evaluate both needs so that the more prepotent need will actually become consciously prepotent for the individual who may have given it up very lightly. Thus, a man who has given up his job rather than lose his self-respect, and who then starves for six months or so, may be willing to take his job back even at the price of losing his self-respect.

(6) Another partial explanation of *apparent* reversals is seen in the fact that we have been talking about the hierarchy of prepotency in terms of consciously felt wants or desires rather than of behavior. Looking at behavior itself may give us the wrong impression. What we have claimed is that the person will *want* the more basic of two needs when deprived in both. There is no necessary implication here that he will act upon his desires. Let us say again that there are many determinants of behavior other than the needs and desires.

(7) Perhaps more important than all these exceptions are the ones that involve ideals, high social standards, high values and the like. With such values people become martyrs; they will give up everything for the sake of a particular ideal, or value. These people may be understood, at least in part, by reference to one basic concept (or hypothesis) which may be called 'increased frustration-tolerance through early gratification'. People who have been satisfied in their basic needs throughout their lives, particularly in their earlier years, seem to develop exceptional power to withstand present or future thwarting of these needs simply because they have strong, healthy character structure as a result of basic satisfaction. They are the 'strong' people who can easily weather disagreement or opposition, who can swim against the stream of public opinion and who can stand up for the truth at great personal cost.

I say all this in spite of the fact that there is a certain amount of sheer habituation which is also involved in any full discussion of frustration tolerance. For instance, it is likely that those persons who have been accustomed to relative starvation for a long time are partially enabled thereby to withstand food deprivation. What sort of balance must be made between these two tendencies, of habituation on the one hand, and of past satisfaction breeding present frustration tolerance on the other hand, remains to be worked out by further research.

Degrees of relative satisfaction. – So far, our theoretical discussion may have given the impression that these five sets of needs are somehow in a step-wise, all-or-none relationship to each other. We have spoken in such terms as the following: 'If one need is satisfied, then another emerges.' This statement might give the false impression that a need must be satisfied 100 per cent before the next need emerges. In actual fact, most members of our society who are normal are partially satisfied in all their basic needs and partially unsatisfied in all their basic needs at the same time. A more realistic description of the hierarchy would be in terms of decreasing percentages of satisfaction as we go up the hierarchy of prepotency.

As for the concept of emergence of a new need after satisfaction of the prepotent need, this emergence is not a sudden, saltatory phenomenon but rather a gradual emergence by slow degrees from nothingness.

Unconscious character of needs. – These needs are neither necessarily conscious nor unconscious. On the whole, however, in the average person, they are more often unconscious rather than conscious. It is not necessary at this point to overhaul the tremendous mass of evidence which indicates the crucial importance of unconscious motivation. It would by now be expected, on *a priori* grounds alone, that unconscious motivations would on the whole be rather more important than the conscious motivations. What we have called the basic needs are very often largely unconscious, although they may, with suitable techniques and with sophisticated people, become conscious.

The role of gratified needs. – It has been pointed out above several times that our needs usually emerge only when more prepotent needs have been gratified. Thus gratification has an important role in motivation theory. Apart from this, however, needs cease to play an active determining or organizing role as soon as they are gratified.

What this means is that, e.g., a basically satisfied person no longer has the needs for esteem, love, safety, etc. The only sense in which he might be said to have them is in the almost metaphysical sense that a sated man has hunger, or a filled bottle has emptiness. If we are interested in what *actually* motivates us, and not in what has, will, or might motivate us, then a satisfied need is not a motivator. It must be considered for all practical purposes simply not to exist, to have disappeared. This point should be emphasized because it has been either overlooked or contradicted in every theory of motivation I know.[5] The perfectly healthy, normal, fortunate man has no sex needs or hunger needs, or needs for safety, or for love, or for prestige, or self-esteem, except in stray moments of quickly passing threat. If we were to say otherwise, we should also have to aver that every man had all the pathological reflexes, e.g., Babinski, etc., because if his nervous system were damaged, these would appear.

It is such considerations as these that suggest the bold postulation that a man who is thwarted in any of his basic needs may fairly be envisaged simply as a sick man. This is a fair parallel to our designation as 'sick' of the man who lacks vitamins or minerals. Who is to say that a lack of love is less important than a lack of vitamins? Since we know the pathogenic effects of love starvation, who is to say that we are

[5]Note that acceptance of this theory necessitates basic revision of the Freudian theory.

invoking value-questions in an unscientific or illegitimate way, any more than the physician does who diagnoses and treats pellagra or scurvy? If I were permitted this usage, I should then say simply that a healthy man is primarily motivated by his needs to develop and actualize his fullest potentialities and capacities. If a man has any other basic needs in any active, chronic sense, then he is simply an unhealthy man. He is as surely sick as if he had suddenly developed a strong salt hunger or calcium hunger.[6]

If this statement seems unusual or paradoxical the reader may be assured that this is only one among many such paradoxes that will appear as we revise our ways of looking at man's deeper motivations. When we ask what man wants of life, we deal with his very essence.

SUMMARY

(1) There are at least five sets of goals, which we may call basic needs. These are briefly physiological, safety, love, esteem, and self-actualization. In addition, we are motivated by the desire to achieve or maintain the various conditions upon which these basic satisfactions rest and by certain more intellectual desires.

(2) These basic goals are related to each other, being arranged in a hierarchy of prepotency. This means that the most prepotent goal will monopolize consciousness and will tend of itself to organize the recruitment of the various capacities of the organism. The less prepotent needs are minimized, even forgotten or denied. But when a need is fairly well satisfied, the next prepotent ('higher') need emerges, in turn to dominate the conscious life and to serve as the center of organization of behavior, since gratified needs are not active motivators.

Thus man is a perpetually wanting animal. Ordinarily the satisfaction of these wants is not altogether mutually exclusive, but only tends to be. The average member of our society is most often partially

[6]If we were to use the word 'sick' in this way, we should then also have to face squarely the relations of man to his society. One clear implication of our definition would be that (1) since a man is to be called sick who is basically thwarted, and (2) since such basic thwarting is made possible ultimately only by forces outside the individual, then (3) sickness in the individual must come ultimately from a sickness in the society. The 'good' or healthy society would then be defined as one that permitted man's highest purposes to emerge by satisfying all his prepotent basic needs.

satisfied and partially unsatisfied in all of his wants. The hierarchy principle is usually empirically observed in terms of increasing percentages of non-satisfaction as we go up the hierarchy. Reversals of the average order of the hierarchy are sometimes observed. Also it has been observed that an individual may permanently lose the higher wants in the hierarchy under special conditions. There are not only ordinarily multiple motivations for usual behavior, but in addition many determinants other than motives.

(3) Any thwarting or possibility of thwarting of these basic human goals, or danger to the defenses which protect them, or to the conditions upon which they rest, is considered to be a psychological threat. With a few exceptions, all psychopathology may be partially traced to such threats. A basically thwarted man may actually be defined as a 'sick' man, if we wish.

(4) It is such basic threats which bring about the general emergency reactions.

(5) Certain other basic problems have not been dealt with because of limitations of space. Among these are (a) the problem of values in any definitive motivation theory, (b) the relation between appetites, desires, needs and what is 'good' for the organism, (c) the etiology of the basic needs and their possible derivation in early childhood, (d) redefinition of motivational concepts, i.e., drive, desire, wish, need, goal, (e) implication of our theory for hedonistic theory, (f) the nature of the uncompleted act, of success and failure, and of aspiration-level, (g) the role of association, habit and conditioning, (h) relation to the theory of interpersonal relations, (i) implications for psychotherapy, (j) implication for theory of society, (k) the theory of selfishness, (l) the relation between needs and cultural patterns, (m) the relation between this theory and Allport's theory of functional autonomy. These as well as certain other less important questions must be considered as motivation theory attempts to become definitive.

REFERENCES

Cannon, W. B. (1932), *The Wisdom of the Body*, New York: Norton.

Fromm, E. (1941), *Escape from Freedom*, New York: Farrar & Rinehart.

Goldstein, K. (1939), *The Organism*, New York: American Book Co.

Kardiner, A. (1941), *The Traumatic Neuroses of War*, New York: Hoeber.

Levy, D. M. (1937), 'Primary affect hunger', *American Journal of Psychology*, *94*, 643–52.

Maslow, A. H. (1939), 'Dominance, personality, and social behavior in women', *Journal of*

Social Psychology, *10*, 3–39.

Maslow, A. H. (1942), 'The dynamics of psychological security–insecurity', *Character and Personality*, *10*, 331–44.

Maslow, A. H. (1943), 'A preface to motivation theory', *Psychosomatic Medicine*, *5*, 85–92.

Maslow, A. H., & Mittelmann, B. (1941), *Principles of Abnormal Psychology*, New York: Harper.

Plant, J. (1937), *Personality and the Culture Pattern*, New York: Commonwealth Fund.

3

ROBERT W. WHITE

Motivation Reconsidered:
The Concept of Competence

Abridged from R. W. White, 'Motivation reconsidered: The concept of
competence', *Psychological Review*, Vol. 66, 1959, pp. 297–333.

When parallel trends can be observed in realms as far apart as animal
behavior and psychoanalytic ego psychology, there is reason to suppose
that we are witnessing a significant evolution of ideas. In these two
realms, as in psychology as a whole, there is evidence of deepening
discontent with theories of motivation based upon drives. Despite great
differences in the language and concepts used to express this discontent,
the theme is everywhere the same: Something important is left out
when we make drives the operating forces in animal and human behavior.

The chief theories against which the discontent is directed are those
of Hull and of Freud. In their respective realms, drive-reduction theory
and psychoanalytic instinct theory, which are basically very much alike,
have acquired a considerable air of orthodoxy. Both views have an
appealing simplicity, and both have been argued long enough so that
their main outlines are generally known.

In this paper I shall attempt a conceptualization which gathers up
some of the important things left out by drive theory. To give the
concept a name I have chosen the word *competence*, which is intended
in a broad biological sense rather than in its narrow everyday meaning.
As used here, competence will refer to an organism's capacity to interact
effectively with its environment. In organisms capable of but little
learning, this capacity might be considered an innate attribute, but in
the mammals and especially man, with their highly plastic nervous
systems, fitness to interact with the environment is slowly attained
through prolonged feats of learning. In view of the directedness and
persistence of the behavior that leads to these feats of learning, I consider it necessary to treat competence as having a motivational aspect,
and my central argument will be that the motivation needed to attain
competence cannot be wholly derived from sources of energy currently

conceptualized as drives or instincts. We need a different kind of motivational idea to account fully for the fact that man and the higher mammals develop a competence in dealing with the environment which they certainly do not have at birth and certainly do not arrive at simply through maturation.

The kinds of behavior that are left out or handled poorly by theories of motivation based wholly on organic drives ... [include] the familiar series of learned skills which starts with sucking, grasping, and visual exploration and continues with crawling and walking, acts of focal attention and perception, memory, language and thinking, anticipation, the exploring of novel places and objects, effecting stimulus changes in the environment, manipulating and exploiting the surroundings, and achieving higher levels of motor and mental coordination. These aspects of behavior have long been the province of child psychology, which has attempted to measure the slow course of their development and has shown how heavily their growth depends upon learning. Collectively they are sometimes referred to as adaptive mechanisms or as ego processes, but on the whole we are not accustomed to cast a single name over the diverse feats whereby we learn to deal with the environment.

I now propose that we gather the various kinds of behavior just mentioned, all of which have to do with effective interaction with the environment, under the general heading of competence. According to Webster, competence means fitness or ability, and the suggested synonyms include capability, capacity, efficiency, proficiency, and skill. It is therefore a suitable word to describe such things as grasping and exploring, crawling and walking, attention and perception, language and thinking, manipulating and changing the surroundings, all of which promote an effective – a competent – interaction with the environment.

There is a *competence motivation* as well as competence in its more familiar sense of achieved capacity. The behavior that leads to the building-up of effective grasping, handling, and letting go of objects, to take one example, is not random behavior produced by a general overflow of energy. It is directed, selective, and persistent, and it is continued not because it serves primary drives, which indeed it cannot serve until it is almost perfected, but because it satisfies an intrinsic need to deal with the environment.

No doubt it will at first seem arbitrary to propose a single motivational conception in connection with so many and such diverse kinds of behavior. What do we gain by attributing motivational unity to such a large array of activities? We could, of course, say that each developmental sequence, such as learning to grasp or to walk, has its own built-in bit of motivation – its 'aliment', as Piaget (1952) has expressed it. We could go further and say that each item of behavior has its intrinsic motive – but this makes the concept of motivation redundant. On the other hand, we might follow the lead of the animal psychologists and postulate a limited number of broader motives under such names as curiosity, manipulation, and mastery. I believe that the idea of a competence motivation is more adequate than any of these alternatives and that it points to very vital common properties which have been lost from view amidst the strongly analytical tendencies that go with detailed research.

We shall now attempt to describe more fully the possible nature of the motivational aspect of competence. It needs its own name, and I propose that this name be *effectance*.

EFFECTANCE

The new freedom produced by two decades of research on animal drives is of great help in this undertaking. We are no longer obliged to look for a source of energy external to the nervous system, for a consummatory climax, or for a fixed connection between reinforcement and tension-reduction. Effectance motivation cannot, of course, be conceived as having a source in tissues external to the nervous system. We must assume it to be neurogenic, its 'energies' being simply those of the living cells that make up the nervous system. External stimuli play an important part, but in terms of 'energy' this part is secondary, as one can see most clearly when environmental stimulation is actively sought. Putting it picturesquely, we might say that the effectance urge represents what the neuromuscular system wants to do when it is otherwise unoccupied or is gently stimulated by the environment. Obviously there are no consummatory acts; satisfaction would appear to lie in the arousal and maintaining of activity rather than in its slow decline toward bored passivity. The motive need not be conceived as intense and powerful in the sense that hunger, pain, or fear can be powerful when aroused to high pitch. There are plenty of instances in which children refuse to leave their absorbed play in order to eat or to visit the toilet. Strongly aroused drives, pain, and anxiety, however, can be conceived as overriding the effectance urge and capturing the energies of the neuromuscular system. But effectance motivation is persistent in the sense that it regularly occupies the spare waking time between episodes of homeostatic crisis.

In speculating upon this subject we must bear in mind the continuous nature of behavior. This is easier said than done; habitually we break things down in order to understand them, and such units as the reflex arc, the stimulus–response sequence, and the single transaction with the environment seem like inevitable steps toward clarity. Yet when we apply such an analysis to playful exploration we lose the most essential aspect of the behavior. It is constantly circling from stimulus to perception to action to effect to stimulus to perception, and so on around; or, more properly, these processes are all in continuous action and continuous change. Dealing with the environment means carrying on a continuing transaction which gradually changes one's relation to the environment. Because there is no consummatory climax, satisfaction has to be seen as lying in a considerable series of transactions, in a trend of behavior rather than a goal that is achieved. It is difficult to make the word 'satisfaction' have this connotation, and we shall do well to replace it by 'feeling of efficacy' when attempting to indicate the subjective and affective side of effectance.

It is useful to recall the findings about novelty: the singular effectiveness of novelty in engaging interest and for a time supporting persistent behavior. We also need to consider the selective continuance of transactions in which the animal or child has a more or less pronounced effect upon the environment – in which something happens as a consequence of his activity. Interest is not aroused and sustained when the stimulus field is so familiar that it gives rise at most to reflex acts or automatized habits. It is not sustained when actions produce no effects or changes in the stimulus field. Our conception must therefore be that effectance motivation is aroused by stimulus conditions which offer, as Hebb (1949) puts it, difference-in-sameness. This leads to variability and novelty of response, and interest is best sustained when the resulting action affects the stimulus so as to produce further difference-in-sameness. Interest wanes when action begins to have less effect; effectance motivation subsides when a situation has been explored to the point that it no longer presents new possibilities.

We have to conceive further that the arousal of playful and exploratory interest means the appearance of organization involving both the cognitive and active aspects of behavior. Change in the stimulus field is not an end in itself, so to speak; it happens when one is passively moved about, and it may happen as a consequence of random movements without becoming focalized and instigating exploration. Similarly, action which has effects is not an end in itself, for if one unintentionally kicks away a branch while walking, or knocks something off a table, these effects by no means necessarily become involved in playful investigation. Schachtel's (1954) emphasis on focal attention becomes helpful at this point. Playful and exploratory behavior is not random or casual. It involves focal *attention* to some object – the fixing of some aspect of the stimulus field so that it stays relatively constant – and it also involves the focalizing of *action* upon this object. As Diamond (1939) has expressed it, response under these conditions is 'relevant to the stimulus', and it is change in the *focalized* stimulus that so strongly affects the level of interest. Dealing with the environment means directing focal attention to some part of it and organizing actions to have some effect on this part.

The urge toward competence is inferred specifically from behavior that shows a lasting focalization and that has the characteristics of exploration and experimentation, a kind of variation within the focus. When this particular sort of activity is aroused in the nervous system, effectance motivation is being aroused, for it is characteristic of this particular sort of activity that it is selective, directed, and persistent, and that instrumental acts will be learned for the sole reward of engaging in it.

Some objection may be felt to my introducing the word *competence* in connection with behavior that is so often playful. Certainly the playing child is doing things for fun, not because of a desire to improve his competence in dealing with the stern hard world. In order to forestall misunderstanding, it should be pointed out that the usage here is parallel to what we do when we connect sex with its biological goal of reproduction. The sex drive aims for pleasure and gratification, and reproduction is a consequence that is presumably unforeseen by animals and by man at primitive levels of understanding. Effectance motivation similarly aims for the feeling of efficacy, not for the vitally important learnings that come as its consequence. If we consider the part played by competence motivation in adult human life we can observe the same parallel. Sex may now be completely and purposefully divorced from reproduction but nevertheless pursued for the pleasure it can yield. Similarly, effectance motivation may lead to continuing exploratory interests or active adventures when in fact there is no longer any gain in actual competence or any need for it in terms of survival. In both cases the motive is capable of yielding surplus satisfaction well beyond what is necessary to get the biological work done.

In infants and young children it seems to me sensible to conceive of effectance motivation as undifferentiated. Later in life it becomes profitable to distinguish various motives such as cognizance, construction, mastery, and achievement. It is my view that all such motives have a root in effectance motivation. They are differentiated from it through life experiences which emphasize one or another aspect of the cycle of transaction with environment. Of course, the motives of later childhood and of adult life are no longer simple and can almost never be referred to a single root. They can acquire loadings of anxiety, defense, and compensation, they can become fused with unconscious fantasies of a sexual, aggressive, or omnipotent character, and they can gain force because of their service in producing realistic results in the way of income and career. It is not my intention to cast effectance in the star part in adult motivation. The acquisition of motives is a complicated affair in which simple and sovereign theories grow daily more obsolete. Yet it may be that the satisfaction of effectance contributes significantly to those feelings of interest which often sustain us so well in day-to-day actions, particularly when the things we are doing have continuing elements of novelty.

What an organism does at a given moment does not always give the right clue as to what it does over a period of time. Discussing this problem, Angyal (1941) has proposed that we should look for the general pattern followed by the total organismic process over the course of time. Obviously this makes it necessary to take account of growth. Angyal defines life as 'a process of self-expansion'; the living system 'expands at the expense of its surroundings', assimilating parts of the environment and transforming them into functioning parts of itself. Organisms differ from other things in nature in that they are 'self-governing entities' which are to some extent 'autonomous'. Internal processes govern them as well as external 'heteronomous' forces. In the course of life there is a relative increase in the preponderance of internal over external forces. The living system expands, assimilates more of the environment, transforms its surroundings so as to bring them under greater control. 'We may say,' Angyal writes, 'that the general dynamic trend of the organism is toward an increase of autonomy ... The human being has a characteristic tendency toward self-determination, that is, a tendency to resist external influences and to subordinate the heteronomous forces of the physical and social environment to its own sphere of influence.' The trend toward increased autonomy is characteristic so long as growth of any kind is going on, though in the end the living system is bound to succumb to the pressure of heteronomous forces.

Of all living creatures, it is man who takes the longest strides toward autonomy. This is not because of any unusual tendency toward bodily expansion at the expense of the environment. It is rather that man, with his mobile hands and abundantly developed brain, attains an extremely high level of competence in his transactions with his surroundings. The building of houses, roads and bridges, the making of tools and instruments, the domestication of plants and animals, all qualify as planful changes made in the environment so that it comes more or less under control and serves our purposes rather than intruding upon them. We meet the fluctuations of outdoor temperature, for example, not only with our bodily homeostatic mechanisms, which alone would be painfully unequal to the task, but also with clothing, buildings, controlled fires, and such complicated devices as self-regulating central heating and air conditioning. Man as a species has developed a tremendous power of bringing the environment into his service, and each individual member of the species must attain what is really quite an impressive level of competence if he is to take part in the life around him.

Under primitive conditions survival must depend quite heavily upon achieved competence. We should expect to find things so arranged as to favor and maximize this achievement. Particularly in the case of man, where so little is provided innately and so much has to be learned through experience, we should expect to find highly advantageous arrangements for securing a steady cumulative learning about the properties of the environment and the extent of possible transactions. Under these circumstances we might expect to find a very powerful drive operating to insure progress toward competence, just as the vital goals of nutrition and reproduction are secured by powerful drives, and it might therefore seem paradoxical that the interests of competence should be so much entrusted to times of play and leisurely exploration. There is good reason to suppose, however, that a strong drive would be precisely the wrong arrangement to secure a flexible, knowledgeable power of transaction with the environment. Strong drives cause us to learn certain lessons well, but they do not create maximum familiarity with our surroundings.

This point was demonstrated half a century ago in some experiments by Yerkes and Dodson (1908). They showed that maximum motivation did not lead to the most rapid solving of problems, especially if the problems were complex. For each problem there was an optimum level of motivation, neither the highest nor the lowest, and the optimum was lower for more complex tasks. The same problem has been discussed more recently by Tolman (1948) in his paper on cognitive maps. A cognitive map can be narrow or broad, depending upon the range of cues picked up in the course of learning. Tolman suggests that one of the conditions which tend to narrow the range of cues is a high level of motivation. In everyday terms, a man hurrying to an important business conference is likely to perceive only the cues that help him to get there faster, whereas a man taking a stroll after lunch is likely to pick up a substantial amount of casual information about his environment.

These facts enable us to see the biological appropriateness of an arrangement which uses periods of less intense motivation for the development of competence. This is not to say that the narrower but efficient learnings that go with the reduction of strong drives make no contribution to general effectiveness. They are certainly an important element in capacity to deal with the environment, but a much greater effectiveness results from having this capacity fed also from learnings that take place in quieter times. It is then that the infant can attend to matters of lesser urgency, exploring the properties of things he does not fear and does not need to eat, learning to gauge the force of his string-pulling when the only penalty for failure is silence on the part of the attached rattles, and generally accumulating for himself a broad knowledge and a broad skill in dealing with his surroundings.

The concept of competence can be most easily discussed by choosing, as we have done, examples of interaction with the inanimate environment. It applies equally well, however, to transactions with animals and with other human beings, where the child has the same problem of finding out what effects he can have upon the environment and what effects it can have upon him. The earliest interactions with members of the family may involve needs so strong that they obscure the part played by effectance motivation, but perhaps the example of the well-fed baby diligently exploring the several features of his mother's face will serve as a reminder that here, too, there are less urgent moments when learning for its own sake can be given free rein.

SUMMARY

The main theme of this paper is introduced by showing that there is widespread discontent with theories of motivation built upon primary drives. Signs of this discontent are found in realms as far apart as animal psychology and psychoanalytic ego psychology. In the former, the commonly recognized primary drives have proved to be inadequate in explaining exploratory behavior, manipulation, and general activity. In the latter, the theory of basic instincts has shown serious shortcomings when it is stretched to account for the development of the effective ego. Workers with animals have attempted to meet their problem by invoking secondary reinforcement and anxiety reduction, or by adding exploration and manipulation to the roster of primary drives. In parallel fashion, psychoanalytic workers have relied upon the concept of neutralization of instinctual energies, have seen anxiety reduction as the central motive in ego development, or have hypothesized new instincts such as mastery. These several explanations are not satisfactory and a better conceptualization is possible.

In trying to form this conceptualization, it is first pointed out that many of the earlier tenets of primary drive theory have been discredited by recent experimental work. There is no longer any compelling reason to identify either pleasure or reinforcement with drive reduction, or to think of motivation as requiring a source of energy external to the nervous system. This opens the way for considering in their own right those aspects of animal and human behavior in which stimulation and contact with the environment seem to be sought and welcomed, in which raised tension and even mild excitement seem to be cherished, and in which novelty and variety seem to be enjoyed for their own sake.

Effectance motivation need not be conceived as strong in the sense that sex, hunger, and fear are strong when violently aroused. It is moderate but persistent, and in this, too, we can discern a feature that is favorable for adaptation. Strong motivation reinforces learning in a narrow sphere, whereas moderate motivation is more conducive to an exploratory and experimental attitude which leads to competent interactions in general, without reference to an immediate pressing need. Man's huge cortical association areas might have been a suicidal piece of specialization if they had come without a steady, persistent inclination toward interacting with the environment.

REFERENCES

Angyal, A. (1941), *Foundations for a Science of Personality*, New York: Commonwealth Fund.

Diamond, S. (1939), 'A neglected aspect of motivation', *Sociometry*, 2, 77–85.

Hebb, D. O. (1949), *The Organization of Behavior*, New York: Wiley.

Piaget, J. (1952), *The Origins of Intelligence in Children* (trans. M. Cook), New York: International University Press.

Schachtel, E. G. (1954), 'The development of focal attention and the emergence of reality', *Psychiatry*, 17, 309–24.

Tolman, E. C. (1948), 'Cognitive maps in rats and men', *Psychological Review*, 55, 189–208.

Yerkes, R. M., & Dodson, J. D. (1908), 'The relation of strength of stimulus to rapidity of habit-formation', *Journal of Comparative Neurology and Psychology*, 18, 459–82.

Reinforcements and Goals:
The Process of Motivation

SECTION TWO

Reinforcement and Goals:
The Process of Motivation

4

W. CLAY HAMNER

Reinforcement Theory and Contingency Management in Organizational Settings

Abridged from W. C. Hamner, 'Reinforcement theory and contingency management in organizational settings', in H. L. Tosi and W. C. Hamner (eds.), *Organizational Behavior and Management: A Contingency Approach*, Chicago: St Clair Press, 1974, pp. 86–112.

The purpose of this paper is to describe the determinants of behavior as seen from a reinforcement theory point of view, and to describe how the management of the contingencies of reinforcement in organizational settings is a key to successful management. Hopefully, this paper will enable the manager to understand how his behavior affects the behavior of his subordinates and to see that in most cases the failure or success of the worker at the performance of a task is a direct function of the manager's own behavior. Since a large portion of the manager's time is spent in the process of modifying behavior patterns and shaping them so that they will be more goal-oriented, it is appropriate that this paper begin by describing the processes and principles that govern behavior.

LEARNING AS A PREREQUISITE FOR BEHAVIOR

Learning is such a common phenomenon that we tend to fail to recognize its occurrence. Nevertheless, one of the major premises of reinforcement theory is that all behavior is learned – a worker's skill, a supervisor's attitude and a secretary's manners.

There seems to be general agreement among social scientists that learning can be defined as *a relatively permanent change in behavior potentiality that results from reinforced practice or experience*. Note that this definition states that there is change in behavior potentiality and not necessarily in behavior itself. The reason for this distinction rests on the fact that we can observe other people responding to their environments, see the consequences which accrue to them, and be vicariously conditioned. For example, a boy can watch his older sister burn her hand on a hot stove and 'learn' that pain is the result of touching a hot stove. This definition therefore allows us to account for 'no-trial' learning. Bandura (1969) describes this as imitative learning and says that while behavior can be *acquired* by observing, reading, or other vicarious methods, '*performance* of observationally learned responses will depend to a great extent upon the nature of the reinforcing consequences to the model or to the observer' (p. 128).

Learning is the acquisition of knowledge, and performance is the translation of knowledge into practice. The primary effect of reinforcement is to strengthen and intensify certain aspects of ensuing behavior. Behavior that has become highly differentiated (shaped) can be understood and accounted for only in terms of the history of reinforcement of that behavior (Morse, 1966). Reinforcement generates a reproducible behavior process in time. A response occurs and is followed by a reinforcer, and further responses occur with a characteristic temporal patterning. When a response is reinforced it subsequently occurs more frequently than before it was reinforced. Reinforcement may be assumed to have a characteristic and reproducible effect on a particular behavior, and usually it will enhance and intensify that behavior (Skinner, 1938; 1953).

TWO BASIC LEARNING PROCESSES

Before discussing in any detail exactly how the general laws or principles of reinforcement can be used to predict and influence behavior, we must differentiate between two types of behavior. One kind is known as *voluntary* or *operant* behavior, and the other is known as *reflex* or *respondent* behavior. Respondent behavior takes in all responses of human beings that are *elicited* by special stimulus changes in the environment. An example would be when a person turns a light on in a dark room (stimulus change), his eyes contract (respondent behavior).

Operant behavior includes an even greater amount of human activity. It takes in all the responses of a person that may at some time be said to have an effect upon or do something to the person's outside world (Keller, 1969). Operant behavior *operates* on this world either directly or indirectly. For example, when a person presses the up button at the elevator entrance to 'call' the elevator, he is operating on his environment.

The process of learning or acquiring reflex behavior is different from the processes of learning or acquiring voluntary behavior. The two basic and distinct learning processes are known as *classical conditioning* and *operant conditioning*. It is from studying these two learning processes that much of our knowledge of individual behavior has emerged.

Classical conditioning

Pavlov (1902) noticed, while studying the automatic reflexes associated with digestion, that his laboratory dog salivated (unconditioned response) not only when food (unconditioned stimulus) was placed in the dog's mouth, but also when other stimuli were presented before food was placed in the dog's mouth. In other words, by presenting a neutral stimulus (ringing of a bell) every time food was presented to the dog, Pavlov was able to get the dog to salivate to the bell alone.

A stimulus which is not a part of a reflex relationship (the bell in Pavlov's experiment) becomes a *conditioned stimulus* for the response by repeated, temporal pairing with an *unconditioned* stimulus (food) which already elicits the response. This new relationship is known as a conditioned reflex, and the pairing procedure is known as classical conditioning.

While it is important to understand that reflex behavior is conditioned by a different process than is voluntary behavior, classical conditioning principles are of little use to the practicing manager. Most of the behavior that is of interest to society does not fit in the paradigm of reflex behavior (Michael & Meyerson, 1962). Nevertheless, the ability to generalize from one stimulus setting to another is very important in human learning and problem solving, and for this reason, knowledge of the classical conditioning process is important.

Operant conditioning

The basic distinction between classical and operant conditioning procedures is in terms of the *consequences* of the conditioned response. In classical conditioning, the sequence of events is independent of the subject's behavior. In operant conditioning, consequences (rewards and punishments) are made to occur as a consequence of the subject's response or failure to respond.

For voluntary behavior, the consequence is dependent on the behavior of the individual in a given stimulus setting. Such behavior can be said to 'operate' (Skinner, 1969) on the environment, in contrast to behavior which is 'respondent' to prior eliciting stimuli (Michael & Meyerson, 1962). Reinforcement is not given every time the stimulus is presented, but is *only* given when the correct response is made. For example, if an employee taking a work break puts a penny (R) in the soft-drink machine (S), nothing happens (consequence). However, if he puts a quarter (R) in the machine (S), he gets the soft drink (consequence). In other words, the employee's behavior is *instrumental* in determining the consequences which accrue to him.

The interrelationships between the three components of (1) *stimulus* or environment, (2) *response* or performance, and (3) consequences or *reinforcements* are known as the *contingencies* of reinforcement. Skinner (1969) says, 'The class of responses upon which a reinforcer is *contingent* is called an operant, to suggest the action on the environment followed by reinforcements' (p. 7). Operant conditioning presupposes that human beings explore their environment and act upon it. This behavior, randomly emitted at first, can be constructed as an operant by making a reinforcement contingent on a response. Any stimulus present when an operant is reinforced acquires control in the sense that the rate of response for that individual will be higher when it is present. 'Such a stimulus does not act as a *goal*; it does not elicit the response (as was the case in classical conditioning of reflex behavior)[1] in the sense of forcing it to occur. It is simply an essential aspect of the occasion upon which response is made and reinforced' (Skinner, 1969, p. 7).

Therefore, an adequate formulation of the interaction between an individual and his environment must always specify three things: (1) the occasion upon which a response occurs, (2) the response itself and (3) the reinforcing consequences. Skinner holds that the consequences determine the likelihood that a given operant will be performed in the future. Thus to change behavior, the consequences of the behavior must be changed, i.e. the contingencies must be rearranged (the ways in which the consequences are related to the behavior) (Behling, et al., 1973). For Skinner, this behavior generated by a given set of contingencies can be accounted for without appealing to hypothetical inner states (e.g. awareness or expectancies). 'If a conspicuous stimulus does not have an effect, it is not because the organism has not attended to it or because some central gatekeeper has screened it out, but because the stimulus plays no important role in the prevailing contingencies' (Skinner, 1969, p. 8).

Arrangement of the contingencies of reinforcement

In order to *understand* and *interpret* behavior, we must look at the interrelationship among the components of the contingencies of be-

[1] Parentheses added.

havior. If one expects to influence behavior, he must also be able to manipulate the consequences of the behavior (Skinner, 1969).

After appropriate reinforcers that have sufficient incentive value to maintain stable responsiveness have been chosen, the contingencies between specific performances and reinforcing stimuli must be arranged (Bandura, 1969). Employers intuitively use rewards in their attempt to modify and influence behavior, but their efforts often produce limited results because the methods are used improperly, inconsistently, or inefficiently. In many instances considerable rewards are bestowed upon the workers, but they are not made conditional or contingent on the behavior the manager wishes to promote. Also, 'long delays often intervene between the occurrence of the desired behavior and its intended consequences; special privileges, activities, and rewards are generally furnished according to fixed time schedules rather than performance requirements; and in many cases, positive reinforcers are inadvertently made contingent upon the wrong type of behavior' (Bandura, 1969, pp. 229–30).

One of the primary reasons that managers fail to 'motivate' workers to perform in the desired manner is due to a lack of understanding of the power of the contingencies of reinforcement over the employee and of the manager's role in arranging these contingencies. The laws or principles for arranging the contingencies are not hard to understand, and if students of behavior grasp them firmly, they are powerful managerial tools which can be used to increase supervisory effectiveness.

As we have said, operant conditioning is the process by which behavior is modified by manipulation of the contingencies of the behavior. To understand how this works, we will look at various *types* (arrangements) of contingencies. Rachlin (1970) described the four basic ways available to a manager of arranging the contingencies – *positive reinforcement, avoidance learning, extinction,* and *punishment.* The difference among these types of contingencies depends on the consequence which results from the behavioral act. Positive reinforcement and avoidance learning are methods of strengthening *desired* behavior, and extinction and punishment are methods of weakening *undesired* behavior.

Positive reinforcement. 'A positive reinforcer is a stimulus which, when added to a situation, strengthens the probability of an operant response' (Skinner, 1953, p. 73). The reason it strengthens the response is explained by Thorndike's (1911) Law of Effect. This law states simply that behavior which appears to lead to a positive consequence tends to be repeated, while behavior which appears to lead to a negative consequence tends not to be repeated. A positive consequence is called a reward.

Reinforcers, either positive or negative, are classified as either: (1) unconditioned or primary reinforcers, or (2) conditioned or secondary reinforcers. Primary reinforcers such as food, water, and sex are of biological importance in that they are innately rewarding and have effects which are independent of past experiences. Secondary reinforcers such as job advancement, praise, recognition, and money derive their effects from a consistent pairing with other reinforcers (i.e., they are conditioned). Secondary reinforcement, therefore, depends on the individual and his past reinforcement history. What is rewarding to one person may not be rewarding to another. Managers should look for a reward system which has maximal reinforcing consequences to the group he is supervising.

Regardless of whether the positive reinforcer is primary or secondary in nature, once it has been determined that the consequence has reward value to the worker, it can be used to increase the worker's performance. So the *first step* in the successful application of reinforcement procedures is to select reinforcers that are sufficiently powerful and durable to 'maintain responsiveness while complex patterns of behavior are being established and strengthened' (Bandura, 1969, p. 225).

The *second step* is to design the contingencies in such a way that the reinforcing events are made contingent upon the desired behavior. This is the rule of reinforcement which is most often violated. Rewards must result from performance, and the greater the degree of performance by an employee, the greater should be his reward. Money is not the only reward available. Other forms of rewards, such as recognition, promotion and job assignments, can be made contingent on good performance. Unless a manager is willing to discriminate between employees on the basis of their level of performance, the effectiveness of his power over the employee is nil.

The *third step* is to design the contingencies in such a way that a reliable procedure for eliciting or inducing the desired response patterns is established; otherwise, if they never occur there will be few opportunities to influence the desired behavior through contingent management. If the behavior that a manager wishes to strengthen is already present, and occurs with some frequency, then contingent applications of incentives can, from the outset, increase and maintain the desired performance patterns at a high level. However, as Bandura (1969) states, 'When the initial level of the desired behavior is extremely low, if the criterion for reinforcement is initially set too high, most, if not all, of the person's responses go unrewarded, so that his efforts are gradually extinguished and his motivation diminished' (p. 232).

The nature of the learning process is such that acquiring the new response patterns can be easily established. The principle of operant conditioning says that an operant followed by a positive reinforcement is more likely to occur under similar conditions in the future. Through the process of *generalization*, the more nearly alike the new situation or stimulus is to the original one, the more the old behavior is likely to be emitted in the new environment. For example, if you contract with an electrician to rewire your house, he is able to bring with him enough old behavioral patterns which he generalizes to this unfamiliar, but similar, stimulus setting (the house) in order to accomplish the task. He has learned through his past reinforcement history that, when in a new environment, one way to speed up the correct behavior needed to obtain reward is to generalize from similar settings with which he has had experience. Perhaps one reason an employer wants a person with work experience is that the probability of that person emitting the correct behavior is greater and thus the job of managing that person simplified.

Just as generalization is the ability to react to similarities in the environment, *discrimination* is the ability to react to differences in a new environmental setting. Usually when an employee moves from one environment (a job, a city, an office) to another he finds that only certain dimensions of the stimulus conditions change. While all of the responses of the employee in this new setting will not be correct, by skilled use of the procedures of reinforcement currently being discussed, we can bring about the more precise type of stimulus control called discrimination. When we purchase a new car, we do not have to relearn how to drive a car (generalizable stimulus). Instead we need only learn the differences in the new car and the old car so that we can respond to these differences in order to get reinforced. This procedure is called *discrimination training*. 'If in the presence of a stimulus a response is reinforced, and in the absence of this stimulus it is extinguished, the stimulus will control the probability of the response in high degree. Such a stimulus is called a *discriminative stimulus*' (Michael & Meyerson, 1962).

The development of effective discriminative repertoires is important for dealing with many different people on an interpersonal basis. Effective training techniques will allow the supervisor to develop the necessary discriminative repertoires in his new employees (e.g. see Bass & Vaughan, 1966).

Using the principles of generalization and discrimination in a well-designed training program allows the manager to accomplish the third goal of eliciting or inducing the desired response patterns. Training is a method of *shaping* desired behavior so that it can be conditioned to come under the control of the reinforcement stimuli. Shaping behavior is necessary when the response to be learned is not currently in the individual's repertoire and when it is a fairly complex behavior. In shaping, we teach a desired response by reinforcing the series of successive steps which lead to the final response.

Avoidance learning. The second type of contingency arrangement available to the manager is called escape, or avoidance learning. Just as with positive reinforcement, this is a method of strengthening desired behavior. A contingency arrangement in which an individual's performance can terminate an already noxious stimulus is called *escape* learning. When behavior can prevent the onset of a noxious stimulus the procedure is called *avoidance learning*. In both cases, the result is the development and maintenance of the desired operant behavior (Michael & Meyerson, 1962).

An example of this kind of control can be easily found in a work environment. Punctuality of employees is often maintained by avoidance learning. The noxious stimulus is the criticism by the shop steward or office manager for being late. In order to avoid criticism other employees make a special effort to come to work on time. A supervisor begins criticizing a worker for 'goofing off'. Other workers may intensify their efforts to escape the criticism of the supervisor.

The distinction between the process of strengthening behavior by means of positive reinforcement techniques and avoidance learning techniques should be noted carefully. In one case, the individual works hard to gain the consequences from the environment which result from good work, and in the second case, the individual works hard to avoid the noxious aspects of the environment itself. In both cases the same behavior is strengthened.

While Skinner (1953) recognizes that avoidance learning techniques can be used to condition desired behavior, he does not advocate their use. Instead a Skinnerian approach to operant conditioning is primarily based on the principles of positive reinforcement.

Extinction. While positive reinforcement and avoidance learning techniques can be used by managers to strengthen desired behavior, extinction and punishment techniques are methods available to managers for reducing undesired behavior. When positive reinforcement for a learned or previously conditioned response is withheld, individuals will continue to exhibit that behavior for an extended period of time. Under repeated non-reinforcement, the behavior decreases and eventually disappears.

This decline in response rate as a result of non-rewarded repetition of a task is defined as *extinction*.

This method when combined with a positive reinforcement method is the procedure of behavior modification recommended by Skinner (1953). It leads to the least negative side-effects and when the two methods are used together, it allows the employee to get the rewards he desires and allows the organization to eliminate the undesired behavior.

Punishment. A second method of reducing the frequency of undesired behavior is through the use of punishment. Punishment is the most controversial method of behavior modification, and most of the ethical questions about operant methods of control center around this technique. 'One of the principal objections to aversive control stems from the widespread belief that internal, and often unconscious, forces are the major determinant of behavior. From this perspective, punishment may temporarily suppress certain expressions, but the underlying impulses retain their strength and press continuously for discharge through alternative actions' (Bandura, 1969, p. 292). While Skinner (1953) discounts the internal state hypothesis, he recommends that extinction rather than punishment be used to decrease the probability of the occurrence of a particular behavior.

Punishment is defined as presenting an aversive or noxious consequence contingent upon a response, or removing a positive consequence contingent upon a response. Based on the Law of Effect, as rewards strengthen behavior, punishment weakens it.

Notice carefully the difference in the withholding of rewards in the punishment process and the withholding of rewards in the extinction process. In the extinction process, we withhold rewards for behavior that has previously been administered the rewards because the behavior was desired. In punishment, we withhold a reward because the behavior is undesired, has never been associated with the reward before, and is in fact a noxious consequence. For example, if your young son began imitating an older neighborhood boy's use of profanity and you thought it was 'cute', you might reinforce the behavior by laughing or by calling public attention to it. Soon, the son learns one way to get the recognition he craves is to use profanity – even though he may have no concept of its meaning. As the child reaches an accountable age, you decide that his use of profanity is no longer as cute as it once was. To stop the behavior you can do one of three things: (1) You can withhold the previous recognition you gave the child by ignoring him (extinction), (2) You can give the child a spanking (punishment by noxious consequence), or (3) You can withhold his allowance or refuse to let him watch television (punishment by withholding of positive consequences not previously connected with the act).

It should be noted that method 2 and perhaps method 3 would be considered cruel because of the parent's own inconsistencies. Punishment should rarely be used to extinguish behavior that has previously been reinforced if the person administering the punishment is the same person who previously reinforced the behavior. However, had the parent failed to extinguish the use of profanity prior to sending the child out in society (e.g. school, church), it is possible that the society may punish the child for behavior that the parent is reinforcing or at least tolerating. It is often argued therefore that the failure to use punishment early in the life of a child for socially unacceptable behavior (e.g. stealing, driving at excessive speeds, poor table manners) is more cruel than the punishment itself, simply because the society will withhold rewards or administer adversive consequences for the behavior which the parents should have extinguished.

Rules for using operant conditioning techniques

Several rules concerning the arrangement of the contingencies of reinforcement should be discussed. While these rules have common-sense appeal, the research findings indicate that they are often violated by managers when they design control systems.

Rule 1. Don't reward all people the same. In other words, differentiate the rewards based on performance as compared to some defined objective or standard. We know that people compare their own performance to that of their peers to determine how well they are doing ('Social Comparison Theory', Festinger, 1954) and they compare their rewards to the rewards of their peers ('Equity Theory', Adams, 1965) in order to determine how to evaluate their rewards. While some managers seem to think that the fairest system of compensation is one where everyone in the same job classification gets the same pay, employees want differentiation so that they know their importance to the organization. On the basis of social comparison and equity theory assumptions, it can be argued that managers who reward all people the same are encouraging, at best, only average performance. Behavior of high-performance workers is being extinguished (ignored) while the behavior of average-performance and poor-performance workers is being strengthened by positive reinforcement.

Rule 2. Failure to respond has reinforcing consequences. Managers who find the job of differentiating between workers so unpleasant that they fail to respond must recognize that failure to respond modifies behavior. 'Indeed, whether he is conscious of it or not, the superior is bound to be constantly shaping the behavior of his subordinates by the way in which he utilizes the rewards that are at his disposal, and he will inevitably modify the behavior of his work group' (Haire, 1964). Managers must be careful that they examine the performance consequence of their non-action as well as their action.

Rule 3. Be sure to tell a person what he can do to get reinforced. By making clear the contingencies of reinforcement to the worker, a manager may be actually increasing the individual freedom of the worker. The employee who has a standard against which to measure his job will have a built-in feedback system which allows him to make judgements about his own work. The awarding of the reinforcement in an organization where the worker's goal is specified will be associated with the performance of the worker and not based on the biases of the supervisor. The assumption is that the supervisor rates the employee accurately (see Scott & Hamner, 1973a) and that he then reinforces the employee on the basis of his ratings (see Scott & Hamner, 1973b). If the supervisor fails to rate accurately or administer rewards based on performance, then the stated goals for the worker will lose stimulus control, and the worker will be forced to search for the 'true' contingencies, i.e. what behavior should he perform in order to get rewarded (e.g., ingratiation? loyalty? positive attitude?).

Rule 4. Be sure to tell a person what he is doing wrong. As a general rule, very few people find the act of failing rewarding. One assumption of behavior therefore is that a worker wants to be rewarded in a positive manner. A supervisor should never use extinction or punishment as a sole method for modifying behavior, but if used judiciously in conjunction with other techniques designed to promote more effective response options (Rule 3) such combined procedures can hasten the change process. If the supervisor fails to specify why a reward is being withheld, the employee may associate it with past desired behavior instead of the undesired behavior that the supervisor is trying to extinguish. The supervisor then extinguishes good performance while having no effect on the undesired behavior.

Rules 3 and 4, when used in combination, should allow the manager to control behavior in the best interest of reaching organizational goals. At the same time they should give the employee the clarity he needs to see that his own behavior and not the behavior of the supervisor controls his outcomes.

Rule 5. Don't punish in front of others. The reason for this rule is quite simple. The punishment (e.g., reprimand) should be enough to extinguish the undesired behavior. By administering the punishment in front of the work group, the worker is doubly punished in the sense that he is also put out of face (Goffman, 1959). This additional punishment may lead to negative side-effects in three ways. First, the worker whose self-image is damaged may feel that he must retaliate in order to protect himself. Therefore, the supervisor has actually increased undesired responses. Secondly, the work group may misunderstand the reason for the punishment and through 'avoidance learning' may modify their own behavior in ways not intended by the supervisor. Third, the work group is also being punished in the sense that observing a member of their team being reprimanded has noxious or aversive properties for most people. This may result in a decrease in the performance of the total work group.

Rule 6. Make the consequences equal to the behavior. In other words be fair. Don't cheat the worker out of his just rewards. If he is a good worker, tell him. Many supervisors find it very difficult to praise an employee. Others find it very difficult to counsel an employee about what he is doing wrong. When a manager fails to use these reinforcement tools, he is actually reducing his effectiveness. When a worker is over-rewarded he may feel guilty (Adams, 1965) and on the basis of the principles of reinforcement, the worker's current level of performance is being conditioned. If his performance level is less than others who get the same reward, he has no reason to increase his output. When a worker is under-rewarded, he becomes angry with the system (Adams, 1965). His behavior is being extinguished and the company may be forcing the good employee (under-rewarded) to seek employment elsewhere while encouraging the poor employee (over-rewarded) to stay.

REFERENCES

Adams, J. S. (1965), 'Inequity in social exchange', in L. Berkowitz (ed.), *Advances in Experimental Social Psychology*, New York: Academic Press, 157–89.

Bandura, A. (1969), *Principles of Behavior Modification*, New York: Holt, Rinehart & Winston.

Bass, B. M., & Vaughan, J. A. (1966), *Training in Industry: The Management of Learning*, Belmont, Calif.: Wadsworth.

Behling, O., Schriesheim, C., & Tolliver, J. (1973), 'Present theories and new directions in theories of work effort', *Journal Supplement Abstract Catalog of Selected Documents in Psychology*, American Psychological Corporation, Ms. 385.

Festinger, L. (1954), 'A theory of social comparison processes', *Human Relations, 7*, 117–40.

Goffman, E. (1959), *The Presentation of Self in Everyday Life*, New York: Doubleday.

Haire, Mason (1964), *Psychology in Management* (2nd edn.), New York: McGraw-Hill.

Keller, F. S. (1969), *Learning: Reinforcement Theory*, New York: Random House.

Michael, J., & Meyerson, L. (1962), 'A behavioral approach to counseling and guidance', *Harvard Educational Review*, *32*, 382–402.

Morse, W. H. (1966), 'Intermittent reinforcement', in W. K. Honig (ed.), *Operant Behavior*, New York: Appleton-Century-Crofts.

Pavlov, I. P. (1902), *The Work of the Digestive Glands* (trans. W. H. Thompson), London: Charles Griffin.

Rachlin, H. (1970), *Modern Behaviorism*, New York: W. H. Freeman.

Scott, W. E., & Hamner, W. Clay (1973a), 'The effects of order and variance in performance on supervisory ratings of workers', paper presented at the 45th Annual Meeting, Midwestern Psychological Association, Chicago, 1973.

Scott, W. E., & Hamner, W. Clay (1973b), 'The effect of order and variance in performance on the rewards given workers by supervisory personnel', mimeo, Indiana University.

Skinner, B. F. (1938), *The Behavior of Organisms*, New York: Appleton-Century.

Skinner, B. F. (1953), *Science and Human Behavior*, New York: Macmillan.

Skinner, B. F. (1969), *Contingencies of Reinforcement*, New York: Appleton-Century-Crofts.

Thorndike, E. L. (1911), *Animal Intelligence*, New York: Macmillan.

5

ALBERT BANDURA

Self-Efficacy: Toward a Unifying Theory of Behavioral Change

Abridged from A. Bandura, 'Self-efficacy: Toward a unifying theory of behavioral change', *Psychological Review*, Vol. 84, 1977, pp. 191–215.

Current developments in the field of behavioral change reflect two major divergent trends. The difference is especially evident in the treatment of dysfunctional inhibitions and defensive behavior. On the one hand, the mechanisms by which human behavior is acquired and regulated are increasingly formulated in terms of cognitive processes. On the other hand, it is performance-based procedures that are proving to be most powerful for effecting psychological changes. As a consequence, successful performance is replacing symbolically based experiences as the principle vehicle of change.

The present article presents the view that changes achieved by different methods derive from a common cognitive mechanism. The apparent divergence of theory and practice can be reconciled by postulating that cognitive processes mediate change but that cognitive events are induced and altered most readily by experience of mastery arising from effective performance. The distinction between process and means is underscored, because it is often assumed that a cognitive mode of operation requires a symbolic means of induction. Psychological changes can be produced through other means than performance accomplishments. Therefore, the explanatory mechanism developed in this article is designed to account for changes in behavior resulting from diverse modes of treatment.

COGNITIVE LOCUS OF OPERATION

Psychological treatments based on learning principles were originally conceptualized to operate through peripheral mechanisms. New behavior was presumably shaped automatically by its effects. Contingency learning through paired stimulation was construed in connectionist terms as a process in which responses were linked directly to stimuli. Altering the rate of pre-existing behavior by reinforcement was portrayed as a process wherein responses were regulated by their immediate consequences without requiring any conscious involvement of the responders.

Growing evidence from several lines of research altered theoretical perspectives on how behavior is acquired and regulated. Theoretical formulations emphasizing peripheral mechanisms began to give way to cognitively oriented theories that explained behavior in terms of central processing of direct, vicarious, and symbolic sources of information. Detailed analysis of the empirical and conceptual issues (see Bandura, 1977) falls beyond the scope of the present article. To summarize briefly, however, it has now been amply documented that cognitive processes play a prominent role in the acquisition and retention of new behavior patterns. Transitory experiences leave lasting effects by being coded and retained in symbols for memory representation. Because acquisition of response information is a major aspect of learning, much human behavior is developed through modeling. From observing others, one forms a conception of how new behavior patterns are performed, and on later occasions the symbolic construction serves as a guide for action (Bandura, 1977). The initial approximations of response patterns learned observationally are further refined through self-corrective adjustments based on informative feedback from performance.

Learning from response consequences is also conceived of largely as a cognitive process. Consequences serve as an unarticulated way of informing performers what they must do to gain beneficial outcomes and to avoid punishing ones. By observing the differential effects of their own actions, individuals discern which responses are appropriate in which settings and behave accordingly (Dulany, 1968). Viewed from the cognitive framework, learning from differential outcomes becomes a special case of observational learning. In this mode of conveying response information, the conception of the appropriate behavior is gradually constructed from observing the effects of one's actions rather than from the examples provided by others.

Changes in behavior produced by stimuli that either signify events to come or indicate probable response consequences also have been shown to rely heavily on cognitive representations of contingencies. People are not much affected by paired stimulation unless they recognize that the events are correlated (Dawson & Furedy, 1976; Grings, 1973). Stimuli influence the likelihood of a behavior's being performed by virtue of their predictive function, not because the stimuli are automatically connected to responses by their having occurred together. Reinterpretation of antecedent determinants as predictive cues, rather than as controlling stimuli, has shifted the locus of the regulation of behavior from the stimulus to the individual.

The issue of the locus at which behavioral determinants operate applies to reinforcement influences as well as to antecedent environmental stimuli. Contrary to the common view that behavior is controlled by its immediate consequences, behavior is related to its outcomes at the level of aggregate consequences rather than momentary effects (Baum, 1973). People process and synthesize feedback information from sequences of events over long intervals about the situational circumstances and the patterns and rates of actions that are necessary to produce given outcomes. Since consequences affect behavior through the influence of thought, beliefs about schedules of reinforcement can exert greater influence on behavior than the reinforcement itself (Baron, Kaufman, & Stauber, 1969; Kaufman, Baron, & Kopp, 1966). Incidence of behavior that has been positively reinforced does not increase if individuals believe, on the basis of other information, that the same actions will not be rewarded on future occasions (Estes, 1972); and the same consequences can increase, reduce, or have no effect on incidence of behavior depending on whether individuals are led to believe that the consequences signify correct responses, incorrect responses, or occur non-contingently (Dulany, 1968).

The discussion thus far has examined the role of cognition in the acquisition and regulation of behavior. Motivation, which is primarily concerned with activation and persistence of behavior, is also partly rooted in cognitive activities. The capacity to represent future consequences in thought provides one cognitively based source of motivation. Through cognitive representation of future outcomes individuals can generate current motivators of behavior. Seen from this perspective, reinforcement operations affect behavior largely by creating expectations that behaving in a certain way will produce anticipated benefits or avert future difficulties (Bolles, 1972). In the enhancement of previously learned behavior, reinforcement is conceived of mainly as a motivational device rather than as an automatic response strengthener.

A second cognitively based source of motivation operates through the intervening influences of goal setting and self-evaluative reactions (Bandura, 1976, 1977). Self-motivation involves standards against which to evaluate performance. By making self-rewarding reactions conditional on attaining a certain level of behavior, individuals create self-inducements to persist in their efforts until their performances match self-prescribed standards. Perceived negative discrepancies between performance and standards create dissatisfactions that motivate corrective changes in behavior. Both the anticipated satisfactions of desired accomplishments and the negative appraisals of insufficient performance thus provide incentives for action. Having accomplished a given level of performance, individuals often are no longer satisfied with it and make further self-reward contingent on higher attainments.

The reconceptualization of human learning and motivation in terms of cognitive processes has major implications for the mechanisms through which therapeutic procedures alter behavioral functioning. Although the advances in cognitive psychology are a subject of increasing interest in speculations about behavioral change processes, few new theories of psychotherapy have been proposed that might prove useful in stimulating research on explanatory mechanisms and in integrating the results accompanying diverse modes of treatment. The present article outlines a theoretical framework, in which the concept of *self-efficacy* is assigned a central role, for analyzing changes achieved in fearful and avoidant behavior. The explanatory value of this conceptual system is then evaluated by its ability to predict behavioral changes produced through different methods of treatment.

EFFICACY EXPECTATIONS AS A MECHANISM OF OPERATION

The present theory is based on the principal assumption that psychological procedures, whatever their form, serve as means of creating and strengthening expectations of personal efficacy. Within this analysis, efficacy expectations are distinguished from response–outcome expectancies. The difference is presented schematically in Figure 1.

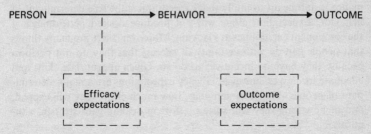

Figure 1. Diagrammatic representation of the difference between efficacy expectations and outcome expectations.

An outcome expectancy is defined as a person's estimate that a given behavior will lead to certain outcomes. An efficacy expectation is the conviction that one can successfully execute the behavior required to produce the outcomes. Outcome and efficacy expectations are differentiated, because individuals can believe that a particular course of action will produce certain outcomes, but if they entertain serious doubts about whether they can perform the necessary activities such information does not influence their behavior.

In this conceptual system, expectations of personal mastery affect both initiation and persistence of coping behavior. The strength of people's convictions in their own effectiveness is likely to affect whether they will even try to cope with given situations. At this initial level, perceived self-efficacy influences choice of behavioral settings. People fear and tend to avoid threatening situations they believe exceed their coping skills, whereas they get involved in activities and behave assuredly when they judge themselves capable of handling situations that would otherwise be intimidating.

Not only can perceived self-efficacy have directive influence on choice of activities and settings, but, through expectations of eventual success, it can affect coping efforts once they are initiated. Efficacy expectations determine how much effort people will expend and how long they will persist in the face of obstacles and aversive experiences. The stronger the perceived self-efficacy, the more active the efforts. Those who persist in subjectively threatening activities that are in fact relatively safe will gain corrective experiences that reinforce their sense of efficacy, thereby eventually eliminating their defensive behavior. Those who cease their coping efforts prematurely will retain their self-debilitating expectations and fears for a long time.

The preceding analysis of how perceived self-efficacy influences performance is not meant to imply that expectation is the sole determinant of behavior. Expectation alone will not produce desired performance if the component capabilities are lacking. Moreover, there are many things that people can do with certainty of success that they do not perform because they have no incentives to do so. Given appropriate skills and adequate incentives, however, efficacy expectations are a major determinant of people's choice of activities, how much effort they will expend, and of how long they will sustain effort in dealing with stressful situations.

DIMENSIONS OF EFFICACY EXPECTATIONS

Empirical tests of the relationship between expectancy and performance of threatening activities have been hampered by inadequacy of the expectancy analysis. In most studies the measures of expectations are mainly concerned with people's hopes for favorable outcomes rather than with their sense of personal mastery. Moreover, expectations are usually assessed globally only at a single point in a change process as though they represent a static, unidimensional factor. Participants in experiments of this type are simply asked to judge how much they expect to benefit from a given procedure. When asked to make such estimates, participants assume, more often than not, that the benefits will be produced by the external ministrations rather than gained through the development of self-efficacy. Such global measures reflect a mixture of, among other things, hope, wishful thinking, belief in the potency of the procedures, and faith in the therapist. It therefore comes as no surprise that outcome expectations of this type have little relation to magnitude of behavioral change (Davison & Wilson, 1973, Lick & Bootzin, 1975).

Efficacy expectations vary on several dimensions that have important performance implications. They differ in *magnitude*. Thus when tasks are ordered in level of difficulty, the efficacy expectations of different individuals may be limited to the simpler tasks, extend to moderately difficult ones, or include even the most taxing performances. Efficacy expectations also differ in *generality*. Some experiences create circumscribed mastery expectations. Others instill a more generalized sense of efficacy that extends well beyond the specific treatment situation. In addition, expectancies vary in *strength*. Weak expectations are easily extinguishable by disconfirming experiences, whereas individuals who possess strong expectations of mastery will persevere in their coping efforts despite disconfirming experiences.

An adequate expectancy analysis, therefore, requires detailed assessment of the magnitude, generality, and strength of efficacy expectations commensurate with the precision with which behavioral processes are measured. Both efficacy expectations and performance should be assessed at significant junctures in the change process to clarify their reciprocal effects on each other. Mastery expectations influence performance and are, in turn, altered by the cumulative effects of one's efforts.

SOURCES OF EFFICACY EXPECTATIONS

In this social learning analysis, expectations of personal efficacy are based on four major sources of information: performance accomplishments, vicarious experience, verbal persuasion, and physiological states.

Performance accomplishments

This source of efficacy information is especially influential because it is based on personal mastery experiences. Successes raise mastery expectations; repeated failures lower them, particularly if the mishaps occur early in the course of events. After strong efficacy expectations are developed through repeated success, the negative impact of occasional failures is likely to be reduced. Indeed, occasional failures that are later overcome by determined effort can strengthen self-motivated persistence if one finds through experience that even the most difficult obstacles can be mastered by sustained effort. The effects of failure on personal efficacy therefore partly depend on the timing and the total pattern of experiences in which the failures occur.

Once established, enhanced self-efficacy tends to generalize to other situations in which performance was self-debilitated by preoccupation with personal inadequacies (Bandura, Adams, & Beyer, 1977; Bandura, Jeffery, & Gajdos, 1975). As a result, improvements in behavioral functioning transfer not only to similar situations but to activities that are substantially different from those on which the treatment was focused.

Vicarious experience

People do not rely on experienced mastery as the sole source of information concerning their level of self-efficacy. Many expectations are derived from vicarious experience. Seeing others perform threatening activities without adverse consequences can generate expectations in observers that they too will improve if they intensify and persist in their efforts. They persuade themselves that if others can do it, they should be able to achieve at least some improvement in performance (Bandura & Barab, 1973). Vicarious experience, relying as it does on inferences from social comparison, is a less dependable source of information about one's capabilities than is direct evidence of personal accomplishments. Consequently, the efficacy expectations induced by modeling alone are likely to be weaker and more vulnerable to change.

Verbal persuasion

In attempts to influence human behavior, verbal persuasion is widely used because of its ease and ready availability. People are led, through suggestion, into believing they can cope successfully with what has overwhelmed them in the past. Efficacy expectations induced in this manner are also likely to be weaker than those arising from one's own accomplishments because they do not provide an authentic experiential base for them. In the face of distressing threats and a long history of failure in coping with them, whatever mastery expectations are induced by suggestion can be readily extinguished by disconfirming experiences.

Although social persuasion alone may have definite limitations as a means of creating an enduring sense of personal efficacy, it can contribute to the successes achieved through corrective performance. That is, people who are socially persuaded that they possess the capabilities to master difficult situations and are provided with provisional aids for effective action are likely to mobilize greater effort than those who receive only the performance aids. However, to raise by persuasion expectations of personal competence without arranging conditions to facilitate effective performance will most likely lead to failures that discredit the persuaders and further undermine the recipients' perceived self-efficacy. It is therefore the interactive, as well as the independent, effects of social persuasion on self-efficacy that merit experimental consideration.

Emotional arousal
Stressful and taxing situations generally elicit emotional arousal that, depending on the circumstances, might have informative value concerning personal competency. Therefore, emotional arousal is another constituent source of information that can affect perceived self-efficacy in coping with threatening situations. People rely partly on their state of physiological arousal in judging their anxiety and vulnerability to stress. Because high arousal usually debilitates performance, individuals are more likely to expect success when they are not beset by aversive arousal than if they are tense and viscerally agitated. Fear reactions generate further fear of impending stressful situations through anticipatory self-arousal. By conjuring up fear-provoking thoughts about their ineptitude, individuals can rouse themselves to elevated levels of anxiety that far exceed the fear experienced during the actual threatening situation.

COGNITIVE PROCESSING OF EFFICACY
INFORMATION

The discussion thus far has centered primarily on the many sources of information – enactive, vicarious, exhortative, and emotive – that people use to judge their level of self-efficacy. At this point a distinction must be drawn between information contained in environmental events and information as processed and transformed by the individual. The impact of information on efficacy expectations will depend on how it is cognitively appraised. A number of contextual factors, including the social, situational, and temporal circumstances under which events occur, enter into such appraisals. For this reason, even success experiences do not necessarily create strong generalized expectations of personal efficacy. Expectations that have served self-protective functions for years are not quickly discarded. When experience contradicts firmly established expectations of self-efficacy, they may undergo little change if the conditions of performance are such as to lead one to discount the import of the experience.

The corrective value of information derived from successful performance can be attenuated in several ways. The first involves discrimination processes. The consequences individuals anticipate were they to perform feared activities differ in circumstances which vary in safeguards. As a result, they may behave boldly in situations signifying safety, but retain unchanged their self-doubts under less secure conditions.

Cognitive appraisals of the causes of one's behavior, which have been examined extensively in investigations of self-attributional processes (Bem, 1972), can similarly delimit gains in self-efficacy from behavioral attainments. It was previously shown that attributions of affect and actions to illusory competence have little, if any, effect on refractory behavior. This does not, of course, mean that causal appraisals are of limited importance in the process of behavior change. Quite the contrary, performance attainment is a prominent source of efficacy information, but it is by no means unambiguous. People can gain competence through authentic means but, because of faulty appraisals of the circumstances under which they improve, will credit their achievements to external factors rather than to their own capabilities. Here the problem is one of inaccurate ascription of personal competency to situational factors. Successes are more likely to enhance self-efficacy if performances are perceived as resulting from skill than from fortuitous or special external aids. Conversely, failures would be expected to produce greater reductions in self-efficacy when attributed to ability rather than to unusual situational circumstances. The more extensive the situational aids for performance, the greater are the chances that behavior will be ascribed to external factors (Bem, 1972; Weiner, 1972).

Even under conditions of perceived self-determination of outcomes, the impact of performance attainments on self-efficacy will vary depending on whether one's accomplishments are ascribed mainly to ability or to effort. Success with minimal effort fosters ability ascriptions that reinforce a strong sense of self-efficacy. By contrast, analogous successes achieved through high expenditure of effort connote a lesser ability and are thus likely to have a weaker effect on perceived self-efficacy. Cognitive appraisals of the difficulty level of the tasks will further affect the impact of performance accomplishments on perceived self-efficacy. To succeed at easy tasks provides no new information for altering one's sense of self-efficacy, whereas mastery of challenging tasks conveys salient evidence of enhanced competence.

We have already examined how cognitive processing of information conveyed by modeling might influence the extent to which vicarious experience effects changes in self-efficacy. Among the especially informative elements are the models' characteristics (e.g., adeptness, perseverance, age, expertness), the similarity between models and observers, the difficulty of the performance tasks, the situational arrangements under which the modeled achievements occur, and the diversity of modeled attainments.

Just as the value of efficacy information generated enactively and vicariously depends on cognitive appraisal, so does the information arising from exhortative and emotive sources. The impact of verbal persuasion on self-efficacy may vary substantially depending on the perceived credibility of the persuaders, their prestige, trustworthiness, expertise, and assuredness. The more believable the source of the information, the more likely are efficacy expectations to change. The influence of credibility on attitudinal change has, of course, received intensive study. But its effects on perceived self-efficacy remain to be investigated.

People judge their physiological arousal largely on the basis of their appraisal of the instigating conditions. Thus, visceral arousal occurring in situations perceived to be threatening is interpreted as fear, arousal in thwarting situations is experienced as anger, and that resulting from irretrievable loss of valued objects as sorrow (Hunt, Cole, & Reis, 1958). Even the same source of physiological arousal may be interpreted differently in ambiguous situations depending on the emotional reactions of others in the same setting (Mandler, 1975; Schachter & Singer, 1962).

When tasks are performed in ambiguous or complex situations in which there is a variety of evocative stimuli, the informational value of the resultant arousal will depend on the meaning imposed upon it. People who perceive their arousal as stemming from personal inadequacies are more likely to lower their efficacy expectations than those who attribute their arousal to certain situational factors. Given a proneness to ascribe arousal to personal deficiencies, the heightened attention to internal events can result in reciprocally escalating arousal. Indeed, as Sarason (1976) has amply documented, individuals who are especially susceptible to anxiety arousal readily become self-preoccupied with their perceived inadequacies in the face of difficulties rather than with the task at hand.

CONCLUDING REMARKS

The present theoretical formulation orders variations in the level of behavioral changes produced by different modes of treatment; it accounts for behavioral variations displayed by individuals receiving the same type of treatment; and it predicts performance successes at the level of individual tasks during and after treatment. It is possible to generate alternative explanations for particular subsets of data, but the mechanism proposed in the present theory appears to account equally well for the different sets of findings. It might be argued, for example, that self-efficacy proved to be an accurate predictor of performance in the enactive mode of treatment because subjects were simply judging their future performance from their past behavior. However, an interpretation of this type has no explanatory value for the vicarious and emotive treatments, in which perceived self-efficacy was an equally accurate predictor of performance although subjects engaged in no overt behavior. Even in the enactive treatment, perceived self-efficacy proved to be a better predictor of behavior toward unfamiliar threats than did past performance. Moreover, self-efficacy derived from partial enactive mastery during the course of treatment predicted performance on stressful tasks that the individuals had never done before.

REFERENCES

Bandura, A. (ed.) (1971), *Psychological Modeling: Conflicting Theories*, Chicago: Aldine-Atherton.

Bandura, A. (1976), 'Self-reinforcement: Theoretical and methodological considerations', *Behaviorism*, *4*, 135–55.

Bandura, A. (1977), *Social Learning Theory*, Englewood Cliffs, NJ: Prentice Hall.

Bandura, A., Adams, N. E., & Beyer, J. (1977), 'Cognitive processes mediating behavioral changes', *Journal of Personality and Social Psychology*, *35*, 125–39.

Bandura, A., & Barab, P. G. (1973), 'Processes governing disinhibitory effects through symbolic modeling', *Journal of Abnormal Psychology*, *82*, 1–9.

Bandura, A., Jeffery, R. W., & Gajdos, E. (1975), 'Generalizing change through participant modeling with self-directed mastery', *Behavior Research and Therapy*, *13*, 141–52.

Baron, A., Kaufman, A., & Stauber, K. A. (1969), 'Effects of instructions and reinforcement-feedback on human operant behavior maintained by fixed-interval reinforcement', *Journal of the Experimental Analysis of Behavior*, *12*, 701–12.

Baum, W. M. (1973), 'The correlation-based law of effect', *Journal of the Experimental Analysis of Behavior*, *20*, 137–53.

Bem, D. J. (1972), 'Self-perception theory', in L. Berkowitz (ed.), *Advances in Experimental Social Psychology* (Vol. 6), New York: Academic Press.

Bolles, R. C. (1972), 'Reinforcement, expectancy, and learning', *Psychological Review*, *79*, 394–409.

Davison, G. C., & Wilson, G. T. (1973), 'Processes of fear-reduction in systematic desensitization: Cognitive and social reinforcement factors in humans', *Behavior Therapy*, *4*, 1–21.

Dawson, M. E., & Furedy, J. J. (1976), 'The role of awareness in human differential autonomic classical conditioning: The necessary-gate hypothesis', *Psychophysiology*, *13*, 50–53.

Dulany, D. E. (1968), 'Awareness, rules, and propositional control: A confrontation with S–R behavior theory', in T. R. Dixon & D. L. Horton (eds.), *Verbal Behavior and General Behavior Theory*, Englewood Cliffs, NJ: Prentice Hall.

Estes, W. K. (1972), 'Reinforcement in human behavior', *American Scientist*, *60*, 723–9.

Grings, W. W. (1973), 'The role of consciousness and cognition in autonomic behavior change', in F. J. McGuigan & R. A. Schoonover (eds.), *The Psychophysiology of Thinking*, New York: Academic Press.

Hunt, J. McV., Cole, M. W., & Reis, E. E. S. (1958), 'Situational cues distinguishing anger, fear, and sorrow', *American Journal of Psychology*, *71*, 136–51.

Kaufman, A., Baron, A., & Kopp, E. (1966), 'Some effects of instructions on human operant behavior', *Psychonomic Monograph Supplements*, *1*, 243–50.

Lick, J., & Bootzin, R. (1975), 'Expectancy factors in the treatment of fear: Methodological and theoretical issues', *Psychological Bulletin*, *82*, 917–31.

Mandler, G. (1975), *Mind and Emotion*, New York: Wiley.

Sarason, I. G. (1976), 'Anxiety and self-preoccupation', in I. G. Sarason & C. D. Spielberger (eds.), *Stress and Anxiety* (Vol. 2), Washington, DC: Hemisphere.

Schachter, S., & Singer, J. E. (1962), 'Cognitive, social, and physiological determinants of emotional state', *Psychological Review*, *69*, 379–99.

Weiner, B. (1972), *Theories of Motivation*, Chicago: Markham.

6

CRAIG C. PINDER

Valence–Instrumentality–Expectancy Theory

Excerpt from C. C. Pinder, *Work Motivation*, Chapter 7, Glenview, Ill.: Scott, Foresman, 1984

Probably the most popular theory of work motivation among organizational scientists in recent years has been that which is referred to as Valence–Instrumentality–Expectancy Theory or Expectancy Theory (Locke, 1975). Actually, there are a variety of theories included under these general titles, although the similarities among them are more important than are the differences. Each of these theories has its modern roots in Vroom's (1964) book on work motivation, although earlier theory in psychology relating to general human motivation quite clearly predates Vroom's interpretation for organizational science (e.g., Atkinson, 1958; Davidson, Suppes, & Siegel, 1957; Lewin, 1938; Peak, 1955; Rotter, 1955; Tolman, 1959), and an early study by Georgopoulos, Mahoney, and Jones (1957) demonstrated the relevance of the theory for work behavior.

VROOM'S ORIGINAL THEORY

Vroom's theory assumes that ' . . . the choices made by a person among alternative courses of action are lawfully related to psychological events occurring contemporaneously with the behavior' (1964, pp. 14–15). In other words, people's behavior results from choices among alternatives, and these choices (behaviors) are systematically related to psychological processes, particularly perception and the formation of beliefs and attitudes. The purpose of the choices, generally, is to maximize pleasure and minimize pain. VIE Theory assumes that people base their acts on perceptions and beliefs, although we need not anticipate any one-to-one relationships between particular beliefs and specific behaviors (such as job behaviors).

To understand why Vroom's theory and those which have followed it are referred to as *VIE Theory*, we must examine the three key mental components that are seen as instigating and directing behavior. Referred to as Valence, Instrumentality, and Expectancy, each of these components is, in fact, a *belief*.

The concept of valence

VIE Theory assumes that people hold preferences among various outcomes or states of nature. For example, the reader probably prefers, other things equal, a higher rate of pay for a particular job over a lower rate of pay. Here, pay level is the *outcome* in question, and the preference for high pay over low pay reflects the strength of the reader's basic underlying need state. Likewise, some people hold preferences among different types of outcomes (as opposed to greater or lesser amounts of a particular outcome). For example, many employees would seem to prefer an opportunity to work with people, even if the only jobs featuring high levels of social interaction entail less comfortable surroundings, lower pay, or some other trade-off. The point is that people have more or less well-defined preferences for the outcomes they derive from their actions.

Vroom uses the term *valence* to refer to the affective (emotional) orientations people hold with regard to outcomes. An outcome is said to be positively valent for an individual if she would prefer having it to not having it. For example, we would say that a promotion is positively valent for an employee who would rather be promoted than not be promoted. Likewise, we say that an outcome which a person would prefer to avoid has negative valence for her, or simply that it is negatively valent. For example, fatigue, stress, and layoffs are three outcomes that are usually negatively valent among employees. Finally, it is sometimes the case that an employee is indifferent toward certain outcomes; in such cases, the outcome is said to hold zero valence for that individual.

The most important feature of people's valences concerning work-related outcomes is that they refer to the level of satisfaction the person *expects* to receive from them, *not from the real value the person actually derives from them*. So, for example, the reader may be enrolled in a program of business management because she expects that the outcomes to follow (an education and a diploma, among others) will be of value to her when she is finished. It may be the case, however, that when the student graduates there will be little or no market demand for the services she has to offer the world of business and administration, so the degree may have little real value. The point here is that people attribute either positive or negative preferences (or indifference) to outcomes according to the satisfaction or dissatisfaction they *expect* to receive from them. It is often the case that the true value of an outcome (such as a diploma) is either greater or lesser than the valence (expected value) that outcome once held for the individual who was motivated either to pursue it or to avoid it. As a final example, consider the individual who fears being fired, but learns after actually being dismissed from a job that she is healthier, happier, and better off financially in the new job she acquired after having been terminated by her former employer. In this case, being fired was a negatively valent outcome before it occurred, but eventually turned out to be of positive value after it occurred.

Performance as an outcome. Of the many outcomes that follow an employee's work effort, one of the most important, of course, is the level of performance that is accomplished. In fact, for the sake of understanding Vroom's theory, the strength of the connection in the mind of the employee between his effort and the performance level he achieves is very important, as we will see shortly. Further, the degree to which the employee believes that his performance will be connected to other outcomes (such as pay) is also critical. The point here is that work effort results in a variety of outcomes, some of them directly, others indirectly. The level of job performance is the most important outcome for understanding work motivation from a VIE Theory perspective. So, V stands for valence – the expected levels of satisfaction and/or dissatisfaction brought by work-related outcomes.

The concept of instrumentality

We have just stated that outcomes carry valences for people. But what determines the valence of a particular outcome for an employee? For example, we noted that performance level is an important outcome of a person's work effort, but what determines the valence associated with a given level of performance? For Vroom, the answer is that a given level of performance is positively valent if the employee believes that it will lead to other outcomes, which are called *second-level outcomes*. In other words, if an employee believes . . . that a high level of performance is *instrumental* for the acquisition of other outcomes that he expects will be gratifying (such as a promotion, for example), and/or if he believes that a high performance level will be instrumental for avoiding other outcomes that he wishes to avoid (such as being fired), then that employee will place a high valence upon performing the job well.

Consider the meaning of the adjective *instrumental*. The author's typewriter at the present time is instrumental in the preparation of this book. It contributes to the job; it helps. Something is said to be instrumental if it is believed to lead to something else, if it helps achieve or attain something else. Hence, studying is commonly seen by students as instrumental for passing exams. In turn, passing exams is often *believed* instrumental for the acquisition of diplomas, which, in turn, are *believed* to be instrumental for landing jobs in tight labor market conditions.

Vroom (1964) suggests that we consider instrumentality as a probability belief linking one outcome (performance level) to other outcomes, ranging from 1.0 (meaning that the attainment of the second outcome is certain if the first outcome is achieved), through zero (meaning that there is no likely relationship between the attainment of the first outcome and the attainment of the second), to − 1.0 (meaning that the attainment of the second outcome is certain without the first and that it is impossible with it). For example, bonus pay that is distributed at random would lead to employee instrumentality perceptions linking bonus pay to performance equal to zero. ('Performance and pay have no connection around here!') On the other hand, commission pay schemes which tie pay directly to performance, and only to performance, are designed to make employees perceive that performance is positively instrumental for the acquisition of money. Finally, an employee who has been threatened with dismissal for being drunk on the job may be told by his supervisor, in effect, that lack of sobriety at work is negatively instrumental for continued employment, or, alternatively, that further imbibing will be positively instrumental for termination. (The notion of negative instrumentalities makes Vroom's original formulation of VIE Theory somewhat more difficult and cumbersome than it might otherwise be, so subsequent versions of the theory have avoided it, choosing instead to speak only of positive instrumentalities.)

Consider the case of an employee who perceives that high performance will *not* lead to things he desires, but that it will be more instrumental for attaining outcomes to which he attributes negative valences. High performance will not be positively valent for such a person, so we would not expect to see him striving to perform well. As a further example, an employee might perceive that taking a job as a traveling salesman will be instrumental for attaining a number of outcomes, some of which he expects will be positive, some of which he believes will be negative. On the positively valent side, meeting new people and seeing the countryside may be appealing to him, because he expects that these outcomes will be instrumental for satisfying his relatedness and growth needs, while the possible threat to his family life may be aversive to him, the popularly acknowledged exploits to traveling salesmen notwithstanding!

In short, the *I* in VIE Theory stands for instrumentality – an outcome is positively valent if the person believes that it holds high instrumentality for the acquisition of positively valent consequences (goals or other outcomes), and the avoidance of negatively valent outcomes. But in order for an outcome to be positively valent, the outcomes to which the person believes it is connected must themselves, in turn, be seen as positively valent. If an employee anticipates that high levels of performance will lead primarily to things he dislikes, then high performance will not be positively valent to him. Likewise, if the individual perceives that high performance is generally rewarded with things he desires, he will place high valence on high performance and – other things being equal – he will strive for high performance. Of course, the valence of such second-level outcomes is determined by the nature of the person's most salient needs and values.

Already, the reader should be able to distill a few implications for the design of reward systems in organizations: if management wants high performance levels, it must tie positively valent outcomes to high performance *and be sure that employees understand the connection*. Likewise, low performance must be seen as connected to consequences that are of either zero or negative valence.

The concept of expectancy

The third major component of VIE Theory is referred to as *expectancy*. Expectancy is the strength of a person's belief about whether a particular outcome is possible. The author, for example, would place very little expectancy on the prospect of becoming an astronaut. The reasons are, of course, personal, but the point is that he doesn't believe that any amount of trying on his part will see him aboard the space shuttle! If a person believes that he can achieve an outcome, he will be more motivated to try for it, assuming that other things are equal (the other things, of course, consist of the person's beliefs about the valence of the outcome, which, in turn, is determined by the person's beliefs about the odds that the outcome will be instrumental for acquiring and avoiding those things he either wishes to acquire or avoid, respectively).

Vroom (1964) spoke of expectancy beliefs as *action–outcome* associations held in the minds of individuals, and suggested that we think of them in probability terms ranging from zero (in the case where the person's subjective probability of attaining an outcome is psychologically zero – 'I can't do it') through to 1.0, indicating that the person has no doubt about his capacity to attain the outcome. In practice, of course, people's estimates tend to range between these two extremes.

There are a variety of factors that contribute to an employee's expectancy perceptions about various levels of job performance. For example, his level of confidence in his skills for the task at hand, the degree of help he expects to receive from his supervisor and subordinates, the quality of the materials and equipment available, the availability of pertinent information and control over sufficient budget, are common examples of factors that can influence a person's expectancy beliefs about being able to achieve a particular level of performance. Previous success experiences at a task and a generally high level of self-esteem also strengthen expectancy beliefs (Lawler, 1973). The point is that an employee's subjective estimate of the odds that he can achieve a given level of performance is determined by a variety of factors, both within his own control and beyond it.

The concept of force

Vroom (1964) suggests that a person's beliefs about expectancies, instrumentalities, and valences interact psychologically to create a motivational force to act in those ways that seem most likely to bring pleasure or to avoid pain. 'Behavior on the part of a person is assumed to be the result of a field of forces each of which has a direction and magnitude' (p. 18). Vroom likens his concept of force to a variety of other metaphorical concepts, including things such as *performance vectors* and *behavior potential*. We can think of the force as representing the strength of a person's *intention* to act in a certain way. For example, if a person elects to strive for a particular level of job performance, we might say that the person's beliefs cause the greatest amount of force to be directed toward that level, or that he intends to strive for that level rather than for other levels.

Symbolically, Vroom (1964, p. 18) summarizes his own theory as follows:

$$F_i = f \sum_{i=1}^{n} (E_{ij} V_j) \quad \text{and} \quad V_j = f \left[\sum_{j=1}^{n} I_{jk} V_k \right]$$

where F_i = the psychological force to perform an act (i) (such as strive for a particular level of performance)

E_{ij} = the strength of the expectancy that the act will be followed by the outcome j

V_j = the valence for the individual of outcome j

I_{jk} = instrumentality of outcome j for attaining second-level outcome k

V_k = valence of second-level outcome k

or, in his words: 'The force on a person to perform an act is a monotonically increasing function of the algebraic sum of the products of the valences of all outcomes and the strength of his expectancies that the act will be followed by the attainment of these outcomes.'

So people choose from among the alternative acts the one(s) corresponding to the strongest positive (or weakest negative) force. People attempt to maximize their overall best interest, using the information available to them and their evaluations of this information. *In the context of work motivation, this means that people select to pursue that level of performance that they believe will maximize their overall best interest* (or *subjective expected utility*).

Notice from the formula above that there will be little or no motivational force operating on an individual to act in a certain manner if any of three conditions hold: (1) if the person does not believe that she can successfully behave that way (that is, if her expectancy of attaining the outcome is effectively zero); (2) if she believes that there will be no positively valent outcomes associated with behaving in that manner; (3) if she believes the act will result in a sufficient number of outcomes that are negatively valent to her.

The choice of a performance level. When we think of the levels of job performance that an employee might strive for as the outcome of interest, Vroom's theory suggests that the individual will consider the valences, instrumentalities, and expectancies associated with each level of the entire spectrum of performance levels and will elect to pursue the level that generates the greatest positive force (or lowest negative force) for him. If the person sees more good outcomes than bad ones associated with performing at a high level, he will strive to perform at that level. On the other hand, if a lower level of performance results in the greatest degree of psychological force, we can anticipate that he will settle for such a level. The implication is that low motivation levels result from employee choices to perform at low levels, and that these choices, in turn, are the result of beliefs concerning the valences, instrumentalities and expectancies held in the mind of the employee.

REFINEMENTS TO THE THEORY

Since the publication of Vroom's book in 1964, there has been a considerable amount of both theoretical and empirical attention paid to expectancy-type models of work motivation. Aside from attempting to test the validity of the theory in its simple form, most of these efforts have sought to study the characteristics of people and organizations that influence valence, instrumentality, and expectancy beliefs, or to examine the types of conditions within which VIE-type predictions of work motivation can be expected to apply. A complete discussion of these refinements could easily constitute an entire book – well beyond our present purposes. Thorough reviews of the *research evidence* pertaining to VIE Theory are provided by Heneman and Schwab (1972), Mitchell and Biglan (1971), and Campbell and Pritchard (1976).

The Porter/Lawler model

Vroom's (1964) statement of VIE Theory left a number of questions unanswered. Perhaps the most important of these concerned the origins of valence, instrumentality, and expectancy beliefs, and the nature of the relationship, if any, between employee attitudes toward work and job performance. Porter and Lawler (1968) developed a theoretic model and then tested it, using a sample of managers, and revised it to explore these issues. The revised statement of their model is provided in schematic form in Figure 1.

In a nutshell, their theory suggests the following. *Employee effort* is jointly determined by two key factors: the *value* placed on certain outcomes by the individual, and the *degree to which the person believes that his effort will lead to the attainment of these rewards*. As predicted by Vroom, Porter and Lawler found that these two factors interact to determine effort level; in other words, they found that people must both positively value outcomes and believe that these outcomes result from their effort for any further effort to be forthcoming.

However, effort may or may not result in *job performance*, which they defined as the accomplishment of those tasks that comprise a person's job. The reason? The level of *ability* the person has to do his job, and his *role clarity*, the degree of clarity of the understanding the person has concerning just what his job consists of. Thus, a person may be highly motivated (putting out a lot of effort), but that effort will not necessarily result in what can be considered performance, unless he has both the ability to perform the job as well as a clear understanding of the ways in which it is appropriate to direct that effort. The student

reader is probably familiar with at least one colleague who has high
motivation to learn and succeed in university, but who lacks either the
ability or the *savoir faire* needed to direct his energy into what can be
considered performance in the academic context: learning and self-
development. In short, all three ingredients are needed to some degree,
and if any of them is absent, performance cannot result.

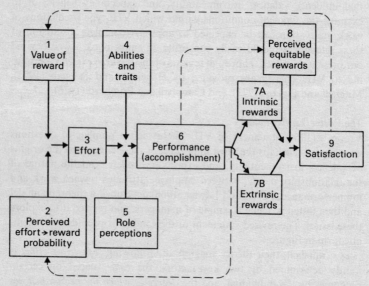

Figure 1. The revised Porter/Lawler model.

Next, what is the relationship between performance (at whatever
level it is accomplished) and *job satisfaction*? As reflected in Figure 1,
Porter and Lawler argue that performance and satisfaction may or may
not be related to one another, depending upon a number of factors.
First, they note that it is not always the case that performance results in
rewards in organizations. Further, they recognize that there are at least
two types of rewards potentially available from performance: intrinsic
and extrinsic. Porter and Lawler recognize that intrinsic rewards can be
much more closely connected with good performance than extrinsic
rewards, because the former result (almost automatically) from performance itself, whereas the latter depend upon outside sources (both to

recognize that performance has been attained and to administer rewards accordingly).

Porter and Lawler suggest that the level of performance a person believes she has attained will influence the level of rewards that she believes will be *equitable*. So, if an employee believes that her efforts have resulted in a high degree of performance, she will expect a greater level of reward than would be the case if she believes that her performance is not as high. As a result, a particular reward, if any is forthcoming, will be assessed in terms of its level of equity in the mind of the employee, rather than in terms of its absolute level. We sometimes hear statements such as 'That pay increase was an insult, considering all I do for this company,' reflecting Porter and Lawler's belief that it is not the absolute amount of reward that follows performance which determines whether it is satisfying; rather, the amount, however large or small, must be seen by the employee as equitable in order for it to be satisfying.

Satisfaction was defined in Porter and Lawler's research as '. . . the extent to which rewards actually received meet or exceed the perceived equitable level of rewards' (p. 31). And, as suggested by the feedback loop at the top of Figure 1, the level of satisfaction or dissatisfaction experienced by the person as a result of his treatment by the organization helps determine the value he places in the future on the rewards in question. Moreover, notice the feedback loop at the bottom of the diagram. It suggests that the strength of the person's belief that effort will result in rewards is also determined through experience.

IMPLICATIONS OF VIE THEORY FOR MANAGEMENT

Beliefs about work (or about life in general) are based on the individual's perceptions of the surrounding environment, and these perceptions are influenced by information stored in the person's memory. It is assumed here that valence, instrumentality, and expectancy beliefs are established and influenced in the same manner as are other beliefs. Therefore, it also follows that because beliefs may not be valid or accurate, the person's behavior may not seem appropriate to observers. And it also follows that because these three beliefs are merely beliefs (as opposed to intentions), they may not result in behavior at all, or at least, they may not result in any specifically predictable behaviors. They should, however, influence an individual's *intentions* to act certain ways. Accordingly, a number of implications follow from VIE Theory for any supervisor who wishes to try to 'motivate' his staff.

First, in order to generate positive expectancy forces, the supervisor must assign his personnel to jobs for which they are trained, and which they are capable of performing. This requires that the supervisor understand the skills, strengths, and weaknesses of each of his subordinates, as well as the nature of the skill requirements of the jobs to which he is assigning them. If people are assigned to tasks that they are not capable of performing, according to VIE Theory, their expectancy perceptions will be low, and we will not expect to see them trying to perform.

But adequate skill levels are not sufficient to assure positive expectancy perceptions. In addition, the employee must *believe* that the other circumstances surrounding his effort are favorable and conducive to his success. For example, the supervisor must be sure that machinery and equipment are in good repair, and that the employee's own staff, if any, are trained and capable of being of assistance. Likewise, there must be sufficient budget to make successful performance possible. In short, the job must be capable of being performed by an employee if we are to expect the employee to try to perform it, and – more importantly – the person must perceive that it is so.

Of particular importance for supervisors is the structuring of the expectancy beliefs of newcomers to a work setting (Hall, 1976). Success experiences are necessary for developing strong expectancy beliefs, and for maintaining a positive self-concept about one's work – a feeling of competence, self-determination, and high self-esteem (cf. Deci, 1975; Hall, 1976; Korman, 1970, 1976)

In order to operationalize the concepts of instrumentality and valence, supervisors must make sure that positively valent rewards are associated with good job performance, *and that their employees perceive this connection.*

Where does the notion of valence fit into practice? VIE Theory would prescribe that those rewards which are distributed for good performance should be the types of things that employees desire. All that we know from common sense, as well as that which we have learned from research into human needs, tells us that different people have different need profiles at different times, so it follows that different outcomes will be rewarding for different people at different times. Hence, even the same outcome (such as a job transfer to another city) may be positively valent for some people, while being negatively valent for others. And to the extent that satisfied needs tend to lose their capacity to motivate behavior, we can expect certain organizationally distributed rewards to be satisfying and perhaps motivating for a particular individual in some circumstances, but not so in other circumstances. Hence, older employees often have no desire to meet and befriend new employees on the job: their relatedness needs are already well met and secured by interactions with old friends and acquaintances.

REFERENCES

Atkinson, J. W. (1958), 'Towards experimental analysis of human motivation in terms of motives, expectancies, and incentives', in J. W. Atkinson (ed.), *Motives in Fantasy, Action, and Society*, Princeton, NJ.: Van Nostrand.

Campbell, J. P., & Pritchard, R. D. (1976), 'Motivation theory in industrial and organizational psychology', in M. D. Dunnette (ed.), *Handbook of Industrial and Organizational Psychology*, Chicago: Rand McNally.

Davidson, D., Suppes, P., & Siegel, S. (1957), *Decision Making: An Experimental Approach*, Stanford, Calif.: Stanford University Press.

Deci, E. L. (1975), *Intrinsic Motivation*, New York: Plenum.

Georgopoulos, B. S., Mahoney, G. M., & Jones, N. W. (1957), 'A path–goal approach to productivity', *Journal of Applied Psychology*, *41*, 345–53.

Hall, D. T. (1976), *Careers in Organizations*, Pacific Palisades, Calif.: Goodyear.

Heneman, H. G, III, & Schwab, D. P. (1972), 'Evaluation of research on expectancy theory predictions of employee performance', *Psychological Bulletin*, *78*(1), 1–9.

Korman, A. K. (1970), 'Toward a hypothesis of work behavior', *Journal of Applied Psychology*, *54*, 31–41.

Korman, A. K. (1976), 'Hypothesis of work behavior revisited and an extension', *Academy of Management Review*, *1*, 50–63.

Lawler, E. E., III (1973), *Motivation in Work Organizations*, Monterey, Calif.: Brooks/Cole.

Lewin, K. (1938), 'The conceptual representation and the measurement of psychological forces', *Contributions to Psychological Theory*, Durham, NC: Duke University Press, *1* (4).

Locke, E. A. (1975), 'Personnel attitudes and motivation', *Annual Review of Psychology*, *26*, 457–80.

Mitchell, T. R., & Biglan, A. (1971), 'Instrumentality theories: Current uses in psychology', *Psychological Bulletin*, *76*, 432–54.

Peak, H. (1955), 'Attitude and motivation', in M. R. Jones (ed.), *Nebraska Symposium on Motivation*, Lincoln, Nebr: University of Nebraska Press.

Porter, L. W., & Lawler, E. E., III (1968), *Managerial Attitudes and Performance*, Homewood, Ill.: Irwin-Dorsey.

Rotter, J. B. (1955), 'The role of the psychological situation in determining the direction of human behavior', in M. R. Jones (ed.), *Nebraska Symposium on Motivation*, Lincoln, Nebr.: University of Nebraska Press.

Tolman, E. C. (1959), 'Principles of Purposive Behavior', in S. Koch (ed.), *Psychology: A Study of a Science*, Vol. 2, New York: McGraw-Hill.

Vroom, V. H. (1964), *Work and Motivation*, New York: Wiley.

7

ZUR SHAPIRA

Expectancy Determinants of Instrinsically Motivated Behavior

Abridged from Z. Shapira, 'Expectancy determinants of intrinsically motivated behavior', *Journal of Personality and Social Psychology*, Vol. 34, 1976, pp. 235–44.

Most cognitive theories of motivation (e.g., Atkinson, 1964; Lewin, 1938; Peak, 1955; Rotter, 1954; Tolman, 1959, Vroom, 1964) postulate two main determinants of motivated behavior: expectancy and valence. Expectancy simply means subjective probability or a degree of belief that a certain action is followed by specific outcomes. Valence (cf. Lewin, 1938) is the psychological value that is attached to an outcome. Thus, a person's motivation to do a particular behavior is a function of the valence of the outcomes which might follow the behavior, and the person's subjective probability that the outcomes actually follow the behavior. The expectancy–valence models of motivated behavior which have generated the greatest amount of empirical research are those of Atkinson (1964) and Vroom (1964).

VROOM'S MODEL

Vroom's (1964) expectancy theory is a decision-making model of work motivation which utilizes the concepts of expectancy and valence. There are two propositions in Vroom's model. The first proposition allows one to assign valence to outcomes of a behavior (these are called first-order outcomes). Vroom hypothesized that the valence of a first-order outcome is determined by the value of other outcomes (called second-order outcomes) to which the first order outcomes can lead. For example, the valence of getting a college degree (a first-order outcome) is determined by its possible consequences such as being admitted to a graduate school, getting a better job and a higher salary, and so on. More specifically, Vroom asserted that the valence of a first-order outcome is a function of the valence of the second-order outcomes which it can lead to and the instrumentality of the first-order outcome for the achievement of each second-order outcome.

Instrumentality takes on values from $+1$ to -1, where $+1$ represents certainty that the second-order outcome follows from the first-order outcome, and -1 represents certainty that the second-order outcome cannot follow the first-order outcome. Mathematically, the valence of an outcome is said to be a monotonically increasing function of the sum of the product of valences of all second-order outcomes times the instrumentalities of the first-order outcomes for the attainment of these second-order outcomes.

The second proposition in Vroom's model allows one to determine the motivation to do a particular behavior. Motivation (which Vroom calls force toward action) is determined by the sum of the products of the valences of the different first-order outcomes times the expectancies that the specific action being considered results in that outcome.

The model further assumes that people choose the action which has the strongest positive (or weakest negative) force, which is similar to the notion, in decision theory, that people choose in a way which maximizes their subjective expected utility.[1]

ATKINSON'S MODEL

Atkinson (1964) suggested a theory of achievement motivation which is also within the expectancy–valence framework. The basic multiplicative relationship in his model is $P_s \times I_s$ where P_s stands for the subjective probability of success on the task, and I_s is the incentive value associated with success on the task.

Atkinson asserted that there are two conflicting tendencies operating in people who are faced with achievement-related tasks. The first is the tendency to approach success (T_s), and the second is the tendency to avoid failure (T_{af}). The resultant tendency to approach or avoid achievement-oriented activity (T_A) was postulated by Atkinson to be the sum of these conflicting tendencies, that is $T_A = T_s + (-T_{af})$. According to Atkinson, the tendency to approach success in any specific case (T_s) is determined by the product of the motive for success (M_s, a personality variable) and the basic multiplicative relation $P_s \times I_s$. Similarly, the

[1]Vroom's model is described in more detail in the previous reading by C. C. Pinder

tendency to avoid failure in any specific case (T_{af}) is determined by the product of M_{af} (the motive to avoid failure) times a multiplicative relation which corresponds to the basic multiplicative relation which was introduced above, that is, the probability of failure (P_f) times the incentive value of failure ($-I_f$). Thus, $T_s = M_s(P_s \times I_s)$ and $T_{af} = M_{af}$ $[P_f(-I_f)]$. Atkinson assumed that the incentive value of success is negatively related to the probability of success, that is, people desire those successes which they are least likely to attain. He suggested a specific linear function to describe the relation between the two, that is, $I_s = 1 - P_s$, a postulate which he called a 'special assumption' (1964, p. 242). Since $P_f = 1 - P_s$, and $I_f = 1 - P_f$, a simple substitution yields the following equation describing the resultant motivation:

$$T_A = (M_s - M_{af})[P_s \times (1 - P_s)].$$

This function gets its maximum at $P_s = .5$, when $M_s > M_{af}$. Hence, Atkinson predicted that people who are high-need achievers (for whom $M_s > M_{af}$) choose moderately difficult tasks since in these situations their motivation (i.e., their resultant tendency) is highest.

COMPARISON OF THE MODELS

The two models predict different results in certain situations. Assume that we have a series of similar tasks which vary in their degree of difficulty. Assume also that there are equal monetary rewards associated with successful performance on the tasks. Suppose that we present these tasks to people in an attempt to find out on which tasks they would be most motivated to work. If all the monetary outcomes which follow the completion of the tasks at each difficulty level are the same, then the valences for the completion of each task are equal. Hence, Vroom's model predicts that people select the task with the greatest force toward action. The greatest force toward action is associated with the easiest task, since if all valences are the same, then the differences among the alternatives lie in their expectancies, and the higher the expectancy (i.e., the easier the task) the greater the motivation to pursue the specific alternative. Atkinson, on the other hand, postulated that the incentive value is inversely related to the probability of success. His model predicts that motivation which is determined by the multiplication of the probability of success times the incentive value is the highest for intermediately difficult tasks, for people who are high in need achievement. In sum, in certain situations Vroom's model predicts that people choose easy tasks, and Atkinson's model predicts that they choose moderately difficult tasks.

The main difference between Vroom's and Atkinson's models lies in their different conceptions of valence or incentive value. Vroom's model does not specify any particular relationship between the valence of an outcome and its expectancy. In line with the requirement of decision models, we can infer that Vroom's model assumes that the two (i.e., valence and expectancy) are independent. Atkinson (1964), on the other hand, argued that the incentive value of success on a task is an inverse linear function of its expectancy. As pointed out by Deci (1975), the differences between these two formulations can be explained in terms of intrinsic versus extrinsic motivation.

Intrinsically motivated behavior is operationally defined as choice behavior which is exhibited for no apparent external reward. The psychological basis of this is in people's need to be competent and self-determining (cf. de Charms, 1968; Deci, 1975; White, 1959). In other words, people behave in ways which they think allow them to feel competent and self-determining in relation to their environment. Extrinsically motivated behavior, on the other hand, is behavior directed toward some external reward such as money, so people are extrinsically motivated if they engage in activities to get external rewards.

Vroom's model is one of extrinsic motivation. The outcomes take on their valence in accord with the other outcomes (rewards) which they have instrumentalities for achieving. Several authors have proposed adding an intrinsic factor to Vroom's model (cf. Campbell, Dunnette, Lawler, & Weick, 1970; Galbraith & Cummings, 1967; Porter & Lawler, 1968), yet the basic formulation of the model is extrinsic in orientation.

In contrast to Vroom, Atkinson's (1964) model is primarily one of intrinsically motivated behavior. He defined incentive value purely as an intrinsic source of valence, that is, the incentive value is related to the relative degree of success on the task irrespective of other rewards which may follow. There is no extrinsic aspect in Atkinson's (1957) original formulation, though Feather (1961) has proposed the addition of an extrinsic factor to the model.

This study tested (a) whether people's choice behavior in a situation where there is a salient monetary reward could be better accounted for by Vroom's model than Atkinson's model and (b) whether, if extrinsic rewards are not available, Atkinson's model predicts people's choice behavior better than Vroom's model.

The question of concern in this study was how the difficulty of tasks relates to subjects' motivation for doing the tasks in the presence or absence of extrinsic rewards. Vroom's theory led to the prediction that subjects choose the easiest task when equivalent extrinsic rewards are attached to the completion of each task. The present experiment provided support for Vroom's prediction in that subjects who were offered $2.50 for solving the puzzle of their choice selected relatively easy tasks. They did not however choose the easiest tasks. Thus, it seems that subjects tend to choose easy paths to extrinsic rewards, though they may desire some intrinsic satisfaction from doing challenging tasks, so they select tasks which have a fairly high probability of success but provide slightly more than minimal challenge.[2]

This study was also concerned with the relations between task difficulty and motivation in the absence of extrinsic rewards. It was reasoned that only in the no-pay condition is it possible to have an unconfounded investigation of the determinants of intrinsic motivation. Subjects actually chose tasks of more than intermediate difficulty (the median was 20.83 per cent probability of success). This finding lent support to the proposition that intrinsic valence can best be described as a positively accelerated function of task difficulty rather than a linear function as Atkinson suggested. In other words, given the choices (and thus the motivation) of the subjects, and assuming that choices are a function of expectation times valence, the valence function which allows us to account most accurately for the choices is a positively accelerated function of task difficulty. Such a function implies that a person who is intrinsically motivated chooses fairly difficult tasks rather than moderately difficult tasks as predicted by Atkinson's achievement theory.

While the present study helps clarify the nature of intrinsic motivation, it does not attempt to explain human choice behavior solely as a function of intrinsic motivation. Extrinsic rewards also play a crucial role in choice behavior, as we saw, and motivation to do a task is a function of both intrinsic and extrinsic motivation. How the two types of motivation are combined is still an unanswered question, although they were shown to be interactive rather than additive (cf. Calder & Staw, 1975; Deci, 1971).

---

[2] This article presents a research study to test this hypothesis. The present abridged version includes only the theoretical discussion and summary of findings.

108 / Understanding Human Motivation

REFERENCES

Atkinson, J. W. (1957), 'Motivational determinants of risk-taking behavior', *Psychological Review*, *64*, 359–72.

Atkinson, J. W. (1964), *An Introduction to Motivation*, Princeton, NJ: Van Nostrand.

Calder, B. J., & Staw, B. M. (1975), 'Self-perception of intrinsic and extrinsic motivation', *Journal of Personality and Social Psychology*, *31*, 599–605.

Campbell, J. P., Dunnette, M. D., Lawler, E. E., III, & Weick, K. E. (1970), *Managerial Behavior, Performance and Effectiveness*, New York: McGraw-Hill.

deCharms, R. (1968), *Personal Causation: The Internal Affective Determinants of Behavior*, New York: Academic Press.

Deci, E. L. (1971), 'Effects of externally mediated rewards on intrinsic motivation', *Journal of Personality and Social Psychology*, *18*, 105–15.

Deci, E. L. (1975), *Intrinsic Motivation*, New York: Plenum.

Feather, N. T. (1961), 'The relationship of persistence at a task to expectation of success and achievement related motives', *Journal of Abnormal and Social Psychology*, *63*, 552–61.

Galbraith, J., & Cummings, L. L. (1967), 'An empirical investigation of the motivational determinants of task performance: Interactive effects between instrumentality-valence and motivation-ability', *Organizational Behavior and Human Performance*, *2*, 237–57.

Lewin, K. (1938), *The Conceptual Representation and the Measurement of Psychological Forces*, Durham, NC: Duke University Press.

Peak, H. (1955), 'Attitudes and Motivation', in M. R. Jones (ed.), *Nebraska Symposium on Motivation* (Vol. 3), Lincoln, Nebr.: University of Nebraska Press.

Porter, L. W., & Lawler, E. E., III (1968), *Managerial Attitudes and Performance*, Homewood, Ill.: Irwin-Dorsey.

Rotter, J. B. (1954), *Social Learning and Clinical Psychology*, Englewood Cliffs, NJ: Prentice Hall.

Tolman, E. C. (1959), 'Principles of purposive behavior', in S. Koch (ed.), *Psychology: A Study of a Science* (Vol. 2), New York: McGraw-Hill.

Vroom, V. H. (1964), *Work and Motivation*, New York: Wiley.

White, R. W. (1959), 'Motivation reconsidered: The concept of competence', *Psychological Review*, *66*, 297–333.

8

PAUL E. SPECTOR

Behavior in Organizations as a Function of Employee's Locus of Control

Abridged from P. E. Spector, 'Behavior in organizations as a function of employee's Locus of Control', *Psychological Bulletin*, Vol. 91, 1982, pp. 482–97.

Little attention has been given to individual personality in research on job motivation and satisfaction. For the most part, the major theories in organizational psychology assume that the same basic processes account for behavior across all individuals and that situational characteristics cause predictable behavior across people.[1] This article attempts to demonstrate the usefulness of personality in explaining human behavior in organizations and focuses on locus of control as it relates to behavior in organizational settings.

The general theory of locus of control arose from observation and research in clinical psychology. Both the measurement and theory have been refined so that the concept is heuristically useful. Over two dozen studies of locus of control have been related specifically to attitudinal, motivational, and behavioral variables in organizational settings. One major task of this article is to integrate the general theory with the organizational findings.

THE CONCEPT OF LOCUS OF CONTROL

People attribute the cause or control of events either to themselves or

---

[1] Some notable exceptions are Hulin and Blood's (1968) suggestion that subscription to middle-class values moderates the job satisfaction–enlargement relation and Hackman and Lawler's (1971) finding that higher order need strength moderates the relation between job characteristics and satisfaction.

to the external environment. Those who ascribe control of events to themselves are said to have an internal locus of control and are referred to as *internals*. People who attribute control to outside forces are said to have an external locus of control and are termed *externals*.

Rotter (1966) and his colleagues developed the concept of locus of control from Rotter's (1954) social learning theory. According to Phares (1976), the concept was developed to explain the seeming tendency of some individuals to ignore reinforcement contingencies. Their failure to respond as predicted to rewards and punishments was attributed to a 'generalized expectancy' that their own actions would not lead to attainment of rewards or avoidance of punishment. The tendency for internals to believe they can control events and externals to believe they cannot leads to a number of predictions about their behavior that are discussed at length below.

MEASUREMENT OF LOCUS OF CONTROL

The most widely used instrument to measure locus of control is Rotter's (1966) Internal–External (I–E) scale, which consists of twenty-three locus of control and six filler items in a forced-choice format. Scores are calculated by summing the total number of externally oriented responses for each pair. Thus, scores range from 0–23 with low scores representing internality and high scores, externality.

VALIDITY OF THE CONCEPT OF LOCUS OF CONTROL

The first basic question to address concerns the basic validity of the locus of control concept itself, that is, whether internals perceive more often than externals that events are due to their own actions and whether they have more choices in situations. Roark (1978) reported that among the employees she surveyed, internals were more inclined to attribute to their own actions the obtaining of their present jobs. Hammer and Vardi (1981) found among manufacturing employees that internals were more likely than externals to attribute past job changes to their own initiative. Finally, Harvey, Barnes, Sperry, and Harris (1974) demonstrated in a laboratory study that internals tended to perceive more alternatives in a choice situation than did externals.

Not only do internals perceive greater control, but they may actually seek situations in which control is possible. Kabanoff and O'Brien (1980) described leisure-time activities of internals and externals along five dimensions, including skill utilization (the amount of skill necessary for success) and influence (the amount of personal control involved). They found a small but statistically significant tendency for internals to engage in leisure activities that required greater skill and allowed more personal control. Julian and Katz (1968) conducted a laboratory study of competitive game behavior in which subjects were given the choice of relying either on their own skill or on a more competent opponent. Externals were more likely to rely on the opponent, and internals preferred to rely on themselves. Kahle (1980) gave laboratory subjects the choice of a task requiring either luck or skill. As might be expected, externals were more likely to choose luck, whereas internals tended to prefer skill.

Phares (1976) summarized findings concerning differential behavior by internals and externals. Specifically, he noted that in contrast to externals, internals exert greater efforts to control their environment, exhibit better learning, seek new information more actively when that information has personal relevance, use information better, and seem more concerned with information rather than with social demands of situations.

Several studies linking locus of control to learning and problem solving have demonstrated superior performance by internals (e.g., DuCette & Wolk, 1973; Ude & Vogler, 1969; Wolk & DuCette, 1974). Phares (1968) found that internals were superior to externals in the use of memorized information for problem solving even though there were no differences in acquisition. Apparently, internals made better use of information in a complex problem-solving situation.

LOCUS OF CONTROL IN AN ORGANIZATIONAL CONTEXT

The basic distinguishing characteristic between internals and externals, belief in personal control, should have direct and powerful effects on organizations in several ways. First, because internals tend to believe that they can control the work setting through their behavior, they should attempt to exert more control than would externals, *provided that* control is perceived to lead to desired outcomes or rewards. If a situation cannot provide desired outcomes, the internal should not differ from the external in attempts at control. For some individuals, however, control itself might be rewarding, leading some internals to attempt control for its own sake.

The attempt of internals to control the work setting might be manifested in many ways. The internal would probably attempt control in the following areas: work flow, task accomplishment, operating procedures, work assignments, relationships with supervisors and subordinates, working conditions, goal setting, work scheduling, and organizational policy. The factors on which control attempts focused would be determined by the potential rewards each carried and by the constraints within the organizational setting.

Internals, as previously mentioned, perform better in learning and problem-solving situations, apparently because of their better use of information (Phares, 1976). It would certainly be expected that internals would exert more effort toward collecting relevant information in situations where they attempt control. This would lead one to predict better performance by internals in training and in performing tasks that necessitate the use of information. Internals, because of their generalized expectancies of environmental control, should be easier to motivate. Thus, one should find internals more responsive than externals if the appropriate performance–reward contingencies can be presented.

Internals look to themselves for direction; externals look to others. Thus, externals make more compliant followers or subordinates than do internals, who are likely to be independent and resist control by superiors and other individuals. This compliance by externals may seem reminiscent of the submissiveness of authoritarians (Adorno, Frenkel-Brunswik, Levinson, & Sanford, 1950), and in fact, Lefcourt (1966) cited two theses (Holden, 1958; Simmons, 1959) that report a moderately high correlation ($r = .51$) between locus of control and the California F Scale. One further piece of data suggesting similarities between authoritarians and externals is provided by Goodstadt and Hjelle's (1973) finding that externals tend to use a coercive leadership style in dealing with subordinates.

The nature of a job within the context of organizational factors and demands would determine whether an internal or external would be best suited. If a job requires complex information processing and frequent complex learning, internals would be expected to perform better; for simple tasks, however, the performance differential would disappear. When tasks or organizational demands require initiative and independence of action, the internal would be more suitable; when the requirement is for compliance, however, the external would be more appropriate. Finally, for jobs requiring high motivation, internals would be more likely to believe that their efforts will lead to rewards, especially when they actually do, and thus internals would tend to exhibit higher motivation. Therefore, it would seem that internals are best suited for highly technical or skilled jobs, professional jobs, and managerial or supervisory jobs. Externals would be more suited to factory-line jobs, unskilled labor jobs, clerical jobs, and jobs of a routine nature.

Motivation

It might be expected that internals would display greater job motivation than would externals because they perceive themselves to have greater control over the environment. It is not that externals are less oriented toward valued rewards or personal goals but rather that internals will exert greater efforts toward acquiring rewards or achieving goals because they are more likely to believe their efforts will be successful. In the specific job or organizational setting, the internal will exhibit more task-oriented and goal-oriented behavior, and for that reason will exhibit more job motivation, although underlying personal motivations may be the same. Job motivation that is operationalized in terms of effort and task orientation will appear to be higher in internals.

Although internals will tend to exhibit greater job motivation than externals do, job settings in which rewards do not follow performance will not long show the internal–external differences. As discussed above, internals are sensitive to reinforcement contingencies, and when effort on the job does not lead to rewards, internals may adopt a more external perspective.

Expectancy Theory

Most of the job motivation studies involving locus of control have been attempts to validate expectancy theory hypotheses. The most popular expectancy theory application to organizations has been developed by Vroom (1964). This theory proposes two types of expectancies, namely, that effort will lead to good job performance and that good performance will lead to rewards. The first is actually the belief in personal effectiveness; that is, the individual can perform well if he or she makes the effort. It is in many ways similar to self-esteem, at least in terms of self-perceived ability on the job. The second is the belief that good performance will be rewarded; that is, good performers get rewarded. This is similar to a belief in justice in the work world that is much like the concept of equity – the person who provides more inputs (good performance) receives more outcomes (rewards). Basically, if an individual holds both expectancies strongly, he or she will have high job motivation and will (within limits of ability and organizational constraints) perform well.

Theoretically, internals should hold higher expectancies of both varieties than externals would. Internals are more likely to believe that their efforts will result in good performance, and they exhibit stronger beliefs in their own competence. Therefore, they should exhibit greater self-esteem, a hypothesis supported by Lied and Pritchard (1976). Internals should also hold greater expectancies that good performance leads to rewards and should tend to perceive the job situation as more equitable than externals do.

Results are consistent in demonstrating the hypothesized relation between locus of control and expectancy. That is, internals hold higher expectancies that effort will lead to performance and that performance will lead to rewards. Lawler (1971, p. 177) argued that this tendency makes only internals suitable for pay-incentive systems. That is, internals develop expectancies that will lead them to exert greater job effort for monetary or other rewards. Externals do not develop these expectancies and therefore seem oblivious or insensitive to pay incentives. Lawler suggested using locus of control to select internals for jobs with incentive systems.

Job performance

For at least two reasons one would predict that internals would perform better on the job than externals. First, they hold greater expectancies that effort will lead to good performance and good performance to reward. Thus, they exert greater effort in situations where rewards are tied to performance, and ultimately, greater effort should lead to better performance across individuals. In fact, Lawler (1968) provided evidence that expectancies of good performance leading to rewards is a causal factor in high job performance. Using cross-lagged and dynamic correlations, Lawler found that self-reported expectancies were related to both peer and supervisor ratings of performance in a manner that was consistent with the notion that expectancies affect performance. Second, internals seek more relevant information and perform better than externals in complex task situations. Again, this should lead to better performance by internals for tasks involving complex information and learning, assuming the internals are motivated to perform.

The existing evidence suggests that internals do perform better than externals. Internals seem to exhibit greater personal career effectiveness, exert greater effort, and perform better on the job. One should keep in mind, however, that internals will only display better performance if they perceive that effort will lead to *valued* rewards. In many situations, internals may hold higher performance–reward expectancies but not value the rewards. Furthermore, if there are no rewards for performance (either immediate or long-term career), internals might not differ from externals in their performance–reward expectancies. In addition, the advantage that internals have over externals in information seeking and utilization is only an advantage in situations involving complex information, so simple situations may yield no internal–external differences. Future studies that attempt to confirm the relation between locus of control and performance should take into account the moderating influence of situation complexity and real performance–reward contingencies as well as the contribution of trait anxiety.

Job satisfaction

Internals should demonstrate greater job satisfaction than externals do for at least four reasons. First, because internals tend to take action more frequently than externals do, the dissatisfied internal is more likely to quit a dissatisfying job. Thus, there would be fewer dissatisfied internals than externals. Second, internals may perform better and receive the benefits of that performance. In situations where rewards follow performance, internals are likely to be more satisfied. Third, internals tend to advance more quickly and receive more raises than do externals. More frequent promotions and salary increases should be expected to lead to greater satisfaction. Organizational level has been shown to be positively correlated with satisfaction, although direction of causality has not been established (Porter & Lawler, 1965). Finally, cognitive consistency theory would predict that individuals who have perceived personal control to leave the situation and who choose to stay will tend to re-evaluate the situation favorably to retain consistency between their attitudes and behavior (Salancik & Pfeffer, 1978). Internals who perceive greater control and ability to leave are more likely to leave in dissatisfying situations. If they perceive the opportunity to leave but do not, they will be under some internal cognitive pressure to evaluate the job situation as favorable, thus justifying their behavior. Externals who perceive no options are under only external constraints to remain on the job and feel little pressure to change their job attitudes in a positive direction.

The research supports the locus of control–satisfaction hypothesis. Internals have been found to be more satisfied generally than externals, although there have been some interesting interactions involving satisfaction with supervision.

Leadership

There are two sides to the leadership process that have been studied – the subordinate's reaction to his or her supervisor's behavior or style and the behavior of the supervisors themselves. It would be expected that locus of control affects both the supervisor's behavior and the subordinate's reaction to it.

The research suggests that internals and externals differ in their personal supervisory styles and in their reactions to the supervisory styles of their superiors. Externals seem to prefer supervisors who are directive, and they themselves rely more on coercion with their subordinates. In addition, they seem more concerned with the social rather than the task aspects of the job. Internals, on the other hand, prefer participative approaches from their supervisors, rely more on personal persuasion with their own subordinates, and seem more task oriented and less socially oriented.

One further note is that internals seem to behave in ways that validate much theory in organizational psychology. That is, internals respond to reinforcement contingencies (incentive systems) on the job, they seem to prefer participative supervision, they demonstrate initiative, and they tend to take personal action on the job. Externals on the other hand seem unresponsive to incentives (they want them but will not necessarily work harder for them) and prefer directive supervision. Thus, much organizational theory might well be limited to internals.

REFERENCES

Adorno, T. W., Frenkel-Brunswik, E., Levinson, D. J., & Sanford, R. N. (1950), *The Authoritarian Personality*, New York: Harper & Row.

DuCette, J., & Wolk, S. (1973), 'Cognitive and motivational correlates of generalized expectancies for control', *Journal of Personality and Social Psychology*, 26, 420–26.

Goodstadt, B. E., & Hjelle, L. A. (1973), 'Power to the powerless: Locus of control and the use of power', *Journal of Personality and Social Psychology*, 27, 190–96.

Hackman, J. R., & Lawler, E. E., III (1971), 'Employee reactions to job characteristics', *Journal of Applied Psychology*, 55, 259–86.

Hammer, T. H., & Vardi, Y. (1981), 'Locus of control and career self-management among nonsupervisory employees in industrial settings', *Journal of Vocational Behavior*, 18, 13–29.

Harvey, J. H., Barnes, R. D., Sperry, D. L., & Harris, B. (1974), 'Perceived choice as a function of internal–external locus of control', *Journal of Personality*, 42, 437–52.

Holden, K. B. (1958), 'Attitude toward external versus internal control of reinforcement and learning of reinforcement sequences', unpublished master's thesis, Ohio State

University. Cited in H. M. Lefcourt, 'Internal versus external control of reinforcement: A review', *Psychological Bulletin*, 1966, *65*, 206–20.

Hulin, C. L., & Blood, M. R. (1968), 'Job enlargement, individual differences, and worker responses', *Psychological Bulletin*, *69*, 41–55.

Julian, J. W., & Katz, S. B. (1968), 'Internal versus external control and the value of reinforcement', *Journal of Personality and Social Psychology*, *8*, 89–94.

Kabanoff, B., & O'Brien, G. E. (1980), 'Work and leisure: A task-attributes analysis', *Journal of Applied Psychology*, *65*, 596–609.

Kahle, L. R. (1980), 'Stimulus condition self-selection by males in the interaction of locus of control and skill–chance situations', *Journal of Personality and Social Psychology*, *38*, 50–56.

Lawler, E. E., III (1968), 'A correlational–causal analysis of the relationship between expectancy attitudes and job performance', *Journal of Applied Psychology*, *52*, 462–8.

Lawler, E. E., III (1971), *Pay and Organizational Effectiveness: A Psychological View*, New York: McGraw-Hill.

Lefcourt, H. M. (1966), 'Internal versus external control of reinforcement: A review', *Psychological Bulletin*, *65*, 206–20.

Lied, T. R., & Pritchard, R. D. (1976), 'Relationships between personality variables and components of the expectancy–valence model', *Journal of Applied Psychology*, *61*, 463–7.

Phares, E. J. (1968), 'Differential utilization of information as a function of internal–external control', *Journal of Personality*, *36*, 649–62.

Phares, E. J. (1976), *Locus of Control in Personality*, Morristown, NJ: General Learning Press.

Porter, L. W., & Lawler, E. E., III (1965), 'Properties of organizational structure in relation to job attitudes and job behavior', *Psychological Bulletin*, *64*, 23–51.

Roark, M. H. (1978), 'The relationship of perception of chance in finding jobs to locus of control and to job search variables on the part of human resource agency personnel', (Doctoral dissertation, Virginia Polytechnic University, 1978), *Dissertation Abstracts International*, *38*, 2070A (University Microfilms No. 78–18558).

Rotter, J. B. (1954), *Social Learning and Clinical Psychology*, Englewood Cliffs, NJ: Prentice Hall.

Rotter, J. B. (1966), 'Generalized expectancies for internal versus external control of reinforcement', *Psychological Monographs*, *80* (1, Whole No. 609), pp. 1–28.

Salancik, G. R., & Pfeffer, J. (1978), 'A social information processing approach to job attitudes and task design', *Administrative Science Quarterly*, *23*, 224–53.

Simmons, W. (1959), 'Personality correlates of the James–Phares scale', unpublished master's thesis, Ohio State University. Cited in H. M. Lefcourt, 'Internal versus external control of reinforcement: A review', *Psychological Bulletin*, 1966, *65*, 206–20.

Ude, L. K., & Vogler, R. E. (1969), 'Internal versus external control of reinforcement and awareness in a conditioning task', *Journal of Psychology*, *73*, 63–7.

Vroom, V. H. (1964), *Work and Motivation*, New York: Wiley.

Wolk, S., & DuCette, J. (1974), 'Intentional performance and incidental learning as a function of personality and task dimensions', *Journal of Personality and Social Psychology*, *29*, 90–101.

Social and Group Influences on Motivation

9

ARNOLD S. TANNENBAUM

The Group in Organizations

Abridged from A. S. Tannenbaum, *Social Psychology of the Work Organization*, Chapter 5, Belmont, Calif.: Wadsworth, 1966.

CONFORMITY

In the 1920s F. H. Allport (1924) reported the results of several experiments he conducted among graduate students at Harvard. In these experiments the students made judgements about the weights of objects and the unpleasantness of odors. The students made these judgements alone and in the presence of others, and each subject recorded his judgements on paper without revealing them to the other subjects. Allport found that subjects made less extreme evaluations in the presence of others than when alone. Although the subjects did not know the judgements of others in the group, they imagined how the others were reacting and they avoided what they thought would be extreme and deviant responses. Allport attributed this moderation of judgement to an 'attitude of social conformity' that persons adopt in social situations, even in the absence of communication among them.

Normally, members of a group communicate with one another, and Sherif (1936) demonstrated how members develop common standards as they become aware of the opinions of others in the group. He placed subjects in a darkened room where they could observe a pinpoint of light. Although the light does not move, the persons experience the illusion of movement, an illusion known as the *autokinetic effect*. Subjects who experience this effect while alone establish individual norms representing the average distances which they judge the light to move. However, subjects tested in groups gradually alter their individual judgements to agree more closely with the judgements reported by the others in their group. A common standard thus becomes established as the norm for the group.

Once a norm is established, members do not deviate easily from it, and some members may conform even against their 'better' judgement. Asch (1958) asked persons in groups to estimate which of three lines of varying lengths was equal to a fourth line. Only one person in each experimental group, however, was a real subject; the others pretended to be subjects but were really confederates of the experimenter, instructed to make erroneous judgements. The lone subject was therefore confronted with others who, in direct contradiction to the subject's own senses, unanimously and repeatedly chose the wrong line. About one-third of the real subjects who underwent this experience changed their reported judgements to conform to that of the group – even though the lengths of the lines were not the least bit ambiguous, as demonstrated by subjects who made virtually no errors in judgement when not confronted with contrary group pressures

These studies illustrate the power of the group as an instrument of influence or control over members. However, not all groups are equally effective in establishing or maintaining conformity. Festinger (1950, 1951), Schachter (1951), Back (1951), and others have investigated group conditions that are conducive to conformity. These psychologists find support in their research for a number of propositions, of which we list three:

1. The more attractive a group is to members, the more likely members are to change their views to conform with those of others in the group.

2. If an individual fails to conform, the group is likely to reject him; and the more attractive the group is to its members, the more decisively they will reject this individual.

3. Members are more likely to be rejected for deviancy on an issue that is important to the group than on an issue that is unimportant.

These propositions suggest that members, implicitly or explicitly, demand conformity because it helps maintain the group that is 'attractive' to them. A general basis for the attractiveness of the group is the satisfaction that people derive from their social relations in it. In the work organization informal social behaviors – friendly remarks, jokes and conversations about matters of mutual interest – give expression to many personal needs that are frustrated by the formal limits of work roles. Groups also provide *support* to their members, and this is an especially important basis for members' attraction to the group in the context of the frustration members face on the job.

SUPPORT

Support by a group occurs in several forms. When members face a frustrating or threatening environment, the group may (a) afford some sense of comfort or consolation to members, (b) help or protect members by acting against the source of threat or frustration and (c) strengthen the individual member in his own opposition to the source of adversity.

Research by Schachter (1951) illustrates the comfort that persons undergoing threat derive through associating with others in a group. This psychologist compared the behavior of two groups of college students. Subjects in the first group were told they would undergo an experiment involving severe electric shock, while those in the second group were instructed that the experiment would involve only a very slight shock, equivalent to a tickle. The experimenter then informed the subjects that they might choose to wait their turns alone or together with others. They were also told that in the 'together' situation they would not be permitted to talk to one another. Schachter thus ruled out the possibility that the subjects who waited together might plan some joint action. None the less nearly two-thirds of the subjects in the 'severe-shock' group preferred to wait in a room with others, whereas approximately the same proportion of subjects in the second group did not care whether they waited with others or alone.

Schachter's research suggests that people are drawn to each other *psychologically* under conditions of threat or frustration. We stress the word *psychologically* because there may be no apparent benefit to members from their affiliation beyond whatever gratification or comfort is derived from the mere presence of others. The group, in other words, need not *do* anything about the source of threat in order to attract members. However, groups can sometimes act or attempt to act against the source of threat, and they may in this way afford protection or hope of protection to members. Thus a pragmatic form of support may be added to the 'psychological' support that comes from the mere presence of others.

A group may also provide support to a member by strengthening him psychologically in his opposition to a source of frustration. Stotland, for example (1959), found that subjects' reactions to a restrictive authority figure during the course of an experiment were affected by their opportunities to talk to other subjects. Unlike those who had no social contact, subjects who spent some time with other subjects (a) were more aggressive and hostile toward their supervisor, (b) disagreed with the supervisor more often, (c) expressed greater dissatisfaction with the supervisor's failure to give reasons for his behavior and (d) argued strenuously for *their own* positions as opposed to that of the supervisor.

IMPLICATIONS OF THE GROUP FOR THE WORK ORGANIZATION

Organizations are full of informal face-to-face groups that offer satisfying interpersonal relations and support to their members in the face of frustrations on the job. These groups form among workers operating around a common machine, or among workers who are near one another on the shop floor, or among workers who meet at lunch or in rest rooms or while moving around the plant. Many such groups develop norms that are relevant to the performance of the job. Members who do not conform to the group's norms face disapproval, ostracism or expulsion from the group. And if these sanctions fail, physical force may be employed. Thus relationships within these informal groups – particularly groups that are highly attractive to members – imply control and conformity as well as satisfaction and support. These characteristics help make group action the *concerted* or *mobilized* effort that it sometimes is.

Effects of the group on adjustment

Near the end of the Second World War, mass-production technology was introduced into British coal mines, in order to make mining more efficient. However, the new methods produced some unexpected results (Trist & Bamforth, 1951). For instance, psychosomatic ailments of epidemic proportions broke out among miners, and worker morale dropped to a low ebb. Absenteeism, conflicts and tensions among workers rapidly increased – and productivity did not rise as it should have. At fault was the new technology, which – however sound from an engineering standpoint – did not take into account some of the social and psychological facts of life for the miner on the job; it did not consider the function of the social group.

Coal mines are dark, lonely and dangerous. The miners had coped with these adverse working conditions by forming small, tight-knit work groups. The members of these groups chose one another, knew one another and relied on one another. Thus, they gained some sense of security against the dark, the danger and other hardships of mining.

Outside the mine, these supportive groups operated through the friendship and kinship relations within the community. When a miner died as a result of a mine accident, the members of his group often assumed responsibility for his family.

These group relations changed radically under the new technology. The new method of extracting coal relocated workers over a large area in the mine, so that they could no longer talk with one another easily. Their jobs, redefined by the new, large-scale machinery, isolated them further; they no longer collaborated closely and directly in getting the coal from the seam and out of the mine. Because of the new machinery, each worker specialized in a very limited part of the total process of extracting coal, which formerly was the responsibility of the group. Thus, the groups of mutually interdependent miners, which were functionally compatible with the earlier system of mining, became inappropriate. The mass-production technology disrupted these important social ties and, where adjustments were not made to substitute new social arrangements for the old, the mental health, morale, and productive efforts of the miners suffered.

Research on absenteeism and turnover in industry also suggest the importance of the group. Trist and Bamforth's study of British miners (1951) illustrates some of the possible effects of groups on morale and on absenteeism. Research in other organizations generally supports the hypothesis that membership in a cohesive group helps increase job satisfaction and reduce absenteeism and turnover. Coch and French, for example (1948), studied a group of textile workers who were required to adapt to changes in work methods. The turnover rates for these workers were quite high, but those who belonged to groups with strong 'we feeling' quit at a much lower rate – even though they had strong antagonistic feelings toward the company – than those who did not belong to 'cohesive' groups. Mann and Baumgartel (1952) show how a sense of group belongingness, group spirit, group pride or group solidarity on the part of workers relates inversely to rates of absenteeism. In groups where workers were absent at least four times during a six-month period, only 21 per cent report that their crew is better than others in sticking together. However, 62 per cent of workers in groups with an average of only one absence during the six-month period report this kind of cohesiveness among members.

The group also appears to have important effects on the adjustment of organization members. In a number of respects, workers who belong to cohesive groups appear 'better adjusted' in the organization than those who do not have these informal attachments. Workers who belong to such groups are likely to have higher rates of job satisfaction and lower rates of tension, absenteeism and turnover than workers who do not belong to cohesive groups. The better adjustment of members of cohesive groups is due in part to the satisfactions and the psychological support that groups provide. The better adjustment may also reflect the lesser tendency for persons who are inept in social relations to join groups in the first place. But what implications does the group have for workers' productive efforts?

Effects of the group on productivity

In the Hawthorne research,[1] the formation of a tight-knit group in the relay-assembly test room seemed to be responsible for the steadily increasing productivity (Roethlisberger & Dixon, 1939). Increased productivity, however, is not the inevitable result of cohesive groups. Quite the contrary: when cohesive groups are formed in opposition to the organization, productivity drops.

The men in the test room at Hawthorne established norms to which they all conformed. One of these norms concerned the way they acted when the supervisor was present and when he was away: all was seriousness and industry in his presence; but in his absence, levity and relaxation were the rule. Furthermore the wiremen established their own standard for production, and each employee consistently produced about what the group considered the 'proper' amount of work.

It was apparent to the observer that the men maintained a lower level of production than they could very easily have achieved. They did this despite the 'logic' of a wage-incentive system that would have rewarded them with larger pay checks, had they been less restrictive. In the *workers'* 'logic', higher production would only lead the company to raise the piece-rates, canceling out whatever additional earnings they might have made. The group, its restrictive norm and its control over members were natural consequences of this state of conflict. This control applied to members who produced at levels below the informal norm as well as to those who exceeded it. Low producers were called 'chiselers' and were admonished for not carrying their own weight. More often, however, the group imposed its sanctions on the 'rate busters' or 'slaves', who were producing at dangerously high levels.

Hawthorne drew the attention of social scientists to the group in

---

[1] See Reading 31 by J.A.C. Brown in this volume for further details on the Hawthorne studies – *Editors*.

industry, and soon a number of other researchers conducted studies on the effects of the group on worker productivity. Coch and French (1948) found that workers in informal social groups lowered their productivity in order to resist innovations in work methods introduced by the company, and that more cohesive groups – those with strong 'we feeling' – provided greater support to members who opposed the innovations. Seashore (1954) showed that workers in cohesive groups were neither more nor less productive on the average than workers in non-cohesive groups, but in the cohesive groups workers were more *uniform* in their productivity – they all produced pretty much the same amount.

This uniformity is brought about through pressures against deviancy. These pressures can have an effect in changing the behavior of a newcomer to a group. Coch and French (1948) illustrate this with an example of a female textile worker. The newcomer unwittingly learned her job too well; and she began, after only a few days on the job, to exceed the group's production norm of about fifty units. On the thirteenth day, the group began to express its antagonism, with the desired effect: her productivity dropped. On the twentieth day, however, when all the members except the newcomer were transferred to other jobs, the group disbanded. Without the group to guide her productive efforts, her production climbed to an almost impossible level compared to what she and the group had been doing just a few days earlier.

SOME QUESTIONS ABOUT THE GROUP IN ORGANIZATIONS

The informal group in organizations poses a paradox: groups can act with considerable effectiveness as law-enforcement agencies within the larger formal structure of the organization, but groups can direct the efforts of their members in opposition to organizational goals just as readily as they can direct members' efforts towards the support of these goals. This paradox caused students of organization to wonder how they might harness the power of the cohesive group. The answer seemed to lie in the approach taken by the Hawthorne experimenters in the relay-assembly test room, where the group worked towards the goal of efficient production. Why was the group so productive there and not in the bank-wiring room or on the shop floor?

Although part of the answer seemed to be the morale and job satisfaction – the 'fun' – that the girls felt in the relay test room, job satisfaction alone is not the answer. Neither is the mere existence of friendly social relations and a tight-knit group. The results of the Hawthorne study suggested another element in the puzzle – namely, the friendly and permissive behavior of the test-room supervisor.

REFERENCES

Allport, F. H. (1924), *Social Psychology*, Boston, Mass.: Houghton Mifflin.

Asch, S. E. (1958), 'The effects of group pressure upon the modification and distortion of judgements', in E. E. Maccoby, T. E. Newcomb & E.L. Hartley (eds.), *Readings in Social Psychology*, (pp. 174–83), New York: Holt.

Back, K. (1951), 'The exertion of influence through social communication', *Journal of Abnormal and Social Psychology*, 46, 9–23.

Coch, L., & French, J. R. P., Jr (1948), 'Overcoming resistance to change', *Human Relations*, 1, 512–33.

Festinger, L., Schachter, S., & Back, K. (1950), *Social Pressures in Informal Groups: A Study of a Housing Project*, New York: Harper.

Festinger, L., & Thibaut, J. (1951), 'Interpersonal communication in small groups', *Journal of Abnormal and Social Psychology*, 46, 92–9.

Mann, F. C., & Baumgartel, H. G. (1952), *Absences and Employee Attitudes in an Electric Power Company*, Survey Research Center, University of Michigan.

Roethlisberger, F. J., & Dickson, W. J. (1939), *Management and the Worker*, Cambridge, Mass.: Harvard University Press.

Schachter, S. (1951), 'Deviation, rejection and communication', *Journal of Abnormal and Social Psychology*, 46, 190–207.

Seashore, S. E. (1954), *Group Cohesiveness in the Industrial Work Group*, Survey Research Center, University of Michigan.

Sherif, M. (1936), *The Psychology of Social Norms*, New York: Harper.

Stotland, E. (1959), 'Peer groups and reactions to power figures', in D. Cartwright (ed.), *Studies in Social Power* (pp. 53–68), Institute for Social Research, University of Michigan.

Trist, E., & Bamforth, K. (1951), 'Some social and psychological consequences of the Longwall method of coal-getting', *Human Relations*, 4, 3–38.

10

J. STACY ADAMS

Inequity in Social Exchange

Abridged from J. S. Adams, 'Inequity in Social Exchange', in L. Berkowitz (ed.), *Advances in Experimental Social Psychology*, Vol. 2, New York: Academic Press, 1965, pp. 267–99.

ANTECEDENTS OF INEQUITY

Whenever two individuals exchange anything, there is the possibility that one or both of them will feel that the exchange was inequitable. Such is frequently the case when a man exchanges his services for pay. On the man's side of the exchange are his education, intelligence, experience, training, skill, seniority, age, sex, ethnic background, social status, and, of course, the effort he expends on the job. Under special circumstances other attributes will be relevant. These may be personal appearance or attractiveness, health, possession of certain tools, the characteristics of one's spouse, and so on. They are what a man perceives as his contributions to the exchange, for which he expects a just return. A man brings them into an exchange, and henceforth they will be referred to as his *inputs*. These inputs, let us emphasize, are *as perceived by their contributor* and are not necessarily isomorphic with those perceived by the other party to the exchange. This suggests two conceptually distinct characteristics of inputs, *recognition* and *relevance*.

The possessor of an attribute, or the other party to the exchange, or both, may recognize the existence of the attribute in the possessor. If either the possessor or both members of the exchange recognize its existence, the attribute has the potentiality of being an input. Whether or not an attribute having the potential of being an input is in fact an input is contingent upon the possessor's perception of its relevance to the exchange. If he perceives it to be relevant, if he expects a just return for it, it is an input.

On the other side of an exchange are an individual's receipts. These *outcomes*, as they will be termed, include in an employee–employer exchange pay, rewards intrinsic to the job, satisfying supervision, seniority benefits, fringe benefits, job status and status symbols, and a variety of formally and informally sanctioned perquisites, such as the right of a higher-status person to park his car in a privileged location. These are examples of positively valent outcomes. But outcomes may have negative valence. Poor working conditions, monotony, fate uncertainty, and the many 'dissatisfiers' listed by Herzberg et al. (1959) are no less 'received' than, say, wages and are negatively valent. They would be avoided, rather than approached, if it were possible. As in the case of job inputs, job outcomes are often intercorrelated. For example, greater pay and higher job status are likely to go hand-in-hand.

In other than employee–employer exchanges, though they are not precluded from these exchanges, relevant positive outcomes for one or both parties may consist of affection, love, formal courtesies, expressions of friendship, fair value (as in merchandise), and reliability (as part of the purchase of a service). Insult, rudeness, and rejection are the other side of the coin.

In a manner analogous to inputs, outcomes are *as perceived*, and, again, they should be characterized in terms of recognition and relevance. If the recipient or both the recipient and giver of an outcome in an exchange recognize its existence, it has the potentiality of being an outcome psychologically. If the recipient considers it relevant to the exchange and it has some marginal utility for him, it *is* an outcome. Not infrequently the giver may give or yield something which, though of some cost to him, is either irrelevant or of no marginal utility to the recipient.

In classifying some variables as inputs and others as outcomes, it is not implied that they are independent, except conceptually. Inputs and outcomes are, in fact, intercorrelated, but imperfectly so. Indeed, it is because they are imperfectly correlated that there need be concern with inequity. There exist normative expectations of what constitute 'fair' correlations between inputs and outcomes. The expectations are formed – learned – during the process of socialization, at home, at school, at work. They are based by observation of the correlations obtaining for a reference person or group – a co-worker or a colleague, a relative or neighbor, a group of co-workers, a craft group, an industry-wide pattern. A bank clerk, for example, may determine whether her outcomes and inputs are fairly correlated, in balance so to speak, by comparing them with the ratio of the outcomes to the inputs of other female clerks in her section. For a particular professor the relevant reference group may be professors in the same discipline and of the same academic 'vintage'.

When the normative expectations of the person making social comparisons are violated, when he finds that his outcomes and inputs are not in balance in relation to those of others, feelings of inequity result. But before a formal definition of inequity is offered, two terms of reference will be introduced to facilitate later discussion, *Person* and *Other*. *Person* is any individual for whom equity or inequity exists. *Other* is any individual with whom Person is in an exchange relationship, or with whom Person compares himself when both he and Other are in an exchange relationship with a third party, such as an employer, or with third parties who are considered by Person as being comparable, such as employers in a particular industry or geographic location.

DEFINITION OF INEQUITY

Inequity exists for Person whenever he perceives that the ratio of his outcomes to inputs and the ratio of Other's outcomes to Other's inputs are unequal. This may happen either (a) when he and Other are in a direct exchange relationship or (b) when both are in an exchange relationship with a third party and Person compares himself to Other. The values of outcomes and inputs are, of course, as perceived by Person. Schematically, inequality is experienced when either

$$\frac{O_p}{I_p} < \frac{O_a}{I_a} \quad \text{or} \quad \frac{O_p}{I_p} > \frac{O_a}{I_a},$$

where $O = \Sigma O_i$, $I = \Sigma I_i$ and p and a are subscripts denoting Person and Other, respectively. A condition of equity exists when

$$\frac{O_p}{I_p} = \frac{O_a}{I_a}$$

The outcomes and inputs in each of the ratios are conceived as being the sum of such outcomes and inputs as are perceived to be relevant to a particular exchange. Furthermore, each sum is conceived of as a weighted sum, on the assumption that individuals probably do not weight elemental outcomes or inputs equally. The work of Herzberg et al. (1959) on job 'satisfiers' and 'dissatisfiers' implies strongly that different outcomes, as they are labeled here, have widely varying utilities, negative as well as positive. It also appears reasonable to assume that inputs as diverse as seniority, skill, effort, and sex are not weighted equally.

From the definition of inequity it follows that inequity results for Person not only when he is, so to speak, relatively underpaid, but also when he is relatively overpaid. Person will, for example, feel inequity exists not only when his effort is high and his pay low, while Other's effort and pay are high, but also when his effort is low and his pay high, while Other's effort and pay are low. This proposition receives direct support from experiments by Adams and Rosenbaum (1962), Adams (1963), and Adams and Jacobsen (1964) in which subjects were inequitably overpaid. It receives some support also from an observation by Thibaut (1950) that subjects in whose favor the experimenter discriminated displayed 'guilty smirks' and 'sheepishness'. The magnitude of the inequity experienced will be a monotonically increasing function of the size of the discrepancy between the ratios of outcomes to inputs.

Although there is no direct, reliable evidence on this point, it is probable, as Homans (1961) conjectured, that the thresholds for inequity are different (in absolute terms from a base of equity) in cases of under- and over-reward. The threshold would be higher presumably in cases of over-reward, for a certain amount of incongruity in these cases can be acceptably rationalized as 'good fortune' without attendant discomfort. In his work on pay differentials, Jaques (1961) notes that in instances of under-compensation, British workers paid 10 per cent less than the equitable level show 'an active sense of grievance, complaints or the desire to complain, and, if no redress is given, an active desire to change jobs, or to take action . . .' (p. 26). In cases of over-compensation, he observes that at the 10 to 15 per cent level above equity 'there is a strong sense of receiving preferential treatment, which may harden into bravado, with underlying feelings of unease . . .' (p. 26). He states further, 'The results suggest that it is not necessarily the case that each one is simply out to get as much as he can for his work. There appear to be equally strong desires that each one should earn the right amount – a fair and reasonable amount relative to others' (p. 26).

CONSEQUENCES OF INEQUITY

Although there can be little doubt that inequity results in dissatisfaction, in an unpleasant emotional state, be it anger or guilt, there will be other effects. A major purpose of this paper is to specify these in terms that permit specific predictions to be made. Before turning to this task, two general postulates are presented, closely following propositions from cognitive dissonance theory (Festinger, 1957). First, the presence of inequity in Person creates tension in him. The tension is proportional to the magnitude of inequity present. Second, the tension created in Person will motivate him to eliminate or reduce it. The strength of the motivation is proportional to the tension created. In short, the presence of inequity will motivate Person to achieve equity or to reduce inequity, and the strength of motivation to do so will vary directly with the magnitude of inequity experienced.

Person altering his inputs

Person may vary his inputs, either increasing them or decreasing them, depending on whether the inequity is advantageous or disadvantageous. Increasing inputs will reduce felt inequity, if

$$\frac{O_p}{I_p} > \frac{O_a}{I_a}.$$

conversely, decreasing inputs will be effective, if

$$\frac{O_p}{I_p} < \frac{O_a}{I_a};$$

In the former instance, Person might increase either his productivity or the quality of his work, provided that it is possible, which is not always the case. In the second instance, Person might engage in 'production restriction', for example. Whether Person does, or can, reduce inequity by altering his inputs is partially contingent upon whether relevant inputs are susceptible to change. Sex, age, seniority, and ethnicity are not modifiable. Education and skill are more easily altered, but changing these requires time. Varying inputs will also be a function of Person's perception of the principal 'cause' of the inequity. If the discrepancy between outcome–input ratios is primarily a function of his inputs being at variance with those of Other, Person is more likely to alter them than if the discrepancy is largely a result of differences in outcomes. Additionally, it is postulated that given equal opportunity to alter inputs and outcomes, Person will be more likely to lower his inputs when

$$\frac{O_p}{I_p} < \frac{O_a}{I_a}.$$

than he is to increase his inputs when

$$\frac{O_p}{I_p} > \frac{O_a}{I_a};$$

This is derived from two assumptions: first, the assumption stated earlier that the threshold for the perception of inequity is higher when Person is over-rewarded than when he is under-rewarded; secondly, the assumption that Person is motivated to minimize his costs and to maximize his gains. By the second assumption, Person will reduce inequity, in so far as possible, in a manner that will yield him the largest outcomes.

Person altering his outcomes
Person may vary his outcomes, either decreasing or increasing them, depending on whether the inequity is advantageous or disadvantageous to him. Increasing outcomes will reduce inequity, if

$$\frac{O_p}{I_p} < \frac{O_a}{I_a}$$

conversely, decreasing outcomes will serve the same function, if

$$\frac{O_p}{I_p} > \frac{O_a}{I_a}.$$

Of these two possibilities, the second is far less likely, and there is no good evidence of the use of this means of reducing inequity, though some may be available in the clinical literature. There are, however, data bearing on attempts to increase outcomes, data other than those related to wage increase demands in union–management negotiations, probably only a part of which are directly traceable to wage inequities.

Person distorting his inputs and outcomes cognitively

Person may cognitively distort his inputs and outcomes, the direction of the distortion being the same as if he had actually altered his inputs and outcomes, as discussed above. Since most individuals are heavily influenced by reality, substantial distortion is generally difficult. It is pretty difficult to distort to oneself, to change one's cognitions about the fact, for example, that one has a BA degree, that one has been an accountant for seven years, and that one's salary is $700 per month. However, it is possible, within limits, to alter the utility of these. For example, State College is a small backwoods school with no reputation, or, alternatively, State College has one of the best business schools in the state and the dean is an adviser to the Bureau of the Budget. Or, one can consider the fact that $700 per month will buy all of the essential things of life and a few luxuries, or, conversely, that it will never permit one to purchase a Wyeth oil painting or an Aston Martin DB5. There is ample evidence in the psychological literature, especially that related to cognitive dissonance theory, that individuals do modify or rearrange their cognitions in an effort to reduce perceived incongruities (for a review, see Brehm & Cohen, 1962). Since it has been postulated that the experience of inequity is equivalent to the experience of dissonance, it is reasonable to believe that cognitive distortion may be adopted as a means of reducing inequity. In a variety of work situations, for example in paced production-line jobs, actually altering one's inputs and outcomes may be difficult; as a consequence these may be cognitively changed in relatively subtle ways.

Person leaving the field

Leaving the field may take any of several ways of severing social relationships. Quitting a job, obtaining a transfer, and absenteeism are common forms of leaving the field in an employment situation. These are fairly radical means of coping with inequity. The probability of using them is assumed to increase with magnitude of inequity and to decrease with the availability of other means.

Person acting on other

In the face of injustice, Person may attempt to alter or cognitively distort Other's inputs and outcomes, or try to force Other to leave the field. These means of reducing inequity vary in the ease of their use. Getting Other to accept greater outcomes, which was a possible interpretation of some of the findings by Leventhal et al. (1964), would obviously be easier than the opposite. Similarly, inducing Other to lower his inputs may be easier than the reverse. For example, all other things being equal, such as work-group cohesiveness and the needs and ability of an individual worker, it is probably easier to induce a 'rate buster' to lower his inputs than to get a laggard to increase them. The direction of the change attempted in the inputs and outcomes of Other is the reverse of the change that Person would make in his own inputs and outcomes, whether the change be actual or cognitive. By way of illustration, if Person experienced feelings of inequity because he lacked job experience compared to Other, he could try to induce Other to decrease a relevant input instead of increasing his own inputs.

Cognitive distortion of Other's inputs and outcomes may be somewhat less difficult than distortion of one's own, since cognitions about Other are probably less well anchored than are those concerning oneself. This assumption is consistent with the finding that 'where alternatives to change in central attitudes are possible, they will be selected' (Pilisuk, 1962, p. 102).

Person changing the object of his comparison

Person may change Other with whom he compares himself when he experiences inequity and he and Other stand in an exchange relationship with a third party. This mode is limited to the relationship specified; it is not applicable when Person and Other are in a direct exchange. Changing the object of comparison in the latter situation would reduce to severing the relationship.

The resolution of inequity by changing comparison object is undoubtedly difficult of accomplishment, particularly if Person has been comparing himself to Other for some time.

Choice among modes of inequity reduction

Although reference has been made previously to conditions that may affect the use of one or another method of reducing inequity, there is need for a general statement of conditions that will govern the adoption of one method over another. Given the existence of inequity, any of the means of reduction described earlier are potentially available to Person.

Set forth below are some propositions about conditions determining the choice of modes by Person. As will be noted, the propositions are not all independent of one another, and each should be prefaced by the condition, *ceteris paribus*.

(a) Person will maximize positively valent outcomes and the valence of outcomes.

(b) He will minimize increasing inputs that are effortful and costly to change.

(c) He will resist real and cognitive changes in inputs that are central to self-concept and to his self-esteem. To the extent that any of Person's outcomes are related to his self-concept and to his self-esteem, this proposition is extended to cover his outcomes.

(d) He will be more resistant to changing cognitions about his own outcomes and inputs than to changing his cognitions about Other's outcomes and inputs.

(e) Leaving the field will be resorted to only when the magnitude of inequity experienced is high and other means of reducing it are unavailable. Partial withdrawal, such as absenteeism, will occur more frequently and under conditions of lower inequity.

(f) Person will be highly resistant to changing the object of his comparisons, Other, once it has stabilized over time and, in effect, has become an anchor.

REFERENCES

Adams, J. S. (1963), 'Toward an understanding of inequity', *Journal of Abnormal and Social Psychology*, 67, 422–36.

Adams, J. S., & Jacobsen, Patricia R. (1964), 'Effects of wage inequities on work quality', *Journal of Abnormal and Social Psychology*, 69, 19–25.

Adams, J. S. & Rosenbaum, W. B. (1962), 'The relationship of worker productivity to cognitive dissonance about wage inequities', *Journal of Applied Psychology*, 46, 161–4.

Brehm, J. W., & Cohen, A. R. (1962), *Exploration in Cognitive Dissonance*, New York: Wiley.

Festinger, L. (1957), *A Theory of Cognitive Dissonance*, Evanston, Ill.: Row, Peterson.

Herzberg, F., Mausner, B., & Snyderman, Barbara B. (1959), *The Motivation to Work*, New York: Wiley.

Homans, G. C. (1961), *Social Behavior: Its Elementary Forms*, New York: Harcourt, Brace.

Jaques, E. (1961), 'An objective approach to pay differentials', *Time Motion Study*, 10, 25–8.

Leventhal, G., Reilly, Ellen, & Lehrer, P. (1964), 'Change in reward as a determinant of satisfaction and reward expectancy', paper read at Western Psychological Association, Portland, Ore.

Pilisuk, M. (1962), 'Cognitive balance and self-relevant attitudes', *Journal of Abnormal and Social Psychology*, 65, 95–103.

Thibaut, J. (1950), 'An experimental study of the cohesiveness of underprivileged groups', *Human Relations*, 3, 251–78.

11

ROBERT B. ZAJONC

Social Facilitation

Abridged from R. B. Zajonc, 'Social facilitation', *Science*, Vol. 149, 1965, pp. 269–74.

The influences of individuals on each other's behavior which are of interest to social psychologists today take on very complex forms. Often they involve vast networks of inter-individual effects such as one finds in studying the process of group decision making, competition, or conformity to a group norm. But the fundamental forms of inter-individual influence are represented by the oldest experimental paradigm of social psychology: social facilitation. This paradigm, dating back to Triplett's original experiments on pacing and competition, carried out in 1897, examines the consequences upon behavior which derive from the sheer presence of other individuals.

Research in the area of social facilitation may be classified in terms of two experimental paradigms: audience effects and co-action effects. The first experimental paradigm involves the observation of behavior when it occurs in the presence of passive spectators. The second examines behavior when it occurs in the presence of other individuals also engaged in the same activity. We shall consider past literature in these two areas separately.

AUDIENCE EFFECTS

Simple motor responses are particularly sensitive to social facilitation effects. In 1925 Travis obtained such effects in a study in which he used the pursuit-rotor task. Travis found a clear improvement in performance when his subjects were confronted with an audience. Their accuracy on the ten trials before an audience was greater than on any ten previous trials, including those on which they had scored highest.

A considerably greater improvement in performance was recently obtained in a somewhat different setting and on a different task (Bergum & Lehr, 1963).

Dashiell (1930), who carried out an extensive program of research on social facilitation, also found considerable improvement in performance due to audience effects on such tasks as simple multiplication or word association. But, as is the case in many other areas, negative audience effects were also found. In 1933 Pessin asked college students to learn lists of nonsense syllables under two conditions, alone and in the presence of several spectators. When confronted with an audience, his subjects required an average of 11.27 trials to learn a seven-item list. When working alone they needed only 9.85 trials. The average number of errors made in the 'audience' condition was considerably higher than the number in the 'alone' condition. In 1931 Husband found that the presence of spectators interferes with the learning of a finger maze, and in 1933 Pessin and Husband confirmed Husband's results.

The results thus far reviewed seem to contradict one another. On a pursuit-rotor task Travis found that the presence of an audience improves performance. The learning of nonsense syllables and maze learning, however, seem to be inhibited by the presence of an audience, as shown by Pessin's experiment. The picture is further complicated by the fact that when Pessin's subjects were asked, several days later, to recall the nonsense syllables they had learned, a reversal was found. The subjects who tried to recall the lists in the presence of spectators did considerably better than those who tried to recall them alone. Why are the learning of nonsense syllables and maze learning inhibited by the presence of spectators? And why, on the other hand, does performance on a pursuit-rotor, word-association, multiplication, or a vigilance task improve in the presence of others?

There is just one, rather subtle, consistency in the above results. It would appear that the emission of well-learned responses is facilitated by the presence of spectators, while the acquisition of new responses is impaired. To put the statement in conventional psychological language, performance is facilitated and learning is impaired by the presence of spectators.

This tentative generalization can be reformulated so that different features of the problem are placed into focus. During the early stages of learning, especially of the type involved in social facilitation studies, the subject's responses are mostly the wrong ones. A person learning a finger maze, or a person learning a list of nonsense syllables, emits more wrong responses than right ones in the early stages of training. Most learning experiments continue until he ceases to make mistakes – until his performance is perfect. It may be said, therefore, that during training it is primarily the wrong responses which are dominant and strong; they are the ones which have the highest probability of occurrence. But after the individual has mastered the task, correct responses necessarily gain ascendancy in his task-relevant behavioral repertoire. Now they are the ones which are more probable – in other words, dominant. Our tentative generalization may now be simplified: audience enhances the emission of dominant responses. If the dominant responses are the correct ones, as is the case upon achieving mastery, the presence of an audience will be of benefit to the individual. But if they are mostly wrong, as is the case in the early stages of learning, then these wrong responses will be enhanced in the presence of an audience, and the emission of correct responses will be postponed or prevented.

There is a class of psychological processes which are known to enhance the emission of dominant responses. They are subsumed under the concepts of drive, arousal, and activation (Duffy, 1962; Spence, 1956; Zajonc & Nieuwenhuyse, 1964). If we could show that the presence of an audience has arousal consequences for the subject, we would be a step further along in trying to arrange the results of social-facilitation experiments into a neater package. But let us first consider another set of experimental findings.

CO-ACTION EFFECTS

The experimental paradigm of co-action is somewhat more complex than the paradigm involved in the study of audience effects. Here we observe individuals all simultaneously engaged in the same activity and in full view of each other. One of the clearest effects of such simultaneous action, or co-action, is found in eating behavior. It is well known that animals simply eat more in the presence of others. In an extensive study of social-facilitation effects among albino rats, Harlow (1932) found dramatic increases in eating. Considerably more food was consumed by the animals when they were in pairs than when they were fed alone. James (1953, 1960) and James and Cannon (1955), too, found very clear evidence of increased eating among puppies fed in groups.

Perhaps the most dramatic effect of co-action is reported by Chen (1937). Chen observed groups of ants working alone, and in groups of two. There is absolutely no question that the amount of work an ant accomplishes [in nest-building] increases markedly in the presence of another ant. In all pairs except one, the presence of a companion increased output by a factor of at least 2.

If one assumes that under the conditions of Chen's experiment nest-building *is* the dominant response, then there is no reason why his findings could not be embraced by the generalization just proposed. Nest-building is a response which Chen's ants have fully mastered. Certainly it is something that a mature ant need not learn. And this is simply an instance where the generalization that the presence of others enhances the emission of dominant and well-developed responses holds.

If the process involved in audience effects is also involved in co-action effects, then learning should be inhibited in the presence of other learners. Let us examine some literature in this field. Klopfer (1958) observed greenfinches – in isolation and in heterosexual pairs – which were learning to discriminate between sources of palatable and of un-palatable food. And, as one would by now expect, his birds learned this discrimination task considerably more efficiently when working alone. I hasten to add that the subjects' sexual interests cannot be held responsible for the inhibition of learning in the paired birds. Allee and Masure (1936), using Australian parakeets, obtained the same result for homosexual pairs as well. The speed of learning was considerably greater for the isolated birds than for the paired birds, regardless of whether the birds were of the same sex or of the opposite sex.

Similar results are found with cockroaches. Gates and Allee (1933) compared data for cockroaches learning a maze in isolation, in groups of two, and in groups of three. It is clear from the data that the solitary cockroaches required considerably less time to learn the maze than the grouped animals. Gates and Allee believe that the group situation produced inhibition.

The experiments on social facilitation performed by Floyd Allport in 1920 and continued by Dashiell in 1930, both of whom used human subjects, are the ones best known. Allport's subjects worked either in separate cubicles or sitting around a common table. When working in isolation they did the various tasks at the same time and were monitored by common time signals. Allport did everything possible to reduce the tendency to compete. The subjects were told that the results of their tests would not be compared and would not be shown to other staff members, and that they themselves should refrain from making any such comparisons.

Among the tasks used were the following: chain word association, vowel cancellation, reversible perspective, multiplication, problem solving, and judgements of odors and weights. The results of Allport's experiments are well known: in all but the problem-solving and judgements tests, performance was better in groups than in the 'alone' condition. How do these results fit our generalization? Word association, multiplication, the cancellation of vowels, and the reversal of the perceived orientation of an ambiguous figure all involve responses which are well established. They are responses which are either very well learned or under a very strong influence of the stimulus, as in the word-association task or the reversible-perspective test. The problem-solving test consists of disproving arguments of ancient philosophers. In contrast to the other tests, it does not involve well-learned responses. On the contrary, the probability of wrong (that is, logically incorrect) responses on tasks of this sort is rather high; in other words, wrong responses are dominant. Of interest, however, is the finding that while intellectual work suffered in the group situation, sheer output of words was increased. When working together, Allport's subjects tended consistently to write more. Therefore, the generalization proposed in the previous section can again be applied: if the presence of others raises the probability of dominant responses, and if strong (and many) incorrect response tendencies prevail, then the presence of others can only be detrimental to performance. The results of the judgement tests have little bearing on the present argument, since Allport gives no accuracy figures for evaluating performance. The data reported only show that the presence of others was associated with the avoidance of extreme judgements.

In 1928 Travis, whose work on the pursuit rotor I have already noted, repeated Allport's chain-word-association experiment. In contrast to Allport's results, Travis found that the presence of others decreased performance. The number of associations given by his subjects was greater when they worked in isolation. It is very significant, however, that Travis used stutterers as his subjects. In a way, stuttering is a manifestation of a struggle between conflicting response tendencies, all of which are strong and all of which compete for expression. The stutterer, momentarily hung up in the middle of a sentence, waits for the correct response to reach full ascendancy. He stammers because other competing tendencies are dominant at that moment. It is reasonable to assume that, to the extent that the verbal habits of a stutterer are characterized by conflicting response tendencies, the presence of others, by enhancing each of these response tendencies, simply heightens his conflict. Performance is thus impaired.

PRESENCE OF OTHERS
AS A SOURCE OF AROUSAL

The results I have discussed thus far lead to one generalization and to one hypothesis. The generalization which organizes these results is that the presence of others, as spectators or as co-actors, enhances the emission of dominant responses. We also know from extensive research literature that arousal, activation, or drive all have as a consequence the enhancement of dominant responses (Spence, 1956). We now need to examine the hypothesis that the presence of others increases the individual's general arousal or drive level.

The evidence that the mere presence of others raises the arousal level is indirect and scanty. And, as a matter of fact, some work seems to suggest that there are conditions, such as stress, under which the presence of others may lower the animal's arousal level (Bovard, 1959). Evidence for Bovard's hypothesis, however, is as indirect as evidence for the one which predicts arousal as a consequence of the presence of others, and even more scanty.

SUMMARY AND CONCLUSION

If one were to draw one practical suggestion from the review of the social-facilitation effects which are summarized in this article he would advise the student to study all alone, preferably in an isolated cubicle, and to arrange to take his examinations in the company of many other students, on stage, and in the presence of a large audience. The results of his examination would be beyond his wildest expectations, provided, of course, he had learned his material quite thoroughly.

I have tried in this article to pull together the early, almost forgotten work on social facilitation and to explain the seemingly conflicting results. This explanation is, of course, tentative, and it has never been put to a direct experimental test. It is, moreover, not far removed from the one originally proposed by Allport. He theorized (1924, p. 261) that 'the sights and sounds of others doing the same thing' augment ongoing responses. Allport, however, proposed this effect only for *overt* motor responses, assuming that '*intellectual* or *implicit responses* of thought are hampered rather than facilitated' by the presence of others (1924, p. 274). This latter conclusion was probably suggested to him by the negative results he observed in his research on the effects of co-action on problem solving.

Needless to say, the presence of others may have effects considerably more complex than that of increasing the individual's arousal level. The presence of others may provide cues as to appropriate or inappropriate responses, as in the case of imitation or vicarious learning. Or it may supply the individual with cues as to the measure of danger in an ambiguous or stressful situation. Davitz and Mason (1955), for instance, have shown that the presence of an unafraid rat reduces the fear of another rat in stress. Bovard (1959) believes that the calming of the rat in stress which is in the presence of an unafraid companion is mediated by inhibition of activity of the posterior hypothalamus. But in their experimental situations (that is, the open field test) the possibility that cues for appropriate escape or avoidance responses are provided by the co-actor is not ruled out. We might therefore be dealing not with the effects of the mere presence of others but with the considerably more complex case of imitation. The animal may not be calming *because* of his companion's presence. He may be calming *after* having copied his companion's attempted escape responses. The paradigm which I have examined in this article pertains only to the effects of the mere presence of others and to the consequences for the arousal level. The exact parameters involved in social facilitation still must be specified.

REFERENCES

Allee, W. C., & Masure, R. H. (1936), 'A comparison of maze behavior in paired and isolated shell parakeets (*Melopsittacas undulatus*, Shaw)', *Physiological Zoology*, *22*, 131–56.

Allport, F. H. (1920), 'The influence of the group upon association and thought', *Journal of Experimental Psychology*, *3*, 159–82.

Allport, F. H. (1924), *Social Psychology*, Boston, Mass.: Houghton Mifflin.

Bergum, B. O., & Lehr, D. J. (1963), 'Effects of authoritarianism on vigilance performance', *Journal of Applied Psychology*, *47*, 75–7.

Bovard, E. W. (1959), 'The effect of social stimuli on the response to stress', *Psychological Review*, *66*, 267–77.

Chen, S. C. (1937), 'Social modification of the activity of ants in nest-building', *Physiological Zoology*, *10*, 420–36.

Dashiell, J. F. (1930), 'An experimental analysis of some group effects', *Journal of Abnormal and Social Psychology*, *25*, 190–99.

Davitz, J. R., & Mason, D. J. (1955), 'Socially facilitated reduction of a fear response in rats', *Journal of Comparative and Physiological Psychology*, *48*, 149–51.

Duffy, E. (1962), *Activation and Behavior*, New York: Wiley.

Gates, M. F., & Allee, W. C. (1933), 'Conditioned behavior of isolated and grouped cockroaches on a simple maze', *Journal of Comparative Psychology*, *15*, 331 – 58.

Harlow, H. F. (1932), 'Social facilitation of feeding in the albino rat', *Journal of Genetic Psychology*, *41*, 211–21.

Husband, R. W. (1931), 'Analysis of methods in human maze learning', *Journal of Genetic Psychology*, *39*, 258–77.

James, W. T. (1953), 'Social facilitation of eating behavior in puppies after satiation', *Journal of Comparative and Physiological Psychology*, *46*, 427–8.

James, W. T. (1960), 'The development of social facilitation of eating in puppies', *Journal of Genetic Psychology*, *96*, 123–7.

James, W. T., & Cannon, D. J. (1955), 'Variation in social facilitation of eating behavior in puppies', *Journal of Genetic Psychology*, *87*, 225–8.

Klopfer, P. H. (1958), 'Influence of social interaction on learning rates in birds', *Science*, *128*, 903–4.

Pessin, J. (1933), 'The comparative effects of social and mechanical stimulation on memorizing', *American Journal of Psychology*, *45*, 263–70.

Pessin, J., & Husband, R. W. (1933), 'Effects of social stimulation on human maze learning', *Journal of Abnormal and Social Psychology*, *28*, 148–54.

Spence, K. W. (1956), *Behavior Theory and Conditioning*, New Haven, Conn.: Yale University Press.

Travis, L. E. (1925), 'The effect of a small audience upon eye-hand coordination', *Journal of Abnormal and Social Psychology*, *20*, 142–6.

Travis, L. E. (1928), 'The influence of the group upon the stutterer's speed in free association', *Journal of Abnormal and Social Psychology*, *23*, 45–51.

Triplett, N. (1897), 'The dynamogenic factors in pacemaking and competition', *American Journal of Psychology*, *9*, 507–33.

Zajonc, R. B., & Nieuwenhuyse, B. (1964), 'Relationship between word frequency and recognition: Perceptual process or response bias?', *Journal of Experimental Psychology*, *67*, 276–85.

12

MORTON DEUTSCH

Socially Relevant Science: Reflections on Some Studies of Interpersonal Conflict

Abridged from M. Deutsch, 'Socially relevant science: Reflections on some studies of interpersonal conflict', *American Psychologist*, Vol. 24, 1969, pp. 1076–92.

I have hoped that my intellectual work on cooperation and competition combined with the work of other social scientists on related problems might significantly affect ways of thinking about types of social relations and that, as a consequence, systematic, and possibly new, ideas about preventing destructive conflicts among nations might emerge. If anyone wishes to accuse me of being optimistic, of course, he would be right. After all, my initial theoretical and empirical work in the area of cooperation–competition centered on the differential *effects* of these types of relationships. Only later did I work on the factors influencing whether a cooperative or competitive relationship would develop. This later work (which has been described under such labels as 'interpersonal conflict', 'bargaining', 'conflict resolution') is much more directly related to the question of preventing destructive conflicts. Yet, it turns out that one of the major simplifying ideas about factors affecting conflict resolution arising out of my more recent work complements my earlier theoretical analysis of the effects of cooperation and competition. Namely, the characteristic processes and effects elicited by a given type of social relationship (cooperative or competitive) tend also to elicit that type of social relationship. Thus, the strategy of power and the tactics of coercion, threat, and deception result from and also result in a competitive relationship. Similarly, the strategy of mutual problem solving and the tactics of persuasion, openness, and mutual enhancement elicit and also are elicited by a cooperative orientation.

Table 1 presents in condensed, outline form some of the basic ideas involved in my analysis of the effect of cooperation and competition. In essence, the theory states that the effects of one person's actions upon another will be a function of the nature of their interdependence and the nature of the action that takes place. Skillfully executed actions of an antagonist will elicit rather different responses than skillful actions from an ally, but a bumbling collaborator may evoke as much negative reaction as an adroit opponent. The theory links type of interdependence and type of action with three basic social–psychological processes – which I have labeled 'substitutability', 'cathexis', and 'inducibility' – and it then proliferates a variety of social–psychological consequences from these processes as they are affected by the variables with which the theory is concerned. I shall not attempt here to spell out how this is done. The theory has been published (Deutsch, 1949, 1962), and my interest in this presentation is on the conditions determining the initiation of cooperation and competition rather than upon their effects.

The point I wish to make is that if you take a situation in which there is a mixture of cooperative and competitive elements (most bargaining and 'conflict' situations are of this nature), you can move it in one direction or the other by creating as initial states the typical consequences of effective cooperation and competition. In such indeterminate situations, the tendency to relate cooperatively will be increased by anything that will 'highlight mutual interests', 'enhance mutual power', lead to 'trusting, friendly attitudes, and a positive responsiveness to the other's needs', 'minimize the salience of opposed interests', lead to 'open, honest communication', etc. On the other hand, the likelihood of a competitive relation will be increased by attempts to 'reduce the other's power', 'suspicious, hostile, exploitative attitudes', 'the magnification of the opposed interests', the use of tactics of 'threat, intimidation, or coercion', 'devious communication and espionage', etc.

I now turn to a consideration of three experimental studies [that] employ the Acme–Bolt bargaining game.

The bargaining game involves two players, each of whom operates a trucking firm ('Acme' or 'Bolt'); each gets paid a constant sum of money minus a variable cost for carrying a load of merchandise from his starting point to his destination. The cost is a function of how much time the trip takes. Each player has two routes to his destination: a short main route and a long alternate route. Let me note several characteristics of the routes: If a player takes his alternate route, he will lose at least 10¢ on the trip; if both players take the main route they will meet on the one-lane section of this route and will be deadlocked unless one of them backs down. The players are presented with a very simple conflict. It is to each player's interest to go through the one-lane section first; in doing so he earns more; if he backs down or waits, he earns less. It is also to their mutual interest to work out some agreement for using the main route since otherwise they may both end up with a loss.

The game, like most bargaining and conflict situations, contains a mixture of cooperative and competitive features. On the face of it, the bargaining problem is a reasonably simple one. An obvious solution is for the players to agree to 'take turns' in going through the one-lane segment of the main route 'first'. The game took the simple form it did because of the research question I was posing: 'What are the factors which affect the ease or difficulty with which bargainers conclude an agreement, when an obviously fair agreement is available?' This question is part of my broader interest in what determines whether a conflict will be resolved cooperatively or competitively.

THE EFFECT OF THREAT

Our first bargaining study was concerned with the effect of threat (Deutsch & Krauss, 1960, 1962). In certain experimental conditions, we introduced 'weapons' into the game in the form of gates that a player could close and, by so doing, indicate to the other player that he might be prevented from completing his trip on the main path; by keeping it closed, he would, of course, prevent the other from finishing on the main path. In our first experiment, we ran three basic conditions that varied with regard to the presence or absence of the gates such that both players, only one player, or neither player in a bargaining pair possessed a gate.

Our experiment was guided by two assumptions about threat:

1. If there is a conflict of interest and one person is able to threaten the other, he will tend to use the threat in an attempt to force the other person to yield. This tendency should be stronger, the more irreconcilable (i.e., the more competitive) the conflict is perceived to be. Let me note that I have not suggested that it is inevitable that threat be employed if it is available but rather that the tendency to employ threat will be more likely the stronger the competitive interests and less likely the stronger the cooperative interests of the bargainers in relation to one another.

2. If a person uses threat in an attempt to intimidate another, the threatened person (if he considers himself to be of equal or superior status) will feel hostility toward the threatener and tend to respond with counter-threat and/or increased resistance to yielding. Such a response is more likely the greater the perceived detriment to the other and the lesser the perceived detriment to the self for making such a response.

Table 1 Basic Concepts in the Analysis of the Effects of Cooperation and Competition

Type of perceived interdependence between P and O	Type of action by O	Effects of O's action on P	Some theoretically expected consequences of an exchange of *effective* actions between P and O in cooperative and competitive relationships
Cooperative: P's and O's goals are linked in such a way that their probabilities of goal attainment are positively correlated; as one's chances increase or decrease so do the other's chances.	Effective: (O's action increases O's chances of goal attainment and, thus, also P's).	Positive substitutability: P will not need to act to accomplish what O has accomplished.	Task orientation: highlighting of mutual interests; coordinated effort with division of labor and specialization of function; substitutability of effort rather than duplication; the enhancement of mutual power becomes an objective.
		Positive cathexis: P will value O's actions and will be attracted to O in similar, future situations (i.e., as a fellow cooperator).	Attitudes: trusting, friendly attitudes with a positive interest in the other's welfare and a readiness to respond helpfully to the other's needs and requests.
		Positive inducibility: P will facilitate O's actions and be open to positive influence from O.	Perception: increased sensitivity to common interests while minimizing the salience of opposed interests; a sense of convergence of beliefs and values.
	Ineffective: (O's action decreases O's chances of goal attainment and, thus, also P's).	Negative substitutability: P will need to act to accomplish what O has failed to accomplish.	Communication: open, honest communication of relevant information; each is interested in accurately informing as well as being informed; communication is persuasive rather than coercive in intent.
		Negative cathexis: P will reject O's actions and will reject O in similar, future situations (i.e., as a fellow cooperator).	
		Negative inducibility: P will hinder O's actions and be negatively influenced by O.	

Competitive: P's and O's goals are linked in such a way that their probabilities of goal attainment are negatively correlated; as one's chances increase, the other's decrease.	Effective: (O's action increases O's chances of goal attainment and, thus, decreases P's chances.)	Negative substitutability: P will need to act to accomplish what O has accomplished.
		Negative cathexis: P will dislike the occurrence of O's successes and will reject O as a future competitor.
		Negative inducibility: P will hinder or block O's actions and react negatively to O's influence attempts.
	Ineffective: (O's action decreases O's chances of goal attainment and, thus, increases P's chances.	Positive substitutability: P will not need to repeat O's mistakes.
		Positive cathexis: P will value the occurrence of O's failures and will prefer O as a future competitor.
		Positive inducibility: P will facilitate O's blunders and be ready to help O make mistakes.

Task orientation: emphasis on antagonistic interests; the minimization of the other's power becomes an objective.

Attitudes: suspicious, hostile attitudes with a readiness to exploit the other's needs and weakness and a negative responsiveness to the other's requests.

Perception: increased sensitivity to opposed interests, to threats, and to power differences while minimizing the awareness of similarities.

Communication: little communication or misleading communication; espionage or other techniques to obtain information the other is unwilling to give; each seeks to obtain accurate information about the other but to mislead, discourage, or intimidate the other; coercive tactics are employed.

From these assumptions, given the conditions of our experiment, we expected that the subjects would use the gates and, in doing so, would strengthen the competitive interests of the bargainers in relationship to one another by introducing or enhancing the competitive struggle for self-esteem. Strengthening the competitive interests would make it more difficult for the players to come to a cooperative agreement about use of the main route, and the consequence would be that they would have lower joint payoffs. We expected that agreement would be most difficult to arrive at in the 'two-gate' situation and least difficult in the 'no-gate' situation. The results of the experiment clearly support our assumptions; the joint outcomes were best in the no-gate and worst in the two-gate condition.

A comparison of the outcomes of the two players in the 'one-gate' condition indicated that the player with the gate did better than the one without it in the early periods but that he gradually relinquished his advantage so that at the end both players were cooperating optimally. Comparisons of the two players with and without a weapon in the one-gate and no-gate conditions, respectively, each of whom faced someone without a weapon, indicated that the player with a weapon in the one-gate situation had poorer outcomes than the player without the weapon in the no-gate condition. Similarly comparisons of the two players with and without weapons, in the two-gate and one-gate situations, respectively, each of whom faced someone with a weapon, indicated that the player in the two-gate condition had poorer outcomes than the player without a weapon in the one-gate condition. In other words, if one member of a bargaining pair has a weapon, you are better off if you are the one who has it; but you may be even better off if neither of you has a weapon.

THE EFFECT OF COMMITMENT

Such terms as 'brinksmanship', 'the rationality of irrationality', and 'the doctrine of the last clear chance' have been much in vogue among intellectuals who are concerned with formulating a rationale to guide strategic choices in a situation of international conflict. The basic notion underlying these different terms is that a bargainer will gain an advantage if he can commit himself irrevocably so that the last clear chance of avoiding mutual disaster rests with his opponent.

It is evident that this type of bargaining maneuver can sometimes be very effective. Yet I wonder, had we not blundered into the atrocities and stupidities of the war in Vietnam partially under the influence of such thinking? Would one expect this type of bargaining tactic to be effective when both sides could resort to it? I also wondered whether it is a ploy that is as suitable for a continuing relationship as it might be for a single, unrepeated encounter? To investigate these questions, Lewicki and I employed a modified version of the Acme–Bolt bargaining game.

Two basic modifications were made. The game was altered so as to resemble more closely the adolescent game of 'chicken' by instructing the subjects that if their two trucks met at any point along the one-way section of the main path, the encounter would be defined as a 'collision'. If there were a collision, the trial would be terminated; both subjects would then be penalized the amount of time taken from the start of the trial to the time of the collision at the cost 1¢ per second. (A collision would cost each player at least 20¢.) The second modification entailed introducing a commitment device as a replacement for the gates. The commitment device (called 'the lock') enabled the subject to lock his truck into forward gear so that his truck had to move forward. Once locked, the position of the gear could not be altered during the trial, and, hence, the truck was committed irreversibly to moving forward. When a subject used the lock, the other player was informed of this action by a clear, unambiguous signal.

The subjects in all of the experiments described below were adolescent males attending high schools in New York City.

One-trial game. In this experiment the subjects were led to believe it was a one-trial game; however, following completion of the initial trial, they played an additional trial. In the second trial, the 'no-lock' pairs became the 'bilateral-lock' pairs and the bilateral-lock became the no-lock pairs; 'Bolt' got the lock from 'Acme' in the second 'unilateral-lock' condition. They played under instructions to make as much money as they could for themselves regardless of how the other player did. The subjects played in one of three experimental conditions: *bilateral lock*, both possessed locks; *unilateral lock*, only Acme possessed the lock; and *no lock*, neither player possessed the lock.

The results indicated that a one-sided possession of a commitment device provided a relative advantage to the player, comparing him with the one with whom he was paired. There was no evidence that he had any advantage compared with players in the no-lock condition, in which neither player had such a device. There was, however, evidence to indicate that when both players were able publicly to commit themselves irreversibly to 'going through first', they did worse than when neither could do so. These were the results for the single encounter for a one-trial game.

Twenty-trial game. What would happen if the players expect the encounters to be repeated? To investigate this question, we conducted another experiment that completely paralleled the one just described except that the pairs played the game for twenty trials. At the outset they knew that there would be more than one trial but they did not know how many until they finished.

If we compare the results for the first trial of the twenty-trial game with those of the first one-trial game, it is evident that the bargaining pairs did better when they were anticipating a longer game, the difference being most marked for the bilateral-lock condition. Again, there was no advantage for Acme, who possessed the lock, in the unilateral lock condition as compared to Acme in the no-lock condition; however, he did better than Bolt with whom he was paired in the one-sided condition.

The overall results were not surprising since the one-trial game is clearly more competitive in structure than the longer game, which permits an equitable solution of alternation. Although the differences among conditions in the first trial of the twenty-trial game were not statistically significant, I was surprised by the relatively favorable outcomes in the bilateral-lock condition.

If we examine the overall results for the twenty trials, we find much the same findings as for the first trial: No significant differences in mean joint payoffs among the conditions, but the bilateral-lock condition tended to do best; the possessor of the commitment device did relatively better than the other player with whom he was paired in the one-sided condition, but had no advantage over the players in the other conditions; there was some improvement in outcomes from the initial to the final block of trials for all conditions, but it was most marked in the no-lock condition. A dominance–submission pattern occurred in only four of the ten pairs in the unilateral-lock condition (rarely in the other conditions), the other six pairs were characterized by frequent collisions before settling down to an alternation pattern that gave them low but essentially equal outcomes.

It was evident that many of the pairs in the bilateral-lock condition used their locks as a device for coordination rather than as a means of committing themselves to obtaining a favored outcome. Questionnaire data indicated that the subjects felt about as much desire to 'cooperate with the other player' as to 'maximize their own outcome' and very much less desire to 'do better than the other person'.

'Chicken' versus 'problem-solving' instructions. The further experiment involved two additional bilateral-lock conditions: a cooperative and competitive one. Our assumption was that the results for the cooperative condition would parallel our prior results with the bilateral lock (i.e., the use of the lock for coordination purposes), but this would not be so for the competitive condition. We created the cooperative condition by using 'social problem-solving' instructions and the competitive condition by using 'chicken' instructions.

The major results [indicate] that the original bilateral-lock condition had effects that were rather similar to the cooperative bilateral-lock condition. Our explanation of the findings for the bilateral condition seems reasonably well supported.

There is no evidence to suggest that the bargainer with a commitment device does better than the bargainer without such a device when each is facing a player who does not have one. Perhaps all of this can be summed up by saying that 'locking oneself in' to an irreversible position in order to gain an advantage is rarely more beneficial than cooperating with the other for mutual gain, and it has the prospect of leading to a mutually destructive contest of willpower.

THE EFFECT OF SIZE OF CONFLICT

Roger Fisher, a professor of international law, in a brilliant paper entitled 'Fractionating Conflict' (1964), pointed out that the issues over which nations go to war are big issues that rarely can be adjudicated, whereas little issues can be. In the Cuban missile crisis, neither the United States nor the Soviet Union would have been willing to negotiate about an issue such as 'freedom' or 'communism' in the Western hemisphere, although they were able to negotiate about the much smaller issue of the location of seventy-two weapon systems. Fisher's thesis is the familiar one that small conflicts are easier to resolve than large ones.

In the Acme–Bolt trucking game there was a very simple method for varying the size of conflict; therefore we decided to conduct an experiment on the effect of size using this game.[1]

Conflict size was manipulated experimentally by varying the length

---

[1] This experiment was done with the collaboration of D. Canavan and J. Rubin; L. Rogers helped in the data analysis.

of the one-lane-wide section of road on the main route. In low-conflict conditions this one-lane section was only 4 units in length, while in middle- and high-conflict conditions it was 10 and 18 units long, respectively. The total length of the main route was held constant at 20 units in all conditions. Thus, while in low-conflict conditions only 20 per cent of the main route was one lane wide, in high-conflict conditions it was one lane wide for 90 per cent of the total distance. In order to hold constant the maximum amount of money that subjects in different conflict-size conditions could make, the subjects started with different amounts of money in the three conflict conditions.

The results can be summarized briefly as follows: As the size of conflict increased, the bargainers experienced significantly greater difficulty in reaching a cooperative agreement about how to use the one-lane path. This increased difficulty was exemplified by a significant deterioration in cooperative behaviour (i.e., fewer 'cooperative trials', fewer alternations) resulting in significantly poorer bargaining outcomes (lower joint pay).

These results support the idea that decreasing the size of the conflict makes it easier for bargainers to come to an agreement that is mutually rewarding. It may well be, as Fisher has suggested, that 'issue control' is as crucial as 'arms control' to the peace of the world.

CONCLUSION

I have been brash enough to claim that the games people play as subjects in laboratory experiments may have some relevance to war and peace. I have implied that the study of interpersonal conflict can provide some insights into international conflict and, let me add, that I believe the reverse is also true: the study of international conflict can give new understanding of interpersonal conflict. It is not only that such terms as 'aggression', 'deterrence', 'threat', 'cooperation', 'competition', 'credibility', and the like seem appropriate in the interpersonal as well as the international context, but also there is, I believe, a real conceptual similarity between the processes at the two levels.

I hope it is clear that I am not saying that the mechanisms or capabilities of acquiring information, making decisions, and acting are similar in individuals, groups, and nations. Nor am I stating that the behavior of individuals and nations will parallel one another if there is no parallel in their relevant properties and external circumstances. Rather, I am asserting that nations as well as individuals acquire information, make decisions, and take actions, and that they will act in similar ways under similar conditions. Thus, each type of unit in a social interaction responds to the other in terms of its information and views of the other; these may or may not correspond to the other's actualities. Moreover, characteristic distortions of the other tend to develop as a function of the type of social interaction, cooperative or competitive, that is occurring between them, whether the interacting units be nations, groups, or individuals.

REFERENCES

Deutsch, M. (1949), 'A theory of cooperation and competition', *Human Relations*, 2, 129–51.

Deutsch, M. (1962), 'Cooperation and trust: Some theoretical notes', *Nebraska Symposium on Motivation*, 10, 275–319.

Deutsch, M., & Krauss, R. M. (1960), 'The effect of threat on interpersonal bargaining', *Journal of Abnormal and Social Psychology*, 61 181–9.

Deutsch, M., & Krauss, R. M. (1962), 'Studies of interpersonal bargaining', *Journal of Conflict Resolution*, 6, 52–76.

Fisher, R. (1964), 'Fractionating conflict', in R. Fisher (ed.), *International Conflict and Behavioral Science: The Craigville Papers*, New York: Basic Books.

13

JOHN R. P. FRENCH, JR, AND BERTRAM RAVEN

The Bases of Social Power

Abridged from J. R. P. French, Jr, and B. Raven, 'The bases of social power', in D. Cartwright (ed.), *Studies in Social Power*, Ann Arbor, Mich.: Institute for Social Research, 1959, pp. 150–67.

Recent empirical work, especially on small groups, has demonstrated the necessity of distinguishing different types of power in order to account for the different effects found in studies of social influence. Yet there is no doubt that more empirical knowledge will be needed to make final decisions concerning the necessary differentiations, but this knowledge will be obtained only by research based on some preliminary theoretical distinctions. We present such preliminary concepts and some of the hypotheses they suggest.

Since we shall define power in terms of influence, and influence in terms of psychological change, we begin with a discussion of change. We want to define change at a level of generality which includes changes in behavior, opinions, attitudes, goals, needs, values and all other aspects of the person's psychological field. We shall use the word 'system' to refer to any such part of the life space.

Our theory of social influence and power is limited to influence on the person, P, produced by a social agent, O, where O can be either another person, a role, a norm, a group or a part of a group. We do not consider social influence exerted on a group.

THE BASES OF POWER

By the basis of power we mean the relationship between O and P which is the source of that power. It is rare that we can say with certainty that a given empirical case of power is limited to one source. Normally, the relation between O and P will be characterized by several qualitatively different variables which are bases of power (Lippitt, et al., 1952). Although there are undoubtedly many possible bases of power which may be distinguished, we shall here define five which seem especially common and important. These five bases of O's power are: (1) reward power, based on P's perception that O has the ability to mediate rewards for him; (2) coercive power, based on P's perception that O has the ability to mediate punishments for him; (3) legitimate power, based on the perception by P that O has a legitimate right to prescribe behavior for him; (4) referent power, based on P's identification with O; (5) expert power, based on the perception that O has some special knowledge or expertness.

Reward power

Reward power is defined as power whose basis is the ability to reward. The strength of the reward power of O/P increases with the magnitude of the rewards which P perceives that O can mediate for him. Reward power depends on O's ability to administer positive valences and to remove or decrease negative valences. The strength of reward power also depends upon the probability that O can mediate the reward, as perceived by P. A common example of reward power is the addition of a piece-work rate in the factory as an incentive to increase production.

The new state of the system induced by a promise of reward (for example the factory worker's increased level of production) will be highly dependent on O. Since O mediates the reward, he controls the probability that P will receive it. Thus P's new rate of production will be dependent on his subjective probability that O will reward him for conformity minus his subjective probability that O will reward him even if he returns to his old level. Both probabilities will be greatly affected by the level of observability of P's behavior. Incidentally, a piece-rate often seems to have more effect on production than a merit rating system because it yields a higher probability of reward for conformity and a much lower probability of reward for nonconformity.

The utilization of actual rewards (instead of promises) by O will tend over time to increase the attraction of P toward O and therefore the referent power of O over P.

The range of reward power is specific to those regions within which O can reward P for conforming. The use of rewards to change systems within the range of reward power tends to increase reward power by increasing the probability attached to future promises.

Coercive power

Coercive power is similar to reward power in that it also involves O's ability to manipulate the attainment of valences. Coercive power of O/P stems from the expectation on the part of P that he will be punished by O if he fails to conform to the influence attempt. Thus negative valences will exist in given regions of P's life space, corresponding to the threatened punishment by O. The strength of coercive power depends on the magnitude of the negative valence of the threatened punishment multiplied by the perceived probability that P can avoid the punishment by conformity, i.e., the probability of punishment for nonconformity minus the probability of punishment for conformity (French, et al., 1960). Just as an offer of a piece-rate bonus in a factory can serve as a basis for reward power, so the ability to fire a worker if he falls below a given level of production will result in coercive power.

Coercive power leads to dependent change also; and the degree of dependence varies with the level of observability of P's conformity. An excellent illustration of coercive power leading to dependent change is provided by a clothes presser in a factory observed by Coch and French (1948). As her efficiency rating climbed above average for the group the other workers began to 'scapegoat' her. That the resulting plateau in her production was not independent of the group was evident once she was removed from the presence of the other workers. Her production immediately climbed to new heights.

There is some evidence that conformity to group norms in order to gain acceptance (reward power) should be distinguished from conformity as a means of forestalling rejection (coercive power) (Dittes & Kelley, 1956).

The distinction between these two types of power is important because the dynamics are different. The concept of 'sanctions' sometimes lumps the two together despite their opposite effects. While reward power may eventually result in an independent system, the effects of coercive power will continue to be dependent. Reward power will tend to increase the attraction of P toward O; coercive power will decrease this attraction (French, et al., 1960; Raven & French, 1958).

Legitimate power

Legitimate power is probably the most complex of those treated here, embodying notions from the structural sociologist, the group-norm and role-oriented social psychologist, and the clinical psychologist.

There has been considerable investigation and speculation about socially prescribed behavior, particularly that which is specific to a given role or position. Linton (1945) distinguishes group norms according to whether they are universals for everyone in the culture, alternatives (the individual having a choice as to whether or not to accept them), or specialities (specific to given positions). Whether we speak of internalized norms, role prescriptions and expectations (Newcomb, 1950), or internalized pressures (Herbst, 1953), the fact remains that each individual sees certain regions toward which he should locomote, some regions toward which he should not locomote, and some regions toward which he may locomote if they are generally attractive for him. This applies to specific behaviors in which he may, should, or should not engage; it applies to certain attitudes or beliefs which he may, should, or should not hold. The feeling of 'oughtness' may be an internalization from his parents, from his teachers, from his religion, or may have been logically developed from some idiosyncratic system of ethics. He will speak of such behaviors with expressions like 'should', 'ought to', or 'has a right to'. In many cases, the original source of the requirement is not recalled.

Conceptually, we may think of legitimacy as a valence in a region which is induced by some internalized norm or value. This value has the same conceptual property as power, namely an ability to induce force fields (Lewin, 1951, pp. 40–41). It may or may not be correct that values (or the super-ego) are internalized parents, but at least they can set up force fields which have a phenomenal 'oughtness' similar to a parent's prescription.

Legitimate power of O/P is here defined as that power which stems from internalized values in P which dictate that O has a legitimate right to influence P and that P has an obligation to accept this influence.

In all cases, the notion of legitimacy involves some sort of code or standard, accepted by the individual, by virtue of which the external agent can assert his power. We shall attempt to describe a few of these values here.

Bases for legitimate power. Cultural values constitute one common basis for the legitimate power of one individual over another. O has characteristics which are specified by the culture as giving him the right to prescribe behavior for P, who may not have these characteristics.

Acceptance of the social structure is another basis for legitimate power. If P accepts as right the social structure of his group, organization, or society, especially the social structure involving a hierarchy of authority, P will accept the legitimate authority of O who occupies a superior office in the hierarchy. Thus legitimate power in a formal organization is largely a relationship between offices rather than between persons.

Designation by a legitimizing agent is a third basis for legitimate power. An influencer O may be seen as legitimate in prescribing behavior for P because he has been granted such power by a legitimizing agent whom P accepts. Thus a department head may accept the authority of his vice-president in a certain area because that authority has been specifically delegated by the president.

Range of legitimate power of O/P. The areas in which legitimate power may be exercised are generally specified along with the designation of that power. A job description, for example, usually specifies supervisory activities and also designates the person to whom the jobholder is responsible for the duties described.

The attempted use of legitimate power which is outside of the range of legitimate power will decrease the legitimate power of the authority figure. Such use of power which is not legitimate will also decrease the attractiveness of O (French, et al., 1960; Raven & French, 1958).

Referent power

The referent power of O/P has its basis in the identification of P with O. By identification, we mean a feeling of oneness of P with O, or a desire for such an identity. If O is a person toward whom P is highly attracted, P will have a desire to become closely associated with O. If O is an attractive group, P will have a feeling of membership or a desire to join. If P is already closely associated with O he will want to maintain this relationship (Torrance & Mason, 1956). P's identification with O can be established or maintained if P behaves, believes, and perceives as O does. Accordingly O has the ability to influence P, even though P may be unaware of this referent power. A verbalization of such power by P might be, 'I am like O, and therefore I shall behave or believe as O does,' or 'I want to be like O, and will be more like O if I behave or believe as O does.' The stronger the identification of P with O the greater the referent power of O/P.

We must try to distinguish between referent power and other types of power which might be operative at the same time. If a member is attracted to a group and he conforms to its norms only because he fears ridicule or expulsion from the group for nonconformity, we would call this coercive power. On the other hand if he conforms in order to obtain praise for conformity, it is a case of reward power. The basic criterion for distinguishing referent power from both coercive and reward power is the mediation of the punishment and the reward by O: to the extent that O mediates the sanctions (i.e., has means control over P) we are dealing with coercive and reward power; but to the extent that P avoids discomfort or gains satisfaction by conformity based on identification, regardless of O's responses, we are dealing with referent power.

Expert power

The strength of the expert power of O/P varies with the extent of the knowledge or perception which P attributes to O within a given area. Probably P evaluates O's expertness in relation to his own knowledge as well as against an absolute standard. In any case expert power results in primary social influence on P's cognitive structure and probably not on other types of systems. Of course changes in the cognitive structure can change the direction of forces and hence of locomotion, but such a change of behavior is secondary social influence. Expert power has been demonstrated experimentally (Festinger, et al., 1952; Moore, 1921). Accepting an attorney's advice in legal matters is a common example of expert influence; but there are many instances based on much less knowledge, such as the acceptance by a stranger of directions given by a native villager.

Wherever expert influence occurs it seems to be necessary both for P to think that O knows and for P to trust that O is telling the truth (rather than trying to deceive him).

The range of expert power, we assume, is more delimited than that of referent power. Not only is it restricted to cognitive systems but the expert is seen as having superior knowledge or ability in very specific areas, and his power will be limited to these areas, though some 'halo effect' might occur.

SUMMARY

We have distinguished five types of power: referent power, expert power, reward power, coercive power, and legitimate power. These distinctions led to the following hypotheses.

1. For all five types, the stronger the basis of power the greater the power.

2. For any type of power the size of the range may vary greatly, but in general referent power will have the broadest range.

3. Any attempt to utilize power outside the range of power will tend to reduce the power.

4. A new state of a system produced by reward power or coercive power will be highly dependent on O, and the more observable P's conformity the more dependent the state. For the other three types of power, the new state is usually dependent, at least in the beginning, but in any case the level of observability has no effect on the degree of dependence.

5. Coercion results in decreased attraction of P toward O and high resistance; reward power results in increased attraction and low resistance.

6. The more legitimate the coercion the less it will produce resistance and decreased attraction.

REFERENCES

Coch, L., & French, J. R. P., Jr (1948), 'Overcoming resistance to change', *Human Relations*, *1*, 512–32.

Dittes, J., & Kelley, H. (1956), 'Effects of different conditions of acceptance upon conformity to group norms', *Journal of Abnormal and Social Psychology*, *53*, 629–36.

Festinger, L., et al. (1952), 'The influence process of extreme deviates', *Human Relations*, *5*, 327–46.

French, J. R. P., Jr, Morrison, H. W., & Levinger, G. (1960), 'Coercive power and forces affecting conformity', *Journal of Abnormal and Social Psychology*, *61*, 93–101.

Herbst, P. (1953), 'Analysis and measurement of a situation', *Human Relations*, *2*, 113–40.

Lewin, K. (1951), *Field Theory in Social Science*, New York: Harper.

Linton, R. (1945), *The Cultural Background of Personality*, New York: Appleton-Century-Crofts.

Lippitt, R., et al. (1952), 'The dynamics of power', *Human Relations*, *5*, 37–64.

Moore, H. (1921), 'The comparative influence of majority and expert opinion', *American Journal of Psychology*, *32*, 16–20.

Newcomb, T. (1950), *Social Psychology*, New York: Dryden.

Raven, B., & French, J. (1958), 'Group support, legitimate power, and social influence', *Journal of Personality*, *26*, 400–409.

Torrance, E., & Mason, R. (1956), 'Instructor effort to influence: An experimental evaluation of six approaches', paper presented at USAF–NRC Symposium on Personnel, Training, and Human Engineering, Washington, DC.

Motivation in Work Settings

EDWARD L. DECI

Motivation Research in Industrial/Organizational Psychology

It is widely believed, as Lewin (1938) and others have stated, that motivation interacts with ability to predict effective performance. Thus, managers have the possibility of promoting such performance by their subordinates through enhancing either ability or motivation. Enhancing ability, as was mentioned in the introduction, can be done through improved selection practices and well-designed training experiences, but both can be slow and costly and often are not under the control of individual supervisors. An understanding of human motivation in the workplace, therefore, would seem to hold great potential as an avenue through which managers could enhance subordinates' performance.

The study of work motivation within the field of industrial/organizational psychology has been concerned with specifying variables that are reliably linked, through individuals' motivation, to effective performance. The majority of this research has focused on characteristics of the work environment over which managers have control and which could lead to enhanced motivation and performance in subordinates. Accordingly, that work will receive primary attention in the readings of Part B. Secondarily, we will examine research on work motivation that has explored the relations between individual differences in motivation and work performance. That work is included not only because of its potential significance for selecting and placing highly motivated workers, but also because the concepts embodied by the individual differences may have implications for creating appropriate work contexts.

Approaches to the study of motivation, as we saw in Part A, have been extremely diverse. However, research on work motivation in organizational settings can generally, as we will see, be distinguished from the study of motivation in other areas of psychology.

As was evident in the readings of Part A, personality psychology tends to involve broad macro-theories that state general principles about people rather than specific, testable hypotheses about the person–environment interaction. That work tends to be aimed more at explicating aspects of human nature and individual differences than at establishing specific, cause–effect relations between variables or events. The personality theories that have motivational concepts at their core tend to focus on general innate and acquired psychological needs and on the process through which the regulation of behavior is related to the satisfaction of these needs (Deci & Ryan, 1985; McClelland, 1985; Murray, 1938; White, 1959).

In contrast, social psychologists have been less broad in their theorizing, tending instead to develop mini-theories about the effects on individuals of social situations. These theories have stimulated countless empirical tests of the causal links between specific social variables and individuals' attitudes and behavior.

The three sections in Part A of this volume featured readings from personality psychology and social psychology. Those readings were ordered so as to reflect a movement from personality theories toward social psychological theories. Thus, they moved from broader to narrower theories, and they moved from theories less likely to specify manipulable social variables to those more likely to make such specification. The work of industrial/organizational psychologists is more like that of empirical social psychologists than that of personality theorists, because most of their work attempts to establish links between contextual conditions and the performance of individuals in those contexts. The work of industrial/organizational psychologists has differed from that of social psychologists, however, in the extent to which its results are directly applicable to management practices. Typically, the research by industrial/organizational psychologists deals with solving specific problems in work settings or with hypotheses that relate work conditions to organizational effectiveness.

PERFORMANCE, MOTIVATION, SATISFACTION

In part because of the nature of research on work motivation, the obvious criterion variables have been performance, absenteeism, and turnover. In other words, research on work motivation has typically tried to relate motivation variables such as individuals' needs and goals or contextual variables such as pay or supervisory style to the criteria of productivity and job attendance. However, because of the widely held belief, prompted in part by the Human Relations movement in management, that workers who are satisfied (who have more positive job attitudes) will perform better, stay longer, and attend more regularly, employee satisfaction has also been widely used as a criterion variable.

Interestingly, as early as 1955, Brayfield and Crockett reviewed all the research that had explored the relation of job satisfaction to productivity, and they concluded that although satisfaction does correlate reliably with lower absenteeism and turnover, there was, at best, a low positive correlation between satisfaction and performance. Some studies did show strong positive relations between satisfaction and performance, though others yielded negative correlations, and many found no correlation. It would seem, therefore, that the relation between the two variables is relatively complex and that one cannot conclude that a satisfied worker will necessarily be productive or that the conditions that promote satisfaction will necessarily promote productivity. This issue is elaborated in Reading 15 by Schwab and Cummings.

Porter and Lawler (1968) took an interesting approach to reconsidering the lack of consistency in the correlational studies on attitudes and performance. Employing an expectancy–valence formulation derived from Vroom (1964), they outlined a model in which satisfaction was hypothesized to be a *consequence*, rather than an *antecedent*, of performance. They advocated enlarging jobs so people will experience intrinsic satisfaction from performing them well and then providing extrinsic rewards for effective performance so the people will also experience extrinsic satisfaction when they perform effectively. This, Porter and Lawler suggested, will lead to a direct and strong relation between performance and satisfaction because both intrinsic and extrinsic satisfaction will accrue from performing well. This approach to job motivation can be found in Reading 20 by Lawler.

As mentioned, much of the research on motivation within industrial/organizational psychology has related situational factors to motivation and performance. Still, researchers (e.g., Staw & Ross, 1985, Reading 18) have shown that satisfaction is to some extent dispositionally based, and various studies have attempted to specify personality predictors of motivation and performance of workers (e.g., Spector, 1982, Reading 8) and of managers (e.g., McClelland & Burnham, 1976, Reading 19).

Section IV of this volume includes readings pertinent to both situational and personality predictors of motivation, satisfaction, and performance, as well as to the most appropriate ways to conceptualize and explore such relations.

Common to most of the research and theory on work motivation are the beliefs that behaviors are goal directed and/or are undertaken to satisfy human needs. Although the work of the editors (e.g., Deci, 1975; Vroom, 1964) falls within this general category, Section IV includes for your consideration an article by Salancik and Pfeffer (1977, Reading 17) which criticizes the general needs/goal perspective. They argue, alternatively, that attitudes and behaviors are largely a function of social contextual forces – a position similar to that presented in Hamner's discussion of reinforcement theory (1974, Reading 4).

JOB CONTENT

Implicit in the Porter/Lawler model mentioned earlier (which falls in the general category of goal theories) is the idea that jobs can be made more intrinsically motivating, in other words that they can be designed so the content will be more compelling and satisfying for the people who perform them. Section V of this book deals with that matter in depth.

In his motivation–hygiene theory of motivation and satisfaction, Herzberg (1966; see also Reading 21) emphasized that only intrinsic or 'content' factors within the work itself are effective motivators and that extrinsic or 'context' factors can ameliorate dissatisfaction but will not serve to motivate effective job performance. This idea, that jobs can be restructured to make them more motivating, is clearly evident in the theory and research pertaining to job enlargement. Job enlargement takes two essential forms, captured by the notions of horizontal job enlargement and vertical job enlargement. In the former, activities themselves are changed, so that employees might, for example, be given greater variety in their tasks, whereas in the latter, the focus is on providing greater choice in how a task is accomplished and how decisions are made. Vertical job enlargement entails giving employees greater say in how and when they do various aspects of their jobs.

Hackman and Oldham (1980, Reading 22) addressed the core aspects of jobs that lead to greater internal work motivation. Specifically, they suggested that meaningful, motivating work requires: using varied skills, being able to identify the product of one's labors, knowing that the 'product' will affect other people, feeling a sense of autonomy, and receiving meaningful feedback. It is clear from this and other theories that emphasize autonomy and participation that the issue of vertical job enlargement has a great deal to do with the leadership behavior and style of the supervisor. Deci, Connell, and Ryan (1989, Reading 23), for example, reported that managers' tendency to support their subordinates' autonomy is positively related to the satisfaction and trust of those subordinates.

PAY, REWARDS, AND EVALUATION

Extrinsic incentives are an integral part of all employment, so it is not surprising that there has been a tremendous amount of research and discussion about this topic. There are many aspects of the broad topic, and many issues have been debated. Among these issues is how closely one's rewards should be tied to the quality or quantity of one's performance. There is considerable diversity in the opinions expressed by different writers, but there is fairly widespread agreement, at least within the free-market system, that people should be required to perform at some minimum level of effectiveness to retain their jobs and receive their pay. Thus, the issue of performance appraisal, of evaluating employees' performance, is an important one that is closely related to the topic of pay. Section VI of this volume is concerned with the topics of performance evaluation and reward policies.

There are two central issues that appear in most writing on performance appraisal. The first concerns whether employees' performance evaluation should be based only on the results or outcomes of their performance or should also include an evaluation of their actual behavior – of the way in which the results or outcomes were achieved. Implicit in the approach called Management by Objectives (Drucker, 1954; see also Reading 34 by Tosi & Carroll) is the idea that achieving objectives or reaching goals (Latham & Locke, 1979, Reading 16) is the critical consideration in the evaluation of one's performance. In contrast, others (e.g., Levinson, 1976, Reading 25) have argued that it is the responsibility of managers to be aware of the means their subordinates use to obtain the desired ends and that the evaluation of performance should take account of both means and ends.

A second point of discussion concerns the degree to which employees should participate in the process of their own evaluation. In an autocratic or top-down view managers set the goals for the subordinate to achieve, dictate the methods for achieving them, determine the criteria for evaluating performance, and then actually do the evaluation, all with little or no input from the subordinate. In contrast, proponents of Participative or Theory Y Management (Likert, 1967, Reading 33; McGregor, 1960, Reading 32) advocate that subordinates should play an active role in setting the goals, choosing how to achieve them, and then evaluating their own performance. Such an approach, as outlined in Reading 24 by McGregor, is useful not only as a means of fostering subordinates' internal motivation and commitment to the job but also as a strategy for employee development. By participating in this process, the subordinates will be learning how to accept greater responsibility and will be more prepared to move to higher-level positions within the organization.

The design and use of payment and reward structures has generated even more controversy than evaluation systems, and the advocates of various reward structures have relied on different motivation theories to support their prescriptions. The central tenet of operant psychology (Skinner, 1953) is that behaviors are under the control of external reinforcements and that reinforcements are most effective in shaping behavior when administered in close succession to the desired behavior. This has led some people to suggest that payments should be closely tied to clearly specifiable behaviors, and the piece-rate payment system advocated, for example, within Scientific Management (Taylor, 1911, Reading 30) is perhaps the most palpable instantiation of the operant principle.

In a somewhat similar vein the cognitive expectancy theories of motivation (e.g., Vroom, 1964) provide a rationale for the use of pay-for-performance plans, based on the idea that, if good performance is understood to be instrumental for rewards, people will be more inclined to perform well. The cognitive theories, however, understand the underlying processes of motivation to involve cognitive processing of information about the relation between behaviors and outcomes. Thus, since people's expectations are said to be determinative of their behavior, prescriptions based on this perspective do not require close proximity between the behaviors and outcomes and, in fact, rewards can be made contingent on reaching a reasonably long-term goal rather than on emitting a particular behavior. The Porter and Lawler (1968) model mentioned earlier (see also Reading 15 by Schwab & Cummings) is a typical example of this type of theorizing, as is the Kanter (1987) paper included in Section VI (Reading 29).

A quite different set of prescriptions has been employed by various theorists who focus on intrinsic aspects of work. As mentioned, Herzberg (1966) has maintained that money and other so-called context factors do not serve as motivators, so tying pay closely to performance would not be advocated. Instead, equitable pay should be provided to prevent dissatisfaction, and motivation should be fostered by appropriate job content.

The debate over whether to tie rewards closely to performance was further stimulated by the empirical evidence that monetary rewards can undermine intrinsic motivation (Deci, 1972; Pritchard, Campbell & Campbell, 1977). This work indicates that the effects of intrinsic and extrinsic rewards are not simply additive, as had been suggested in the Porter and Lawler model, and it further indicates that when a job is intrinsically rewarding relying on the use of contingent rewards as a motivational strategy could be counter-productive. Unlike Herzberg, Deci (1975) has agreed that contingently administered rewards do motivate performance – they motivate extrinsically. However, considerable research suggests that the quality of extrinsically controlled behavior is often inferior to the quality of intrinsically motivated behavior if the job involves interesting, challenging, or heuristic activities (Amabile, 1983; McGraw & McCullers, 1979). Thus, this work has led scholars interested in intrinsic motivation to advocate focusing on designing interesting and challenging jobs rather than on using task-contingent monetary rewards as a means of controlling behavior. The extrinsic rewards (which of course must be given) should be used primarily to acknowledge good performance. Deci and Ryan (1985) have referred to this as administering rewards informationally rather than controllingly.

Ryan, Mims, and Koestner (1983, Reading 27) pointed out not only that different monetary reward structures tend to have different effects on intrinsic motivation but, even more importantly, that the interpersonal context within which the reward is administered explains even more variance than the reward structure itself. Rewards are administered by supervisors, and the orientation of the supervisors – whether they are oriented toward supporting subordinates' autonomy or controlling subordinates' behavior – may be the most critical factor in determining the effects of rewards. In fact, Deci, Connell, and Ryan (1989, Reading 23) found that supervisors' orientations toward autonomy support versus control have an important influence on their subordinates, even independent of the reward administration.

A final, quite interesting development and source of controversy concerning pay structures deals with whether incentives should be based on individual performance or on the performance of a group. For example, the productivity and profitability of a small work group, or even of a reasonably large organizational unit, could be used as the basis for providing bonus or incentive pay to the members of that group. The well-known Scanlon Plan (Lesieur & Puckett, 1969, Reading 28) includes such a group-incentive system and has been found to be quite effective in some situations. The central idea contained in such a plan is that shared incentives will lead group members to work together toward a common goal of high productivity.

The idea of group incentives stands in clear contrast to the fairly widely held view that motivation can be enhanced by pitting members of the group against each other in the kind of competition that results in a 'stack ranking' of the group members on the basis of one or more criteria. It seems increasingly clear from research both in the laboratory and in work organizations that incentives will be most effective when they are given to individuals for meeting their own self-selected goals or bettering their own previous performance or, alternatively, are given to members of a group on the basis of the group's being productive. Incentive systems that turn members of a group against each other in competitions are likely to lead to poor morale and poor-quality work.

In Part B of this book, we have selected a set of readings that explicate the points and controversies mentioned here and that give a representative sampling of the types of research and theorizing that have been done on motivation in the work place. Following that, Part C will present a discussion of general theories of management and the motivational assumptions (whether implicit or explicit) that underlie them.

REFERENCES

Amabile, T. M. (1983), *The Social Psychology of Creativity*, New York: Springer-Verlag.

Brayfield, A. H., & Crockett, W. H. (1955), 'Employee attitudes and employee performance', *Psychological Bulletin, 52*, 396–424.

Deci, E. L. (1972), 'Effects of contingent and non-contingent rewards and controls on intrinsic motivation', *Organizational Behavior and Human Performance, 8*, 217–29.

Deci, E. L. (1975), *Intrinsic Motivation*, New York: Plenum.

Deci, E. L., Connell, J. P., & Ryan, R. M. (1989), 'Self-determination in a work organization', *Journal of Applied Psychology, 74*, 580–90.

Deci, E. L., & Ryan, R. M. (1985), *Intrinsic Motivation and Self-Determination in Human Behavior*, New York: Plenum.

Drucker, P. (1954), *The Practice of Management*, New York: Harper.

Hackman, J. R., & Oldham, G. R. (1980), *Work Redesign*, Reading, Mass.: Addison-Wesley.

Hamner, W. C. (1974), 'Reinforcement theory and contingency management in organizational settings' in H. L. Tosi & W. C. Hamner (eds.), *Organizational Behavior and Management: A Contingency Approach*, Chicago: St Clair Press.

Herzberg, F. (1966), *Work and the Nature of Man*, Cleveland, Ohio: World.

Kanter, R. M. (1987), 'The attack on pay', *Harvard Business Review, 65*, 60–67.

Latham, G. P., & Locke, E. A. (1979), 'Goal setting – A motivational technique that works', *Organizational Dynamics, 8*(2), 68–80.

Lesieur, F. G.., & Puckett, E. S. (1969), 'The Scanlon Plan has proved itself', *Harvard Business Review, 47*, 109–18.

Levinson, H. (1976), 'Appraisal of *what* performance?', *Harvard Business Review, 54*(4), 30–46.

Lewin, K. (1938), *The Conceptual Representation and the Measurement of Psychological*

Forces, Durham, NC: Duke University Press.

Likert, R. (1967), *The Human Organization*, New York: McGraw-Hill.

McClelland, D. C. (1985), *Human Motivation*, Glenview, Ill.: Scott, Foresman.

McClelland, D. C., & Burnham, D. H. (1976), 'Power is the great motivator', *Harvard Business Review*, *54*, 100–10.

McGraw, K. O., & McCullers, J. C. (1979), 'Evidence of a detrimental effect of extrinsic incentives on breaking a mental set', *Journal of Experimental Social Psychology*, *15*, 285–94.

McGregor, D. (1960), *The Human Side of Enterprise*, New York: McGraw-Hill.

Murray, H. A. (1938), *Explorations in Personality*, New York: Oxford University Press.

Porter, L. W., & Lawler, E. E., III (1968), *Managerial Attitudes and Performance*, Homewood, Ill.: Irwin-Dorsey.

Pritchard, R. D., Campbell, K. M., & Campbell, D. J. (1977), 'Effects of extrinsic financial rewards on intrinsic motivation', *Journal of Applied Psychology*, *62*, 9–15.

Ryan, R. M., Mims, V., & Koestner, R. (1983), 'Relation of reward contingency and interpersonal context to intrinsic motivation: A review and test using cognitive evaluation theory', *Journal of Personality and Social Psychology*, *45*, 736–50.

Salancik, G. R., & Pfeffer, J. (1977), 'An examination of need-satisfaction models of job attitudes', *Administration Science Quarterly*, *22*, 427–56.

Skinner, B. F. (1953), *Science and Human Behavior*, New York: Macmillan.

Spector, P. E. (1982), 'Behavior in organizations as a function of employees' locus of control', *Psychological Bulletin*, *91*, 482–97.

Staw, B. M., & Ross, J. (1985), 'Stability in the midst of change: A dispositional approach to job attitudes', *Journal of Applied Psychology*, *70*, 469–80.

Taylor, F. W. (1911), *Principles of Scientific Management*, New York: Harper.

Vroom, V. H. (1964), *Work and Motivation*, New York: Wiley.

White, R. W. (1959), 'Motivation reconsidered: The concept of competence', *Psychological Review*, *66*, 297–333.

Motivation, Satisfaction, and Performance: Persons and Contexts

14

DANIEL KATZ AND ROBERT L. KAHN

Motivational Patterns and Performance

Abridged from D. Katz and R. L. Kahn, *The Social Psychology of Organizations* (2nd edn), Chapter 13, New York: Wiley, 1978.

BEHAVIORAL REQUIREMENTS FOR ORGANIZATIONS

First of all, enough people must be kept within the system to perform its essential functions. People must be induced to enter the system at a sufficiently rapid rate to counteract retirement and defection. They must also be induced to remain within the system. The optimum period of tenure will vary for different individuals and situations, but high turnover is almost always costly. Moreover, while people are members of a system they must validate their membership by regular attendance. Thus turnover and absenteeism are both measures of organizational effectiveness, albeit partial measures.

Secondly, there must be dependable activity. The great range of variable human behavior must be reduced to a limited number of predictable patterns. In other words, the assigned roles must be carried out in ways that meet some minimal level of quantity and quality. A common measure of productivity is the amount of work turned out within some stipulated period by an individual or by a group. Quality of performance is not as easily measured, and the problem is met by quality controls which set minimal standards for the pieces of work sampled. In general, the major content of the member's role is clearly set forth by organizational protocol, observable characteristics of the situation, and instructions of leaders. The worker on the assembly line, the nurse in the hospital, the teacher in the elementary school all know what their major job is. To do a lot of it and to do it well are the most conspicuous behavioral requirements of the organization.

A third and often neglected set of requirements includes those actions not specified by role prescriptions but which facilitate the accomplishment of organizational goals. The organizational need for actions of an innovative, relatively spontaneous sort is inevitable and unending. No organizational plan can foresee all contingencies within its own operations, can anticipate with perfect accuracy all environmental changes, or can control perfectly all human variability. The resources of people for innovation, for spontaneous cooperation, for protective and creative behavior are thus vital to organizational survival and effectiveness. An organization that depends solely on its blueprints of prescribed behavior is a very fragile social system.

Acts beyond the line of duty also take the form of creative suggestions for improving methods of production or maintenance [and] the self-educative activities of members who learn to do their own jobs better and prepare to assume more responsible positions in the organization. Members of an organization can [also] contribute to its operations by helping to create a favorable climate for it in the community that surrounds the organization. In short, for effective organizational functioning many members must be willing on occasion to do more than their job prescriptions specify.

TYPES OF MOTIVATIONAL PATTERNS

It is profitable to consider our three motivational patterns as they affect organizational behavior.

Type A. Rule enforcement

The first pattern is the acceptance of role prescriptions and of organizational directives because of their legitimacy. The group member obeys the rules because they stem from legitimate sources of authority and because they can be enforced by legal sanctions. This is the basic pattern of motivation in simple machine theory. Motivation bears no relation to the activity itself. Any rule or directive from the proper authority must be obeyed because it is the law of the nation, of the organization, or of the group.

Type B. External rewards

Incentives can be linked to desired behaviors. Actions can become instrumental to achieving specific rewards. Four sub-types of such instrumental rewards are often employed in social systems. In the first place, rewards can be earned merely through membership in the system and increased through seniority in it. For example, government, industry, and educational institutions offer retirement pensions, sick leave, health examinations, and other fringe benefits. They furnish cost-of-living raises and other across-the-board wage increases. They may provide attractive working conditions and recreational facilities.

In addition to these general system rewards are the individual rewards of pay increases, promotion, and recognition accorded to people on the basis of individual merit. They may take the form of a piece-rate system in which each individual is paid according to the amount he or she produces. They may take the form of giving oustanding workers some priority with respect to promotion. Or a suggestion system may reward individuals in proportion to the value of their suggestions to the company.

Another form of instrumental motivation for group members derives from the approval they receive from their leaders. This category refers to the gratification a person may find in the praise of a powerful and respected figure.

A similar type of individual reward is social approval of one's own group. Social approval of the immediate work group motivates members toward organizational requirements, however, only to the extent that those requirements are congruent with the norms of the group. This type of motivation can facilitate or prevent attainment of organizational objectives, depending on the nature of the group norms.

Type C. Internalized motivation

This motivational pattern refers both to intrinsic job satisfaction and to the internalization of the goals of the group or organization as part of the individual's own value system.

Self-expression and self-determination are the basis for *identification with the job*, that is, for satisfactions deriving directly from role performance. The scientist derives gratification from scientific inquiry, the musical composer from creating a symphony, the craftsman from the exercise of skill in a job well done.

Value expression and self-idealization lead to the *internalization of organizational goals*. The goals of the group become incorporated as part of the individual's value system or conception of self. As a result, satisfactions accrue to the person from the expression of attitudes and behavior reflecting his or her cherished beliefs and self-image. The reward is not so much a matter of social recognition or monetary advantage as of establishing one's self-identity, confirming one's notion of the sort of person one sees oneself to be, and expressing the values appropriate to this self-concept.

CONSEQUENCES OF DIFFERENT MOTIVATIONAL PATTERNS

The preceding analysis of the various types of behavior required for organizational effectiveness and the different motivational patterns available for energizing and directing such behavior strongly suggests that there will be costs and gains in emphasizing any single desired outcome. Maximizing dependable role performance may involve motivational conditions that inhibit spontaneous and innovative behavior. Attracting people to a system and holding them in it may not lead to a high level of productivity. We need to examine in detail the differential effects of the three patterns of motivation on organizational behavior, and to analyse the conditions most likely to arouse these patterns.

Legal compliance and the punishment model

There is some evidence that clarity of rules is a condition of some importance in holding people in the system. If people know what to expect and are clear about the roles they fulfill they are more likely to remain in the system. Weitz (1956), Youngberg (1963), and Macedonia (1969) found that prior knowledge and understanding of role requirements was a significant factor in keeping people in the company. In these investigations the experimental groups received information through booklets and the control groups did not. In a more subjective study Lyons (1971) reported that staff nurses who perceived their role demands as clear were less likely to leave or think of leaving.

Emphasis on legal compliance can bring about acceptable levels of individual performance both in quantity and quality. The more routine the activity, the more likely this is to be true. Creativity is difficult if not impossible to legislate. Legality, moreover, needs the reinforcement of situational reminders. The time clock, the use of mechanical 'speeds and feeds' beyond the control of the worker, and the occasional policing of rules and regulations are characteristic of the legal motif in organizations.

Emphasis on the legalities of organizational control tends in practice to mean that the minimal acceptable standard for quantity and quality of performance becomes the maximal standard. If it is legitimate and proper according to company and union standards to turn out forty pieces on a machine, then there is no point in exceeding this standard. One cannot be more legal or proper than the norm, though there are degrees of nonconformity in failing to meet it.

The legal basis of influencing people is notoriously deficient in affecting performance beyond the narrow role prescriptions for quantity and quality of work. What is not covered by rules is by definition not the responsibility of the organizational member. 'Working to the rules' thus becomes the traditional revenge of the legally constrained work-force.

The attempt is usually made to extend the rules to cover more and more of the behavior required for good overall organizational perform-ance. But several considerations argue against such extension. Acts of creativity or spontaneous, mutual helpfulness cannot be legislated. Major role requirements will be obscured if the legal specifications become too numerous. Finally, building up the role of every member would entail some upgrading of even the lowliest positions and would run counter to the machine-theoretical basis of many hierarchical organi-zations.

Extrinsic rewards: system and individual

The first logical extension of machine theory beyond rules and sanctions is the addition of rewards to motivate performance. It is important to distinguish between rewards administered in relation to individual effort and performance, and the system rewards that accrue to people by virtue of their membership in the system. In the former category are piece-rate incentives, promotion for outstanding performance, or any special recognition bestowed in acknowledgement of differential con-tributions to organizational functioning. The category of system rewards includes fringe benefits, recreational facilities, cost-of-living raises, across-the-board upgrading, job security, and pleasant working conditions.

Individual rewards properly administered help attract people to the system and hold them in it. A major factor in the effectiveness of such rewards is the extent to which they are competitive with individual reward systems in other organizations. Individual rewards can also be effective in motivating people to meet and exceed the quantitative and qualitative standards of role performance. This effectiveness is limited, however, when large numbers of people are performing identical tasks, so that superior individual performance threatens the rewards and secur-ity of the majority. In other words, differential individual rewards are difficult to apply effectively to masses of people doing the same work and sharing a common fate in a mass-production organization. It is no accident that large organizations have moved in the direction of convert-ing individual rewards into system rewards.

Individual rewards are also difficult to apply to contributions that go beyond the formal requirements of role. Spectacular instances of innovative behavior can be singled out for recognition, of course, and heroism beyond the call of duty can be decorated. But the everyday cooperative activities that keep an organization from falling apart are more difficult to recognize and reward. Creative suggestions for organizational improvement are sometimes encouraged through financial rewards. In general, however, singling out of individuals for their extra contributions to the cause is not the most effective and reliable means of evoking high motivation for the accomplishment of organizational objectives.

If rewards such as pay incentives are to work as they are intended they must meet three primary conditions: (1) They must be clearly perceived as large enough in amount to justify the additional effort required to obtain them. (2) They must be perceived as directly related to the required performance and follow directly on its accomplishment. (3) They must be perceived as equitable by the majority of system members, many of whom will not receive them. These conditions suggest some of the reasons why individual rewards can work so well in some situations and yet be so difficult for application in large organizations.

System rewards differ from individual rewards in that they are not allocated on the basis of differential effort and performance but on the basis of membership in the system. The main basis for differential allocation of system rewards is seniority in the system. A higher pension for thirty years of service than for twenty years does not violate the principle of rewarding membership. Management often overlooks the distinction between individual and system rewards, and operates as if rewards administered across the board would produce the same effects as individual rewards.

System rewards are most effective for holding members within the organization. Since these rewards are often distributed on the basis of length of service, people will want to stay on to receive them. The limiting factor is competition with attractions in other systems. As the system increases its attractions, other things being equal, it should reduce its problems of turnover. In fact, it may sometimes have the problem of too little turnover, with many poorly motivated people staying on until retirement.

System rewards will not lead to work of higher quality or greater quantity than is required to stay in the organization. Since rewards are given equally to all members or differentially in terms of seniority, people are not motivated to do more than meet the standards for remaining in the system. It is sometimes assumed that the liking for the organization created by system rewards will generalize to greater productive effort. Such generalization of motivation may occur to a very limited extent, but it is not a reliable basis for the expectation of higher productivity. Management may expect gratitude from workers because it has added some special fringe benefit or some new recreational facility. Employees will be motivated to remain in an enterprise with such advantages, but are unlikely to express gratitude by working harder for the company.

Although system rewards maintain the level of productivity not much above the minimum required to stay in the system, there still may be large differences between systems with respect to the quantity and quality of production as a function of system rewards. An organization with substantially better wage rates and fringe benefits than its competitors may be able to set a higher level of performance as a minimal requirement for its workers and still hold its employees. System rewards can be related to the differential productivity of organizations as a whole though they are not effective in maximizing the potential contributions of the majority of individuals within an organization. They may account for differences in motivation between systems rather than for differences in motivation between individuals in the same system.

Research has frequently not discriminated between system and individual rewards, between intrinsic job satisfaction and satisfaction with aspects of the job other than work content, and even among behavioral outcomes. At a general level we know that high pay rates and bonuses make the system more attractive and so reduce turnover and absenteeism. In their review of such studies Porter and Steers (1973) found that satisfaction with pay and promotion was correlated with turnover in the expected direction in nine out of eleven investigations.

Rewards can also influence absenteeism, as Lawler and Hackman (1969) demonstrated in an experimental field study of part-time janitorial employees. A plan to provide cash bonuses for regular attendance was developed participatively in three work groups and imposed upon two others. The plan worked well in reducing absenteeism for the groups that had participated in its formulation and less well for the groups not involved in its development. A follow-up study a year later (Schefler, Lawler & Hackman, 1971) showed that where the plan remained in effect for the participating workers, absence rates remained low; where the plan had been dropped by management, absences increased. Although the investigators attributed the decreased absenteeism to both the cash bonus and its method of introduction, it is not clear how much of the result was a matter of the bonus as an extrinsic reward and how much a matter of ego motivation deriving from involvement in the bonus plan.

Increasing financial returns on a productivity-contingent basis can lead to more productivity, subject to the conditions already described. Locke and Bryan (1967) demonstrated that in well-controlled laboratory studies increasing the financial rewards increases productivity. Lawler (1968) found that subjects working on a piece-rate system produced 20 per cent more than subjects working on an hourly system. But in these experiments rewards are tied to individual performance whereas in industry the problem is how to create such ties. Increasing wages as such is no guarantee of increased productivity but the company with a high pay rate is in a strong position in attracting and holding employees.

Internalized motivation

We will consider first the organizational consequences of intrinsic job satisfaction, then value expression, and finally shared psychological fields and group cohesiveness.

Self-expression, self-determination and intrinsic job satisfaction

Most of the research on job enlargement and job enrichment reports a rise in satisfaction from the content of the work itself – greater feelings of autonomy, of responsibility, of demonstrating one's worth. When productivity has also been measured in job enrichment experiments, most of them have shown increases in productivity as well. The assumption is that the challenge of the job motivates people toward greater effort. The further assumption is often made that subjective states of being able to express oneself or show one's abilities mediate between the objective characteristics of the enriched job and the increased productivity of the worker. Finally it is assumed that questions directed at these feelings adequately and validly measure the subjective feeling state. Although more research is needed to support these assumptions conclusively, there is considerable backing for them as more and more evidence accumulates in this area of investigation.

Porter and Steers (1973) in their review of studies of job satisfaction report a high degree of agreement on the relationship of job satisfaction and turnover. Fifteen out of sixteen investigations found an association between low turnover and high job satisfaction. Where absenteeism was also measured similar results were obtained – low absenteeism was correlated with high satisfaction.

Four experiments [were done by] Paul, Robertson, and Herzberg (1969) on job enrichment. In one laboratory of an industrial research department, technicians were given the opportunity to participate in planning projects, setting goals, and making fiscal decisions. The measure of performance was the evaluation of research reports and research minutes of experimental and control subjects by a panel of three managers not members of the department. Three such staff assessments were carried out during the course of a year and the only group showing consistent improvement was one of the experimental groups.

With a more objective performance criterion, an experiment on sales representatives (Paul, Robertson, & Herzberg, 1969) showed a more dramatic outcome. For the group with enriched jobs, the gain over the previous year, after allowing for the additional work of making decisions about calls and claims, was almost 19 per cent, amounting to $300,000 in sales value. The control group, on the other hand, declined by 5 per cent. During the same period the control group showed no change in job satisfaction, while the experimental group improved some 11 per cent.

The third Paul–Robertson–Herzberg experimental program was conducted among design engineers, for whom there was no such hard performance criterion as was available for the salespeople. None the less, senior managers felt that the many changes giving the engineers more autonomy had cumulated significantly and positively. There was no evidence of poor decisions, more time was given to technical development rather than routine tasks, and important problems were solved.

In their fourth study the same investigators introduced changes in the work roles of production supervisors and of engineering supervisors. Again in the experimental groups more autonomy was provided for training, recruiting, discipline, and contributing to organizational problems. A number of the supervisors given the opportunity did contribute their experience and expertise to long-standing organizational and technical difficulties. In three cases where financial assessment was possible, the estimated annual savings totaled more that $125,000. Moreover, the production supervisors improved markedly in their training of workers; the number of assistants unable to do the job of the person they assisted fell by 37 per cent. The engineering supervisors also interacted effectively with union officials, and relations between these two groups had long been difficult.

Other case studies of job enlargement for the most part report that increased autonomy and responsibility lead not only to more satisfaction with the content of the work but to improvements in the quality of the work and to higher productivity (Davis & Taylor, 1972; Davis & Cherns, 1975). Not every case provides hard data on productivity but where such figures are available the findings are consistently in the same direction. Often total labor costs go unmeasured but the evidence again suggests that with job enrichment less time has to be spent by management in supervisory control.

Value expression

A motive pattern relating to intrinsic job satisfaction is value expression, which can be tied to organization goals as well as to the content of the work. People can derive feelings of gratification in working for a system whose values they have internalized or whose values coincide with their own. The dedicated party worker or the committed employee is likely to meet all three organizational requirements – staying in the system, doing excellent work, and performing innovative acts supportive of organizational policies. Since many motivational problems would be solved if organizations had such value consensus among their members, it is of interest that research and practice is in its infancy in exploring the matter. Almost no studies have attempted to measure the distribution of organizational values and their relationship to various types of performance.

Perhaps the closest approach is in studies of occupational identification and organizational commitment. But occupational identification transcends the particular organization and so would not predict to turnover or necessarily to innovative acts to advance the goals of one organization.

Dubin, Champoux, and Porter (1975) found a strong relationship between job-oriented life interests and organizational commitment in a sample of 1,014 male and female blue-collar workers drawn from a bank and telephone company. Of the men with low organizational commitment only 14 per cent were job-oriented, as compared to 65 per cent of the highly committed group. Similarly the female clerical workers with low organizational commitment had 14 per cent who were job-oriented, but with high commitment some 54 per cent. The questionnaire measuring organizational commitment was a fifteen-item instrument developed by Porter and Smith (1970), based on their concept of commitment and described by Dubin et al. (1975) thus: 'a highly committed person will indicate: (1) a strong desire to remain a member of a particular organization, (2) a willingness to exert high levels of effort on behalf of the organization, and (3) a definite belief in and acceptance of the values and goals of the organization' (Dubin, Champoux, & Porter, 1975, p. 414). The validity of the instrument is attested by its power in predicting turnover in a sample of managerial trainees over a fifteen-month period (Porter, Crampon & Smith, 1976). The trainees who voluntarily left the company showed a definite decline in commitment prior to their departure.

Shared psychological fields and group cohesiveness

In our discussion of patterns of internalized motivation we emphasized the importance of the primary group, especially the potentiality of the group for providing the sense of task accomplishment and closure that is usually thought of only in individual terms. We called attention to the magnitude and unity of effort that can be motivated by attachment to the group. The great advantage of the cohesive group is that its members can find in group responsibility and group achievement satisfaction for their individual needs for self-expression and self-determination, as well as affiliation.

Research workers at the Tavistock Institute have been leaders in theory and experimentation involving the primary group as the motivational base for performance. Rice's (1958) experiment in a large Indian textile mill is a classic example of their approach and of the motivational power of the primary group. The pre-experimental condition consisted of a highly specialized and fractionated division of labor, in which no worker nor group of workers could be identified with the task outcome; the output could be meaningfully described only as the result of their aggregative specialized roles. The experimental condition created groups of seven people, with each group responsible for specific looms – their maintenance, their servicing, their operation, and their output. There is division of labor within such groups, but each member of the group identifies with the group task and its accomplishment as well as with his or her own contribution to it. Increased motivation, increased performance, and increased satisfaction resulted in this case, as in many others. The discovery of the motivational power of the primary group, and of the fulfillment of individual needs through group achievement, is the greatest contribution of the 'group dynamicists' and of the Tavistock research workers to organizational theory and practice. Its potential impact is no less than the discovery of the informal group by Elton Mayo and his colleagues [Roethlisberger & Dickson, 1939]. Organizational theory and practice has been slow to recognize the implications of these group phenomena, however, and only in recent years has the earlier work of Rice and Trist [at the Tavistock Institute] been extended.

One example of such extension is the research of Thorsrud (1976) and his Norwegian colleagues with 'autonomous work groups' in factory settings. The emphasis on the primary group as the producing unit is also to be seen in the design of the Swedish 'new factories'.

Much remains to be learned about the limits of individual fullfillment through group accomplishment, and about the substitutability of shared outcomes for solitary ones. The potential formation of small cohesive work groups, engaged in tasks of meaningful size and with visible outcomes, seems a desirable objective in the design of production sequences and factories. The gains – psychological and material – would be substantial.

REFERENCES

Davis, L. E., & Cherns, A. B. (1975), *The Quality of Working Life* (Vols. 1 & 2), New York: Free Press.

Davis, L. E., & Taylor, J. C. (eds.) (1972), *Design of Jobs: Selected Readings*, Harmondsworth, England: Penguin.

Dubin, R., Champoux, J. E., & Porter, L. W. (1975), 'Central life interests and organizational commitment of blue-collar and clerical workers', *Administrative Science Quarterly*, *10*, 411–21.

Lawler, E. E., III (1968), 'Equity theory as a predictor of productivity and work quality', *Psychological Bulletin*, *70*, 596–610.

Lawler, E. E., III, & Hackman, J. R. (1969), 'Impact of employee participation in the development of pay incentive plans: A field experiment', *Journal of Applied Psychology*, *53*, 467–71.

Locke, E. A., & Bryan, J. F. (1967), *Goals and Intentions as Determinants of Performance Level, Task Choice and Attitudes*, Washington, DC: American Institute for Research.

Lyons, T. (1971), 'Role clarity, need for clarity, satisfaction, tension and withdrawal', *Organizational Behavior and Human Performance*, *6*, 99–110.

Macedonia, R. M. (1969), 'Expectation-press and survival', unpublished doctoral dissertation, Graduate School of Public Administration, New York University.

Paul, W. J., Robertson, K. B., & Herzberg, F. (1969), 'Job enrichment pays off', *Harvard Business Review*, *47*, 61–78.

Porter, L. W., Crampon, W. J., & Smith, F. J. (1976), 'Organizational commitment and managerial turnover: A longitudinal study', *Organizational Behavior and Human Performance*, *15*, 87–98.

Porter, L. W., & Smith, F. J. (1970), 'The etiology of organizational commitment: A longitudinal study of the initial stages of employee–organization reactions', unpublished paper, Graduate School of Administration, University of California, Irvine.

Porter, L. W., & Steers, R. M. (1973), 'Organizational, work and personal factors in employee turnover and absenteeism', *Psychological Bulletin*, *80*, 151–76.

Rice, A. K. (1958), *Productivity and Social Organization: The Ahmedabad Experiment*, London: Tavistock Publications.

Roethlisberger, F. J., & Dixon, W. J. (1939), *Management and the Worker*, Cambridge, Mass.: Harvard University Press.

Schefler, K. C., Lawler, E. E., III, & Hackman, J. R. (1971), 'Long-term impact of employee participation in the development of pay incentive plans: A field experiment', *Journal of Applied Psychology*, *55*, 182–6.

Thorsrud, E., Sørensen, B. S., & Gustavsen, B. (1976), 'Sociotechnical approach to industrial democracy in Norway', in R. Dubin (ed.), *Handbook of Work, Organization, and Society*, Chicago: Rand McNally.

Weitz, J. (1956), 'Job expectancy and survival', *Journal of Applied Psychology*, *40*, 243–7.

Youngberg, C. F. (1963), 'An experimental study of "job satisfaction" and turnover in relation to job expectancies and self expectations', unpublished doctoral dissertation, New York University.

15

DONALD P. SCHWAB AND LARRY L. CUMMINGS

Theories of Performance and Satisfaction: A Review

Abridged from D. P. Schwab and L. L. Cummings 'Theories of performance and satisfaction: A review', *Industrial Relations*, Vol. 9, 1970, pp. 408–30.

A sizeable portion of behavioral science research in organizations has focused on possible connections between job attitudes, particular job satisfaction, and various job behaviors. Industrial psychologists and labor economists, for example, have explored the relationship between job satisfaction and job tenure. Other scholars from various disciplines have examined the association between job satisfaction and such behavioral variables as absences, accidents, grievances, illness, and even life expectancy. More recently, a growing number of studies suggesting a controversy have emerged concerning the relationship between technology and task design and satisfaction with the job.

Unquestionably, however, it is the hypothesized connection between employee satisfaction and job performance which has generated the greatest research and theoretical interest. In the last forty years, investigators have examined these two variables in a wide variety of work situations: (1) among organization members ranging from the unskilled to managers and professionals, (2) in diverse administrative and technological environments, (3) using individuals or groups as the unit of analysis, and (4) employing various measures of both satisfaction and performance. The methodologies employed in these studies, and their findings have been reviewed by Brayfield and Crockett (1955); Herzberg, Mausner, Peterson and Capwell (1957); and Vroom (1964).

SATISFACTION→PERFORMANCE

... management has at long last discovered that there is greater production, and hence greater profit when workers are satisfied with their jobs. Improve the morale of a company and you improve production. (Parker & Kleemeir, 1951, p. 10)

Historical perspective. Whatever their value as research, the Hawthorne studies had a significant impact on the thinking of a generation of behavioral scientists and business managers (Roethlisberger & Dickson, 1939). The quotation from Parker and Kleemeir was almost certainly inspired by the Hawthorne studies, although the original investigators probably never stated the relationship so unequivocally. Roethlisberger, for example, in discussing the implications of the study for managers, noted that '. . . the factors which make for efficiency in a business organization are not necessarily the same as those factors that make for happiness, collaboration, teamwork, morale, or any other word which may be used to refer to cooperative situations' (Roethlisberger, 1941).

Yet, despite Roethlisberger's caveat, the early human relationists have been interpreted as saying that satisfaction leads to performance. Vroom, for example, argues that '. . . human relations might be described as an attempt to increase productivity by satisfying the needs of employees' (Vroom, 1964, p. 181). Strauss (1968) states that '. . . early human relationists viewed the morale–productivity relationship quite simply: higher morale would lead to improved productivity' (p. 264). In the final analysis the interpretation is perhaps more significant than the original views expressed.

A current satisfaction→performance interpretation. The work of Herzberg and his colleagues provides perhaps the best illustration of current theory and research formulated on the view that satisfaction leads to performance. These researchers separate job variables into two groups, hygiene factors and motivators (Herzberg, Mausner, & Snyderman, 1959). Included in the hygiene group are such variables as supervision, physical working conditions, regular salary and benefits, company policies, etc. These are viewed as potential sources of dissatisfaction, but not as sources of positive work attitudes. Among the motivators, Herzberg lists factors closely associated with work itself and its accomplishment, i.e., challenging assignments, recognition, the opportunity for professional growth, etc. These factors presumably contribute to work satisfaction and are the key factors associated with performance. Thus, Herzberg feels that low performance–satisfaction correlations obtained in other research studies can thus be explained since '. . . the usual morale measures are confounded . . . they tap both kinds of attitudes . . .' (i.e., satisfiers and dissatisfiers) (Herzberg, et al., 1959, p. 87).

In fairness to the original authors of *The Motivation to Work*, it should be recognized that the conclusion relating performance to the satisfiers but not to the dissatisfiers has escalated somewhat with the passage of time. In the original study, care was taken to report the actual percentages obtained and at least to raise alternative explanations of the findings (Herzberg, et al., 1959, pp. 86–7).

Although there have been a number of partial replications of the two-factory theory, they have not investigated the hypothesized performance consequences of job satisfaction and dissatisfaction. Thus, the empirical validity of the satisfaction–performance relationship specified in the two-factor theory rests entirely on the original study of 200 accountants and engineers.

Moreover, the evidence employed to support the premise that satisfaction leads to performance has been non-experimental in design. As such, the studies obviously do not show causality. In fact, neither human relationists in general, nor Herzberg in particular, have provided an adequate theoretical explanation for the causal relationship which they postulated.

A capstone to 'the development' of uncertainty regarding the satisfaction–performance relationship was provided by Brayfield and Crockett in 1955. Their review of over fifty studies represents, depending on one's point of view, either a council of despair or a challenge for theory development and extended research. As we will illustrate, the latter (at least the theoretical dimension) seems to have prevailed.

Brayfield and Crockett hypothesized that employees govern their job-seeking, job-performing, and job-terminating behavior by the law of effect, subsequently elaborated and relabeled by Vroom (1964) and Porter and Lawler (1968) as expectancy theory. Regarding job-terminating behavior, Brayfield and Crockett argued that: 'One principal generalization suffices to set up an expectation that morale should be related to absenteeism and turnover, namely, that organisms tend to avoid those situations which are punishing and to seek out situations that are rewarding' (1955, p. 415).

Brayfield and Crockett encountered greater difficulty explaining satisfaction and job-performance linkages through the simple application of the hedonistic principle. They suggested that satisfaction and job performance might be concomitantly rather than causally related. In addition, one '. . . might expect high satisfaction and high productivity to occur together when productivity is perceived as a path to certain important goals and when these goals are achieved. Under other conditions, satisfaction and productivity might be unrelated or even negatively related' (1955, p. 416).

Satisfaction and the motivation to produce. A model proposed by

March and Simon perhaps best bridges the theoretical gap between the satisfaction→performance view of the human relationists and the performance→satisfaction view to be discussed in the following section. The model suggests that both performance and satisfaction can serve as dependent variables (March & Simon, 1958).

Beginning with performance as the dependent variable, March and Simon hypothesized: 'Motivation to produce stems from a present or anticipated state of discontent and a perception of a direct connection between individual production and a new state of satisfaction' (p. 51). The hypothesis states that performance is a function of two variables: (1) the degree of dissatisfaction experienced, and (2) the perceived instrumentality of performance for the attainment of valued rewards.

Thus, the model suggests that a state of dissatisfaction is a necessary, but not sufficient, condition for performance. It is necessary because dissatisfaction of some sort is assumed to be required to activate the organism toward search behavior. It lacks sufficiency, however, because a dissatisfied employee may not perceive performance as leading to satisfaction or may perceive non-performance as leading to greater perceived satisfaction.

PERFORMANCE→SATISFACTION

> ... good performance may lead to rewards, which in turn lead to satisfaction; this formulation then would say that satisfaction, rather than causing performance, as was previously assumed, is caused by it. (Lawler & Porter, 1967a, p. 23)

The performance→satisfaction theory represents an important departure from earlier views about the relationship between these two variables. Human relationists, not without some qualification, postulated that high levels of satisfaction would result in high levels of performance. The performance→satisfaction theory stresses the importance of variations in effort and performance as causes of variations in job satisfaction.

The Porter–Lawler model. Just as the Brayfield and Crockett review significantly influenced subsequent theoretical developments on the satisfaction→performance issue, a later review published by Vroom in 1964 has apparently had a similar impact on recent theorizing. While noting the generally low correspondence observed between measured satisfaction and performance, Vroom nevertheless found that in twenty of

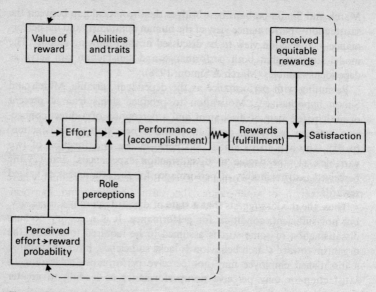

Figure 1. Performance→Satisfaction

Adapted from Porter and Lawler, *Managerial Attitudes and Performance*, (1968), p. 17.

twenty-three cases the correlation was positive and that the median correlation reported was + .14 (Vroom, 1964, p. 183). Porter and Lawler have cited this review and the generally positive nature of this association as a basis for suggesting that premature, pessimistic closure would be unwise and have expounded their model through a series of recent publications (Lawler & Porter, 1967b).

Although the Porter–Lawler model posits circularity in the relationship between performance and satisfaction, Figure 1 shows that the most direct linkage has performance as the causal and satisfaction as the dependent variable. That relationship is mediated only by rewards (intrinsic and extrinsic) and the perceived equity of those rewards. When performance leads to rewards which are seen by the individual as equitable, it is hypothesized that high satisfaction will result. The model suggests that the generally low performance–satisfaction relationships observed in previous empirical research may result from rewards, particularly extrinsic rewards, which are often not closely tied to performance.

For satisfaction to exert an influence on performance in the Porter–Lawler model, it must affect the value of the rewards received, which in turn interacts with the perceived effort→reward linkage to determine the level of actual work effort. Finally, effort moderated by role perceptions and abilities and traits determines performance. Because of the number of intervening variables involved, it seems unlikely that satisfaction (or dissatisfaction) has as much impact on performance as performance has on satisfaction.

Implications for administrative practice. The Porter–Lawler model is quite rich in terms of its administrative implications. For example, it shares with the theory of work adjustment implications for high performance through the modification of abilities and traits via selection and training processes. In addition, their theory more than the others suggests a role for performance appraisal and salary administration in increasing employee performance levels. Both activities presumably have the potential of influencing the effort→reward and performance→reward probabilities. Furthermore, salary level, and particularly salary structure, would appear to be important determinants of perceived equity of rewards.

REFERENCES

Brayfield, A. H., & Crockett, W. H. (1955), 'Employee attitudes and employee performance', *Psychological Bulletin, 52,* 396–424.

Herzberg, F. H., Mausner, B. M., Peterson, R. O., Capwell, D. F. (1957), *Job Attitudes: Review of Research and Opinion,* Pittsburgh: Psychological Service of Pittsburgh.

Herzberg, F. H., Mausner, B. M., & Snyderman, B. (1959), *The Motivation to Work* (2nd edn), New York: Wiley.

Lawler, E. E., III, & Porter, L. W. (1967a), 'The effect of performance on job satisfaction', *Industrial Relations, 7,* 20–28.

Lawler, E. E., III, & Porter, L. W. (1967b), 'Antecedent attitudes of effective managerial performance', *Organizational Behavior and Human Performance, 2,* 122–42.

March, J. G., & Simon, H. A. (1958), *Organizations,* New York: Wiley.

Parker, W. E., & Kleemeir, R. W. (1951), *Human Relations in Supervision: Leadership in Management,* New York: McGraw-Hill.

Porter, L. W., & Lawler, E. E., III (1968), *Managerial Attitudes and Performance,* Homewood, Ill.: Irwin-Dorsey.

Roethlisberger, F. J. (1941), *Management and Morale,* Cambridge, Mass.: Harvard University Press.

Roethlisberger, F. J., & Dickson, W. J. (1939), *Management and the Worker,* Cambridge, Mass.: Harvard University Press.

Strauss, G. (1968), 'Human relations – 1968 style', *Industrial Relations, 7,* 264.

Vroom, V. H. (1964), *Work and Motivation,* New York: Wiley.

16

GARY P. LATHAM AND EDWIN A. LOCKE

Goal Setting – A Motivational Technique That Works

Abridged from G. P. Latham and E. A. Locke, 'Goal setting: A motivational technique that works', *Organizational Dynamics*, Vol. 8 (2), 1979, pp. 68–80.

The problem of how to motivate employees has puzzled and frustrated managers for generations. One reason the problem has seemed difficult, if not mysterious, is that motivation ultimately comes from within the individual and therefore cannot be observed directly. Moreover, most managers are not in a position to change an employee's basic personality structure. The best they can do is try to use incentives to direct the energies of their employees toward organizational objectives.

Money is obviously the primary incentive, since without it few if any employees would come to work. But money alone is not always enough to motivate high performance. Other incentives, such as participation in decision making, job enrichment, behavior modification, and organizational development, have been tried with varying degrees of success. A large number of research studies have shown, however, that one very straightforward technique – goal setting – is probably not only more effective than alternative methods, but may be the major mechanism by which these other incentives affect motivation.

THE GOAL-SETTING CONCEPT

The idea of assigning employees a specific amount of work to be accomplished – a specific task, a quota, a performance standard, an objective, or a deadline – is not new. The task concept, along with time and motion study and incentive pay, was the cornerstone of scientific management, founded by Frederick W. Taylor more than seventy years ago (see Reading 30). He used his system to increase the productivity of blue-collar workers. About twenty years ago the idea of goal setting reappeared under a new name, management by objectives, but this technique was designed for managers (see Reading 34).

In a fourteen-year program of research, we have found that goal setting does not necessarily have to be part of a wider management system to motivate performance effectively. It can be used as a technique in its own right.

Laboratory and field research

Our research program began in the laboratory. In a series of experiments, individuals were assigned different types of goals on a variety of simple tasks – addition, brain-storming, assembling toys. Repeatedly it was found that those assigned hard goals performed better than did people assigned moderately difficult or easy goals. Furthermore, individuals who had specific, challenging goals out-performed those who were given such vague goals as to 'do your best'. Finally, we observed that pay and performance feedback led to improved performance only when these incentives led the individual to set higher goals.

While results were quite consistent in the laboratory, there was no proof that they could be applied to actual work settings. Fortunately, just as Locke published a summary of the laboratory studies in 1968, Latham began a separate series of experiments in the wood-products industry that demonstrated the practical significance of these findings. The field studies did not start out as a validity test of a laboratory theory, but rather as a response to a practical problem.

In 1968, six sponsors of the American Pulpwood Association became concerned about increasing the productivity of independent loggers in the South. These loggers were entrepreneurs on whom the multimillion-dollar companies are largely dependent for their raw material. The problem was twofold. First, these entrepreneurs did not work for a single company; they worked for themselves. Thus they were free to (and often did) work two days one week, four days a second week, five half-days a third week, or whatever schedule they preferred. In short, these workers could be classified as marginal from the standpoint of their productivity and attendance, which were considered highly unsatisfactory by conventional company standards. Second, the major approach taken to alleviate this problem had been to develop equipment that would make the industry less dependent on this type of worker. A limitation of this approach was that many of the logging supervisors were unable to obtain the financing necessary to purchase a small tractor, let alone a rubber-tired skidder.

Consequently, we designed a survey that would help managers

determine 'what makes these people tick'. The survey was conducted orally in the field with 292 logging supervisors. Complex statistical analyses of the data identified three basic types of supervisor. One type stayed on the job with their men, gave them instructions and explanations, provided them with training, read the trade magazines, and had little difficulty financing the equipment they needed. Still, the productivity of their units was at best mediocre.

The operation of the second group of supervisors was slightly less mechanized. These supervisors provided little training for their workforce. They simply drove their employees to the woods, gave them a specific production goal to attain for the day or week, left them alone in the woods unsupervised, and returned at night to take them home. Labor turnover was high and productivity was again average.

The operation of the third group of supervisors was relatively unmechanized. These leaders stayed on the job with their men, provided training, gave instructions and explanations, and in addition, set a specific production goal for the day or week. Not only was the crew's productivity high, but their injury rate was well below average.

Two conclusions were discussed with the managers of the companies sponsoring this study. First, mechanization alone will not increase the productivity of logging crews. The second conclusion of the survey was that setting a specific production goal combined with supervisory presence to ensure goal commitment will bring about a significant increase in productivity.

One of the companies decided to replicate the survey in order to check our findings. The company's study placed each of 892 independent logging supervisors who sold wood to the company into one of three categories of supervisory styles our survey had identified – namely, (1) stays on the job but does not set specific production goals; (2) sets specific production goals but does not stay on the job; and (3) stays on the job and sets specific production goals. Once again, goal setting, in combination with the on-site presence of a supervisor, was shown to be the key to improved productivity.

We were granted permission to run one more project to test the effectiveness of goal setting.

Twenty independent logging crews who were all but identical in size, mechanization level, terrain on which they worked, productivity, and attendance were located. The logging supervisors of these crews were in the habit of staying on the job with their men, but they did not set production goals. Half the crews were randomly selected to receive training in goal setting; the remaining crews served as a control group.

The logging supervisors who were to set goals were told that we had found a way to increase productivity at no financial expense to anyone. We gave the ten supervisors in the training group production tables developed through time-and-motion studies by the company's engineers. These tables made it possible to determine how much wood should be harvested in a given number of manhours. They were asked to use these tables as a guide in determining a specific production goal to assign their employees. In addition, each sawhand was given a tallymeter (counter) that he could wear on his belt. The sawhand was asked to punch the counter each time he felled a tree. Finally, permission was requested to measure the crew's performance on a weekly basis.

The ten supervisors in the control group – those who were not asked to set production goals – were told that the researchers were interested in learning the extent to which productivity is affected by absenteeism and injuries. They were urged to 'do your best' to maximize the crew's productivity and attendance and to minimize injuries. It was explained that the data might be useful in finding ways to increase productivity at little or no cost to the wood harvester.

Performance was measured for twelve weeks. During this time, the productivity of the goal-setting group was significantly higher than that of the control group. Moreover, absenteeism was significantly lower in the groups that set goals than in the groups who were simply urged to do their best. Injury and turnover rates were low in both groups.

Why should anything so simple and inexpensive as goal setting influence the work of these employees so significantly? Anecdotal evidence from conversations with both the loggers and the company foresters who visited them suggested several reasons.

Harvesting timber can be a monotonous, tiring job with little or no meaning for most workers. Introducing a goal that is difficult, but attainable, increases the challenge of the job. In addition, a specific goal makes it clear to the worker what it is he is expected to do. Goal feedback via the tallymeter and weekly record-keeping provide the worker with a sense of achievement, recognition, and accomplishment. He can see how well he is doing now as against his past performance and, in some cases, how well he is doing in comparison with others. Thus the worker not only may expend greater effort, but may also devise better or more creative tactics for attaining the goal than those he previously used.

NEW APPLICATIONS

Management was finally convinced that goal setting was an effective motivational technique for increasing the productivity of the independent woods worker in the South. The issue now raised by the management of another wood-products company was whether the procedure could be used in the West with company logging operations in which the employees were unionized and paid by the hour. The previous study had involved employees on a piece-rate system, which was the practice in the South.

The immediate problem confronting this company involved the loading of logging trucks. If the trucks were underloaded, the company lost money. If the trucks were overloaded, however, the driver could be fined by the Highway Department and could ultimately lose his job. The drivers opted for underloading the trucks.

For three months management tried to solve this problem by urging the drivers to try harder to fill the truck to its legal net weight, and by developing weighing scales that could be attached to the truck. But this approach did not prove cost effective, because the scales continually broke down when subjected to the rough terrain on which the trucks traveled. Consequently, the drivers reverted to their former practice of underloading. For the three months in which the problem was under study the trucks were seldom loaded in excess of 58 to 63 per cent of capacity.

At the end of the three-month period, the results of the previous goal-setting experiments were explained to the union. They were told three things – that the company would like to set a specific net weight goal for the drivers, that no monetary reward or fringe benefits other than verbal praise could be expected for improved performance, and that no one would be criticized for failing to attain the goal. Once again, the idea that simply setting a specific goal would solve a production problem seemed too incredible to be taken seriously by the union. However, they reached an agreement that a difficult, but attainable, goal of 94 per cent of the truck's legal net weight would be assigned to the drivers, provided that no one could be reprimanded for failing to attain the goal. This latter point was emphasized to the company foremen in particular.

Within the first month, performance increased to 80 per cent of the truck's net weight. After the second month, however, performance decreased to 70 per cent. Interviews with the drivers indicated that they were testing management's statement that no punitive steps would be taken against them if their performance suddenly dropped. Fortunately for all concerned, no such steps were taken by the foremen, and performance exceeded 90 per cent of the truck's capacity after the third month. Their performance has remained at this level to this day, seven years later.

The results over the nine-month period during which this study was conducted saved the company $250,000. This figure, determined by the company's accountants, is based on the cost of additional trucks that would have been required to deliver the same quantity of logs to the mill if goal setting had not been implemented. The dollar-saved figure is even higher when you factor in the cost of the additional diesel fuel that would have been consumed and the expenses incurred in recruiting and hiring the additional truck drivers.

Why could this procedure work without the union's demanding an increase in hourly wages? First, the drivers did not feel that they were really doing anything differently. This, of course, was not true. As a result of goal setting, the men began to record their truck weight in a pocket notebook, and they found themselves bragging about their accomplishments to their peers. Second, they viewed goal setting as a challenging game: 'It was great to beat the other guy.'

Competition was a crucial factor in bringing about goal acceptance and commitment in this study. However, we can reject the hypothesis that improved performance resulted solely from competition, because no special prizes or formal recognition programs were provided for those who came closest to, or exceeded, the goal. No effort was made by the company to single out one 'winner'. In short, competition affected productivity only in the sense that it led to the acceptance of, and commitment to, the goal. It was the setting of the goal itself and the working toward it that brought about increased performance and decreased costs.

The concept of goal setting is a very simple one. Interestingly, however, we have gotten two contradictory types of reaction when the idea was introduced to managers. Some claimed it was so simple and self-evident that everyone, including themselves, already used it. This, we have found, is not true. Time after time we have gotten the following response from subordinates after goal setting was introduced: 'This is the first time I knew what my supervisor expected of me on this job.' Conversely, other managers have argued that the idea would not work, precisely *because* it is so simple (implying that something more radical and complex was needed). Again, results proved them wrong.

But these successes should not mislead managers into thinking that goal setting can be used without careful planning and forethought. Research and experience suggest that the best results are obtained when the following steps are followed:

Setting the goal. The goal set should have two main characteristics. First, it should be specific rather than vague: 'Increase sales by 10 per cent' rather than 'Try to improve sales.' Whenever possible, there should be a time limit for goal accomplishment: 'Cut costs by 3 per cent in the next six months.'

Second, the goal should be challenging yet reachable. If accepted, difficult goals lead to better performance than do easy goals. In contrast, if the goals are perceived as unreachable, employees will not accept them. Nor will employees get a sense of achievement from pursuing goals that are never attained. Employees with low self-confidence or ability should be given more easily attainable goals than those with high self-confidence and ability.

Another issue that needs to be considered when setting goals is whether they should be designed for individuals or for groups. Rensis Likert and a number of other human relations experts argue for group goal setting on grounds that it promotes cooperation and team spirit. But one could argue that individual goals better promote individual responsibility and make it easier to appraise individual performance. The degree of task interdependence involved would also be a factor to consider.

Obtaining goal commitment. If goal setting is to work, then the manager must ensure that subordinates will accept and remain committed to the goals. Simple instruction backed by positive support and an absence of threats or intimidation were enough to ensure goal acceptance in most of our studies. Subordinates must perceive the goals as fair and reasonable and they must trust management, for if they perceive the goals as no more than a means of exploitation, they will be likely to reject the goals.

It may seem surprising that goal acceptance was achieved so readily in the field studies. Remember, however, that in all cases the employees were receiving wages or a salary (although these were not necessarily directly contingent on goal attainment). Pay in combination with the supervisor's benevolent authority and supportiveness were sufficient to bring about goal acceptance. Recent research indicates that whether goals are assigned or set participatively, supportiveness on the part of the immediate superior is critical. A supportive manager or supervisor does not use goals to threaten subordinates, but rather to clarify what is expected of them. His or her role is that of a helper and goal facilitator.

Providing support elements. A third step to take when introducing goal setting is to ensure the availability of necessary support elements. That is, the employee must be given adequate resources – money, equipment, time, help – as well as the freedom to utilize them in attaining goals, and company policies must not work to block goal attainment.

CONCLUSION

We believe that goal setting is a simple, straightforward, and highly effective technique for motivating employee performance. It is a basic technique, a method on which most other methods depend for their motivational effectiveness. The currently popular technique of behavior modification, for example, is mainly goal setting plus feedback, dressed up in academic terminology.

However, goal setting is no panacea. It will not compensate for under-payment of employees or for poor management. Used incorrectly, goal setting may cause rather than solve problems. If, for example, the goals set are unfair, arbitrary, or unreachable, dissatisfaction and poor performance may result. If difficult goals are set without proper quality controls, quantity may be achieved at the expense of quality. If pressure for immediate results is exerted without regard to how they are attained, short-term improvement may occur at the expense of long-run profits. That is, such pressure often triggers the use of expedient and ultimately costly methods – such as dishonesty, high-pressure tactics, postponing of maintenance expenses, and so on – to attain immediate results. Furthermore, performance goals are more easily set in some areas than in others. It's all too easy, for example, to concentrate on setting readily measured production goals and ignore employee development goals. Like any other management tool, goal setting works only when combined with good managerial judgement.

REFERENCE

Locke, E. A. (1968), 'Toward a theory of task motivation and incentives', *Organizational Behavior and Human Performance*, 3, 157–89.

17

GERALD R. SALANCIK AND JEFFREY PFEFFER

An Examination of Need-Satisfaction Models of Job Attitudes

Abridged from G. R. Salancik and J. Pfeffer, 'An examination of need-satisfaction models of job attitudes', *Administrative Science Quarterly*, Vol. 22, 1977, pp. 427–56.

One of the most prominent areas of study in organizational behavior is job attitudes, or how people feel about what they do when they work. This interest in job satisfaction persists to attract research attention. Affective responses to job conditions are the bases for several different organizational development strategies (Bowers, 1973) and an important component of recent interest in work and job design (Hackman & Suttle, 1977).

It is fair to state that a need-satisfaction model has been the theoretical framework almost universally applied to understand job satisfaction and, occasionally, motivation.

The need-satisfaction model, in its basic structure, is quite simple. The model posits that persons have basic, stable, relatively unchanging and identifiable attributes, including needs (and personality (Argyris, 1957)). The model also assumes that jobs have a stable, identifiable set of characteristics that are relevant to those needs of individuals. Job attitudes and, occasionally, motivation are presumed to result from the correspondence between the needs of the individual and the characteristics of the job or the job situation. When the characteristics of the job are compatible with the person's needs, the assumption is made that the person is satisfied and, on occasion, the further argument is made that the person will be more motivated to perform the job. Jobs which fulfill a person's needs are satisfying; those that do not are not satisfying. If the person is satisfied with his job, it is presumably because the job has characteristics compatible with his needs. If the person is unhappy with his job, it is because the job is presumably not satisfying his needs.

IMPLICATIONS OF NEED-SATISFACTION MODELS FOR MANAGEMENT

Models of job attitudes historically have been developed to enable organizational managers to manipulate job attitudes, and through job attitudes, motivation and performance to enhance the outcomes achieved by the organization (Gallagher & Einhorn, 1976). This initial interest in the attitudes of workers to work settings has persisted. While the rationale used to justify the interest in job attitudes has changed over time, three concerns can be identified. The first concern assumed that, by providing for the satisfaction of workers, one could increase their motivation and, holding ability constant, their performance on the job. From Brayfield and Crockett's (1955) early review of the satisfaction–performance literature, through Vroom's (1964) review, to the review by Schwab and Cummings (1970), the link beween satisfaction and performance has been hard to discern, and it is generally accepted currently that job satisfaction does not inevitably cause higher job performance. Indeed, Lawler and Porter (1967) have explicitly postulated that the reverse causal ordering may be true.

But, the satisfaction–performance link is apparently a theoretically compelling one, because it has recently begun to recur, though in a slightly different guise, to provide a second justification for job attitude research. Proceeding from an expectancy theory framework (Vroom, 1964), researchers have argued that: (1) an individual will engage in a behavior to the extent that he believes he can obtain a valued outcome; (2) outcomes are valued to the extent they satisfy needs; (3) employees will tend to work hard if conditions at work are arranged so that by working hard, the employees' needs will be satisfied; and (4) individuals will experience need satisfaction when they learn that they have accomplished something (Hackman & Lawler, 1971, p. 262). These authors, therefore, argued that 'higher-order need satisfactions . . . are seen both as (a) a result of [rather than a determinant of] effective performance . . . and (b) an incentive for continued efforts to perform effectively' (1971, p. 263). Hackman and Lawler have identified motivation with the satisfaction of higher-order needs, and therefore can list motivation and satisfaction together (1971, p. 273) as outcomes or employee reactions to job characteristics. Need satisfaction, an attitude, becomes identified with motivation, and through motivation, with performance (Oldham, 1976).

A third justification for the interest in job attitudes makes fewer direct links with performances and motivation. Recently, there has been concern with the satisfaction of workers because of social concern for the quality of working life (Hackman & Suttle, 1977). This concern is epitomized in the United States government's report *Work in America*. Work organizations because of their pervasive impact on members of society, it argues, have an obligation to ensure the mental health of those who work for them. Work can be a cause of role stress and tension (Kahn, et al., 1964) and alienation (Blauner, 1964). Since society is interested in the quality of life in general, it has an interest in the specific quality of work life apart from any immediate interest in productivity or profits.

The need-satisfaction model makes two recommendations for how job attitudes can be managed. The first recommendation is to select those individuals with needs appropriate to the job characteristics. While this is clearly one implication of the need-satisfaction model, it is not a course of action frequently recommended. Some authors, such as Argyris (1957), believe that all normal, healthy, adult personalities have similar requirements in terms of work characteristics and that, therefore, it is not right to find maladjusted or deficient persons to work at jobs that fit those characteristics. A strong normative orientation guides much of this literature about what are appropriate job characteristics and what are appropriate needs. The idea of finding persons with appropriate needs to fill jobs lacking in variety, autonomy, or feedback, while consistent with the model, is inconsistent with the normative orientation of most of its proponents.

The second strategy, and the one most frequently advocated, is to design jobs that have characteristics which are satisfying to the needs of the individuals. Programs of job extension, job enrichment, and job enlargement are all applications of the need-satisfaction model. Each tends to define job design in terms of the need-satisfaction model: '. . . specifications of the contents, methods, and relationship of jobs in order to satisfy technological and organizational requirements as well as the social and personal requirements of the job holder' (Rush, 1971, p. 5). Alderfer (1969a) reported on the successful implementation of a job-enlargement program, and Lawler (1969) reviewed literature indicating that job enlargement was successful particularly in increasing the quality, though not the amount, of production. Job design as a strategy to improve motivation, and through motivation, job performance, was advocated by Herzberg (1966) and has been an increasingly important focus of organizational development efforts. In this context, job design can be seen as an extension of other efforts to redesign the conditions of the workplace to enhance employee satisfaction. Such redesigns have occasionally focused on supervisory style and leadership behavior. Once again, with only limited success from this research, the attention has shifted to emphasize the objective content of the work and focus less on contextual factors such as the supervisor–employee relationship.

The implications of the need-satisfaction model for the management of job attitudes are, of course, logical consequences of the basic assumptions of the model. Thus, a model that posits stable needs and fixed job characteristics leads only to strategies of either matching needs with characteristics or changing characteristics of the job to fit the needs of the job holders. Since assumptions made about how job attitudes develop are critical to determining the strategies used to change such attitudes, it is necessary to test these assumptions occasionally and abandon them when they do not hold. To refute an assumption, however, one must attempt to violate it. This procedure is not often followed by researchers; more often, the search is for support of beliefs than tests of their validity.

If one's assumptions become more flexible about the permanence of needs and the reality of job characteristics, a variety of strategies for managing job attitudes becomes possible. Some of the strategies include: (1) redesigning or changing people to have different needs (as in socialization or consciousness-raising); (2) affecting a person's awareness, comprehension, or interpretation of job characteristics; (3) altering the context of the job to develop desired attitudes; (4) affecting the relationship of the person to the job (such as expected length of tenure, or degree of commitment) to obtain desired attitudes; or (5) affecting behavior or the conditions of behavior to provoke, create, or change attitudes. The evidence for the effectiveness of such strategies is precisely evidence against the assumptions associated with the need-satisfaction model, and, therefore, evidence that invalidates the model.

In suggesting that there are a variety of alternate strategies for affecting job attitudes we are, of course, not suggesting anything about the value or feasibility of changing attitudes through job redesign. Indeed, for reasons not related to the need-satisfaction model, we suspect that job redesign would affect job attitudes. But that fact alone does not indicate the relative merit of need-satisfaction models, as other conceptualizations could be equally compatible with such a result. Consistent evidence alone cannot validate a model, if the evidence is also consistent with alternative theories.

VERSIONS OF THE NEED-SATISFACTION MODEL

The basic need-satisfaction model is largely an outgrowth of Maslow's (1943, 1954) theory of human needs [see Reading 2]. Maslow asserted that human motives emerge sequentially according to a hierarchy of five need levels: (1) physiological needs, (2) safety needs, (3) affiliation needs, (4) achievement and esteem needs, and (5) self-actualization. Maslow further argued that the satisfied need was not a motivator of behavior. Thus, the importance of higher needs increases as lower needs become satisfied and decrease. Maslow (1970, Chapter 6) claimed that this need hierarchy was instinctual, or that such needs could be almost universally observed, even in different cultures. Maslow's theory of human needs formed the basis for Porter's (1962) need-deficiency scales, and is probably the theory most commonly known to managers and others.

In spite of the central position of Maslow's need theory, it has been subjected to slight empirical testing; the tests that have been conducted have, in general, failed to support the theory. Hall and Nougaim (1968) found little evidence for Maslow's original hierarchy or their revised, two-level hierarchy. While the authors did find that as managers advanced, safety needs became less important while higher-order needs were more important, Hall and Nougaim argued that might be explained by a process of career change and advancement. Wahba and Bridwell (1976) recently reviewed ten factor-analytic and three ranking studies examining Maslow's need hierarchy, and concluded that the concept of a need hierarchy was only partially supported.

Alderfer (1969b) attempted to redefine Maslow's need hierarchy into three needs: existence, relatedness, and growth. Alderfer's theory was less insistent on the hierarchical arrangement of the need categories, and was somewhat more consistent with the data than Maslow's theory. Alderfer and Argyris (1957) shared the belief with Maslow that need structures were virtually universal among individuals. Argyris was willing to define mental health or normal personality growth in terms of a universal standard based on the emergence of higher-order needs.

Herzberg, Mausner, and Snyderman (1959) redefined needs into two categories, which they labeled as 'hygienes' and 'motivators'. They advanced the interesting thesis that satisfaction and dissatisfaction were not just opposite ends of a single continuum. While the absence of hygienes could make employees unhappy, merely furnishing ever more hygienes, such as pay, air conditioning, pleasant working conditions, and vacation, could not provide additional motivation. For there to be additional motivation, the critical variable was the nature of the work itself. While this study has been subjected to extensive, and well-deserved, methodological criticism (Dunnette, Campbell, & Hakel, 1967; Hinton, 1968; King, 1970; Schneider & Locke, 1971) and is currently regarded as theoretically weak, it was one of the first attempts to draw the distinction between intrinsic and extrinsic motivation, a distinction which has drawn increasing research attention (Staw, 1976). Herzberg shared with Maslow, Argyris, and Alderfer the belief that need structures were rather universally distributed.

The repeated failures to find empirical support for theories of universal human needs (Turner & Lawrence, 1965; Hulin & Blood, 1968) led to an acceptance of the idea that different individuals had different needs, or at least differing strengths of the same needs. The current research on job satisfaction and job redesign generally proceeds from the premise that different individuals have different need strengths and, therefore, will respond differently to the same job characteristics (Hackman & Lawler, 1971). The research examining the moderating effect of need strength on the relation between job satisfaction and job features has been equivocal. White and Ruh (1973) found no relation between workers' values and favorable attitudes toward parts of the job. Umstot, Bell, and Mitchell (1976) found no differences between the attitude–job correlations for individuals with presumed high- and low-need strengths; Oldham, Hackman, and Pearce (1976) found only partial support for this moderating role of need strength.

Another possible modification to need-satisfaction theories has been proposed, however, which does not necessarily require the rejection of the idea of universal human needs. Argyris (1973) argued that different individuals, although sharing the same needs, come to expect different things from their jobs. Individuals with an instrumental orientation look on the job as a means toward another end, such as making sufficient money to do things they really enjoy. Those persons with an expressive orientation toward work tend to attempt to find fulfillment of higher-order needs, such as esteem and self-actualization, on the job. Strauss (1974) focused on this distinction in criticizing need-satisfaction models, arguing that jobs serve different needs for different people. Note that this supposed criticism of the need-satisfaction formulation is not much of a radical revision. Persons still have needs, and jobs still have characteristics, but now there has been some movement toward the position that, perhaps persons have different needs, or, alternatively, persons look on their jobs for different satisfactions. O'Reilly (1977) attempted an empirical examination of the different work-orientations idea distinguishing between those who perceive work as an instrumental activity in contrast to those who perceive it as an expressive activity. While the hypothesized interaction between orientation toward work and the relationship between job characteristics and job attitudes was found, it accounted for only 1 per cent of the variance in job attitudes. Furthermore, this formulation does not describe how different individuals develop different orientations toward work.

Expectancy theories (Hackman & Lawler, 1971; Mitchell & Biglan, 1971) are the natural outgrowth of this progression of research. Most current research on job satisfaction, motivation, and job design proceeds from an expectancy-theory formulation. Expectancy theories admit the possibility that individuals may have different goals or needs, and that individuals may perceive different connections between actions and their achievement of these goals. By permitting individual differences in both need and perceptions, the expectancy-theory formulation is quite flexible. Yet, even this formulation retains the questionable premise that people have needs and jobs have characteristics.

The evolution of thinking about job attitudes and needs has followed a course from assumptions about the universality of humans to adopt positions that permit more and more contingencies and individual differences. The flexibility in the need-satisfaction model has been bought, however, at the cost of theoretical elegance and precision. Job satisfaction became increasingly contingent and difficult to predict. First, it became contingent on the person's particular needs. Then, it became simultaneously contingent on a person's expectations from the job, whether work is viewed as an instrumental or expressive activity. Again, it became contingent on a person's perceptions of the connections between job activities and characteristics and that person's satisfaction. While no studies have attempted to take these various contingencies into account simultaneously, it is clear that these modifications made to fit the need-satisfaction model with empirically described reality have weakened its one great strength, the intuitive appeal of its simplicity.

THE POPULARITY OF NEED-SATISFACTION MODELS

The need-satisfaction model, in one of its versions, is virtually ubiquitous in writing about job attitudes. To reduce the hold of a need-satisfaction perspective, one must first understand some of its sources of persistence as a theoretical framework for thinking about persons in the work situation.

Need-satisfaction models are consistent with other models of human behavior that promote beliefs about human rationality. As Mitchell and Biglan (1971) noted, expectancy models are to be found not only in organizational behavior but also in marketing, in the studies of attitudes

(Fishbein, 1963), and in theories of rational decision making (Edwards, 1959). The need-satisfaction model is similar to the rational–economic man model of decision making, which argues that people make decisions consistent with the extent to which choice alternatives satisfy or do not satisfy their preferences or self-interest. By suggesting that individuals develop preferences according to the manner in which states of the world satisfy their needs, it is suggested that individual responses are rationally linked to the environment. The idea suggests that people pursue their interests and shape their behavior and attitudes to achieve their goals. Thus, the underlying structure of need-satisfaction models presumes rational action. In this, they are consistent in important respects with other models of rational choice.

Need-satisfaction models also have the benefit of attributing potency and freedom to individuals. The idea that individuals shape their actions to satisfy their needs gives individual activity purpose and direction. While a person is, to some extent, a captive to his needs, he is pictured as directing activities according to his needs, and potentially, choosing situations in which his needs will be more or less well met. A person has the freedom to decide and, through his decisions, to attain need satisfaction.

Although need-satisfaction models apparently attribute freedom to an individual, in one important respect they also deny a person freedom to behave. Implicit in the idea that a person is motivated to satisfy his needs is that needs serve as inevitable determinants of action. Maslow (1943) even speaks of self-actualizing behavior as a somewhat compulsive thing, as musicians who *must* make music, and artists who *must* paint. Such a formulation provides a ready explanation for behavior – I had to do it – and can aid in maintaining the behaviors in the face of negative reactions about their worth or acceptability. In other words, needs make it acceptable not to change. Children who fail at a task have been found to avoid trying further if they attribute their failure to unchangeable personal characteristics (Dweck, 1975). Thus needs, by providing explanations for behavior, help to stabilize individual action and provide continuity.

Need-satisfaction models offer the further advantage of being simple, easily expressed views of human behavior. And, as with most persistent theories, need-satisfaction models, if carefully formulated, are almost impossible to disprove, and can provide an explanation for behavior that is almost as pervasive as the idea of motivation (Weick, 1969). Needs, used for explanation by scientists and lay people alike, are indeed a seductive concept.

THEORETICAL DIFFICULTIES CONFRONTING
NEED-SATISFACTION MODELS

When the principal features of the need-satisfaction model were outlined, an allusion was made to some conceptual ambiguities facing this perspective, such as the calculus by which needs, job characteristics, and attitudes were interrelated. The major theoretical problems confronting need-satisfaction models, however, have to do with the two basic components of these models, the concepts of needs and job characteristics. Given the relatively large number of studies devoted to job attitudes, it is reasonable to expect that the theoretical problems inherent in the use of concepts such as needs and job characteristics would have been addressed long ago. Such is not the case, and any critique of the model must proceed from an examination of these two major building blocks.

The concept of needs

The concept of needs is a concept that has been widely used in psychology. One irreverent observer has commented that psychologists must have a need to construct lists of needs. The idea of needs is one of the basic foundations of the need-satisfaction model. Whether the needs are arranged in a hierarchy, in categories, are widely distributed through the population, are acquired in childhood or are instinctual, need-satisfaction models all assume that persons have needs. Most models assert hypotheses about needs as if these hypotheses were established truths, and then move quickly on to the interesting problem of the interrelationship of needs, jobs, and attitudes.

Such a cavalier attitude is scarcely warranted. The concept of needs may be potentially misleading and unnecessary for the development of theories of human behavior. The first question to be asked about needs is their origin. As noted, some believe that virtually all needs are instinctual (for example, Maslow, 1970), and most psychologists believe that at least some needs are instinctual. If some needs are instinctual and some are learned, then an interesting issue becomes which needs are acquired and which are inherent. One general finding of the research on the concept of instinct is that the further the inquiries progress, less tends to be attributed to instinct. Such is the case with the concept of human needs as well. Even the presumably basic human needs such as hunger, thirst, and sex are, in part, socially conditioned, as is evidenced from the research on obesity and human sexual dysfunctions. It is difficult to maintain the position that needs, particularly higher-order needs, are instinctual in the face of little evidence for the generality of needs (Turner & Lawrence, 1965; Hulin & Blood, 1968) and of the convincing social learning literature (Bandura, 1969) which argues that most behavioral dispositions are acquired through learning.

Needs must be relatively stable if they are to have any explanatory power over time, and, therefore, theorists who do argue that needs are learned tend to argue that such learning occurs early in a person's life. For example, McClelland (1961) believed that the need for achievement could be inculcated to affect future economic development in a nation, and even undertook programs in developing nations to change the level of the need for achievement. Yet, McClelland stressed the inculcation of this need in childhood, and did not address the issue of the extent to which the need for achievement varies over short periods during a person's adult life. In this case, it is difficult to distinguish between needs and cultural expectations for behavior.

An additional difficulty with the learned-needs concept is to be found in the idea that such learning is terminated relatively early in life. Operant conditioning has been used on persons of all ages, and there is little theoretical justification for believing that learning terminates at pubescence. As long as there is some possibility that learning continues, including the learning of needs, then need models must attempt to incorporate changes in needs and acknowledge the cause of such changes over time.

But, the concept of needs faces an even great problem than the mystery of origin and development. The descriptions of the needs most frequently used to explain job-related behavior are frequently ambiguous. This is the case with Maslow's arrangement of need hierarchy. The sequence in which the needs are activated also represents a sequence of increasing ambiguity and indefiniteness. The basic physiological needs of hunger and thirst are well defined. Deprivation can be measured and metered physiologically, and, more importantly, there are precise objects associated with need satisfaction. Such precision in definition is lost as the need hierarchy is ascended. Self-actualization is a concept so poorly articulated that there continue to be debates about its essential properties: Is it an ever increasing need or can it be satisfied like the lower-order needs? What is the precise distinction between self-actualization and esteem (competence needs)? Is self-actualization the most intrinsically controlled need? To the extent that needs are loosely defined, it becomes difficult to do research that has any chance of refuting their applicability. The ambiguity of need concepts facilitates the finding of support for the need-satisfaction model. It is much easier to find empirical support for a concept which is vague.

The concept of job characteristics

Needs are related to attitudes through the experience of the individual on the job. Thus, theories of need satisfaction must define jobs in terms of characteristics that could then be related somehow to need satisfaction. There have been two major approaches to developing job characteristics – asking people directly about what makes them happy, and hypothesizing about what should make them happy.

Herzberg, Mausner, and Snyderman's (1959) approach was to ask people to describe what made them feel good and what did not make them feel good about their job. When people described what they liked about work, they tended to use concepts relating to accomplishment, achievement, and personal growth. When they described what they disliked about their job, they tended to use concepts such as poor pay, company rules, working conditions, and characteristics of the supervisor. The generalization Herzberg, Mausner, and Snyderman drew, though not perfectly consistent with the data they reported, was that persons tended to describe good feelings toward factors intrinsic to themselves or toward their work activities, while bad feelings were due to things outside of themselves or their immediate job. This tendency is similar to the common attributional phenomenon of attributing success to personal causes and failure to external causes as noted by Weiner and Sierad (1975).

The second approach to developing dimensions for characterizing jobs involves proceeding from thinking of human needs and uncovering job characteristics that would appear to be, a priori, relevant to these needs. The lists of job characteristics developed have tended to emphasize the higher-order needs from Maslow's hierarchy. Turner and Lawrence (1965) developed the Requisite Task Attribute Index which included the job attributes of variety, autonomy, required interaction, optional interaction, knowledge and skill required, and responsibility. Hackman and Lawler (1971) described jobs in terms of their variety, autonomy, task identity, feedback, opportunity for dealing with others, and friendship opportunities. More recently, Hackman and Oldham (1975) developed the Job Diagnostic Survey, measuring the five dimensions of skill variety, task identity, task significance, autonomy, and feedback, as well as a dimension measuring the extent to which the job facilitates dealing with others. The important contribution of this second approach is that a theory is used to generate the list of job characteristics and therefore, can be tested. If the defined job characteristics do provide for the satisfaction of higher-order needs, then individuals with those needs should be more or less satisfied to the extent the jobs have those characteristics. This is what has been empirically found (Hackman & Lawler, 1971) to some extent.

Regardless of the strategy used to develop a list of job characteristics, there are some problems with the concept and its operationalization. First and most important, the reader should recognize that the characterization of jobs is a process. When one sees well-developed lists of job characteristics, one is tempted to take such lists as descriptions of reality and forget to ask how the lists were developed in the first place. Saying that a job has certain characteristics orients the reader and the researcher to the characteristics, and the characteristics therefore become real and meaningful. However, if one asks the question of how did particular characteristics come to be identified with a job, one recognizes that the characteristics are defined into the situation by someone. Characterization of jobs, therefore, is a process which says as much about the researcher as it does about the jobs.

The problem with the concept of job characteristics is that it must ultimately be arbitrarily defined. Inevitably, jobs can be characterized along multiple dimensions, and the choice of the dimensions used may affect what the researcher observes. The fact that job characterization is a process, providing information about the observer, also implies that job characterization is a process with information about the worker and his social context. Characteristics are imputed to jobs, and this imputation may be a consequence of a social process.

An important research task is to discover the factors which determine what selections individuals make in characterizing their jobs. We have already alluded to Herzberg's finding that attributions differ when outcomes differ. Research from cognitive psychology and dissonance theory shows different factors affect the perceptions of the environment. To the extent that job dimensions are cognitively constructed and behaviorally enacted (Weick, 1976), additional research on the processes is required to understand individual behaviors in work settings.

REFERENCES

Alderfer, C. P. (1969a), 'Job enlargement and the organizational context', *Personnel Psychology*, *22*, 418–26.

Alderfer, C. P. (1969b), 'An empirical test of a new theory of human needs', *Organizational Behavior and Human Performance*, *4*, 142–75.

Argyris, C. (1957), *Personality and Organization*, New York: Harper.

Argyris, C. (1973), 'Personality and organization theory revisited', *Administration Science Quarterly*, *18*, 141–67.

Bandura, A. (1969), *Principles of Behavior Modification*, New York: Holt, Rinehart & Winston.

Blauner, R. (1964), *Alienation and Freedom*, Chicago: University of Chicago Press.

Bowers, D. G. (1973), 'OD techniques and their results in 23 organizations: the Michigan ICL study', *Journal of Applied Behavioral Science, 9*, 21–43.

Brayfield, A. H., & Crockett, W. H. (1955), 'Employee attitudes and employee performance', *Psychological Bulletin, 52*, 396–424.

Dunnette, M. D., Campbell, J. P., & Hakel, M. D. (1967), 'Factors contributing to job satisfaction and dissatisfaction in six occupational groups', *Organizational Behavior and Human Performance, 2*, 143–74.

Dweck, C. S. (1975), 'The role of expectations and attributions in the alleviation of learned helplessness', *Journal of Personality and Social Psychology, 31*, 674–85.

Edwards, W. (1959), 'The theory of decision making', *Psychological Bulletin, 51*, 380–414.

Fishbein, M. (1963), 'An investigation of the relationship between beliefs about an object and the attitude toward that object', *Human Relations, 16*, 233–40.

Gallagher, W. E., Jr, & Einhorn, H. J. (1976), 'Motivation theory and job design', *Journal of Business, 49*, 358–73.

Hackman, J. R., & Lawler, E. E., III (1971), 'Employee reactions to job characteristics', *Journal of Applied Psychology, 55*, 259–86.

Hackman, J. R., & Oldham, G. R. (1975), 'Development of the job diagnostic survey', *Journal of Applied Psychology, 60*, 159–70.

Hackman, J. R., & Suttle, J. L. (1977), *Improving Life at Work: Behavioral Science Approaches to Organizational Change*, Santa Monica, Calif.: Goodyear.

Hall, D. T. & Nougaim, K. E. (1968), 'An examination of Maslow's need hierarchy in an organizational setting', *Organizational Behavior and Human Performance, 3*, 12–35.

Herzberg, F. (1966), *Work and the Nature of Man*, Cleveland, Ohio: World.

Herzberg, F., Mausner, B., and Bloch Snyderman, B. (1959), *The Motivation to Work*, New York: Wiley.

Hinton, B. L. (1968), 'An empirical investigation of the Herzberg methodology and two-factor theory', *Organizational Behavior and Human Performance, 3*, 286–309.

Hulin, C. L., & Blood, M. R. (1968), 'Job enlargement, individual differences, and worker responses', *Psychological Bulletin, 69*, 41–55.

Kahn, R. L., Wolfe, D. M., Quinn, R. P., Snoek, J. D., & Rosenthal, R. A. (1964), *Organizational Stress*, New York: Wiley.

King, N. (1970) 'A clarification and evaluation of the two-factor theory of job satisfaction', *Psychological Bulletin, 74*, 18–31.

Lawler, E. E., III (1969), 'Job design and employee motivation', *Personnel Psychology, 22*, 426–35.

Lawler, E. E., III, & Porter, L. W. (1967), 'Antecedent attitudes of effective managerial performance', *Organizational Behavior and Human Performance, 2*, 122–42.

McClelland, D. C. (1961), *The Achieving Society*, Princeton, NJ: Van Nostrand.

Maslow, A. H. (1943), 'A theory of human motivation', *Psychological Review, 50*, 370–96.

Maslow, A. H. (1954), *Motivation and Personality*, New York: Harper.

Maslow, A. H. (1970), *Motivation and Personality*, 2nd edn, New York: Harper and Row.

Mitchell, T. R., & Biglan, A. (1971), 'Instrumentality theories: Current uses in psychology', *Psychological Bulletin, 76*, 432–54.

Oldham, G. R. (1976), 'Job characteristics and internal motivation: The moderating effect of interpersonal and individual variables', *Human Relations, 29*, 559–69.

Oldham, G. R., Hackman, J. R., & Pearce, J. L. (1976), 'Conditions under which employees respond positively to enriched work', *Journal of Applied Psychology, 61*, 395–403.

O'Reilly, C. A. (1977), 'Personality-job fit: implications for individual attitudes and performance', *Organizational Behavior and Human Performance*, *18*, 36–46.

Porter, L. W. (1962), 'Job attitudes in management: 1. Perceived deficiencies in need fulfillment as a function of job level', *Journal of Applied Psychology*, *46*, 375–84.

Rush, H. M. F. (1971), *Job Design for Motivation*, New York: The Conference Board.

Schneider, J., & Locke, E. A. (1971), 'A critique of Herzberg's incident classification system and a suggested revision', *Organizational Behavior and Human Performance*, *6*, 441–57.

Schwab, D. P., & Cummings, L. L. (1970), 'Theories of performance and satisfaction: A review', *Industrial Relations*, *9*, 408–30.

Staw, B. M. (1976), *Intrinsic and Extrinsic Motivation*, Morristown, NJ: General Learning Press.

Strauss, G. (1974), 'Job satisfaction, motivation, and job redesign', in G. Strauss, R. E. Miles, C. C. Snow, & A. S. Tannenbaum (eds.), *Organizational Behavior: Research and Issues: 19–49*, Madison, Wis.: Industrial Relations Research Association.

Turner, A. N., & Lawrence, P. R. (1965), *Industrial Jobs and the Worker*, Boston, Mass.: Harvard Graduate School of Business Administration.

Umstot, D. D., Bell, C. H., Jr, & Mitchell, T. R. (1976), 'Effects of job enrichment and task goals on satisfaction and productivity: Implications for job design', *Journal of Applied Psychology*, *61*, 379–94.

Vroom, V. (1964), *Work and Motivation*, New York: Wiley.

Wahba, M. A., & Bridwell, L. G. (1976), 'Maslow reconsidered: A review of research on the need hierarchy theory', *Organizational Behavior and Human Performance*, *15*, 212–40.

Weick, K. E. (1969), *The Social Psychology of Organizing*, Reading, Mass.: Addison-Wesley.

Weick, K. E. (1976), 'Educational organizations as loosely coupled systems', *Administrative Science Quarterly*, *21*, 1–19.

Weiner, B., & Sierad, J. (1975) 'Misattribution for failure and enhancement of achievement strivings', *Journal of Personality and Social Psychology*, *31*, 415–21.

White, J. K., & Ruh, R. A. (1973), 'The effects of personal values on the relationship between participation and job attitudes', *Administrative Science Quarterly*, *18*, 506–14.

18

BARRY M. STAW AND JERRY ROSS

Stability in the Midst of Change: A Dispositional Approach to Job Attitudes

Abridged from B. M. Staw and J. Ross, 'Stability in the midst of change: A dispositional approach to job attitudes', *Journal of Applied Psychology*, Vol. 70, 1985, pp. 469–80.

In recent years almost all research on job attitudes has been situationally based. Situational variables such as task characteristics, supervision, pay, and working conditions have been commonly isolated as determinants of job attitudes (Locke, 1976), and perceptions of these aspects of the work context are frequently aggregated into indices of job satisfaction (e.g., Quinn & Shepard, 1974; Weiss, Dawis, England, & Lofquist, 1967). Rarely, however, are job attitudes formulated as having an endogenous source of variance, one that is reflective of the ongoing state of the person as opposed to being a product of the situation.

The prevailing emphasis on situational determinants of job attitudes is probably best exemplified in the recent controversy over the effects of job design. In one camp have been job-design researchers who have posited that objective job characteristics are the major determinants of work attitudes and behavior, with improvements in job satisfaction coming as a product of job enrichment and enlargement interventions (e.g., Hackman & Oldham, 1976, 1980; Lawler, 1982). In a second camp have been researchers who have taken a social information processing perspective, arguing that job attitudes can be altered by social influence and contextual cues (e.g., Salancik & Pfeffer, 1977, 1978; O'Reilly & Caldwell, 1979; White & Mitchell, 1979). Although these two approaches are generally considered to be diametrically opposed, it should be recognized that they both emphasize the role of situational forces on job attitudes. Although job-design researchers often use individual characteristics as a moderating variable, neither the job design nor the information processing perspectives recognize that work attitudes can be directly affected by dispositional variables.

The confrontation between social information processing and more traditional job-design approaches has contributed to two recent shifts in theories about how people react to work environments. The first change has been greater emphasis on subjective factors that can condition work attitudes, leading to a more malleable model of job satisfaction. The second shift has been a greater emphasis on situational rather than personal determinants of job attitudes. Need-based theories of job attitudes have come under severe criticism (Salancik & Pfeffer, 1977), and, as a result, the field's approach to job satisfaction has moved from models positing some interaction of the person and environment toward greater situational determinism.

The research reported here takes a dispositional rather than situational approach to job satisfaction. We will argue that in criticizing need-based theories the field may have underestimated the contribution of dispositional determinants.

DISPOSITIONAL APPROACH

The dispositional approach involves the measurement of personal characteristics and the assumption that such measures can aid in explaining individual attitudes and behavior. Although distinctions are sometimes made between the concepts of *personal dispositions*, *traits*, *personality*, and *individual characteristics*, these terms are used almost interchangeably in the literature. Each of these terms is based on a set of common assumptions: that it is possible to characterize people on certain dimensions, that these dimensions have some stability over time, and that these dimensions are useful in predicting individual behavior across situations.

Dispositional concepts have been criticized on many grounds, but the most telling has been Mischel's (1968) argument that personality scales or traits have accounted for little variance in human action across situations. Recently, however, several counter-arguments have been made in defense of personality determinants of behavior. Bem and Allen (1974) have noted that the behavior of some but not all individuals is consistent across situations. Block (1977) has noted that in-depth assessments of personality by trained specialists are much more predictive than the paper-and-pencil measures of traits that are commonly used. McGowan and Gormly (1976) and Aries, Gold, and Weigel (1983) have noted that personality traits are more predictive of multiple instances of behavior than behavior in a single situation. Monson, Hesley, and Chernick (1982) have noted that personality is more predictive of behavior in ambiguous situations than in settings where role demands are so strong that behavior is externally determined regardless of personal dispositions. And, finally, Funder and Ozer (1983) have argued that the statistical magnitude of many of the most famous situational effects (e.g., forced compliance, bystander intervention, and obedience) is no greater than that achieved by the more heavily criticized dispositional research.

The dispositional approach to predicting attitudes and behavior has also been unpopular in organizational research. Aside from its use in personnel selection (Dunnette, 1976), the assessment of personality traits and other individual characteristics has usually been relegated to the back of questionnaires designed principally to demonstrate situational relationships. Weiss and Adler (1984) have argued that personality effects have not explained a great deal of variance in organizational psychology because they have seldom been the focus of research or the product of serious theorizing. Off-the-shelf measures of personality have typically been included in cross-sectional surveys and experiments so as to explain some additional variance in situational behavior. But, seldom have situational variables been specifically chosen or manipulated so as to develop the construct validity of personality dimensions. Nor have there been many longitudinal studies devoted to understanding when and under what conditions individual dispositions will best explain attitudes or behavior. As noted by Weiss and Adler, because we have put our theoretical energies and research skills into demonstrating the influence of situational factors, it is little wonder that situational explanations have appeared so much more robust than dispositional effects.

A DISPOSITIONAL APPROACH TO JOB ATTITUDES

A dispositional formulation of job attitudes could take many forms. Research could be directed toward the study of transitory moods and how they affect individual reactions to job characteristics; toward stable individual characteristics and how they may influence job attitudes over time; or toward the interaction of individual and job characteristics. Although the crucial aspect of dispositional approaches is the search for coherence rather than consistency in individual responses over time (Magnusson & Endler, 1977; Terborg, 1981; Schneider, 1983), this article will investigate one of the most parsimonious of the dispositional approaches. We will hypothesize that there are stable individual characteristics that predispose people to respond positively or negatively to job contexts. We will also hypothesize that the predisposition to like or dislike jobs can be as important a determinant of job attitudes as the content of the work itself.

The hypothesis that individuals may have stable predispositions toward jobs can be drawn from a number of theoretical formulations. One rather radical possibility is that job attitudes may reflect a biologically based trait that predisposes individuals to see positive or negative content in their lives (cf. Buss, Plomin, & Willerman, 1973; Thomas, Chess, & Birch, 1970). Differences in individual temperament (Buss & Plomin, 1975), ranging from clinical depression to a very positive disposition, could influence the information individuals input, recall, and interpret within various social situations, including work. Alternatively, job attitudes could reflect a socialized or learned response to a broad class of situations. Individuals may have come to associate work positively or negatively (e.g., due to family or early job experiences), and this affective orientation may influence the way individuals react subsequently to a variety of job contexts.

The purpose of this article is not to choose among various underlying causes of personal dispositions but to explore the more general implications of a dispositional approach to job attitudes. The possibility that individuals have a positive or negative predisposition toward work implies that there may be much more continuity to job attitudes than we have previously recognized. Such continuity does not of course deny the role of situational influence, because it would be naïve to assume that individuals are unaffected by strong external stimuli, either from others or the job itself, in forming attitudes about work. However, it may be just as naïve to believe that individuals enter job contexts as blank slates, ready to be influenced by the slightest set of external cues. Thus, although individual attitudes may be determined by both dispositional and situational variables, we would argue that recent research has emphasized only half of this equation.

The possibility that there is a dispositional source of job satisfaction is at least indirectly consistent with three findings from the job attitude literature. First, research has shown substantial individual variation in the way jobs are perceived, even if formal job descriptions and tasks are relatively constant (O'Reilly, Parlette, & Bloom, 1980). The implication of this finding is that there is probably enough ambiguity in most job situations to allow individuals to interpret the context in ways that fit their own dispositions. Second, field experiments on job redesign have had only mixed success in producing long-term changes in work responses. Oldham and Hackman (1980) have argued that changes in job characteristics are often not large enough to have an effect on individuals and that competing organizational forces may mask such effects over time. However, a dispositional explanation of these same data would argue that there is consistency in individual job attitudes and that, in spite of changes in the job context, individuals may have a tendency to return to their own attitudinal equilibriums (cf. Landy, 1978).

The third source of data bearing on the dispositional approach comes from a recent study by Pulakos and Schmitt (1983). This research demonstrates that pre-employment expectations were a significant predictor of subsequent job satisfaction. The results showed that high-school students who expected jobs to be psychologically rewarding tended to be more satisfied when they were subsequently employed (nine and twenty-nine months later) than those who were originally more negative in their expectations. Thus, it appears at least possible that job satisfaction is as much a function of individual dispositions as organizational or job characteristics (cf. Blood, 1969; Schneider, 1976).

Research on consistency in attitudes

If there are dispositional characteristics that affect job attitudes, we would expect some consistency in attitudes over time. However, to date, there has been little research on the consistency of job attitudes. So far, the strongest evidence for attitudinal consistency, though not from the work context, comes from a recent study by Epstein (1979). Epstein found that the emotional experiences of individuals were highly consistent when aggregated over a large number of measurements, with the self-report of 'happy' experiences reaching a correlation of .92 between even and odd days in his sample. Epstein argued that some personal reactions to situations (e.g., feeling tired or impulsive) are less stable than others (e.g., happiness) but that much of the problem with demonstrating temporal consistency has to do with inadequate measurement. Epstein noted that consistency can be increased dramatically with an increase in the number of observations as well as data aggregation. Of course, as noted by other personality theorists, consistency might also be expected to be high when the situation has remained constant or when the context is ambiguous enough to allow personal dispositions to be manifested.

Schneider and Dachler (1978) have provided some recent evidence for consistency in attitudes about work. In a longitudinal study two JDI measurements of satisfaction were gathered over a sixteen-month time period. The results showed a strong temporal consistency in satisfaction scores (averaging .56 for managers and .58 for non-managers) and a tendency for the JDI to retain its internal factor structure over time. In discussing these results, Schneider and Dachler were uncertain whether satisfaction was best conceived as a dispositional variable in which stability coefficients should be high, or whether satisfaction is a dynamic variable for which stability coefficients should be low.

As we noted, most organizational research has at least implicitly assumed job satisfaction to be a dynamic variable that is reflective of situational change. Therefore, as an early test of the dispositional perspective it would be useful to demonstrate whether there is simple consistency in attitudes over time. Without temporal stability, dispositional researchers would be forced to search for more subtle patterns of attitude change (e.g., due to life stage) or to examine how attitudes interact with contextual changes in a way that is coherent over time (Schneider, 1983; Terborg, 1981). As a second test of the dispositional perspective, it is important to examine whether there is some consistency in attitudes across situations. Without cross-situational consistency, the dispositional argument remains subordinate to the usual contextual approach that emphasizes the environmental determination of attitudes. Finally, it is important to investigate whether attitudinal consistency is as strong a force as the effect of common situational changes. If situational changes are a stronger predictor of job attitudes than the consistency of work affect, then the dispositional explanation may be inherently weaker than the situational approach.

Method

To assess the consistency of attitudes over time, longitudinal data are needed on both job attitudes and on situational variables. One of the best available data sets for these tests of consistency is the Longitudinal Survey of Mature Men collected by the Center for Human Resource Research at Ohio State University (Center for Human Resource Research, 1977). This survey comprises a national random sample of over 5,000 men aged forty-five to fifty-nine. Data were collected over multiple waves, with the majority of the sample assessed on job satisfaction during 1966, 1969, and 1971.

The National Longitudinal Survey was designed primarily to test labor market and economic behavior hypotheses. Its measurement of job attitudes was much less sophisticated than, for example, the Minnesota Satisfaction Questionnaire (Weiss et al., 1967) or the Michigan measure of facet satisfaction (Quinn & Staines, 1979). However, the chief advantage of using the National Longitudinal Survey is its documentation of changes in the job situation. The National Longitudinal Survey documents objective changes in employer, occupation, job status and pay, whereas most surveys rely primarily on perceptions of the job situation (e.g., job challenge) that may be confounded with job attitudes.

Job attitudes were assessed by a one-item global satisfaction measure with four levels of possible response (ranging from *highly satisfied* to *highly dissatisfied*). To test for attitudinal consistency across situations, changes in the situation need to be documented in a way that is independent of the measurement of satisfaction. Situational theories of both job design and social information processing would argue that there are many potential sources of environmental influence on an individual's attitudes. Therefore, a strong test of the dispositional approach would be to examine attitudinal consistency when people have made large-scale changes in their work lives. The National Longitudinal Survey documented changes in both employer and occupation.

Data on both pay rates and job status were available in the National Longitudinal Survey. Pay rate was coded by hourly rate (or its equivalent for those employed on a salary basis), whereas status was assessed using the Duncan occupational index for the job held by the individual.

Discussion

The data on job satisfaction from the National Longitudinal Survey proved useful for testing consistency in attitudes over time and across situations. The first hypothesis, that there is a strong and significant relationship in attitudes over time, was at least partially confirmed by the data. All temporal relationships were significant, even though the magnitude of the correlations was not extremely high. Aggregating measures did improve the relationships, however, as did using a subsample of respondents who had not experienced changes in occupation or employer.

The second major hypothesis, that there would be a strong and significant relationship in attitudes across situations, was also partially confirmed. The correlations of attitudes over time were all statistically significant under conditions of maximum situational change, and these relationships were improved through the aggregation of measurement. Job and occupational changes did reduce attitudinal consistency, however. As one might expect, the greater the situational changes the lower was attitudinal consistency. Having experienced either employer or occupational changes served to reduce attitudinal consistency, while having experienced both types of situational changes reduced consistency further. Therefore, although the consistency in attitudes across situations provided support for the dispositional view of attitudes, the attenuation of relationships under situational change also provided evidence for contextual effects.

The third hypothesis, that prior attitudes will be as strong a predictor of subsequent attitudes as situational changes, was supported by the regression results. Using changes in pay and job status as situational determinants, the regression analyses showed that neither of these variables was as good a predictor of job satisfaction as the prior level of attitude. Changes in pay did predict some variance when both employer and occupation were changed, but the strength of its relationship with satisfaction was considerably less than that represented by prior job attitudes.

Situational versus dispositional effects

Despite possible limitations of the data, we believe our results show a much stronger case for dispositional effects than has been presented for many years in organizational psychology. In addition, our results did not show nearly as strong situational effects as one would predict from either the social information processing or job design perspectives. Social information processing would have predicted strong attitudinal changes from changes in job status, because status certainly implies what others in the society think of one's position. Job redesign would likewise have predicted changes in job attitudes as a consequence of greater pay and status, since these two measures would likely serve as proxies for improvements in responsibility and job challenge. Of course, using data previously collected for another purpose, we could not test whether situational effects operationalized exactly as prescribed by job design and social information processing theories might have had larger effects. Also, we did not test for the effects of *perceived* adequacy of pay and job status. One might hypothesize that changes in these variables, like the perceptional measures of task characteristics (e.g., Hackman & Oldham, 1976), would covary highly with job satisfaction. However, because job perceptions may be inherently confounded with job satisfaction (Roberts & Glick, 1981), covariation among perceived variables would *not* imply that changes in objective job situations would actually lead to attitudinal effects.

The strongest evidence for situational effects was the attenuation of attitudinal consistency across situations. The data clearly showed that both the passage of time and the presence of major changes in the work context can weaken attitudinal consistency. Still, it is difficult to conclude from the present data that situational effects will supersede attitudinal consistency in most contexts. Rarely are situational forces so great as to entail an entire change of employer as well as the occupation in which one works, yet attitudinal consistency was demonstrated under these disparate conditions.

In search of individual characteristics

The finding of cross-situational consistency in work attitudes means that there may be potentially explainable dispositional influences on job attitudes. This possibility is also underscored by a finding that was not part of our original research design. Further analysis of the National Longitudinal Survey showed that the consistency of job attitudes was as great as the consistency of items from a well-known personality scale. During the 1969 and 1971 administrations of the Survey, Rotter's (1966) Locus of Control (I/E) Scale was included in the battery of primarily economic data. The median consistency for the 11 items comprising the I/E scale was .27, with the relationship between scores on the 1969 and 1971 items ranging from .19 to .39. Over the same period of time, the job satisfaction measure correlated .42 between the 1969 and 1971 administrations. Thus, job satisfaction was at least as stable over time as one of the most widely used personality measures, thereby indicating that there may well be a dispositional source of variance in job attitudes.

REFERENCES

Aries, E. L., Gold, C., & Weigel, R. H. (1983), 'Dispositional and situational influences on dominance behavior in small groups', *Journal of Personality and Social Psychology, 44*, 779–86.

Bem, D. J., & Allen, A. (1974), 'On predicting some of the people some of the time: The search for cross-situational consistencies in behavior', *Psychological Review, 81*, 506–20.

Block, J. (1977), 'Advancing the science of personality: Paradigmatic shift or improving the quality of research?', in D. Magnusson & N. Endler (eds.), *Personality at the Crossroads: Current Issues in Interactional Psychology* (pp. 37–63), Hillsdale, NJ: Erlbaum.

Blood, M. R. (1969), 'Work values and job satisfaction', *Journal of Applied Psychology, 53*, 456–9.

Buss, A. H., & Plomin, R. A. (1975), *A Temperament Theory of Personality Development*, New York: Wiley.

Buss, A. H., Plomin, R., & Willerman, L. (1973), 'The inheritance of temperaments', *Journal of Personality, 41*, 513–24.

Center for Human Resource Research (1977), *The National Longitudinal Surveys Handbook*, Columbus, Ohio: College of Administrative Science, Ohio State University.

Dunnette, M. D. (1976), 'Aptitudes, abilities and skills' in M. Dunnette (ed.), *Handbook of Industrial and Organizational Psychology* (pp. 473–520), Chicago: Rand McNally.

Epstein, S. (1979), 'The stability of behavior: I. On predicting most of the people much of the time', *Journal of Personality and Social Psychology*, *37*, 1097–126.

Funder, D. C., & Ozer, D. J. (1983), 'Behavior as a function of the situation', *Journal of Personality and Social Psychology*, *44*, 107–12.

Hackman, J. R., & Oldham, G. R. (1976), 'Motivation through the design of work: Test of a theory', *Organizational Behavior and Human Performance*, *16*, 250–79.

Hackman, J. R., & Oldham, G. R. (1980), *Work Redesign*, Reading, Mass.: Addison-Wesley.

Landy, F. J. (1978), 'An opponent process theory of job satisfaction', *Journal of Applied Psychology*, *63*, 533-47.

Lawler, E. E., III (1982), 'Increasing worker involvement to enhance organizational effectiveness', in P. Goodman (ed.), *Change in Organizations* (pp. 280–315), San Francisco: Jossey-Bass.

Locke, E. A. (1976), 'The nature and causes of job satisfaction', in M. Dunnette (ed.), *Handbook of Industrial and Organizational Psychology* (pp. 1297–349), Chicago: Rand McNally.

McGowan, J., & Gormly, J. (1976), 'Validation of personality traits: A multicriteria approach', *Journal of Personality and Social Psychology*, *34*, 791–5.

Magnusson, D., & Endler, N. S. (1977), 'Interactional psychology: Present status and future prospects', in D. Magnusson & N. Endler (eds.), *Personality at the Crossroads: Current Issues in Interactional Psychology* (pp. 3–36), Hillsdale, NJ: Erlbaum

Mischel, W. (1968), *Personality and Assessment*, New York: Wiley.

Monson, T. C., Hesley, J. W., & Chernick, L. (1982), 'Specifying when personality traits can and cannot predict behavior: An alternative to abandoning the attempt to predict single act criteria', *Journal of Personality and Social Psychology*, *43*, 385–99.

Oldham, G. R., & Hackman, J. R. (1980), 'Work design in the organizational context', in B. Staw & L. Cummings (eds.), *Research in Organizational Behavior* (Vol. 2, pp. 247–78), Greenwich, Conn.: JAI Press.

O'Reilly, C. A., Parlette, G. N., & Bloom, J. R. (1980), 'Perceptual measures of task characteristics: The biasing effects of differing frames of reference and job attitudes', *Academy of Management Journal*, *23*, 118–31.

O'Reilly, C. A., & Caldwell, D. (1979), 'Informational influence as a determinant of perceived task characteristics and job satisfaction', *Journal of Applied Psychology*, *64*, 157–65.

Pulakos, E. D., & Schmitt, N. (1983), 'A longitudinal study of a valence model approach for the prediction of job satisfaction of new employees', *Journal of Applied Psychology*, *68*, 307–12.

Quinn, R. P., & Shepard, L. J. (1974), *The 1972–73 Quality of Employment Survey*, Ann Arbor, Mich.: Survey Research Center, University of Michigan.

Quinn, R. P., & Staines, G. L. (1979), *The 1977 Quality of Employment Survey*, Ann Arbor, Mich.: Institute for Social Research.

Roberts, K. H., & Glick, W. (1981), 'The job characteristics approach to task design: A critical review', *Journal of Applied Psychology*, *66*, 193–217.

Rotter, J. B. (1966), 'Generalized expectancies for internal and external locus of control of reinforcement', *Psychological Monographs*, *80* (1, Whole No. 609), 1–28.

Salancik, G. R., & Pfeffer, J. (1977), 'An examination of need–satisfaction models of job attitudes', *Administrative Science Quarterly*, *22*, 427–56.

Salancik, G. R., & Pfeffer, J. (1978), 'A social information processing approach to job attitudes and task design', *Administrative Science Quarterly*, *23*, 224–53.

Schneider, B. (1976), *Staffing Organizations*, Glenview, Ill.: Scott, Foresman.

Schneider, B. (1983), 'International psychology and organization behavior', in L. Cummings & B. Staw (eds.), *Research in Organizational Behavior* (Vol. 5, pp. 1–31), Greenwich, Conn.: JAI Press.

Schneider, B., & Dachler, P. H. (1978), 'A note on the stability of the job description index', *Journal of Applied Psychology*, *63*, 650–53.

Terborg, J. R. (1981), 'Interactional psychology and research on human behavior in organizations', *Academy of Management Review*, *6*, 569–76.

Thomas, A., Chess, S., & Birch, H. (1970), 'The origin of personality', *Scientific American*, *223*, 102–9.

Weiss, D. J., Dawis, R. Y., England, G. W., & Lofquist, L. H. (1967), 'Manual for the Minnesota Satisfaction Questionnaire', *Minnesota Studies in Vocational Rehabilitation* (Vol. 22), Minneapolis: University of Minnesota.

Weiss, H. M., & Adler, S. (1984), 'Personality and organizational behavior', in B. Staw & L. Cummings (eds.), *Research in Organizational Behavior* (Vol. 6, pp. 1–50), Greenwich, Conn.: JAI Press.

White, S. E., & Mitchell, T. R. (1979), 'Job enrichment versus social cues: A comparison and competitive test', *Journal of Applied Psychology*, *64*, 1–9.

19

DAVID C. McCLELLAND AND DAVID H. BURNHAM

Power Is the Great Motivator

Abridged from D. C. McClelland and D. H. Burnham, 'Power is the great motivator', *Harvard Business Review*, Vol. 54 (2), 1976, pp. 100–110.

What makes or motivates a good manager? The question is so enormous in scope that anyone trying to answer it has difficulty knowing where to begin. Some people might say that a good manager is one who is successful; and by now most business researchers and business people themselves know what motivates people who successfully run their own small businesses. The key to their success has turned out to be what psychologists call 'the need for achievement', the desire to do something better or more efficiently than it has been done before. Any number of books and articles summarize research studies explaining how the achievement motive is necessary for people to attain success on their own (e.g., McClelland, 1961; McClelland & Winter, 1969).

But what has achievement motivation got to do with good management? There is no reason on theoretical grounds why a person who has a strong need to be more efficient should make a good manager. While it sounds as if everyone ought to have the need to achieve, in fact, as psychologists define and measure achievement motivation, it leads people to behave in very special ways that do not necessarily lead to good management.

For one thing, because they focus on personal improvement, on doing things better by themselves, achievement-motivated people want to do things themselves. For another, they want concrete short-term feedback on their performance so that they can tell how well they are doing. Yet a manager, particularly one of or in a large complex organization, cannot perform all the tasks necessary for success by him or herself. Managers must manage others so that they will do things for the organization. Also, feedback on subordinates' performance may be a lot vaguer and more delayed than it would be if they were doing everything themselves.

The manager's job seems to call more for people who can influence others than for those who do things better on their own. In motivational terms, then, we might expect the successful manager to have a greater 'need for power' than need to achieve. But there must be other qualities beside the need for power that go into the makeup of a good manager. Just what these qualities are and how they interrelate is the subject of this article.

To measure the motivations of managers, good and bad, we studied a number of individual managers from different large US corporations who were participating in management workshops designed to improve their managerial effectiveness.

The general conclusion of these studies is that the top manager of a company must possess a high need for power, that is, a concern for influencing people. However, this need must be disciplined and controlled so that it is directed toward the benefit of the institution as a whole and not toward the manager's personal aggrandizement. Moreover, top managers' need for power ought to be greater than their need for being liked by people.

Now let us look at what these ideas mean in the context of real individuals in real situations and see what comprises the profile of the good manager.

MEASURING MANAGERIAL EFFECTIVENESS

First off, what does it mean when we say that a good manager has a greater need for 'power' than for 'achievement'? To get a more concrete idea, let us consider the case of Ken Briggs, a sales manager in a large US corporation who joined one of our managerial workshops. Some six or seven years ago, Ken Briggs was promoted to a managerial position at corporate headquarters, where he had responsibility for salespeople who service his company's largest accounts.

In filling out his questionnaire at the workshop, Ken showed that he correctly perceived what his job required of him, namely, that he should influence others' success more than achieve new goals himself or socialize with his subordinates. However, when asked with other members of the workshop to write a story depicting a managerial situation, Ken unwittingly revealed through his fiction that he did not share those concerns. Indeed, he discovered that his need for achievement was very high – in fact over the 90th percentile – and his need for power was very low, in about the 15th percentile. Ken's high need to achieve was no surprise – after all, he had been a very successful salesman – but obviously his motivation to influence others was much less than his job required. Ken was a little disturbed but thought that perhaps the measuring instruments were not too accurate and that the gap between the ideal and his score was not as great as it seemed.

Then came the real shocker. Ken's subordinates confirmed what his stories revealed: he was a poor manager, having little positive impact on those who worked for him. Ken's subordinates felt that they had little responsibility delegated to them, that he never rewarded but only criticized them, and that the office was not well organized, but confused and chaotic. On all three of these scales, his office rated in the 10th to 15th percentile relative to national norms.

As Ken talked the results over privately with a workshop leader, he became more and more upset. He finally agreed, however, that the results of the survey confirmed feelings he had been afraid to admit to himself or others. For years, he had been miserable in his managerial role. He now knew the reason: he simply did not want to nor had he been able to influence or manage others. As he thought back, he realized that he had failed every time he had tried to influence his staff, and he felt worse than ever.

Ken had responded to failure by setting very high standards – his office scored in the 98th percentile on this scale – and by trying to do most things himself, which was close to impossible; his own activity and lack of delegation consequently left his staff demoralized. Ken's experience is typical of those who have a strong need to achieve but low power motivation. They may become very successful salespeople and, as a consequence, may be promoted into managerial jobs for which they, ironically, are unsuited.

If achievement motivation does not make a good manager, what motive does? It is not enough to suspect that power motivation may be important; one needs hard evidence that people who are better managers than Ken Briggs do in fact possess stronger power motivation and perhaps score higher in other characteristics as well. But how does one decide who is the better manager?

Real-world performance measures are hard to come by if one is trying to rate managerial effectiveness in production, marketing, finance, or research and development. In trying to determine who the better managers were in Ken Briggs's company, we did not want to rely only on the opinions of their superiors. For a variety of reasons, superiors' judgements of their subordinates' real-world performance may be inaccurate. In the absence of some standard measure of performance, we decided that the next best index of managers' effectiveness would be the climate they create in the office, reflected in the morale of subordinates.

Almost by definition, a good manager is one who, among other things, helps subordinates feel strong and responsible, who rewards them properly for good performance, and who sees that things are organized in such a way that subordinates feel they know what they should be doing. Above all, managers should foster among subordinates a strong sense of team spirit, of pride in working as part of a particular team. If a manager creates and encourages this spirit, the subordinates certainly should perform better.

In the company Ken Briggs works for, we have direct evidence of a connection between morale and performance in the one area where performance measures are easy to come by – namely, sales. In April 1973, at least three employees from the company's sixteen sales districts filled out questionnaires that rated their office for organizational clarity and team spirit. Their scores were averaged and totaled to give an overall morale score for each office. The percentage gains or losses in sales for each district in 1973 were compared with those for 1972. The difference in sales figures by district ranged from a gain of nearly 30 per cent to a loss of 8 per cent, with a median gain of around 14 per cent. The relationship between sales and morale [was] surprisingly close. The six districts with the lowest morale early in the year showed an average sales gain of only around 7 per cent by year's end (although there was wide variation within this group), whereas the two districts with the highest morale showed an average gain of 28 per cent. When morale scores rise above the 50th percentile in terms of national norms, they seem to lead to better sales performance. In Ken Briggs's company, at least, high morale at the beginning is a good index of how well the sales division actually performed in the coming year.

And it seems very likely that the manager who can create high morale among salespeople can also do the same for employees in other areas (production, design, and so on), leading to better performance. Given that high morale in an office indicates that there is a good manager present, what general characteristics does he or she possess?

A need for power

In examining the motive scores of over fifty managers of both high and low morale units in all sections of the same large company, we found that most of the managers – over 70 per cent – were high in power motivation compared with men in general. This finding confirms the fact that power motivation is important for management. (Remember that as we use the term 'power motivation', it refers not to dictatorial behavior, but to a desire to have impact, to be strong and influential.) The better managers, as judged by the morale of those working for them, tended to score even higher in power motivation. But the most important determining factor of high morale turned out not to be how their power motivation compared to their need to achieve but whether it was higher than their need to be liked. This relationship existed for 80 per cent of the better sales managers as compared with only 10 per cent of the poorer managers. And the same held true for other managers in nearly all parts of the company.

In the research, product development, and operations divisions, 73 per cent of the better managers had a stronger need for power than a need to be liked (or what we term 'affiliation motive') as compared with only 22 per cent of the poorer managers. Why should this be so? Sociologists have long argued that, for a bureaucracy to function effectively, those who manage it must be universalistic in applying rules. That is, if they make exceptions for the particular needs of individuals, the whole system will break down.

The manager with a high need for being liked is precisely the one who wants to stay on good terms with everybody, and, therefore, is the one most likely to make exceptions in terms of particular needs. If an employee asks for time off to stay home with a sick spouse to help look after the kids, the affiliative manager, feeling sorry for the person, agrees almost without thinking.

Sociological theory and our data both argue, however, that the person whose need for affiliation is high does not make a good manager. This kind of person creates poor morale because he or she does not understand that other people in the office will tend to regard exceptions to the rules as unfair to themselves.

Socialized power

But so far our findings are a little alarming. Do they suggest that the good manager is one who cares for power and is not at all concerned about the needs of other people? Not quite, for the good manager has other characteristics which must still be taken into account.

Above all, the good manager's power motivation is not oriented toward personal aggrandizement but toward the institution which he or she serves. In another major research study, we found that the signs of controlled action or inhibition that appear when a person exercises his or her imagination in writing stories tell a great deal about the kind of power that person needs. We discovered that, if a high power motive score is balanced by high inhibition, stories about power tend to be altruistic. That is, the heroes in the story exercise power on behalf of someone else. This is the 'socialized' face of power as distinguished from the concern for personal power, which is characteristic of individuals whose stories are loaded with power imagery but which show no sign of inhibition or self-control. In our earlier study, we found ample evidence that these latter individuals exercise their power impulsively. They are ruder to other people, they drink too much, they try to exploit others sexually, and they collect symbols of personal prestige such as fancy cars or big offices.

Individuals high in power and in control, on the other hand, are more institution minded; they tend to get elected to more offices, to control their drinking, and to want to serve others. Not surprisingly, we found in the workshops that the better managers in the corporation also tend to score high on both power and inhibition.

PROFILE OF A GOOD MANAGER

Let us recapitulate what we have discussed so far and have illustrated with data from one company. The better managers we studied are high in power motivation, low in affiliation motivation, and high in inhibition. They care about institutional power and use it to stimulate their employees to be more productive. Now let us compare them with affiliative managers – those in whom the need for affiliation is higher than the need for power – and with the personal power managers – those in whom the need for power is higher than for affiliation but whose inhibition score is low.

The manager who is concerned about being liked by people tends to have subordinates who feel that they have very little personal responsibility, that organizational procedures are not clear, and that they have little pride in their work group. In short affiliative managers make so many *ad hominem* and *ad hoc* decisions that they almost totally abandon orderly procedures. Their disregard for procedure leaves employees feeling weak, irresponsible, and without a sense of what might happen next, of where they stand in relation to their manager, or even of what they ought to be doing.

The managers who are motivated by a need for personal power are somewhat more effective. They are able to create a greater sense of responsibility in their divisions and, above all, a greater team spirit. They can be thought of as managerial equivalents of successful tank commanders such as General Patton, whose own daring inspired admiration in his troops. But managers motivated by personal power are not disciplined enough to be good institution builders, and often their subordinates are loyal to them as individuals rather than to the institution they both serve. When a personal power manager leaves, disorganization often follows. His subordinates' strong group spirit, which the manager has personally inspired, deflates. The subordinates do not know what to do for themselves.

Of the managerial types, 'institutional' managers (i.e., high-power, low-affiliation, high-inhibition managers) are the most successful in creating an effective work climate. Also, these managers create high morale because they produce the greatest sense of organizational clarity and team spirit. If such a manager leaves, he or she can be more readily replaced by another manager, because the employees have been encouraged to be loyal to the institution rather than to a particular person.

Managerial styles

Since it seems undeniable that either kind of power orientation creates better morale in subordinates than a 'people' orientation, we must consider that a concern for power is essential to good management. Our findings seem to fly in the face of a long and influential tradition of organizational psychology, which insists that authoritarian management is what is wrong with most businesses in this country. Let us say frankly that we think the bogeyman of authoritarianism has in fact been wrongly used to downplay the importance of power in management. After all, management is an influence game. Some proponents of democratic management seem to have forgotten this fact, urging managers to be primarily concerned with people's human needs rather than with helping them to get things done.

But a good deal of the apparent conflict between our findings and those of other behavioral scientists in this area arises from the fact that we are talking about *motives*, and behaviorists are often talking about *actions*. What we are saying is that managers must be interested in playing the influence game in a controlled way. That does not necessarily mean that they are or should be authoritarian in action. On the contrary, it appears that power-motivated managers make their subordinates feel strong rather than weak. The true authoritarian in action would have the reverse effect, making people feel weak and powerless.

Thus another important ingredient in the profile of a manager is his or her managerial style. In the illustrative company, 63 per cent of the better managers (those whose subordinates had higher morale) scored higher on the democratic or coaching styles of management as compared with only 22 per cent of the poorer managers, a statistically significant difference. By contrast, the latter scored higher on authoritarian or coercive management styles. Since the better managers were also higher in power motivation, it seems that, in action, they express their power motivation in a democratic way, which is more likely to be effective.

To see how motivation and style interact, let us consider the case of George Prentice, a manager in the sales division of another company. George had exactly the right motive combination to be an institutional manager. He was high in the need for power, low in the need for affiliation, and high in inhibition. He exercised his power in a controlled, organized way. His stories reflected this fact. In one, for instance, he wrote, 'The men sitting around the table were feeling pretty good; they had just finished plans for reorganizing the company; the company has been beset with a number of organizational problems. This group, headed by a hard-driving, brilliant young executive, has completely reorganized the company structurally with new jobs and responsibilities . . .'

This described how George himself was perceived by the company, and shortly after the workshop he was promoted to vice-president in charge of all sales.

But George was also known to his colleagues as a monster, a tough guy who would 'walk over his grandmother' if she stood in the way of his advancement. He had the right motive combination and, in fact, was more interested in institutional growth than in personal power, but his managerial style was all wrong. Taking his cue from some of the top executives in the corporation, he told people what they had to do and threatened them with dire consequences if they didn't do it.

When George was confronted with his authoritarianism in a workshop, he recognized that this style was counterproductive – in fact, in another part of the study we found that it was associated with low morale – and he subsequently changed to acting more like a coach, which was the scale on which he scored the lowest initially. George saw more clearly that his job was not to force other people to do things but to help them to figure out ways of getting their job done better for the company.

The institutional manager
One reason it was easy for George Prentice to change his managerial style was that in his imaginative stories he was already thinking about helping others, characteristic of people with the institution-building

motivational pattern. In further examining institution builders' thoughts and actions, we found they have four major characteristics:

(1) They are more organization-minded; that is, they tend to join more organizations and to feel responsible for building up these organizations. Furthermore, they believe strongly in the importance of centralized authority.

(2) They report that they like to work. This finding is particularly interesting, because our research on achievement motivation has led many commentators to argue that achievement motivation promotes the 'Protestant work ethic'. Almost the precise opposite is true. People who have a high need to achieve like to get out of work by becoming more efficient. They would like to see the same result obtained in less time or with less effort. But managers who have a need for institutional power actually seem to like the discipline of work. It satisfies their need for getting things done in an orderly way.

(3) They seem quite willing to sacrifice some of their own self-interest for the welfare of the organization they serve. For example, they are more willing to make contributions to charities.

(4) They have a keen sense of justice. It is almost as if they feel that if people work hard and sacrifice for the good of the organization, they should and will get a just reward for their efforts.

It is easy to see how each of these four concerns helps a person become a good manager, concerned about what the institution can achieve.

Maturity

Let us consider one more fact we discovered in studying the better managers at George Prentice's company. They were more mature. Mature people can be most simply described as less egotistic. Somehow their positive self-image is not at stake in what they are doing. They are less defensive, more willing to seek advice from experts, and have a longer-range view. They accumulate fewer personal possessions and seem older and wiser. It is as if they have awakened to the fact that they are not going to live forever and have lost some of the feeling that their own personal future is all that important.

Many US businesspeople fear this kind of maturity. They suspect that it will make them less hard driving, less expansion-minded, and less committed to organizational effectiveness. Our data do not support their fears. These fears are exactly the ones George Prentice had before he went to the workshop. Afterward he was a more effective manager, not despite his loss of some of the sense of his own importance, but because of it. The reason is simple: his subordinates believed afterward that he genuinely was more concerned about the company than about himself. Where once they respected his confidence but feared him, they now trust him. Once he supported their image of him as a 'big man' by talking about the new Porsche and the new Honda he had bought; when we saw him recently he said, almost as an aside, 'I don't buy things anymore.'

REFERENCES

McClelland, D. C. (1961), *The Achieving Society*, Princeton, NJ: Van Nostrand.
McClelland, D. C., & Winter, D. (1969), *Motivating Economic Achievement*, New York: Free Press.

Making the Job More Motivating

20

EDWARD E. LAWLER, III

Job Design and Employee Motivation

Edward E. Lawler, III, 'Job design and employee motivation', *Personnel Psychology*, Vol. 22, 1969, pp. 426–35.

The psychological literature on employee motivation contains many claims that changes in job design can be expected to produce better employee job performance. Very few of these claims, however, are supported by an explanation of why changes in job design should be expected to affect performance except to indicate that they can affect employee motivation. Thus, I would like to begin by considering the *why* question with respect to job design and employee performance. That is, I want to focus on the reasons for expecting changes in job design to affect employee motivation and performance. Once this question is answered, predictions will be made about the effects on performance of specific changes in job design (e.g. job enlargement and job rotation).

A THEORY OF MOTIVATION

Basic to any explanation of why people behave in a certain manner is a theory of motivation. As Jones (1959) has pointed out, motivation theory attempts to explain 'how behavior gets started, is energized, is sustained, is directed, is stopped and what kind of subjective reaction is present in the organism'. The theory of motivation that will be used to understand the effects of job design is 'expectancy theory'. Georgopoulos, Mahoney and Jones (1957), Vroom (1964) and others have recently stated expectancy theories of job performance. The particular expectancy theory that will be used in this paper is based upon this earlier work and has been more completely described elsewhere (e.g. Lawler & Porter, 1967; Porter & Lawler, 1968). According to this theory, an employee's motivation to perform effectively is determined by two variables. The first of these is contained in the concept of an effort–reward probability. This is the individual's subjective probability that directing a given amount of effort toward performing effectively will result in his obtaining a given reward or positively valued outcome. This effort–reward probability is determined by two subsidiary subjective probabilities: the probability that effort will result in performance and the probability that performance will result in the reward. Vroom refers to the first of these subjective probabilities as an 'expectancy' and to the second as an 'instrumentality'.

The second variable that is relevant here is the concept of reward value or valence. This refers to the individual's perception of the value of the reward or outcome that might be obtained by performing effectively. Although most expectancy theories do not specify why certain outcomes have reward value, for the purpose of this paper I would like to argue that the reward value of outcomes stems from their perceived ability to satisfy one or more needs. Specifically relevant here is the list of needs suggested by Maslow that includes security needs, social needs, esteem needs and self-actualization needs.

The evidence indicates that, for a given reward, reward value and the effort–reward probability combine multiplicatively in order to determine an individual's motivation. This means that if either is low or non-existent then no motivation will be present. As an illustration of this point, consider the case of a manager who very much values getting promoted but who sees no relationship between working hard and getting promoted. For him, promotion is not serving as a motivator just as it is not for a manager who sees a close connection between being promoted and working hard but who doesn't want to be promoted. In order for motivation to be present, the manager must both value promotion and see the relationship between his efforts and promotion. Thus, for an individual reward or outcome the argument is that a multiplicative combination of its value and the appropriate effort–reward probability is necessary. However, an individual's motivation is influenced by more than one outcome. Thus, in order to determine an individual's motivation it is necessary to combine data concerned with a number of different outcomes. This can be done for an individual worker by considering all the outcomes he values and then by summing the products obtained from multiplying the value of these outcomes to him by their respective effort–reward probabilities.

According to this theory, if changes in job design are going to affect an individual's motivation they must either change the value of the outcomes that are seen to depend upon effort or positively affect the individual's beliefs about the probability that certain outcomes are dependent upon effort. The argument in this paper is that job-design changes can have a positive effect on motivation, because they can change an individual's beliefs about the probability that certain rewards will result from putting forth high levels of effort. They can do this because they have the power to influence the probability that certain rewards will be seen to result from good performance, not because they can influence the perceived probability that effort will result in good performance. Stated in Vroom's language, the argument is that job-design changes are more likely to affect the instrumentality of good performance than to affect the expectancy that effort will lead to performance.

But before elaborating on this point, it is important to distinguish between two kinds of rewards. The first type are those that are extrinsic to the individual. These rewards are part of the job situation and are given by others. Hence, they are externally mediated and are rewards that can best be thought of as satisfying lower-order needs. The second type of rewards are intrinsic to the individual and stem directly from the performance itself. These rewards are internally mediated since the individual rewards himself. These rewards can be thought of as satisfying higher-order needs such as self-esteem and self-actualization. They involve such outcomes as feelings of accomplishment, feelings of achievement and feelings of using and developing one's skills and abilities. The fact that these rewards are internally mediated sets them apart from the extrinsic rewards in an important way. It means that the connection between their reception and performance is more direct than is the connection between the reception of externally mediated rewards and performance. Hence potentially they can be excellent motivators because higher effort–reward probabilities can be established for them than can be established for extrinsic rewards. They also have the advantage that for many people rewards of this nature have a high positive value.

Job content is the critical determinant of whether employees believe that good performance on the job leads to feelings of accomplishment, growth and self-esteem. That is whether individuals will find jobs to be intrinsically motivating. Job content is important here because it serves a motive arousal function where higher-order needs are concerned and because it influences what rewards will be seen to stem from good performance. Certain tasks are more likely to arouse motives like achievement and self-actualization, and to generate among individuals who have these motives the belief that successful performance will result in outcomes that involve feelings of achievement and growth. It is precisely because changes in job content can affect the relationship between performance and the reception of intrinsically rewarding outcomes that they can have a strong influence on motivation and performance.

There appear to be three characteristics which jobs must possess if they are to arouse higher-order needs and to create conditions such that people who perform them will come to expect that good performance will lead to intrinsic rewards. The first is that the individual must receive meaningful feedback about his performance. This may well mean the individual must himself evaluate his own performance and define the kind of feedback that he is to receive. It may also mean that the person may have to work on a whole product or a meaningful part of it. The second is that the job must be perceived by the individual as requiring him to use abilities that he values in order for him to perform the job effectively. Only if an individual feels that his significant abilities are being tested by a job can feelings of accomplishment and growth be expected to result from good performance. Several laboratory studies have, in fact, shown that when people are given tasks that they see as testing their valued abilities, greater motivation does appear (e.g. Alper, 1964; French, 1955). Finally, the individual must feel he has a high degree of self-control over setting his own goals and over defining the paths to these goals. As Argyris (1964) points out, only if this condition exists will people experience psychological 'success' as a result of good performance.

Thus, it appears that the answer to the *why* question can be found in the ability of job-design factors to influence employees' perceptions of the probability that good performance will be intrinsically rewarding. Certain job designs apparently encourage the perception that it will, while others do not, and because of this job-design factors can determine how motivating a job will be.

JOB-DESIGN CHANGES

Everyone seems to agree that the typical assembly-line job is not likely to fit any of the characteristics of intrinsically motivating jobs. That is, it is not likely to provide meaningful knowledge of results, to test valued abilities or to encourage self-control. Much attention has been focused recently on attempts to enlarge assembly-line jobs, and there is good reason to believe that this can lead to a situation where jobs are more intrinsically motivating. However, many proponents of job enlargement have failed to distinguish between two different kinds of job enlargement. Jobs can be enlarged on both the horizontal dimension and the vertical dimension. The horizontal dimension refers to the number and variety of the operations that an individual performs on the job. The vertical dimension refers to the degree to which the job holder controls the planning and execution of his job and participates in the setting of organization policies. The utility man on the assembly line has a job that is horizontally but not vertically enlarged, while the worker whom Argyris (1964) suggests can participate in decision making about his job while he continues to work on the assembly line has a vertically but not a horizontally enlarged job.

The question that arises is, what kind of job enlargement is necessary if the job is going to provide intrinsic motivation? The answer that is suggested by the three factors that are necessary for a task to be motivating is that jobs must be enlarged both vertically and horizontally. It is hard to see in terms of the theory why the utility man will see more connection between performing well and intrinsic rewards than will the assembly-line worker. The utility man typically has no more self-control, only slightly more knowledge of results and only a slightly greater chance to test his valued abilities. Hence, for him, good performance should be only slightly more rewarding than it would be for the individual who works in one location on the line. In fact, it would seem that jobs can be over-enlarged on the horizontal dimension so that they will be less motivating than they were originally. Excessive horizontal enlargement may well lead to a situation where meaningful feedback is impossible and where the job involves using many additional abilities that the worker does not value. The worker who is allowed to participate in some decisions about his work on the assembly line can hardly be expected to perceive that intrinsic rewards will stem from performing well on the line. His work on the line is still not under his control, he is not likely to get very meaningful feedback about it and his valued abilities still are not being tested by it. Thus, for him it is hard to see why he should feel that intrinsic rewards will result from good performance.

On the other hand, we should expect that a job which is both horizontally and vertically enlarged will be a job that motivates people to perform well. For example, the workers who, as Kuriloff (1966) has described, make a whole electronic instrument, check and ship it should be motivated by their jobs. This kind of job does provide meaningful feedback, it does allow for self-control and there is a good chance that it will be seen as testing valued abilities. It does not, however, guarantee that the person will see it as testing his valued abilities since we don't know what the person's valued abilities are. In summary, then, the argument is that if job enlargement is to be successful in increasing motivation, it must be enlargement that affects both the horizontal and the vertical dimensions of the job. In addition, individual differences must be taken into consideration in two respects. First and most obviously, it must only be tried with people who possess higher-order needs that can be aroused by the job design and who, therefore, will value intrinsic rewards. Second, individuals must be placed on jobs that test their valued abilities.

Let me address myself to the question of how the increased motivation, that can be generated by an enlarged job, will manifest itself in terms of behavior. Obviously, the primary change that can be expected is that the individual will devote more effort to performing well. But will this increased effort result in higher-qualitity work, higher productivity, or both? I think this question can be answered by looking at the reasons that we gave for job content being able to affect motivation. The argument was that it does this by affecting whether intrinsic rewards will be seen to come from successful performance. It would seem that high-quality work is indispensable if most individuals are to feel that they have performed well and are to experience feelings of accomplishment, achievement, and self-actualization. The situation is much less clear with respect to productivity. It does not seem at all certain that an individual must produce great quantities of a product in order to feel that he has performed well. In fact, many individuals probably obtain more satisfaction from producing one very high-quality product than they do from producing a number of lower-quality products.

There is a second factor that may cause job enlargement to be more likely to lead to higher work quality than to higher productivity. This has to do with the advantages of division of labor and mechanization. Many job enlargement changes create a situation where, because of the losses in terms of machine assistance and optimal human movements, people actually have to put forth more energy in order to produce at the pre-job enlargement rate. Thus, people may be in effect working harder but producing less. It seems less likely that the same dilemma would arise in terms of work quality and job enlargement. That is, it would seem that if extra effort is devoted to quality, after job enlargement takes place the effort is likely to be translated into improved quality. This would come about because the machine assistance and other features of the assembly-line jobs are more of an aid in bringing about high productivity than they are in bringing about high quality.

THE RESEARCH EVIDENCE

There have been a number of studies that have attempted to measure the effect of job enlargement programs. Thus, it is possible to determine if the evidence supports the contention stated previously that both horizontal and vertical job enlargement are necessary if intrinsic motivation is to be increased. Also it can be determined if the effects of any increased motivation will be more likely to result in higher-quality work than in high productivity.

In a literature search, reports of ten studies were found where jobs had been enlarged on both the horizontal and the vertical dimensions. Table 1 presents a brief summary of the results of these studies. As can be seen, every study shows that job enlargement did have some positive effect since every study reports that job enlargement resulted in higher-quality work. However, only four out of ten studies report that job enlargement led to higher productivity. This provides support for the view that the motivational effects produced by job enlargement are more likely to result in higher-quality work than in higher productivity.

There are relatively few studies that have enlarged jobs only on either the horizontal or the vertical dimensions so it is difficult to test the predictions that both kinds of enlargement are necessary if motivation is to be increased. There are a few studies which have been concerned with the effects of horizontal job enlargement (e.g., Walker & Guest, 1952) while others have stressed its advantages. However, most of these studies have been concerned with its effects on job satisfaction rather than its effects on motivation. None of these studies appears to show that horizontal enlargement tends to increase either productivity or work quality. Walker and Guest, for example, talk about the higher satisfaction of the utility men but they do not report that they work harder. Thus, with respect to horizontal job enlargement the evidence does not lead to rejecting the view that it must be combined with vertical in order to increase production.

The evidence with respect to whether vertical job enlargement alone can increase motivation is less clear. As Argyris (1964) has pointed out, the Scanlon Plan has stressed this kind of job enlargement with some success. However, it is hard to tell if this success stems from people actually becoming more motivated to perform their own jobs better. It is quite possible that improvements under the plan are due to better over-all decision making rather than to increased motivation. Vroom (1964) has analyzed the evidence with respect to the degree to which participation in decision making *per se* leads to increased motivation.

Table 1

Research study	Higher quality	Higher productivity
Biggane and Stewart (1963)	yes	no
Conant and Kilbridge (1965) Kilbridge (1960)	yes	no
Davis and Valfer (1965)	yes	no
Davis and Werling (1960)	yes	yes
Elliott (1953)	yes	yes
Guest (1957)	yes	no
Kuriloff (1966)	yes	yes
Marks (1954)	yes	no
Rice (1953)	yes	yes
Walker (1950)	yes	no

This evidence is suggestive of the fact that vertical job enlargement can lead to increased motivation when it leads to employees committing themselves to higher production goals.

Perhaps the crucial distinction here is whether the participation involves matters of company policy or whether it involves matters directly related to the employees' work process. Participation of the former type would seem to be much less likely to lead to increased motivation than would participation of the latter type. Thus, it seems to be crucial to distinguish between two quite different types of vertical job enlargement, only one of which leads to increased motivation. Considered together the evidence suggests that of the two types of job enlargement vertical is relatively more important than horizontal. Perhaps this is because it can lead to a situation where subjects do feel that their abilities are being tested and where they can exercise self-control even though horizontal enlargement does not take place. Still, the evidence with respect to situations where both types of enlargement have been jointly installed shows that much more consistent improvements in motivation can be produced by both than can be produced by vertical alone.

SUMMARY

In summary, it has been argued that when jobs are structured in a way that makes intrinsic rewards appear to result from good performance then the jobs themselves can be very effective motivators. In addition, the point was made that if job content is to be a source of motivation, the job must allow for meaningful feedback, test the individual's valued abilities and allow a great amount of self-control by the job holder. In order for this to happen, jobs must be enlarged on both the vertical and horizontal dimensions. Further, it was predicted that job enlargement is more likely to lead to increased quality than to increased productivity. A review of the literature on job enlargement generally tended to confirm these predictions.

REFERENCES

Alper, T. G. (1964), 'Task-orientation *v.* ego-orientation in learning and retention', *American Journal of Psychology*, *38*, 224–38.

Argyris, C. (1964), *Integrating the Individual and the Organization*, New York: Wiley.

Biggane, J. F., & Stewart, P. A. (1963), 'Job enlargement: a case study', *Research Series, Bureau of Labor and Management, State University of Iowa*, *25*.

Conant, E. H., & Kilbridge, M. D. (1965), 'An interdisciplinary analysis of job enlargement: technology, costs, and behavioral implications', *Industrial and Labor Relations Review*, *18*, 377–95.

Davis, L. E., & Valfer, E. S. (1965), 'Intervening responses to changes in supervisor job designs', *Occupational Psychology*, *39*, 171–89.

Davis, L. E., & Werling, R. (1960), 'Job design factors', *Occupational Psychology*, *34*, 109–32.

Elliott, J. D. (1953), 'Increasing office productivity through job enlargement. The human side of the office manager's job', *AMA Office Management Series*, *134*, 5–15.

French, E. G. (1955), 'Some characteristics of achievement motivation', *Journal of Psychology*, *50*, 232–6.

Georgopoulos, B. S., Mahoney, G. M., & Jones, N. W. (1957), 'A path–goal approach to productivity', *Journal of Applied Psychology*, *41*, 345–53.

Guest, R. H. (1957), 'Job enlargement: a revolution in job design', *Personnel Administration*, *20*, 9–16.

Jones, M. R. (ed.) (1959), *Nebraska Symposium on Motivation*, University of Nebraska Press, Vol. 7.

Kilbridge, M. D. (1960), 'Reduced costs through job enlargement: A case', *Journal of Business*, *33*, 357–62.

Kuriloff, A. H. (1966), *Reality in Management*, New York: McGraw-Hill.

Lawler, E. E., III, & Porter, L. W. (1967), 'Antecedent attitudes of effective managerial performance', *Organizational Behavior and Human Performance*, *2*, 122–42.

Marks, A. R. N. (1954), 'An investigation of modifications of job design in an industrialist situation and their effects on some measures of economic productivity', unpublished Ph.D. dissertation, University of California.

Porter, L. W., & Lawler, E. E., III (1968), *Managerial Attitudes and Performance*, Homewood, Ill.: Irwin-Dorsey.

Rice, A. K. (1953), 'Productivity and social organization in an Indian weaving-shed', *Human Relations*, *6*, 297–329.

Vroom, V. H. (1964), *Work and Motivation*, New York: Wiley.

Walker, C. R. (1950), 'The problem of the repetitive job', *Harvard Business Review*, *28*, 54–9.

Walker, C. R., & Guest, R. M. (1952), *The Man on the Assembly Line*, Cambridge, Mass.: Harvard University Press.

21

FREDERICK HERZBERG

One More Time: How Do You Motivate Employees?

Abridged from F. Herzberg, 'One more time: How do you motivate employees?', *Harvard Business Review*, Vol. 46, 1968, pp. 53–62.

How many articles, books, speeches, and workshops have pleaded plaintively, 'How do I get an employee to do what I want him to do?'

In lectures to industry on the problem, I have found that the audiences are anxious for quick and practical answers, so I will begin with a straightforward, practical formula for moving people. The surest and least circumlocuted way of getting someone to do something is to kick him in the pants – give him what might be called the KITA.

There are various forms of KITA, and here are some of them:

☐ *Negative physical KITA*. This is a literal application of the term and was frequently used in the past. It has, however, three major drawbacks: (1) it is inelegant; (2) it contradicts the precious image of benevolence that most organizations cherish; and (3) since it is a physical attack, it directly stimulates the autonomic nervous system, and this often results in negative feedback – the employee may just kick you in return. These factors give rise to certain taboos against negative physical KITA.

The psychologist has come to the rescue of those who are no longer permitted to use negative physical KITA. He has uncovered infinite sources of psychological vulnerabilities and the appropriate methods to play tunes on them. 'He took my rug away'; 'I wonder what he meant by that'; 'The boss is always going around me' – these symptomatic expressions of ego sores that have been rubbed raw are the result of application of:

☐ *Negative psychological KITA*. This has several advantages over negative physical KITA. First, the cruelty is not visible; the bleeding is internal and comes much later. Second, since it affects the higher cortical centers of the brain with its inhibitory powers, it reduces the possibility of physical backlash. Third, since the number of psychological pains that a person can feel is almost infinite, the direction and site possibilities of the KITA are increased many times. Fourth, the person administering the kick can manage to be above it all and let the system accomplish the dirty work. Fifth, those who practice it receive some ego satisfaction (one-upmanship), whereas they would find drawing blood abhorrent. Finally, if the employee does complain, he can always be accused of being paranoid, since there is no tangible evidence of an actual attack.

Now, what does negative KITA accomplish? If I kick you in the rear (physically or psychologically), who is motivated? *I* am motivated; *you* move! Negative KITA does not lead to motivation, but to movement. So:

□ *Positive KITA*. Let us consider motivation. If I say to you, 'Do this for me or the company, and in return I will give you a reward, an incentive, more status, a promotion, all the quid pro quos that exist in the industrial organization,' am I motivating you? The overwhelming opinion I receive from management people is, 'Yes, this is motivation.'

I have a year-old Schnauzer. When it was a small puppy and I wanted it to move, I kicked it in the rear and it moved. Now that I have finished its obedience training, I hold up a dog biscuit when I want the Schnauzer to move. In this instance, who is motivated – I or the dog? The dog wants the biscuit, but it is I who want it to move. Again, I am the one who is motivated, and the dog is the one who moves. In this instance all I did was apply KITA frontally; I exerted a pull instead of a push. When industry wishes to use such positive KITAs, it has available an incredible number and variety of dog biscuits (jelly beans for humans) to wave in front of the employee to get him to jump.

Why is it that managerial audiences are quick to see that negative KITA is *not* motivation, while they are almost unanimous in their judgement that positive KITA *is* motivation? It is because negative KITA is rape, and positive KITA is seduction. But it is infinitely worse to be seduced than to be raped; the latter is an unfortunate occurrence, while the former signifies that you were a party to your own downfall. This is why positive KITA is so popular: it is a tradition; it is in the American way. The organization does not have to kick you; you kick yourself.

Why is KITA not motivation? If I kick my dog (from the front or the back), he will move. And when I want him to move again, what must I do? I must kick him again. Similarly, I can charge a man's battery, and then recharge it, and recharge it again. But it is only when he has his own generator that we can talk about motivation. He then needs no outside stimulation. He *wants* to do it.

HYGIENE VERSUS MOTIVATORS

Let me rephrase the perennial question this way: How do you install a generator in an employee? A brief review of my motivation–hygiene theory of job attitudes is required before theoretical and practical suggestions can be offered. The theory was first drawn from an examination of events in the lives of engineers and accountants. At least sixteen other investigations, using a wide variety of populations (including some in the Communist countries), have since been completed, making the original research one of the most replicated studies in the field of job attitudes.

The findings of these studies, along with corroboration from many other investigations using different procedures, suggest that the factors involved in producing job satisfaction (and motivation) are separate and distinct from the factors that lead to job dissatisfaction. Since separate factors need to be considered, depending on whether job satisfaction or job dissatisfaction is being examined, it follows that these two feelings are not opposites of each other. The opposite of job satisfaction is not job dissatisfaction but, rather, *no* job satisfaction; and, similarly, the opposite of job dissatisfaction is not job satisfaction, but *no* job dissatisfaction.

Stating the concept presents a problem in semantics, for we normally think of satisfaction and dissatisfaction as opposites – i.e., what is not satisfying must be dissatisfying, and vice versa. But when it comes to understanding the behavior of people in their jobs, more than a play on words is involved.

Two different needs of man are involved here. One set of needs can be thought of as stemming from his animal nature – the built-in drive to avoid pain from the environment, plus all the learned drives which become conditioned to the basic biological needs. For example, hunger, a basic biological drive, makes it necessary to earn money, and then money becomes a specific drive. The other set of needs relates to that unique human characteristic, the ability to achieve and, through achievement, to experience psychological growth. The stimuli for the growth needs are tasks that induce growth; in the industrial setting, they are the *job content*. Contrariwise, the stimuli inducing pain-avoidance behavior are found in the *job environment*.

The growth or *motivator* factors that are intrinsic to the job are: achievement, recognition for achievement, the work itself, responsibility, and growth or advancement. The dissatisfaction-avoidance or *hygiene* (KITA) factors that are extrinsic to the job include: company policy and administration, supervision, interpersonal relationships, working conditions, salary, status, and security.

The motivation–hygiene theory suggests that work be *enriched* to bring about effective utilization of personnel. Such a systematic attempt to motivate employees by manipulating the motivator factors is just beginning.

The term *job enrichment* describes this embryonic movement. An older term, job enlargement, should be avoided because it is associated with past failures stemming from a misunderstanding of the problem. Job enrichment [i.e., vertical job loading] provides the opportunity for the employee's psychological growth, while job enlargement merely makes a job structurally bigger.

The principles of vertical loading have not all been worked out as yet, and they remain rather general, but I have furnished seven useful starting points for consideration in Exhibit 1.

Exhibit 1. Principles of vertical job loading

Principle	Motivators involved
A. Removing some controls while retaining accountability	Responsibility and personal achievement
B. Increasing the accountability of individuals for own work	Responsibility and recognition
C. Giving a person a complete natural unit of work (module, division, area, and so on)	Responsibility, achievement, and recognition
D. Granting additional authority to an employee in his activity; job freedom	Responsibility, achievement, and recognition
E. Making periodic reports directly available to the worker himself rather than to the supervisor	Internal recognition
F. Introducing new and more difficult tasks not previously handled	Growth and learning
G. Assigning individuals specific or specialized tasks, enabling them to become experts	Responsibility, growth, and advancement

A successful application

The subjects of this study were the stockholder correspondents employed by a very large corporation. Seemingly, the task required of these carefully selected and highly trained correspondents was quite complex and challenging. But almost all indexes of performance and job attitudes were low, and exit interviewing confirmed that the challenge of the job existed merely as words.

A job-enrichment project was initiated in the form of an experiment with one group, designated as an achieving unit, having its job enriched by the principles described in Exhibit 1. A control group continued to do its job in the traditional way. (There were also two 'uncommitted' groups of correspondents formed to measure the so-called Hawthorne Effect – that is, to gauge whether productivity and attitudes toward the job changed artificially merely because employees sensed that the company was paying more attention to them in doing something different or novel. The results for these groups were substantially the same as for the control group, and for the sake of simplicity I do not deal with them in this summary.) No changes in hygiene were introduced for either group other than those that would have been made anyway, such as normal pay increases.

The changes for the achieving unit were introduced in the first two months, averaging one per week of the seven motivators listed in Exhibit 1. At the end of six months the members of the achieving unit were found to be out-performing their counterparts in the control group, and in addition indicated a marked increase in their liking for their jobs. Other results showed that the achieving group had lower absenteeism and, subsequently, a higher rate of promotion.

The 'achievers' were performing less well before the six-month period started, and their performance service index continued to decline after the introduction of the motivators, evidently because of uncertainty over their newly granted responsibilities. In the third month, however, performance improved, and soon the members of this group had reached a high level of accomplishment.

[Furthermore,] the achievers became much more positive about their job, while the attitude of the control unit remained about the same.

STEPS TO JOB ENRICHMENT

Now that the motivator idea has been described in practice, here are the steps that managers should take in instituting the principle with their employees:

1. Select those jobs in which (a) the investment in industrial engineer-

ing does not make changes too costly, (b) attitudes are poor, (c) hygiene is becoming very costly, and (d) motivation will make a difference in performance.

2. Approach these jobs with the conviction that they can be changed. Years of tradition have led managers to believe that the content of the jobs is sacrosanct and the only scope of action that they have is in ways of stimulating people.

3. Brainstorm a list of changes that may enrich the jobs, without concern for their practicality.

4. Screen the list to eliminate suggestions that involve hygiene, rather than actual motivation.

5. Screen the list for generalities, such as 'give them more responsibility', that are rarely followed in practice. This might seem obvious, but the motivator words have never left industry; the substance has just been rationalized and organized out. Words like 'responsibility', 'growth', 'achievement', and 'challenge', for example, have been elevated to the lyrics of the patriotic anthem for all organizations. It is the old problem typified by the pledge of allegiance to the flag being more important than contributions to the country – of following the form, rather than the substance.

6. Avoid direct participation by the employees whose jobs are to be enriched. Ideas they have expressed previously certainly constitute a valuable source for recommended changes, but their direct involvement contaminates the process with human-relations *hygiene* and, more specifically, gives them only a *sense* of making a contribution. The job is to be changed, and it is the content that will produce the motivation, not attitudes about being involved or the challenge inherent in setting up a job. That process will be over shortly, and it is what the employees will be doing from then on that will determine their motivation. A sense of participation will result only in short-term movement.

7. In the initial attempts at job enrichment, set up a controlled experiment. At least two equivalent groups should be chosen, one an experimental unit in which the motivators are systematically introduced over a period of time, and the other one a control group in which no changes are made. For both groups, hygiene should be allowed to follow its natural course for the duration of the experiment. Pre- and post-installation tests of performance and job attitudes are necessary to evaluate the effectiveness of the job-enrichment program. The attitude test must be limited to motivator items in order to divorce the employee's view of the job he is given from all the surrounding hygiene feelings that he might have.

8. Be prepared for a drop in performance in the experimental group the first few weeks. The changeover to a new job may lead to a temporary reduction in efficiency.

9. Expect your first-line supervisors to experience some anxiety and hostility over the changes you are making. The anxiety comes from their fear that the changes will result in poorer performance for their unit. Hostility will arise when the employees start assuming what the supervisors regard as their own responsibility for performance. The supervisor without checking duties to perform may then be left with little to do.

After a successful experiment, however, the supervisor usually discovers the supervisory and managerial functions he has neglected, or which were never his because all his time was given over to checking the work of his subordinates. For example, in the R&D division of one large chemical company I know of, the supervisors of the laboratory assistants were theoretically responsible for their training and evaluation. These functions, however, had come to be performed in a routine, unsubstantial fashion. After the job-enrichment program, during which the supervisors were not merely passive observers of the assistants' performance, the supervisors actually were devoting their time to reviewing performance and administering thorough training.

What has been called an employee-centered style of supervision will come about not through education of supervisors, but by changing the jobs that they do.

CONCLUDING NOTE

Job enrichment will not be a one-time proposition, but a continuous management function. The initial changes, however, should last for a very long period of time. There are a number of reasons for this:

☐ The changes should bring the job up to the level of challenge commensurate with the skill that was hired.

☐ Those who have still more ability eventually will be able to demonstrate it better and win promotion to higher-level jobs.

☐ The very nature of motivators, as opposed to hygiene factors, is that they have a much longer-term effect on employees' attitudes. Perhaps the job will have to be enriched again, but this will not occur as frequently as the need for hygiene.

Not all jobs can be enriched, nor do all jobs need to be enriched. If only a small percentage of time and money that is now devoted to hygiene, however, were given to job-enrichment efforts, the return in human satisfaction and economic gain would be one of the largest dividends that industry and society have ever reaped through their efforts at better personnel management.

22

J. RICHARD HACKMAN AND GREG R. OLDHAM

Motivation Through the Design of Work

Abridged from J. R. Hackman and G. R. Oldham, *Work Redesign*, Chapter 4, Reading, Mass.: Addison-Wesley, 1980.

When people are well matched with their jobs, it rarely is necessary to force, coerce, bribe, or trick them into working hard and trying to perform the job well. Instead, they try to do well because it is rewarding and satisfying to do so.

The term we use to describe this state of affairs is 'internal motivation'. When someone has high internal work motivation, feelings are closely tied to how well he or she performs on the job. Good performance is an occasion for self-reward, which serves as an incentive for continuing to do well. And because poor performance prompts unhappy feelings, the person may elect to try harder in the future so as to avoid those unpleasant outcomes and regain the internal rewards that good performance can bring.

CREATING CONDITIONS FOR INTERNAL MOTIVATION

When will internal motivation occur on the job? Our theory suggests that there are three key conditions. First, the person must have *knowledge of the results* of his or her work. If things are arranged so that the person who does the work never finds out whether it is being performed well or poorly, then that person has no basis for feeling good about having done well or unhappy about doing poorly.

Secondly, the person must *experience responsibility* for the results of the work, believing that he or she is personally accountable for the work outcomes. If one views the quality of work done as depending more on external factors (such as a procedure manual, the boss, or people in another work section) than on one's own initiatives or efforts, then there is no reason to feel personally proud when one does well or sad when one doesn't.

And finally, the person must *experience the work as meaningful*, as something that 'counts' in one's own system of values. If the work being done is seen as trivial (as might be the case for a job putting paper clips in boxes, for example), then internal work motivation is unlikely to develop – even when the person has sole responsibility for the work and receives ample information about how well he or she is performing.

It appears necessary for *all three* of these factors, labelled 'critical psychological states', to be present for strong internal work motivation to develop and persist.

Most people exhibit 'motivational problems' at work when their tasks are designed so that they have little meaning, when they experience little responsibility for the work outcomes, or when they are protected from data about how well they are performing. If, on the other hand, a task is arranged so that the people who perform it richly experience the three psychological states, then even individuals who view themselves as chronically lazy may find themselves putting out a little extra effort to do the work well. It appears, then, that *motivation at work may actually have more to do with how tasks are designed and managed than with the personal dispositions of the people who do them.* But what are the task characteristics that create conditions for internal work motivation?

THE PROPERTIES OF MOTIVATING JOBS

The three psychological states discussed above are, by definition, internal to persons and therefore not directly manipulable in designing or managing work. What is needed are reasonably objective, measurable, changeable properties of the work itself that foster these psychological states, and through them, enhance internal work motivation. Research suggests that the five job characteristics shown in Figure 1 may be useful in this regard (Hackman & Lawler, 1971; Hackman & Oldham, 1976; Turner & Lawrence, 1965). Three of these five job characteristics are shown in the figure as contributing to the experienced meaningfulness of the work, one contributes to experienced responsibility, and one contributes to knowledge of results.

Toward experienced meaningfulness

There are a number of different ways that work can take on personal meaning for the person who performs it. Three characteristics of jobs that seem especially powerful in influencing the experienced

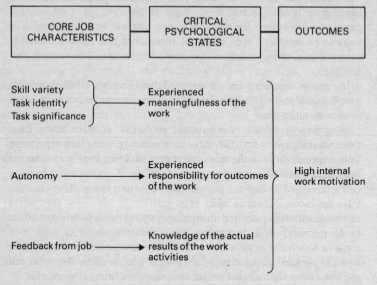

Figure 1. Job characteristics that foster the three psychological states.

meaningfulness of work are (1) *skill variety*, (2) *task identity*, and (3) *task significance*.

Skill variety. The degree to which a job requires a variety of different activities in carrying out the work, involving the use of a number of different skills and talents of the person.

When a task requires workers to engage in activities that challenge or stretch their skills or abilities, they almost invariably experience that task as meaningful, and the more skills involved, the more meaningful the work is likely to be.

Task identity. The degree to which a job requires completion of a 'whole' and identifiable piece of work, that is, doing a job from beginning to end with a visible outcome.

People care about their work more when they are doing a whole job. When workers have an intact task, such as providing a complete unit of service or putting together an entire product, they tend to see that task as more meaningful than is the case when they are responsible for only a small part of the job.

Task significance. The degree to which the job has a substantial impact on the lives of other people, whether those people are in the immediate organization or in the world at large.

Experienced meaningfulness of the work usually is enhanced when workers understand that the work being done will have a substantial impact on the physical or psychological well-being of other people.

Each of the three job characteristics described above contributes to the overall experienced meaningfulness of the work. If a given job is high on all three of the characteristics, an employee is very likely to experience the work as meaningful: putting together a complex heart pacemaker is an example of such a task. Yet because three different task characteristics contribute to experienced meaningfulness, a person can experience the work as meaningful even if one or two of these task characteristics are quite low.

Toward increased responsibility

The characteristic of jobs that fosters increased feelings of personal responsibility for the work outcomes is *autonomy*.

Autonomy. The degree to which the job provides substantial freedom, independence, and discretion to the individual in scheduling the work and in determining the procedures to be used in carrying it out.

When the job provides substantial autonomy to the persons performing it, work outcomes will be viewed by those individuals as depending substantially on their *own* efforts, initiatives, and decisions, rather than on, say, the adequacy of instructions from the boss or on a manual of job procedures. As autonomy increases, individuals tend to feel more personal responsibility for successes and failures that occur on the job and are more willing to accept personal accountability for the outcomes of the work.

Toward knowledge of results

Knowledge of the results of one's work is affected directly by the amount of *feedback* one receives from doing the work.

Job feedback. The degree to which carrying out the work activities required by the job provides the individual with direct and clear information about the effectiveness of his or her performance.

Note that the focus here is on feedback obtained *directly from the job*, as when a television repairman turns on the set and finds that it works (or doesn't work) after being repaired, when a sales representative closes the deal and receives a check from the customer, or when a physician treats a patient and sees the patient get well. In each case, the knowledge of results derives from the work activities themselves, rather than from some other person (such as a co-worker or a supervisor) who collects data or makes a judgement about how well the work is being done. While this second type of feedback (which will be termed 'feedback from agents') can also contribute to the overall knowledge an employee has of the results of his or her work, the focus here is on feedback mechanisms that are designed into the work itself.

THE ROLE OF DIFFERENCES AMONG PEOPLE

Some employees 'take off' on jobs that are high in motivating potential [i.e., that are high in the core job characteristics]; others are more likely to 'turn off'. There are many attributes of people that affect how they respond to their work, and we cannot review all of them here. We have, however, selected for discussion three characteristics of people that seem especially important in understanding who will (and who will not) respond positively to high [motivating potential] jobs.

Knowledge and skill

Recall once again the essential property of internal work motivation: positive feelings follow from good performance, and negative feelings follow from poor performance.

For jobs high in motivating potential, people who have sufficient knowledge and skill to perform well will experience substantially positive feelings as a result of their work activities. But people who are *not* competent enough to perform well will experience a good deal of unhappiness and frustration at work, precisely because the job 'counts' for them and they do poorly at it.

Growth need strength

Jobs high in motivating potential create opportunities for considerable self-direction, learning, and personal accomplishment at work. Not all individuals appreciate such opportunities, even among employees who would be able to perform the work very competently. What determines who will respond positively to a complex, challenging job, and who will not?

The *psychological needs* of people are critical in determining how vigorously an individual will respond to a job high in motivating potential (Hackman & Lawler, 1971; Hackman & Oldham, 1976).

Some people have strong needs for personal accomplishment, for learning, and for developing themselves beyond where they are now.

These people are said to have strong 'growth needs' and are predicted to develop high internal motivation when working on a complex, challenging job. Others have less strong needs for growth and will be less eager to exploit the opportunities for personal accomplishment provided by a job high in motivating potential.

Satisfaction with the work context

Up to this point our discussion has focused on the motivating properties of the work itself and on characteristics of people (specifically their job-relevant knowledge and skill, and their growth need strength) that affect how people respond to jobs that are high or low in motivating potential. However, it is also the case that how satisfied people are with aspects of the work *context* may affect their willingness or ability to take advantage of the opportunities for personal accomplishment provided by enriched work.

We expect that individuals who are relatively satisfied with pay, job security, co-workers, and supervisors will respond more positively to enriched and challenging jobs than individuals who are dissatisfied with these aspects of the work context. And if individuals who are satisfied with the work context also have relatively strong growth need strength, then a *very* high level of internal work motivation would be expected.

Summary

We have reviewed three factors which qualify the general proposition that increases in the motivating potential of a job foster greater internal work motivation on the part of the people who perform it. These factors are a person's job-relevant knowledge and skill; growth need strength; and level of satisfaction with aspects of the work context, particularly satisfaction with job security, compensation, co-workers, and supervision.

While each of these factors may, in its own right, affect the responses of a person to a job, they become especially significant when they occur in combination. The 'worst possible' circumstance for a job that is high in motivating potential, for example, would be when the job incumbent is only marginally competent to perform the work *and* has low needs for personal growth at work *and* is highly dissatisfied with one or more aspects of the work context. The job clearly would be too much for that individual, and negative personal and work outcomes would be predicted. It would be better, for the person as well as for the organization, for the individual to perform relatively more simple and routine work.

On the other hand, if an individual is fully competent to carry out the work required by a complex, challenging task *and* has strong needs for personal growth *and* is well satisfied with the work context, then we would expect both high personal satisfaction and high work motivation and performance. The work, in this case, would fit well both with the talents and the needs of the individual, and the outcomes should be beneficial both to the individual and to the organization.

REFERENCES

Hackman, J. R., & Lawler, E. E., III (1971), 'Employee reactions to job characteristics', *Journal of Applied Psychology*, 55, 259–86.

Hackman, J. R., & Oldham, G. R. (1976), 'Motivation through the design of work: Test of a theory', *Organizational Behavior and Human Performance*, 16, 250–79.

Turner, A. N., & Lawrence, P. R. (1965), *Industrial Jobs and the Worker*, Boston, Mass.: Harvard Graduate School of Business Administration.

23

EDWARD L. DECI, JAMES P. CONNELL, AND
RICHARD M. RYAN

Self-Determination in a Work Organization

Abridged from 'Self-determination in a work organization', *Journal of
Applied Psychology*, Vol. 74, 1989, pp. 580–90.

To be self-determining means to experience a sense of choice in initiating and regulating one's own actions. Recent research linking self-determination to enhanced creativity (Amabile, 1983), conceptual learning (Benware & Deci, 1984), self-esteem (Deci, Schwartz, Sheinman, & Ryan, 1981), and general well-being (Langer & Rodin, 1976) has stimulated psychologists to clarify the antecedent conditions that promote self-determination and to detail the relevance of self-determination to various applied settings.

Concepts related to self-determination have been vigorously researched and discussed in the organizational literature for over a quarter century. Argyris (1957) and McGregor (1960), for example, stressed that organizational contexts providing workers the opportunity to satisfy their higher-order needs (Maslow, 1943) promote effective performance. Furthermore, management styles (e.g., Likert, 1967; Marrow, Bowers, & Seashore 1967) and organizational designs (e.g., Hackman & Oldham, 1980; Herzberg, 1966) that permit greater participation in decision making and greater flexibility in doing one's job have been found to be positively associated with employee satisfaction, quality of work life, and organizational effectiveness (e.g., Lawler, 1986), although these positive effects have emerged more clearly for some employees than for others (Hackman & Lawler, 1971).

Our research tested self-determination theory (Deci & Ryan, 1985) by exploring the interpersonal work climate created by managers for their subordinates. More specifically, it focused on the degree to which managers' interpersonal orientations tend to support subordinates' self-determination, that is, their sense of choice and personal initiative. The idea of managers supporting self-determination is conceptually and philosophically consistent with participative management and vertical job enlargement, although it differs from them by focusing on the interpersonal orientation of managers rather than on the decision-making process or the job design.

The variables in the organizational literature that are perhaps closest to that of a manager's support for self-determination have been systematized in Bowers and Seashore's (1966) theory of leadership. These authors defined the management function of *support* as managers' behaviors that enhance subordinates' feelings of personal worth, and they aligned this concept to Halpin and Winer's (1957) idea of *consideration* and Likert's (1961) principle of *supportive relationships*. Our concept of supporting self-determination is also related to Bowers and Seashore's idea of support, although it extends their idea by specifying the factors that are likely to lead to subordinates' feelings of personal worth. These factors, which comprise the concept of managers' support for self-determination, have emerged from recent motivation research; thus, elaboration of the point requires a brief review of that motivation research.

MOTIVATION RESEARCH

In a recent literature review, Deci and Ryan (1985) argued that the functional significance (i.e., the psychological meaning) of any input affecting the initiation and regulation of intentional behavior can be usefully classified as either *informational* (i.e., as supporting autonomy and promoting competence) or *controlling* (i.e., as pressuring one to think, feel, or behave in specified ways). Experiencing an input as informational fosters self-determination, whereas experiencing it as controlling diminishes self-determination.

Early studies on the contextual factors that affect self-determination were laboratory experiments involving external manipulations from which inferences could be drawn about whether specific events (e.g., reward structures, deadlines, or positive feedback) tend to be experienced as informational (i.e., as supporting self-determination) or controlling (i.e., as thwarting self-determination). These studies indicated, for example, that choice (Zuckerman, Porac, Lathin, Smith, & Deci, 1978) and positive feedback (Blanck, Reis, & Jackson, 1984; Deci 1971) tend to be experienced as informational, whereas task-contingent rewards (e.g., Ryan, Mims, & Koestner, 1983), deadlines (Amabile, DeJong, & Lepper, 1976), threats of punishment (Deci & Cascio, 1972), surveillance (Lepper & Greene, 1975), and evaluations (Smith, 1974) tend to be experienced as controlling.

More recent studies have shown, however, that although a specific event (e.g., positive feedback) tends, on average, to have a particular functional significance, the interpersonal context within which the event is administered has an important influence on the functional significance of the event. Thus, for example, Ryan (1982) reported that positive feedback could be experienced as either informational *or* controlling, depending on the experimenter's style of communication. Similarly, Ryan, Mims, and Koestner (1983) concluded that performance-contingent rewards could be either informational or controlling, and Koestner, Ryan, Bernieri, and Holt (1984) concluded that limit setting could be either informational or controlling, again depending on the interpersonal contexts surrounding the events themselves.

A focus on the interpersonal context within which events occur seems particularly important when applying these concepts to organizational settings, because many events such as reward structures, evaluations, and deadlines are relatively invariant in these settings. Interpersonal contexts within organizations are more variable, however, so they represent an opportunity for explaining variation in employees' attitudes and for designing interventions to enhance them.

The first field studies conducted within this theoretical tradition related the interpersonal contexts of public-school classrooms to students' attitudes and motivation (e.g., Deci, Schwartz, Sheinman, & Ryan, 1981; Ryan & Connell, 1989; Ryan & Grolnick, 1986). These studies showed, for example, that teachers who were oriented toward supporting students' self-determination had a positive effect on the intrinsic motivation, self-esteem, and perceived competence of their students, relative to teachers who were oriented toward controlling their students' behavior.

A synthesis of these and other studies has led to the conclusion that promoting self-determination requires that the significant others in a target person's context (e.g., parents, managers, teachers) take that person's frame of reference. They must understand and acknowledge his or her needs, feelings, and attitudes with respect to the issue or situation at hand. When this is the case, the target person will be more trusting of the context and believe that it will be responsive to his or her initiations and suggestions.

More specifically, the investigations have identified the following three general factors: (a) support for autonomy (e.g., Deci, Nezlek & Sheinman, 1981); (b) non-controlling positive feedback (e.g., Ryan, 1982); and (c) acknowledging the other's perspective (e.g., Koestner et al., 1984). These factors are critical for promoting self-determination (i.e., for increasing the likelihood that an interpersonal context will be experienced as informational).

Although none of these studies on self-determination was done in a work organization, the general conclusions drawn from them are consistent with organizational studies such as those by Coch and French (1948), Lawler and Hackman (1969), Likert (1967), Marrow et al. (1967), and Scheflen, Lawler, and Hackman (1971), which have shown positive, motivationally relevant effects of factors such as participation, support for individual initiative, and open communications. Furthermore, the factors that tend to be experienced as diminishing self-determination are ones that workers tend to complain about in interviews (e.g., Terkel, 1972) and that comprise Likert's (1967) System 1 management. Therefore, it seems useful to test directly the importance of promoting self-determination in the workplace; thus, our research was designed to do that by focusing on interpersonal variables between managers and their subordinates.

The studies exploring the effects of promoting self-determination have used a range of dependent variables, including intrinsic motivation (e.g., Zuckerman et al., 1978), positive emotional tone (Garbarino, 1975), creativity (e.g., Koestner et al., 1984), interest in the activity (Harackiewicz, 1979), conceptual learning (Grolnick & Ryan, 1987), perceived competence and self-esteem (Deci et al., 1981), and internalization of regulations (Eghrari & Deci, 1988). In this study, the dependent variables were the subordinates' perceptions, affects, and satisfactions with respect to their immediate work team and the corporation more generally. We reasoned that when managers provide a context that promotes self-determination, subordinates will trust the context and thus be more active in satisfying their own needs.

This study had two interrelated components. The first explored the relation of managers' interpersonal orientations (i.e., the extent to which they tend to support the self-determination of their subordinates) to a variety of subordinate variables; the second evaluated an intervention that focused on training these same managers to promote the self-determination of their subordinates. The ideas of autonomy support, non-controlling feedback, and acknowledgement of the subordinate's perspective guided the research; these ideas were implicit in the measure of managers' orientations and were the foci of the intervention. With regard to the subordinates, we explored variables related to their attitudes about work and their motivation to perform effectively. These included perceptions of the context, feelings within that context, and satisfaction with various aspects of the context and the job.

The general prediction was that positive outcomes would be associated with managers' interpersonal orientations that are supportive of self-determination, and negative outcomes would be associated with orientations that are controlling and thus undermining of self-determination.

The work setting and the corporate climate

Data for this research were provided by nearly 1,000 employees – technicians and field managers – in the service division of a major office machine corporation. The technicians spend virtually all of their time 'on the road' repairing office machines, whereas their managers work in geographically organized branch offices. The managers and technicians have relatively little direct contact, although the managers are responsible for the work of the eighteen or so technicians on their work team. Their typical contacts include the subordinates' briefly seeing the manager once a week to hand in time cards, occasionally speaking to the manager by phone, and infrequently attending team meetings (monthly, on average).

The data collection in these studies took place over an eighteen-month period, spanning three calendar years (August of Year 1 to February of Year 3), in five different locations (referred to as Locations 1 through 5), from five different states: California, Utah, Washington, New York, and Colorado. In Year 1, the corporation was experiencing profitability and morale problems. The workforce had been reduced and wages had been frozen. People were concerned about their job security and disgruntled about the pay freeze.

Corporate management responded to the troubled times in a variety of ways, although a central feature of their response was a commitment to change the organization climate toward more participative management and employee involvement. During the ensuing years, this resulted in (a) an enormous amount of training for the roughly 15,000 people in the service organization; (b) creation of problem-solving groups, using the quality-circle format; (c) restructuring of work teams to promote technicians' taking greater responsibility for solving their own problems; and (d) establishment of positions for internal, organizational development consultants to work with external consultants in facilitating the desired change.

In motivational terms, with this massive organizational development effort, the company attempted to provide greater self-determination and thus to facilitate greater intrinsic motivation and personal commitment (e.g., Lawler, 1973; Vroom & Deci, 1970). In so far as this could be accomplished, it was expected that a variety of motivationally relevant variables would be positively affected and would result in improved profitability. Our research explored a set of motivationally relevant perceptual, affective, and satisfaction variables.

The training component of this study was merely the first phase of the large change effort in three service branches (Locations 1, 2 and 3), each of which employed approximately 140 people. The training focused on interpersonal issues and was intended to prepare the employees for the structural changes that would be introduced after this study was completed. The intervention took place at a time, during Year 2, when morale was low, and many technicians responded with initial skepticism. Most field managers, on the other hand, tended to be interested in the training because they believed it was relevant to the larger change effort that top management had endorsed.

Overview

In this project we used a dual approach to explore the relation between managers' support for *self-determination* and subordinates' self-reported perceptions, affects, and satisfactions. First, the interpersonal orientations of managers from three branches (Locations 1, 2 and 3) were assessed at three points in time and were correlated with the self-reports of their subordinates at those same three times. Second, an intervention that focused on training the managers to support their subordinates' self-determination was conducted in Location 1 between the first and second assessments of managers and subordinates, and in Locations 2 and 3 between the second and third assessments. Changes in managers' orientations and subordinates' self-reports were calculated to evaluate the intervention. We will now describe the design and time line of the primary assessments and interventions.

At the three points in time (January of Year 2, May of Year 2, and February of Year 3), the managers completed the Problems at Work questionnaire, which assessed their tendency to support the self-determination versus to control the behavior of their subordinates. The subordinates (i.e., the technicians) completed the Work Climate Survey, which assessed their reactions to the immediate workplace and to the corporation and its top management. Correlations between variables from these two questionnaires were calculated for each of the three points in time, using work teams as the unit of analysis. The work teams were reasonably stable over the period of the study, with a low turnover rate, although the people who completed the questionnaire at the three times varied somewhat because of such factors as vacations and illness. Thus, for these correlational analyses, the subjects were somewhat different at each point in time.

During the thirteen-month period between the first and third assessments, a delayed-treatment strategy was used to evaluate an intervention aimed at helping the managers in the project become more supportive of their subordinates' self-determination. From February through April of Year 2, the intervention was conducted in Location 1. Thus, change from the first to the second assessment (i.e., January to May of Year 2) in the orientations of the managers from Location 1 (who had received the intervention) relative to that of the managers from Locations 2 and 3 (who had not yet received the intervention) constituted the first aspect of the evaluation. The data from the first two completions by the managers of the Problems at Work questionnaire provided this outcome variable. Relative changes in subordinates' experience over the same time period constituted the second aspect of the evaluation and provided an indication of whether the effects of the intervention had, over the short term, radiated to the subordinates. This assessment of subordinate variables used the subordinates' responses on the Work Climate Survey at the first two assessment points. For these change analyses, a repeated measures procedure was used; thus, only the subjects who were present at both times were included in those analyses.

Although it seemed reasonable to expect that the managers' orientations would be affected during the intervention period, it was probably not reasonable to expect the change to radiate to the subordinates that quickly, because the managers and subordinates spent so little time together. Yet, the assessment was done at that time because of the organization's needs.

In May and June of Year 2, the intervention was conducted in Location 2, and from September through November of that same year it was conducted in Location 3. By the time of the third data collection (February of Year 3), all three locations had received training. Thus, there was a much larger group for determining longer-term pre-post changes, and it was expected that radiation would have occurred in that amount of time. The problem, however, is that there was no longer a comparison group, because Locations 2 and 3, which had comprised that group, were now part of the intervention group. Consequently, an additional comparison was made by using other subordinate data.

In two of the experimental branches (Locations 1 and 2), an Employee Attitude Survey, which is routinely administered by the organization about every twelve to fourteen months, had coincidentally been administered shortly before and then again several months after the respective interventions. In addition, branches from two other states (Locations 4 and 5) had taken the Employee Attitude Survey on the same schedules as these two intervention branches. More precisely, Locations 1 and 4 completed the survey in August of Year 1 and August of Year 2, whereas Locations 2 and 5 completed it in December of Year 1 and December of Year 2. Because neither Location 4 or 5 had yet been exposed to this intervention or to any of the training or structural changes involved in the large corporate effort to change the organizational climate, they represented an appropriate comparison group. A global satisfaction index derived from the Employee Attitude Survey was used as part of the long-term evaluation of the intervention, and the change for the two intervention branches (Locations 1 and 2) relative to the two control branches (Locations 4 and 5) was the critical comparison.

The intervention

The intervention consisted of an external change agent's spending thirteen days working with the employees of a particular branch. The bulk of the time was spent with the managers (a branch manager and approximately eight field managers who report to the branch manager and each of whom supervises about eighteen technicians), although the technicians also had contact with the change agent on three occasions.

The change agent spent the thirteen days as follows: one day with the branch manager, five days with the management team, and seven days with the various field managers, including some time that each of them spent meeting with his or her team of technicians.

The intervention began with the consultant's spending a day with the branch manager, building trust, explaining the intervention, and listening to the manager give his or her perceptions of the dynamics in the branch. The assessment was then conducted with the field managers by using the Problems at Work questionnaire [to determine their orientation toward autonomy versus control]; this was followed immediately by an orientation to the intervention. Next, the field technicians convened to complete the Work Climate Survey [which assessed their perceptions, affects, and satisfactions] and to receive their orientation. With the preliminary work done, the consultant conducted a two-day, off-site, team-building, management-development session for the management team. At three other times in the ensuing weeks, the management team reassembled with the consultant for follow-up development sessions. During this period, the consultant spent time with each field manager individually, during which he observed the manager leading a team meeting, and provided the manager with feedback on management style and group dynamics. Following the intervention itself, the post-treatment assessment was completed.

The content of the training sessions included discussions and activities that were organized around the three basis themes that prior research (reviewed in the introduction of this article) has shown to be critical for promoting self-determination. The first theme was that of maximizing the opportunity for subordinates to take initiative, that is, to make choices and solve problems relevant to them. This was operationalized in part by demonstrations and discussions about group participation and individual initiative. The second theme was that of informational feedback. According to interviews and anecdotes, the majority of feedback in organizations is critically negative and thus demotivating. Even the positive feedback is all too frequently controlling; it emphasizes how people should behave and implies that the manager is in control. Informational feedback in an organization relates to providing performance feedback that facilitates competence while supporting the subordinates' autonomy. It involves providing positive feedback with a minimum of controlling language and treating poor performance as a problem to be solved rather than as a focus for criticism.

The third theme of the training was recognizing and accepting the subordinates' perspective, that is, their needs and feelings. Working in organizations involves a great deal of accommodating to limits, and limits frequently require that people do things they do not want to do. It is probable that these continual experiences prompt emotions that could interfere with effective functioning and cause interpersonal tension. By recognizing and reflecting such desires and feelings, the manager can ease the tension and increase the likelihood of effective performance. Thus, the workshop included training related to acknowledging the needs and feelings of subordinates. It also focused on feelings among the managers. Perhaps the most common mode of dealing with interpersonal difficulties (e.g., not liking something that a colleague did) is to avoid the topic or the person. In the workshops, considerable time was spent having managers identify and express the feelings they had for each other. The intent was for them to learn to manage feelings more effectively in their everyday work environment.

In the management-development workshops, these three themes predominated. Managers were encouraged to examine their own behavior with respect to these topics and to consider possible changes in their behavior. Through discussions, managers realized, for example, that they sometimes treat their subordinates in ways that leave them (the managers) infuriated when their supervisors do such things to them. This type of learning through examination of one's own behaviors and emotional reactions characterized the intervention.

The other component of the intervention was for the managers to experiment with these practices within their own teams. After the two-day development workshop, each field manager had a meeting with his or her team of field technicians. The idea was for the managers to experiment with facilitating greater subordinate involvement. The change agent observed the meetings and later provided each manager with feedback about his or her behavior and about the group's reactions.

Subsequent meetings with the management group were directed at strengthening the changes that were occurring and planning further activities that could continue the development toward greater participation, involvement, and initiative on the part of each member of that branch.

DISCUSSION

In this research, the first issue explored was whether managers' support for the self-determination of their subordinates would affect a set of perceptual, affective, and satisfaction variables in their subordinates. The data indicate that managers' interpersonal orientations did relate to the target variables, particularly to trust variables, although they did so inconsistently. When the broad corporate conditions were bad (particularly concerning pay and security), there was no relationship; but when broad conditions began to improve and managers began to receive the intervention training, the relations became stronger. It is of course difficult to separate the effects of the improved conditions and the training, although the training was probably viewed by the technicians as an indication that corporate management was committed to improving conditions in the organization. Thus, it seems that when employees were very concerned about extrinsic elements such as pay, benefits, and security, and about tension in the corporate climate, immediate supervisory issues were not as important as we had predicted. Managers' support for self-determination is apparently not enough to buffer employees from major problems that emerge from higher levels in the organization, especially when these problems threaten pay and security. Only when the company showed concrete evidence of being concerned with the workers, by unfreezing wages and by making a commitment to change the general climate, did the immediate supervisory situation become a strong correlate of satisfaction. Under these conditions, providing an informational, autonomy-supportive context was very important.

The data further suggest that the field managers are representatives of the corporation for the technicians, given the fact that the managers' orientations affected the workers' perceptions of the corporation and its top management. It is interesting, however, that this relationship appeared only when top management was not threatening the workers with loss of pay or employment. We had not, of course, predicted these limiting conditions on the relation between managers' support for self-determination and the subordinate variables, although it is an interesting point that deserves further investigation. It could be that these results support the concept of a hierarchy of needs (Alderfer, 1972; Maslow, 1943), in which the higher-order need for self-determination was salient only when lower-order needs for pay and job security were well satisfied and thus not salient. Alternatively, the results could simply indicate that in this situation, in which the actions of top management were extremely salient and were experienced as negative, the technicians were less attuned to their field managers' individual orientations. This would mean that their need for self-determination may still have been salient and strong, but that the relatively small variability among the managers' orientations was not adequate to provide differential satisfaction of the need and thus to affect job attitudes.

The second focus of this research was whether it is possible to change managers' orientations (toward greater support for self-determination) through training and development, and whether any change that might occur in those orientations would in turn affect their subordinates' experience *of work*. The data do provide some indication that it is possible to make a significant change in the workplace by training managers to support their subordinates' self-determination. The effect of the intervention on managers' orientations was reasonably well documented, although its radiation to subordinates was less clear. In this large-scale field experiment, we encountered many of the methodological problems that typically accompany such research, so we did not have an adequate test of the impact of the intervention on subordinates. None the less, by using a two-prong strategy for trying to ascertain whether there was radiation of manager effects, we did obtain some suggestion of positive treatment effects for subordinates.

As we expected, there was no evidence of treatment effects in Location 1 at the end of the intervention when there was still an appropriate control group. Presumably because of the minimal contact between managers and subordinates, it took many weeks before the change in managers' orientations appeared to have influenced subordinates.

In terms of dynamics, it is interesting that subordinate variables concerned with trust in the corporation were more clearly related to managers' styles than were any of the other subordinate variables, even those that supposedly described the managers themselves. This suggests one of two phenomena. It is possible either that (a) field technicians, when they get dissatisfied with their managers, displace those negative feelings onto the less proximal corporation (it is safer to blame top management with whom they have no contact than to blame their immediate supervisors); or, alternatively, (b) the more controlling managers actually attribute their own actions to top management rather than accepting responsibility for their own management behavior. For example, 'There's nothing I can do about it; they said it has to be done' is the kind of disclaimer by a controlling manager that could encourage the displacement.

Previous research has indicated that structural changes, aimed at facilitating participative or autonomy-supportive management, are of great value. It is therefore encouraging to note that even management training, the effects of which are often thought to be transient, may have an impact that persists several months after the completion of the program. Indeed, in this work situation in which managers have minimal contact with their subordinates, the intervention (if it did have an effect on the subordinates) appears to have required a few months have an impact.

In closing, it seems reasonable to conclude that, with certain limitations, the experience of self-determination, promoted by managers' being autonomy-supportive, has positive ramifications for people's work lives.

REFERENCES

Alderfer, C. P. (1972), *Existence Relatedness, and Growth*, New York: Free Press.

Amabile, T. M. (1983), *The Social Psychology of Creativity*, New York: Springer-Verlag.

Amabile, T. M., DeJong, W., & Lepper, M. R. (1976), 'Effects of externally imposed deadlines on subsequent intrinsic motivation', *Journal of Personality and Social Psychology*, 34, 92–8.

Argyris, C. (1957), *Personality and Organization*, New York: Harper.

Benware, C., & Deci, E. L. (1984), 'Quality of learning with an active versus passive motivational set', *American Educational Research Journal*, 21, 755–65.

Blanck, P. D., Reis, H. T., & Jackson, L. (1984), 'The effects of verbal reinforcements on intrinsic motivation for sex-linked tasks', *Sex Roles, 10,* 369–87.

Bowers, D. G., & Seashore, S. E. (1966), 'Predicting organizational effectiveness with a four-factor theory of leadership', *Administrative Science Quarterly, 11,* 238–63.

Coch, L., & French, J. R. P. (1948), 'Overcoming resistance to change', *Human Relations, 11,* 512–32.

Deci, E. L. (1971), 'Effects of externally mediated rewards on intrinsic motivation', *Journal of Personality and Social Psychology, 18,* 105–15.

Deci, E. L., & Cascio, W. F. (1972), 'Changes in intrinsic motivation as a function of negative feedback and threats', paper presented at the meeting of the Eastern Psychological Association, Boston, April.

Deci, E. L., Nezlek, J., & Sheinman, L. (1981), 'Characteristics of the rewarder and intrinsic motivation of the rewardee', *Journal of Personality and Social Psychology, 40,* 1–10.

Deci, E. L., & Ryan, R. M. (1985), *Intrinsic Motivation and Self-Determination in Human Behavior,* New York: Plenum.

Deci, E. L., Schwartz, A. J., Sheinman, L., & Ryan, R. M. (1981), 'An instrument to assess adults' orientations toward control versus autonomy with children: Reflections on intrinsic motivation and perceived competence', *Journal of Educational Psychology, 73,* 642–50.

Eghrari, H., & Deci, E. L. (1988), 'Facilitating internalization: A motivational analysis', unpublished manuscript, University of Rochester.

Garbarino, J. (1975), 'The impact of anticipated reward upon cross-aged tutoring', *Journal of Personality and Social Psychology, 32,* 421–8.

Grolnick, W. S., & Ryan, R. M. (1987), 'Autonomy in children's learning: An experimental and individual difference investigation', *Journal of Personality and Social Psychology, 52,* 890–98.

Hackman, J. R., & Lawler, E. E., III (1971), 'Employee reactions to job characteristics', *Journal of Applied Psychology, 55,* 259–86.

Hackman, J. R., & Oldham, G. R. (1980), *Work Redesign,* Reading, Mass.: Addison-Wesley.

Halpin, A. W., & Winer, J. (1957), 'A factorial study of the Leader Behavior Description Questionnaire', in R. M. Stogdill & A. E. Coons (eds.), *Leader Behavior: Its Description and Measurement* (pp. 6–38), Columbus, Ohio: Bureau of Business Research, Ohio State University.

Harackiewicz, J. (1979),'The effects of reward contingency and performance feedback on intrinsic motivation', *Journal of Personality and Social Psychology, 37,* 1352–63.

Herzberg, F. (1966), *Work and the Nature of Man,* Cleveland, Ohio: World.

Koestner, R., Ryan, R. M., Bernieri, F., & Holt, K. (1984), 'Setting limits on children's behavior: The differential effects of controlling versus informational styles on intrinsic motivation and creativity', *Journal of Personality, 52,* 233–48.

Langer, E. J., & Rodin, J. (1976), 'The effects of choice and personal responsibility for the aged: A field experiment in an institutional setting', *Journal of Personality and Social Psychology, 34,* 191–8.

Lawler, E. E., III (1973), *Motivation in Work Organizations,* Monterey, Calif: Brooks-Cole.

Lawler, E. E., III (1986), *High-Involvement Management,* San Francisco: Jossey-Bass.

Lawler, E. E., III & Hackman, J. R. (1969), 'Impact of employee participation in the development of pay incentive plans: A field experiment', *Journal of Applied Psychology, 53,* 467–71.

Lepper, M. R., & Greene, D. (1975), 'Turning play into work: Effects of adult surveillance and extrinsic rewards on children's intrinsic motivation', *Journal of Personality and Social Psychology, 31,* 479–86.

Likert, R. (1961), *New Patterns of Management*, New York: McGraw-Hill.

Likert, R. (1967), *The Human Organization*, New York: McGraw-Hill.

McGregor, D. (1960), *The Human Side of Enterprise*, New York: McGraw-Hill.

Marrow, A. J., Bowers, D. G., & Seashore, S. E. (1967), *Management by Participation*, New York: Harper & Row.

Maslow, A. H. (1943), 'A theory of human motivation', *Psychological Review*, *50*, 370–96.

Ryan, R. M. (1982), 'Control and information in the intrapersonal sphere: An extension of cognitive evaluation theory', *Journal of Personality and Social Psychology*, *43*, 450–61.

Ryan, R. M., & Connell, J. P. (1989), 'Perceived locus of causality and internalization: Examining reasons for acting in two domains', *Journal of Personality and Social Psychology*, *57*, 749–61.

Ryan, R. M., & Grolnick, W. S. (1986), 'Origins and pawns in the classroom: Self-report and projective assessments of individual differences in children's perceptions', *Journal of Personality and Social Psychology*, *50*, 550–58.

Ryan, R. M., Mims, V., & Koestner, R. (1983), 'Relation of reward contingency and interpersonal context to intrinsic motivation: A review and test using cognitive evaluation theory', *Journal of Personality and Social Psychology*, 45, 736–50.

Scheflen, K. C., Lawler, E. E., & Hackman, J. R. (1971), 'Long-term impact of employee participation in the development of pay incentive plans: A field experiment', *Journal of Applied Psychology*, *55*, 182–6.

Smith, W. E. (1974), 'The effects of social and monetary rewards on intrinsic motivation', unpublished doctoral dissertation, Cornell University.

Terkel, S. (1972), *Working*, New York: Pantheon.

Vroom, V. H., & Deci, E. L. (1970), Introduction, in V. H. Vroom & E. L. Deci (eds.), *Management and Motivation* (pp. 9–19), Harmondsworth, England: Penguin.

Zuckerman, M., Porac, J., Lathin, D., Smith, R., & Deci, E. L. (1978), 'On the importance of self-determination for intrinsically motivated behavior', *Personality and Social Psychology Bulletin*, *4*, 443–6.

Performance Evaluations and Reward Structures

24

DOUGLAS McGREGOR

An Uneasy Look at Performance Appraisal

Abridged from D. McGregor, 'An uneasy look at performance appraisal', *Harvard Business Review*, Vol. 35(3), 1957, pp. 89–94

Performance appraisal within management ranks has become standard practice. The more the method is used, the more uneasy I grow over the unstated assumptions which lie behind it. This article, therefore, has two purposes:

1. To examine the conventional performance appraisal plan which requires the manager to pass judgement on the personal worth of subordinates.

2. To describe an alternative which places on the subordinate the primary responsibility for establishing performance goals and appraising progress toward them.

CURRENT PROGRAMS

Formal performance appraisal plans are designed to meet three needs, one for the organization and two for the individual:

1. They provide systematic judgements to back up salary increases, promotions, transfers, and sometimes demotions or terminations.

2. They are a means of telling a subordinate how he is doing, and suggesting needed changes in his behavior, attitudes, skills, or job knowledge; they let him know 'where he stands' with the boss.

3. They also are being increasingly used as a basis for the coaching and counseling of the individual by the superior.

Problem of resistance

Personnel administrators are aware that appraisal programs tend to run into resistance from the managers who are expected to administer them. Even managers who admit the necessity of such programs frequently balk at the process – especially the interview part. As a result, some companies do not communicate appraisal results to the individual, despite the general conviction that the subordinate has a right to know his superior's opinion so he can correct his weaknesses.

To meet this problem, formal controls – scheduling, reminders, and so on – are often instituted. It is common experience that without them fewer than half the appraisal interviews are actually held. But even controls do not necessarily work. Thus:

In one company with a well-planned and carefully administered appraisal program, an opinion poll included two questions regarding appraisals. More than 90 per cent of those answering the questionnaire approved the idea of appraisals. They wanted to know how they stood. Some 40 per cent went on to say that they had never had the experience of being told – yet the files showed that over four-fifths of them had signed a form testifying that they had been through an appraisal interview, some of them several times!

The respondents had no reason to lie, nor was there the slightest supposition that their superiors had committed forgery. The probable explanation is that the superiors, being basically resistant to the plan, had conducted the interviews in such a perfunctory manner that many subordinates did not realize what was going on. Training programs designed to teach the skills of appraising and interviewing do help, but they seldom eliminate managerial resistance entirely. The difficulties connected with 'negative appraisals' remain a source of genuine concern. There is always some discomfort involved in telling a subordinate he is not doing well. The individual who is 'coasting' during the few years prior to retirement after serving his company competently for many years presents a special dilemma to the boss who is preparing to interview him.

The underlying cause

What should we think about a method – however valuable for meeting organizational needs – which produces such results in a wide range of companies with a variety of appraisal plans? The problem is one that cannot be dismissed lightly.

Perhaps this intuitive managerial reaction to conventional performance appraisal plans shows a deep but unrecognized wisdom. In my view, it does not reflect anything so simple as resistance to change, or dislike for personnel technique, or lack of skill, or mistrust for rating scales. Rather, managers seem to be expressing real misgivings, which they find difficult to put into words. This could be the underlying cause:

The conventional approach, unless handled with consummate skill and delicacy, constitutes something dangerously close to a violation of the integrity of the personality. Managers are uncomfortable when they are put in the position of 'playing God'. The respect we hold for the inherent value of the individual leaves us distressed when we must take responsibility for judging the personal worth of a fellow man. Yet the conventional approach to performance appraisal forces us not only to make such judgements and to see them acted upon but also to communicate them to those we have judged. Small wonder we resist!

Of course, managers cannot escape making judgements about subordinates. Without such evaluations, salary and promotion policies cannot be administered sensibly. But are subordinates like products on an assembly line, to be accepted or rejected as a result of an inspection process? The inspection process may be made more objective or more accurate through research on the appraisal instrument, through training of the 'inspectors', or through introducing group appraisal; the subordinate may be 'reworked' by coaching or counseling before the final decision to accept or reject him; but as far as the assumptions of the conventional appraisal process are concerned, we still have what is practically identical with a program for product inspection.

On this interpretation, then, resistance to conventional appraisal programs is eminently sound. It reflects an unwillingness to treat human beings like physical objects. The needs of the organization are obviously important, but when they come into conflict with our convictions about the worth and the dignity of the human personality, one or the other must give.

Indeed, by the fact of their resistance managers are saying that the organization must yield in the face of this fundamental human value.

A NEW APPROACH

If this analysis is correct, the task is clear. We must find a new plan – not a compromise to hide the dilemma, but a bold move to resolve the issue.

A number of writers are beginning to approach the whole subject of management from the point of view of basic social values. Peter Drucker's (1954), concept of 'management by objectives' offers an unusually promising framework within which we can seek a solution.

Responsibility on subordinate
This approach calls on the subordinate to establish short-term

performance goals *for himself.* The superior enters the process actively only *after* the subordinate has (a) done a good deal of thinking about his job, (b) made a careful assessment of his own strengths and weaknesses, and (c) formulated some specific plans to accomplish his goals. The superior's role is to help the man relate his self-appraisal, his 'targets', and his plans for the ensuing period to the realities of the organization.

The first step in this process is to arrive at a clear statement of the major features of the job. Rather than a formal job description, this is a document drawn up *by the subordinate* after studying the company-approved statement. It defines the broad areas of his responsibility as they actually work out in practice. The boss and employee discuss the draft jointly and modify it as may be necessary until both of them agree that it is adequate.

Working from this statement of responsibilities, the subordinate then establishes his goals or 'targets' for a period of, say, six months. These targets are *specific* actions which the man proposes to take, i.e., setting up regular staff meetings to improve communication, reorganizing the office, completing or undertaking a certain study. Thus they are explicitly stated and accompanied by a detailed account of the actions he proposes to take to reach them. This document is, in turn, discussed with the superior and modified until both are satisfied with it.

At the conclusion of the six-month period, the subordinate makes *his own* appraisal of what he has accomplished relative to the targets he had set earlier. He substantiates it with factual data wherever possible. The 'interview' is an examination by superior and subordinate together of the subordinate's self-appraisal, and it culminates in a resetting of targets for the next six months.

Of course, the superior has veto power at each step of this process; in an organizational hierarchy anything else would be unacceptable. However, in practice he rarely needs to exercise it. Most subordinates tend to underestimate both their potentialities and their achievements. Moreover, subordinates normally have an understandable wish to satisfy their boss, and are quite willing to adjust their targets or appraisals if the superior feels they are unrealistic. Actually, a much more common problem is to resist the subordinates' tendency to want the boss to tell them what to write down.

This approach to performance appraisal differs profoundly from the conventional one, for it shifts the emphasis from *appraisal* to *analysis.* This implies a more positive approach. No longer is the subordinate being examined by the superior so that his weaknesses may be determined; rather, he is examining himself, in order to define not only his weaknesses but also his strengths and potentials. The importance of this shift of emphasis should not be underestimated. It is basic to each of the specific differences which distinguish this approach from the conventional one.

The first of these differences arises from the subordinate's new role in the process. He becomes an active agent, not a passive 'object'. He is no longer a pawn in a chess game called management development.

Effective development of managers does not include coercing them (no matter how benevolently) into acceptance of the goals of the enterprise, nor does it mean manipulating their behavior to suit organizational needs. Rather, it calls for creating a relationship within which a man can take responsibility for developing his own potentialities, plan for himself, and learn from putting his plans into action. In the process, he can gain a genuine sense of satisfaction, for he is utilizing his own capabilities to achieve simultaneously both his objectives and those of the organization. Unless this is the nature of the relationship, 'development' becomes a euphemism.

One of the main differences of this approach is that it rests on the assumption that the individual knows – or can learn – more than anyone else about his own capabilities, needs, strengths and weaknesses, and goals. In the end, only he can determine what is best for his development. The conventional approach, on the other hand, makes the assumption that the superior can know enough about the subordinate to decide what is best for him.

No available methods can provide the superior with the knowledge he needs to make such decisions. Ratings, aptitude and personality tests, and the superior's necessarily limited knowledge of the man's performance yield at best an imperfect picture.

The proper role for the superior, then, is the one that falls naturally to him under the suggested plan: helping the subordinate relate his career planning to the needs and realities of the organization. In the discussions, the boss can use his knowledge of the organization to help the subordinate establish targets and methods for achieving them which will (a) lead to increased knowledge and skill, (b) contribute to organizational objectives, and (c) test the subordinate's appraisal of himself.

This is help which the subordinate wants. He knows well that the rewards and satisfactions he seeks from his career as a manager depend on his contribution to organizational objectives. He is also aware that the superior knows more completely than he what is required for success in this organization and *under this boss*. The superior, then, is the person who can help him test the soundness of his goals and his plans for achieving them. Quite clearly the knowledge and active participation of *both* superior and subordinate are necessary components of this approach.

If the superior accepts this role, he need not become a judge of the subordinate's personal worth.

Another significant difference is that the emphasis is on the future rather than the past. The purpose of the plan is to establish realistic targets and to seek the most effective ways of reaching them. Appraisal thus becomes a means to a *constructive* end.

Finally, the accent is on *performance*, on actions relative to goals. There is less tendency for the personality of the subordinate to become an issue. The superior, instead of finding himself in the position of a psychologist or a therapist, can become a coach helping the subordinate to reach his own decisions on the specific steps that will enable him to reach his targets. Such counseling as may be required demands no deep analysis on the personal motivations or basic adjustment of the subordinate. To illustrate:

Consider a subordinate who is hostile, short-tempered, uncooperative, insecure. The superior need not make any psychological diagnosis. The 'target-setting' approach naturally directs the subordinate's attention to ways and means of obtaining better interdepartmental collaboration, reducing complaints, winning the confidence of the men under him. Rather than facing the troublesome prospect of forcing his own psychological diagnosis on the subordinate, the superior can, for example, help the individual plan ways of getting 'feedback' concerning his impact on his associates and subordinates as a basis for self-appraisal and self-improvement.

There is little chance that a man who is involved in a process like this will be in the dark about where he stands, or that he will forget he is the principal participant of his own development and responsible for it.

As a consequence of these differences we may expect the growth of a different attitude toward appraisal on the part of superior and subordinate alike.

The superior will gain real satisfaction as he learns to help his subordinates integrate their personal goals with the needs of the organization so that both are served. Once the subordinate has worked out a mutually satisfactory plan of action, the superior can delegate to him the responsibility for putting it into effect. He will see himself in a consistent managerial role rather than being forced to adopt the basically incompatible role of either the judge or the psychologist.

Unless there is a basic personal antagonism between the two men (in which case the relationship should be terminated), the superior can conduct these interviews so that both are actively involved in seeking the right basis for constructive action. The organization, the boss, and the subordinate all stand to gain. Under such circumstances the opportunities for learning and for genuine development of both parties are maximal.

It is true that more managerial skill and the investment of a considerable amount of time are required, but the greater motivation and the more effective development of subordinates can justify these added costs.

REFERENCE

Drucker, P. (1954), *The Practice of Management*, New York: Harper.

25

HARRY LEVINSON

Appraisal of *What* Performance?

Abridged from H. Levinson, 'Appraisal of *What* performance?', *Harvard Business Review*, Vol. 54(4), 1976, pp. 30–46, 160.

A corporate president put a senior executive in charge of a failing operation. His only directive was 'Get it in the black.' Within two years of that injunction, the new executive moved the operation from a deficit position to one that showed a profit of several million. Fresh from his triumph, the executive announced himself as a candidate for a higher-level position, and indicated that he was already receiving offers from other companies.

The corporate president, however, did not share the executive's positive opinions of his behavior. In fact, the president was not at all pleased with the way the executive had handled things. Naturally the executive was dismayed, and when he asked what he had done wrong, the corporate president told him that he had indeed accomplished what he had been asked to do, but he had done it singlehandedly, by the sheer force of his own personality. Furthermore, the executive was told, he had replaced people whom the company thought to be good employees with those it regarded as compliant. In effect, by demonstrating his own strength, he had made the organization weaker. Until the executive changed his authoritarian manner, his boss said, it was unlikely that he would be promoted further.

Implicit in this vignette is the major fault in performance appraisal and management by objectives – namely, a fundamental misconception of what is to be appraised.

Performance appraisal has three basic functions: (1) to provide adequate feedback to each person on his or her performance; (2) to serve as a basis for modifying or changing behavior toward more effective working habits; and (3) to provide data to managers with which they may judge future job assignments and compensation. The performance-appraisal concept is central to effective management. Much hard and imaginative work has gone into developing and refining it. In fact, there is a great deal of evidence to indicate how useful and effective performance appraisal is. Yet present systems of performance appraisal do not serve any of these functions well.

As it is customarily defined and used, performance appraisal focuses not on behavior but on outcomes of behavior. But even though the executive in the example achieved his objective, he was evaluated on how he attained it. Thus, while the system purports to appraise results, in practice, people are really appraised on how they do things – which is not formally described in the setting of objectives, and for which there are rarely data on record.

In my experience, the crucial aspect of any manager's job and the source of most failures, which is practically never described, is the 'how'. As long as managers appraise the ends yet actually give greater weight to the means, employ a static job-description base which does not describe the 'how', and do not have support mechanisms for the appraisal process, widespread dissatisfaction with performance appraisal is bound to continue.

When people write their own job descriptions (or make statements from which others will write them) essentially they define their responsibilities and basic functions. Then on performance-appraisal forms, managers comment on these functions by describing what an individual is supposed to accomplish.

In most instances the appraiser is asked to do an overall rating with a five-point scale or some similar device. Finally, he is asked to make a statement about the person's potential for the next step or even for higher-level management.

Nowhere in this set of questions or in any of the performance appraisal systems I have examined is anything asked about how the person is to attain the ends he or she is charged with reaching.

While some may assert that the ideal way of managing is to give a person a charge and leave him or her alone to accomplish it, this principle is over-simplified both in theory and practice. People need to know the topography of the land they are expected to cross, and the routes as perceived by those to whom they report.

DYNAMIC JOB DESCRIPTION

What we are looking for is [a performance-appraisal system] that amplifies statements of job responsibility and desired outcome by describing the emotional and behavioral topography of the task to be done by the individual in the job.

Psychologists describe behavior in many ways, each having his or her own preferences. I have found four major features of behavior to be fundamentally important in a wide range of managerial settings. These features have to do with how a person characteristically manages what some psychologists call aggression, affection, dependency, and also the nature of the person's ego ideal (Levinson, 1973).

Using his preferred system, one can begin formulating a dynamic job description by describing the characteristic behavior required by a job. This is what these terms mean with respect to job descriptions:

1. How does this job require the incumbent to handle his aggression, his attacking capacity?

Must he or she vanquish customers? Must he hold on to his anger in the face of repeated complaints and attacks from others? Will she be the target of hostility and, if so, from whom? Must he give firm direction to others? Must she attack problems vigorously, but handle some areas with great delicacy and finesse? Which problems are to be attacked with vigor and immediacy and which coolly and analytically?

2. How does this job require the incumbent to manage affection, the need to love and to be loved?

Is the person required to be a socially friendly leader of a close-knit work group? Should the person work closely and supportively with subordinates for task accomplishment? Is the task one in which the person will have to be content with the feeling of a job well done, or is it one which involves more public display and recognition? Will he be obscure and unnoticed, or highly visible? Must she lavish attention on the work, a product, a service, or customers? Must he be cold and distant from others and, if so, from whom?

3. How does this job require the incumbent to manage dependency needs?

Will the individual be able to lean on others who have skill and competencies, or will he have to do things himself? How much will she be on her own and in what areas? How much support will there be from superiors and staff functions? How well defined is the nature of the work? What kind of feedback provisions are there? What are the structural and hierarchical relationships? How solid are they and to whom will the person turn and for what? With which people must he interact in order to accomplish what he needs to accomplish, and in what manner?

4. What ego ideal demands does this job fulfill?

If one does the task well, what are the gratifications to be gained? Will the person make a lot of money? Will he achieve considerable organizational and public recognition? Will she be eligible for promotion? Will he feel good about himself and, if so, in what ways? Why? Will she acquire a significant skill, an important element of reputation, or an organizational constituency? Will he acquire power?

Individuals may be described along the same four dynamic dimensions: How does this person characteristically handle aggression? How does he or she characteristically handle affection? How does he or she characteristically handle dependency needs? What is the nature of his or her ego ideal?

Once the subtleties of the task are defined and individuals described, people may be matched to tasks. I am not advocating a return to evaluation of personality traits. I am arguing for a more dynamic conception of the managerial role and a more dynamic assessment of an employee's characteristics. And only when a person's behavior is recognized as basic to how he performs his job will performance-appraisal systems be realistic.

CRITICAL INCIDENT PROCESS

Having established a dynamic job description for a person, the next step is to evolve a complementary performance-appraisal system that will provide feedback on verifiable behavior, do so in a continuous fashion, and serve coaching-, promotion-, and salary-data needs.

Ideally, a manager and his subordinate will have defined together the objectives to be attained in a certain job, and the criteria by which each will know that those objectives have been attained, including the more qualitative aspects of the job. Then they will have spelled out the subtleties of how various aspects of the job must be performed. They will in this way have elaborated the *behavioral* requirements of the task.

In order for performance appraisal to be effective for coaching, teaching, and changing those aspects of an employee's behavior that are amenable to change, an employee needs to know about each piece of behavior that is good, as well as that which for some reason is not acceptable or needs modification. Such incidents will occur randomly and be judged randomly by his manager.

So that there will be useful data, the manager needs to quickly write down what he has said to the subordinate, describing in a paragraph what the subordinate did or did not do, in what setting, under what circumstances, about what problem. This information forms a *behavioral* record, a critical incident report of which the subordinate already has been informed and which is now in his folder, open to his review.

This critical incident technique is not new (Flanagan, 1954; Flanagan & Burns, 1955). In the past it has been used largely for case illustrations and, in modified forms, has been suggested as a method for first-level supervisors to evaluate line employees. Supervisors already record negative incidents concerning line employees because warnings and disciplinary steps must be documented. However, efforts to develop scales from critical incidents for rating behavior have not worked well (Schwab, Heneman, & DeCotis, 1975). Behavior is too complex to be scaled along a few dimensions and then rated.

But instead of scaling behavior, one might directly record the behavior of those being appraised, and evaluate it at a later date. There are other good reasons for adopting this technique as well. At last, here is a process that provides data to help managers perform the basic functions of performance-appraisal systems – namely, provide feedback, coaching, and promotion data.

Here is how behavioral data might be put to use in the critical incident process:

1. *Feedback data:* When there is a semi-annual or annual review, an employee will have no surprises and the manager will have on paper what he is using as a basis for making his summary feedback and appraisal. Because the data are on record, an employee cannot deny having heard what was said earlier, nor must the manager try to remember all year what have been the bases of his judgements.

Also, as each critical incident is recorded, over time there will be data in an individual's folder to be referred to when and if there are suits alleging discrimination. Critical incidents of behavior, which illustrate behavior patterns, will be the only hard evidence acceptable to adjudicating bodies.

2. *Coaching data:* When employees receive feedback information at the time the incident occurs, they may be able to adapt their behavior more easily. With this technique, the employee will receive indications more often on how he is doing, and will be able to correct small problems before they become large ones. Also, if the employee cannot change his behavior, that fact will become evident to him through the repetitive critical incident notes. If the employee feels unfairly judged or criticized, he may appeal immediately rather than long after the fact. If there are few or no incidents on record, that in itself says something about job behavior, and may be used as a basis for discussion. In any

event, both manager and employee will know which behavior is being appraised.

3. *Promotion data:* With such an accumulation of critical incidents, a manager or the personnel department is in a position to evaluate repeatedly how the person characteristically manages aggression, affection, and dependency needs, and the nature of his ego ideal. These successive judgements become cumulative data for better job fit.

When a person is provided continuously with verifiable information, including when he has been passed over for promotion and why, he is able to perceive more accurately the nuances of his behavior and his behavioral patterns. Thus, when offered other opportunities, the employee is in a better position to weigh his own behavioral configurations against those required by the prospective job. A person who knows himself in this way will be more easily able to say about a given job, 'That's not for me.' He will see that the next job in the pyramid is not necessarily rightfully his. In recognizing his own behavioral limitations he may save himself much grief as well as avoid painful difficulty for his superiors and the organization.

But the most important reason for having such information is to increase the chances of success of those who are chosen for greater responsibility. In most personnel folders there is practically no information about how a manager is likely to do when placed on his own. Data about dependency are noticeably absent, and many a shining prospect dims when there is no one to support him in a higher-level job. Managements need to know early on who can stand alone, and they cannot know that without behavioral information.

4. *Long-term data:* Frequently, new managers do not know their employees and all too often have little information in the folder with which to appraise them. This problem is compounded when managers move quickly from one area to another. For his part, the employee just as frequently has to prove himself to transient bosses who hold his fate in their hands but know nothing of his past performance. With little information, managers feel unqualified to make judgements. With the critical incident process, however, managers can report incidents which can be summarized by someone else.

Some may object to 'keeping book' on their people or resist a program of constant reviews and endless reports – both extreme views. Some may argue that supervisors will not follow the method. But if managers cannot get raises for or transfer employees without adequate documentation, they will soon learn the need to follow through. The critical incident process compels superiors to face subordinates, a responsibility too many shirk.

While it might seem difficult to analyze performance in terms of aggression, affection, dependency, the ego ideal, or other psychological concepts, to do so is no different from learning to use economic, financial, or accounting concepts. Many managers already talk about these same issues in other words, for example: 'taking charge' versus 'being a nice guy'; 'needing to be stroked' versus the 'self-starter'; 'fast track' versus the 'shelf-sitter'. A little practice, together with support mechanisms, can go a long way.

WHAT ABOUT RESULTS?

What does adopting the critical incident technique and the dynamic job description mean for judging a person's ability to obtain results? Does quantitative performance lose its importance?

My answer is an unqualified no. There will always be other issues that managers will have to determine, such as level of compensation or promotability – issues which should be dealt with in other sessions after the basic behavioral performance appraisal (Meyer, Kay, & French, 1965).

Some of the performance-appraisal information may be helpful in making such determinations, but neither of these two functions should contaminate the performance-appraisal feedback process. There can still be an annual compensation evaluation, based not only on behavior, which is the basis for coaching, but also on outcome. Did an employee make money? Did he reach quantitative goals? Did she resolve problems in the organization that were her responsibility?

No doubt, there will be some overlapping between behavior and outcome, but the two are qualitatively different. One might behave as it was expected he should, but at the same time not do what had to be done to handle the vagaries of the market-place. He might not have responded with enough speed or flexibility to a problem, even though his behavior corresponded to all that originally was asked of him in the job-description and goal-setting process.

Both behavior and outcome are important, and neither should be overlooked. It is most important, however, that they not be confused.

REFERENCES

Flanagan, J. C. (1954), 'The critical incident techinque', *Psychological Bulletin*, *51*, 327–58.

Flanagan, J. C., & Burns, R. K. (1955), 'The employee performance record: A new appraisal and development tool', *Harvard Business Review, 33*(5), 95–102.

Levinson, H. (1973), *The Great Jackass Fallacy* (Ch.3), Cambridge, Mass.: Harvard University Press.

Meyer, H. H., Kay, E., & French, J. R. P., Jr (1965), 'Split roles in performance appraisal', *Harvard Business Review*, *43*(1), 123–9.

Schwab, D. P., Heneman, H. G., III, & DeCotis, T. A. (1975), 'Behaviorally anchored rating scales: A review of the literature', *Personnel Psychology*, *28*, 549–62.

26

ROBERT L. OPSAHL AND MARVIN D. DUNNETTE

The Role of Financial Compensation in Industrial Motivation

Abridged from R. L. Opsahl and M. D. Dunnette, 'The role of financial
compensation in industrial motivation', *Psychological Bulletin*, Vol. 66,
1966, pp. 94–118.

In this review, we have attempted to identify and summarize research
studies designed to show how opportunities to get money affect the
way people actually do their work. It was decided to focus attention
on the role of money in motivating behavior *on the job*. Thus, we
review here those theories and studies designed to illuminate possible
effects of financial compensation for inducing greater effort in the
job setting, and we ignore those theories and studies related to
money's effects in inducing employees to take jobs, persist in them,
or to leave them.

BEHAVIORAL CONSEQUENCES OF COMPENSATION

The major research problem in industrial compensation is to determine
exactly what effects monetary rewards have for motivating various
behaviors. More specifically, we need to understand more precisely how
money can be used to induce employees to perform at high levels.
Relevant research centers around two major groupings: studies related
to the job or the job content and studies related to personal characteristics – preferences, perceptions, opinions, and other responses – made by
the job incumbent.

JOB AND TASK VARIABLES

Compensation policies

Our assumption is that the manner in which financial compensation is
administered may account for a large amount of the variation in job

behavior. The particular schedule of payment, the degree of secrecy surrounding the amount of pay one receives, how the level of salary or pay is determined, and the individual's long-term or career pay history all have important potential effects on how the employee responds to any specific amount of money.

Schedules of pay. In this review we shall be concerned solely with 'incentive' payment systems which are based on behavioral criteria (usually amount of output) rather than biographical factors such as education, seniority, and experience. Incentive pay schemes of various sorts are believed to function primarily to 'increase or maintain some already initiated activity or . . . to encourage some new form of activity . . .' (Marriott, 1957, p. 12).

There is considerable evidence that installation of such plans usually results in greater output per man hour, lower unit costs, and higher wages in comparison with outcomes associated with straight payment systems (e.g., Dale, 1959; Rath, 1960; Viteles, 1953). However, the installation of an incentive plan is not and can never be an isolated event. Frequently, changes in work methods, management policies, and organization accompany the changeover, and it is difficult to determine the amount of behavioral variance that each of these other events may contribute.

Incentive plans can be based on either the worker's own output or on the total output of his working group. The relative efficiency of the two methods is dependent upon such factors as the nature of the task performed (Babchuk & Goode, 1951; Marriott, 1957), the size of the working group (Campbell, 1952; Marriott, 1949, 1951; Marriott & Denerley, 1955; Shimmin, Williams, & Buck, 1956), the social environment (Selekman, 1941), and the particular group or individual plan employed. The chief disadvantage with group incentives is the likelihood of a low correlation between a worker's own individual performance and his pay in larger groups. There is also evidence (Campbell, 1952) that individual output decreases as the size of the work group increases, and this is apparently due to workers' perceiving a decreased probability that their efforts will yield increased outcomes (i.e., the workers have less knowledge of the relationships between effort and earnings). Both of these effects run counter to the main principle of incentive plans – immediate reward for desired job behaviors.

Not only do financial incentives operate with different efficacy in different situations, but often they do not even lead to increased production. Group standards and social pressures frequently induce workers to perform considerably below their potential.

Hickson (1961) has divided the causes of rate restriction into five categories. Three of the causes are essentially negative or avoidance reasons: uncertainty about the continuance of the existing 'effort-bargain' between the workers and management, uncertainty about the continuance of employment, and uncertainty about the continuance of existing social relationships. The other two causes are positive or approach-type factors: the desire to continue social satisfactions derived from the practice of restriction, and a desire for at least a minimal area of external control over one's own behavior.

Thus, although 'everyone knows' that incentive pay schemes work very effectively some of the time, it is painfully apparent that they are far from uniformly effective.

Secret pay policies. In addition to the particular kind of pay plan, the secrecy surrounding the amount of money given an employee may have motivational implications. Lawler's (1965) recent study indicates that secret pay policies may contribute to dissatisfaction with pay and to the possibility of lowered job performance. He found that managers over-estimated the pay of subordinates and peers, and underestimated their superiors' pay; they saw their own pay as being too low by comparison with all three groups. Moreover, they also underestimated the financial rewards associated with promotion. Lawler argued that these two results of pay secrecy probably reduce the motivation of managers both to perform well on their present jobs and to seek higher-level jobs. Another disadvantage of secrecy is that it lowers money's effectiveness as a knowledge-of-results device to let the manager know how well he is doing in comparison to others. Lawler advocated the abandonment of secrecy policies – 'there is no reason why organizations cannot make salaries public information'(p. 8).

Of course there might be negative outcomes from the sudden implementation of such policies. For example, one obvious possibility is that such action might crystallize present hierarchical 'pecking orders'; group cohesiveness could be disrupted by the sudden awareness of substantial intra-work-group differences. Most such fears stem from the prevalence of actual pay inequities related to inadequate job-performance appraisal systems and current weaknesses in administering salary payments in such a way as to reflect valid relationships with job performance.

Pay curves. An employee's periodic pay increases, as he progresses in his career with a company, constitute another job or task variable with the potential for differentially motivating effects. Wittingly or not, every company 'assigns' each employee a 'pay curve' which is the result of successive alterations in compensation and compensation policies through the years. One way of doing this (the usual way) is with little or no advanced planning; increments are given haphazardly on a year-to-year basis and the resulting career pay curve simply 'grows', somewhat like Topsy. Another alternative is to plan the future compensation program shortly after the individual enters the organization and then to modify it subsequently on the basis of his job behavior as his career unfolds. No matter which pay policy is adopted, the results will most likely affect the employee's job behavior, his aspirations and anticipations of future earnings, and his feelings of fairness with respect to his career-pay 'program'.

Most companies administer pay increments on a periodic (e.g., year-to-year) basis. The rationale for this is quite simple, the usual idea being that differential pay increments may be given for differential results produced by employees on their jobs. Over a span of many years, then, we might expect a consistent pattern of positive correlations for the salary increments received by the individuals comprising any particular group of employees.

In fact, however, career pay histories for employee groups do *not* usually show such patterns of consistently positive relationships between year-to-year salary gains. Haire (1965) mapped the correlations between salary levels at the end of each year and raises over five- and ten-year periods in two large national companies. Haire believed that his results constituted damning evidence that these two companies had no consistent polices with respect to the incentive use of salary increases. He also asserted that a pattern showing extremely low correlations between present salary levels and salary increments indicates that wage increases might just as well be distributed by lottery – that the incentive character of a raise is thereby nullified and that consistent striving for job excellence would seem futile under such circumstances.

SUBJECT VARIABLES

Perceived relations between performance and pay

According to Vroom's (1964) theory of work motivation, the valence of effective performance increases as the instrumentality of effective performance for the attainment of money increases, assuming that the valence of money is positive. Georgopoulos, Mahoney, and Jones' (1957) Path–Goal Approach theory similarly states that if a worker has a desire for a given goal and perceives a given path leading to that goal, he will utilize that path if he has freedom to do so. Georgopoulos et al. found that workers who perceived higher personal productivity as a means to increased earnings performed more effectively than workers who did not perceive this relationship.

The effectiveness of incentive plans in general depends upon the worker's knowledge of the relation between performance and earnings. The lack of this knowledge is one cause of failure in incentive schemes. As already mentioned, Campbell's (1952) study showed that one of the major reasons for lower productivity in large groups under group incentive plans is that the workers often do not perceive the relation between pay and productivity as well as they do in smaller groups. In the Georgopoulos et al. (1957) study, only 38 per cent of the workers perceived increased performance as leading to increased earnings. More amazingly, 35 per cent perceived *low* productivity as an aid to higher earnings in the long run. Lawler (1964) recently found that 600 managers perceived their training and experience to be the most important factors in determining their pay – not how well or how poorly they performed their jobs. Since Lawler found that the relation between their pay and their rated job performance also was low, their perceptions were probably quite accurate. A separate analysis of the most highly motivated managers, however, indicated that they attached greater importance to pay and felt that good job performance would lead to higher pay.

These studies confirm the importance of knowing how job performance and pay are related. The relation between performing certain desired behaviors and attainment of the pay incentive must be explicitly specified. The foregoing statement seems so obvious as hardly to warrant mentioning. Unfortunately, as we have seen, the number of times in industry that the above *rule* is ignored is surprising.

Personality–task interactions

Under some conditions, it appears that even specifying the relation between performance and pay is not sufficient. Early studies (Wyatt & Fraser, 1929; Wyatt, Fraser, & Stock, 1929; Wyatt & Langdon, 1937) conducted on British factory workers showed that feelings of boredom are associated with reduced output even under a carefully developed program of incentive pay.

One possible method of alleviating feelings of boredom is suggested by Wyatt and Fraser's (1929) finding that piece-rate systems lead to fewer symptoms of boredom than does straight hourly pay. This is in keeping with Whyte's (1955) contention that, in addition to money, there are three other sources of reward in a piece-rate situation: escape from fatigue, because the worker has a meaningful goal to shoot at; escape from management pressure and gain of control over one's own time; and 'playing the game' of trying to attain quota.

Even if piece-rate systems relieve boredom, output under such plans may still suffer if the task is disliked. This was Wyatt's (1934) finding when he compared the levels of performance of ten female workers in a British candy factory under hourly, bonus, and piece-rate payment methods. He observed a strong positive relation between an incentive plan's effectiveness (defined as increased productivity) and liking for the job. The best-liked job was wrapping the candy and employees increased their output on it 200 per cent when payment was changed from straight pay to a group bonus and finally to piece-rate payment. In contrast, unwrapping damaged packages was viewed as most onerous – 'an aimless and destructive process' – and output on this task showed no change under different conditions of pay.

The net conclusion from these studies is that repetitive tasks, destructive tasks, boring tasks, and disliked tasks are apparently much less susceptible to monetary incentives. Little has been done, however, to explore other possible interactions in this area. What little data we do have suggest that non-monetary incentives are more effective for subjects who have high ability on the task being measured. Thus, Fleishman (1958) found that subjects high in ability on a complex coordination task increased their performance under incentive conditions significantly more than did low-ability subjects. However, we do not know if such findings would generalize to situations in which monetary incentives are used or how the effectiveness of incentives varies as a function of other important variables such as the type of task, the amount of physical effort demanded, or the degree of interpersonal interaction involved, to mention but a few examples.

Perceived importance of pay

It seems obvious that employees must regard money as a highly desirable commodity before increased amounts of it motivate increased behavior.

In a study by Watson (1939), employees ranked pay third in importance on a list of eight 'morale' factors. However, when their employers were asked to rank the eight factors according to how they thought the employees would respond, pay was selected as the most important factor. This differential perception of the importance of money by employees and higher management has been confirmed in a survey conducted by the National Industrial Conference Board (1947), showing that executives ranking seventy-one morale factors in terms of overall importance gave top rank to compensation, while fewer than 30 per cent of the rank-and-file employees included this among the five most important factors.

Thus, research on the valence of money must move beyond the dependency on self-report measures and strive to establish the actual linkages between money and behavior by more sophisticated observational techniques.

Pay preferences

Although money *per se* is usually accorded a middle position in any ranking of job factors, different ways of making salary payments are differentially preferred. Mahoney (1964) found that managers prefer straight salary over various types of management incentive payments (such as stock options, deferred compensation, etc.). Likewise, Davis (1948) found that 60 per cent of a sample of building operatives were opposed to incentive schemes, with only 21 per cent expressing definite or conditional approval. The main arguments against incentive systems, as reported by Davis, include the fear that the incentive would inhibit other strong and pleasurable motives for working, such as the pleasure of work for its own sake and the solidarity and good fellowship of the working group.

A study conducted by the Michigan Survey Research Center (Larke, 1953) revealed that group incentive payments were favored by fewer than 50 per cent of the employees who already were under such plans. Similarly, Mahoney (1964) found that his sample of managers also preferred individual to group pay plans. On the other hand, Wyatt and Marriott (1956) found more approval than disapproval of group incentives by 62 per cent of the workers sampled in three factories. With respect to particular types of incentives, Spriegal and Dale (1953) found individual piece-work much more popular than group piece-work.

Using paired-comparison techniques, Nealey (1963) found that a large sample ($N = 1,133$) of electrical workers accorded direct pay increases a lower position than such fringe benefits as sick leave, extra vacation time, or hospital insurance.

Although there has been a fair amount of research done in determining the pay preferences of managers and other employees, no work has been done on the relation between preference for a particular plan and the actual incentive value of that plan. The implicit, but unwarranted, assumption in all the above-mentioned studies is that if a person has a pay plan he likes, this plan will motivate behavior more than one that he does not like.

Concept of equitable payment

Several theories have been independently advanced proposing that employees seek a just or equitable return for what they have contributed to the job (Adams, 1963, 1965; Homans, 1961; Jaques, 1961; Patchen, 1961; Sayles, 1958; Zaleznik, Christenson, & Roethlisberger, 1958). A common feature of these theories is the assumption that compensation either above or below that which is perceived by the employee to be 'equitable' results in tension and dissatisfaction due to dissonant cognitions. The tension, in turn, causes the employee to attempt to restore consonance by a variety of behavioral or cognitive methods. [See Reading 10 by Adams for a fuller discussion of equity.]

FUTURE RESEARCH

Although it is generally agreed that money is the major mechanism for rewarding and modifying behavior in industry, very little is known about how it works. Haire remarked at a recent symposium on managerial compensation that, in spite of the tremendous amount of money spent and the obvious relevance of behavioral theory for compensation practices, there is less research and theory in this area than in almost any other field related to management (Haire, 1965). Similarly, Dunnette and Bass (1963), in a critique of current personnel management practices, pointed out that personnel men have relied on faddish and assumptive practices in administering pay which lack empirical support.

As this review shows, very little is known about the behavioral laws regulating the effectiveness of incentives. We continue to dole out large sums of money under the guise of 'incentive pay' without really knowing much about its incentive character. We do not know, for instance, the nature of the effect of a pay raise or the length of time before that effect occurs; or, for that matter, how long the raise may be effective. Nor do we know the optimal reinforcement schedule to be used in giving salary increases for obtaining desired changes in job behavior.

As research on the role of financial compensation in industrial motivation becomes more and more prevalent, answers to many of the questions posed above should be forthcoming. Increased knowledge should be accompanied by more effective use of money in industry. It is hoped that the firm of the future will be able to establish compensation policies and practices based on empirical evidence about the behavioral effects of money as an incentive rather than on the non-tested assumptions, hunches, and time worn 'rules-of-thumb' so common in industry today.

REFERENCES

Adams, J. S. (1963), 'Toward an understanding of inequity', *Journal of Abnormal and Social Psychology*, *67*, 422–36.

Adams, J. S. (1965), 'Inequity in social exchange', in L. Berkowitz (ed.), *Advances in Experimental Social Psychology* (Vol. 2, pp. 267–99), New York: Academic Press.

Babchuk, N., & Goode, W. J. (1951), 'Work incentives in a self-determined group', *American Social Review*, *16*, 679–87.

Campbell, H. (1952), 'Group incentive payment schemes: The effects of lack of understanding and group size', *Occupational Psychology*, *26*, 15–21.

Dale, J. (1959), 'Increase productivity 50 per cent in one year with sound wage incentives', *Management Methods*, *16*, 38–42.

Davis, N. M. (1948), 'Attitudes to work among building operatives', *Occupational Psychology*, *22*, 56–62.

Dunnette, M. D., & Bass, B. M. (1963), 'Behavioral scientists and personnel management', *Industrial Relations*, *2*, 115–30.

Fleishman, E. A. (1958), 'A relationship between incentive motivation and ability level in psychomotor performance', *Journal of Experimental Psychology*, *56*, 78–81.

Georgopoulos, B. S., Mahoney, G. M., & Jones, N. W. (1957), 'A path–goal approach to productivity', *Journal of Applied Psychology*, *41*, 345–53.

Haire, M. (1965), 'The incentive character of pay', in R. Andrews (ed.), *Managerial Compensation* (pp. 13–17), Ann Arbor: Foundation for Research on Human Behavior.

Hickson, D. J. (1961), 'Motives of work people who restrict their output', *Occupational Psychology*, *35*, 110–21.

Homans, G. C. (1961), *Social Behavior: Its Elementary Forms*, New York: Harcourt, Brace & World.

Jaques, E. (1961), *Equitable Payment*, New York: Wiley.

Larke, A. G. (1953), 'Workers' attitudes on incentives', *Dun's Review and Modern Industry*, December, 61–3.

Lawler, E. E., III (1964), 'Managers' job performance and their attitudes toward their pay', unpublished doctoral dissertation, University of California, Berkeley.

Lawler, E. E., III (1965), 'Managerial perceptions of compensation', paper read at Mid-western Psychological Association convention, Chicago, April.

Mahoney, T. (1964), 'Compensation preferences of managers', *Industrial Relations*, *3*, 135–44.

Marriott, R. (1949), 'Size of working group and output', *Occupational Psychology*, *23*, 47–57.

Marriott, R. (1951), 'Socio-psychological factors in productivity', *Occupational Psychology*, *25*, 15–24

Marriott, R. (1957), *Incentive Payment Systems: A Review of Research and Opinion*, London: Staples Press.

Marriott, R., & Denerley, R. A. (1955), 'A method of interviewing used in studies of worker attitudes: II. Validity of the method and discussion of the results', *Occupational Psychology*, *59*, 69–81.

National Industrial Conference Board (1947), 'Factors affecting employee morale' (Studies in Personnel Policy No. 85), New York: Author.

Nealey, S. (1963), 'Pay and benefit preferences', *Industrial Relations*, *1*, 17–28.

Patchen, M. (1961), *The Choice of Wage Comparisons*, Englewood Cliffs, NJ: Prentice Hall.

Rath, A. A. (1960), 'The case for individual incentives', *Personnel Journal*, *39*, 172–5.

Sayles, L. R. (1958), *Behavior of Industrial Work Groups: Prediction and Control*, New York: Wiley.

Selekman, B. M. (1941), 'Living with collective bargaining', *Harvard Business Review*, *22*, 21–3.

Shimmin, S., Williams, J., & Buck, L. (1956), 'Studies of some factors in incentive payment systems', Report to the Medical Research Council. London: Industrial Psychology Research Group, (mimeo).

Spriegal, W. R., & Dale, A. G. (1953), 'Trends in personnel selection and induction', *Personnel*, *30*, 169–75.

Viteles, M. S. (1953), *Motivation and Morale in Industry*, New York: Norton.

Vroom, V. H. (1964), *Work and Motivation*, New York: Wiley.

Watson, G. (1939), 'Work satisfaction', in G. W. Hartmann & T. Newcomb (eds.), *Industrial Conflict* (pp. 114–24), New York: The Cordon Co.

Whyte, W. F. (1955), *Money and Motivation: An Analysis of Incentives in Industry*, New York: Harper.

Wyatt, S. (1934), *Incentives in Repetitive Work: A Practical Experiment in a Factory* (Industrial Health Research Board Report No. 69), London: His Majesty's Stationery Office.

Wyatt, S., & Fraser, J. S. (1929), *The Comparative Effects of Variety and Uniformity in Work* (Industrial Fatigue Research Board Report No. 52), London: His Majesty's Stationery Office.

Wyatt, S., Fraser, J. A., & Stock, F. G. L. (1929), *The Effects of Monotony in Work* (Industrial Fatigue Research Board Report No. 56), London: His Majesty's Stationery Office.

Wyatt, S., & Langdon, J. N. (1937), *Fatigue and Boredom in Repetitive Work* (Industrial Health Research Board Report No. 77), London: His Majesty's Stationery Office.

Wyatt, S., & Marriott, R. (1956), *A Study of Attitudes to Factory Work*, London: Her Majesty's Stationery Office.

Zaleznik, A., Christenson, C. R., & Roethlisberger, F. J. (1958), *The Motivation, Productivity, and Satisfaction of Workers: A Prediction Study*, Boston, Mass.: Harvard University, Graduate School of Business Administration.

27

RICHARD M. RYAN, VALERIE MIMS, AND
RICHARD KOESTNER

Relation of Reward Contingency and Interpersonal Context to Intrinsic Motivation: A Review and Test Using Cognitive Evaluation Theory

Abridged from R. M. Ryan, V. Mims, and R. Koestner, 'Relation of reward contingency and interpersonal context to intrinsic motivation: A review and test using cognitive evaluation theory', *Journal of Personality and Social Psychology*, Vol. 45, 1983, pp. 736–50

The experimental literature on intrinsic motivation includes a complicated set of studies on reward contingency. In all, more than two dozen published studies are relevant to the contingency variable; however, various writers have used different terminology and the results seem inconsistent and at times contradictory. This article reviews and integrates the previous studies and presents some new data to test the proposed integration.

The issue of contingency first appeared in an article in which Deci (1972a) compared the effects of 'contingent' rewards ($1 paid for each puzzle that a subject solved), 'non-contingent' rewards ($2 paid for participating in the experiment), and no rewards. He reported that contingent rewards decreased intrinsic motivation relative to non-contingent rewards and no rewards. Subsequently, several other investigators explored the contingency issue. As early as 1977, Condry presented a lengthy review of studies on contingency effects and concluded that there was need for further clarification.

Perhaps the major obstacle in the integration of this research has been terminological differences. Different researchers have used different terms to mean the same thing and the same terms to mean different things. To review the underlying coherencies and inconsistencies requires a translation of procedures to a standardized vocabulary. We shall begin by establishing one so that the seemingly disparate studies can be compared.

First, the term *task-non-contingent reward* shall be interpreted to mean expected rewards that are given to people for participating in an experimental session, independent of what they do in that session. They are rewarded simply for their presence, without respect to the completion or quality of task activity. This type of reward is essentially comparable to hourly payments in the real world. People are paid for being on the job rather than for particular behaviors. Frequently, this type of reward structure has been labeled non-contingent in the experimental literature (e.g. Condry, 1977; Deci, 1972a). The term *task-non-contingent* prevents confusion with the more frequent use of the term *non-contingent* in the context of helplessness theory (e.g., Seligman, 1975). Task-non-contingent rewards are non-contingent in relation to task behavior, but they are contingent on attendance, so they are quite predictable and controllable and therefore do not induce helplessness.

Second, the term *task-contingent reward* is interpreted to mean that a reward is given for doing a task: for example, a person is paid a set amount for each puzzle solved or each model assembled. Task-contingent rewards are usually given for completion of an activity, but without respect to quality of performance. This payment system is roughly comparable to the piece-rate payment system in the real world and is what Deci (1972a) originally referred to as contingent rewards.

Third, the term *performance-contingent reward* is interpreted to mean a reward that is given for a specified level of performance, that is, for meeting a set criterion, norm, or level of competence. Stated differently, the focus here is on whether people are performing well relative to some type of standard. Although there is no common or uniform real-world pay structure that is directly analogous to these rewards, certain types of bonus or incentive systems would be considered performance contingent. Performance-contingent rewards typically convey that the recipient is skillful or competent at the activity. Of course, task-contingent rewards could also convey competence information; for example, when rewards are administered for each unit of production, obtaining more rewards may mean that one is performing better. However, without specific reference to norms or levels of competence for performance, the rewards would not be considered performance contingent.

Finally, some studies have used the term *contingency* to refer to 'zero-sum' situations in which two or more people compete for a reward. Winning, and thus receiving the reward, demonstrates competence and therefore represents a kind of performance contingency; however, the competition introduces additional considerations that make the situation somewhat different. Thus, we use the term *competitively contingent reward* to refer to situations in which people compete directly with others for a limited number of rewards that are fewer than the number of competitors.

With these categories, we are able to review the experimental literature and integrate the various findings. Before beginning, however, we present one proposition of cognitive evaluation theory (Deci & Ryan, 1980, 1985) that we use in conjunction with the above categories to analyze the experimental findings.

COGNITIVE EVALUATION THEORY

Deci and Ryan asserted that external events such as rewards and communications can have two functional aspects: an informational aspect and a controlling aspect. The informational aspect conveys meaningful feedback in the context of self-determination. There are two important elements in this definition: first, that there be meaningful information and, second, that there be self-determination *vis-à-vis* performance outcomes. For purposes of the present review, the phrase *meaningful feedback* refers to information that is 'effectance' relevant, that is, information that signifies to a person that he or she is competent at the target activity or information that lets the person know how to become more competent at the activity. For any feedback to serve an informational function, it must be received within a context of self-determined performance, as Fisher (1978) demonstrated. Without this context, feedback does not really reflect on one's competence. Several studies have shown the enhancing effect of informational feedback on intrinsic motivation (e.g., Pittman, Davey, Alafat, Wetherill, & Kramer, 1980; Ryan, 1982). Feedback and the informational aspect of rewards are particularly important elements for the present discussion because their presence or absence is a central feature of reward-contingency studies.

The controlling aspect of rewards and communications pressures people toward specified outcomes. If a reward is experienced as making people do something, in other words, if the activity must be done in some particular way, at some particular time, or in some particular place for the person to receive the reward, the reward tends to be experienced as controlling. Just as research has shown that informational rewards or communications tend to enhance intrinsic motivation, an even larger body of data has confirmed that controlling rewards and communications undermine intrinsic motivation (see Deci & Ryan, 1985, for a review).

Cognitive evaluation theory predicts and interprets the effects of external events on intrinsic motivation and other closely related internal variables by providing an analysis of the relative salience of the informational versus controlling aspect of the external events.

SUBJECTS AND THE TASK

In this review, we are concerned only with the effects of rewards on intrinsically interesting tasks. Intrinsically interesting tasks are ones that involve challenge (Deci, 1975), responsiveness (i.e., the possibility for outcomes to be self-determined; Fisher. 1978), and effectance feedback (White, 1959). A person needs to be able to get some sense of how well he or she is doing at the activity to remain intrinsically interested. When building a model, for example, a person sees progress, so feedback is inherent in the activity. Finally, intrinsically interesting tasks need to be ones that a person does not typically do to get rewards. Kruglanski et al. (1975) and Staw, Calder, Hess, and Sandelands (1980) found different, and not directly relevant, results when monetary rewards were offered for a task that is typically done for money.

Some studies have been done with male subjects, some with female subjects, and some with both sexes of subject. There is no indication that various types of tangible reward contingencies affect males and females differently.

Finally, the studies employed subjects of various ages: preschoolers, elementary school children, high-school students, and college students, but across the studies under review there is no clear indication that reward contingencies *per se* had a differential effect depending on age, so that is not addressed systematically.

Having laid the groundwork, we turn now to a review of the literature relevant to the issue of reward contingency.

TASK-NON-CONTINGENT REWARDS

We know of only three studies that have compared task-non-contingent rewards to no rewards. Deci (1972a) offered college-student subjects a $2 reward for participating in a puzzle-solving experiment and found that their intrinsic motivation following the puzzle solving did not differ from that of non-rewarded subjects. Pinder (1976) replicated these results with college students, and Swann and Pittman (1977) reported similar results for elementary school children when the effects of a task-non-contingent good-player award were compared to the effects of no rewards. Thus, it appears that task-non-contingent rewards tend not to decrease intrinsic motivation because they do not create an instrumentality and are not experienced as controlling.

TASK-CONTINGENT REWARDS

Several studies have compared the effects of task-contingent rewards (those given for doing the activity) with either no rewards or task-non-contingent rewards. Generally task-contingent rewards are administered in the absence of additional performance-related feedback from an experimenter because such information is not inherent or necessary in this reward structure. The studies on task contingency reported here all involve no explicit feedback unless otherwise noted.

When the phrase *contingent rewards* (what we call task-contingent rewards now) was first used (Deci, 1972a), it referred to rewards being offered for each of several puzzles that a subject completed in a specified amount of time. The puzzles were sufficiently difficult that subjects were not able to complete all of them, so the amount of their earnings was actually contingent on how well they did at the puzzle activity. Later, the phrase *task contingent* came to be used for rewards that were offered for doing an activity that was easy enough that everyone could do it, so everyone got the same reward. This latter use typically occurred in studies with children in which, for example, they were offered rewards for drawing a picture (e.g., Lepper, Greene, & Nisbett, 1973). Thus, the phrase *task contingent* can mean either that subjects are rewarded for 'working on a task' or for 'completing a task'. Both types of task-contingent administrations create instrumentalities between the activity and the reward, and both have been shown to have the same effects on intrinsic motivation.

Deci (1971, 1972b) reported that task-contingent monetary rewards ($1 for each of four puzzles solved) decreased intrinsic motivation relative to no rewards. Similar results were reported by Weiner and Mander (1978), who actually used both types of task-contingent rewards and found that both decreased intrinsic motivation, though the undermining by rewards that required 'completing' the task was more extreme than that by rewards that merely required 'working on' the task. Pittman, Cooper, and Smith (1977) and Smith and Pittman (1978) also found that task-contingent monetary rewards decreased subjects' intrinsic motivation for game activities. In those studies, as in the Deci (1971, 1972b) studies, subjects' rewards depended on how well they performed; however, the rewards were considered task contingent rather than performance contingent because the rewards were not contingent upon how well subjects performed relative to some type of standard for performance, such as normative information. Better performance led to greater rewards, but subjects had no way of knowing how well they were actually performing. Similar results were reported by Daniel and Esser (1980) when rewards were offered in a way that implied greater rewards for better performance. Finally, Luyten and Lens (1981) and Calder and Staw (1975) reported that task-contingent rewards, offered for completing puzzles, decreased subjects' intrinsic motivation.

Several investigators have also reported that offering task-contingent rewards merely for 'doing' an activity decreased intrinsic motivation relative to no rewards. These diverse studies have included offering money to college students (Wilson, Hull, & Johnson, 1981), prizes to high school students (Harackiewicz, 1979), candy to elementary school children (Ross et al., 1976), and good-player awards to preschool children (Greene & Lepper, 1974; Lepper et al., 1973).

Danner and Lonky (1981), Dollinger and Thelen (1978), Fazio (1981), Loveland and Olley (1979), McLoyd (1979), Morgan (1981), and Ross (1975) provided more support for the hypothesis that task-contingent rewards, offered to children for engaging in an intrinsically interesting activity, decrease the children's intrinsic motivation for the activity. Ross's study showed that the rewards had to be salient to produce this effect; McLoyd's study showed that the rewards had to be desirable to the children to have the effect; Danner and Lonky's study showed that the task had to be optimally challenging (i.e., intrinsically interesting) for the rewards to have the undermining effect; and Fazio's study showed that it is possible to buffer against this effect by reminding the child that he or she was initially interested in the target activity. In the Loveland and Olley study, the undermining effect was apparent one week following the children's being rewarded with a good-player award, although the effect had worn off after seven weeks. Finally, in the Dollinger and Thelen study, tangible rewards (food) were found to decrease intrinsic motivation.

In sum, the weight of evidence makes it clear that task-contingent rewards, whether given for working on an activity or completing an activity, decrease intrinsic motivation relative to no rewards, if the task-contingent rewards are administered without additional explicit performance feedback.

A study by Deci (1972b) combined task-contingent rewards with verbal feedback and compared this combination with a no-feedback, no-reward group. Although task-contingent rewards alone decreased intrinsic motivation relative to no rewards, the addition of positive competence feedback averted this effect such that there was no significant difference between the no-reward group and the task-contingent/verbal-feedback group. Harackiewicz (1979) and Swann and Pittman (1977) also compared task-contingent rewards plus positive feedback to no rewards, no feedback. Both studies found that the two groups did not differ. Thus, these three studies indicate that the effects of task-contingent rewards and positive feedback seem to offset each other.

The case for task-contingent rewards relative to task-non-contingent rewards is less clear, though the evidence provides weak support for the hypothesis that task-contingent rewards are more undermining of intrinsic motivation than task-non-contingent rewards. Deci (1972a) reported a clearly significant difference between groups given the two kinds of rewards, and Phillips and Lord (1980) found the effect on a self-report measure though not on a behavioral measure. Pinder (1976) found some marginal support for the hypothesis that task-contingent rewards are more detrimental than task-non-contingent rewards. Farr, Vance, and McIntyre (1977) reported results that tend to support the hypothesis, although they interpreted their data as being largely non-confirmatory, and Farr (1976) reported no difference between task-contingent and task-non-contingent groups.

Why might one expect that under some conditions, task-contingent rewards would be more detrimental to intrinsic motivation than task-non-contingent rewards? The answer lies in the degree of control conveyed by the reward. When one must complete a task to get a reward, the task is more likely to be seen as instrumental to the reward. The task is something one *must* do to get the reward. This makes it more controlling than a task-non-contingent reward that one gets independent of any particular task performance. On the other hand, that the reward is given for completion of a task could provide some competence feedback; however, with most tasks, completion *per se* (without normative information) provides minimal information or effectance feedback. Simply stated, although conditions of task contingency can in some instances be relatively informational, in most instances it is the controlling aspect of the reward that is relatively more salient, so intrinsic motivation tends to be undermined to a somewhat greater degree than with task-non-contingent rewards. To date, the data appear to support this hypothesis, albeit tentatively.

PERFORMANCE-CONTINGENT REWARDS

Performance-contingent rewards go a step further than task-contingent rewards in making salient both informational and controlling aspects of rewards. By requiring a specified level of performance, the reward is even more controlling, but it also increases the informational value of the reward considerably. As we suggest later, performance-contingent rewards can be made to be either primarily informational or primarily controlling, depending on the context of administration. First, however, let us review the studies.

In considering the effects of performance-contingent rewards, we begin by comparing performance-contingent rewards to no rewards. One important issue to keep in mind is that performance-contingent rewards, by definition, provide competence feedback. That raises the question of whether the appropriate comparison group is a no-reward group with comparable feedback or without comparable feedback. First, we consider a no-reward group with positive feedback.

Karniol and Ross (1977) did a study with four nine-year-old children who received either performance-contingent rewards or no rewards, but got positive feedback. Their results indicated no difference between the performance-contingent-rewards group that conveyed positive competence feedback and the no-reward/positive feedback control group. Rosenfield, Folger, and Adelman (1980) compared what they called a contingent-reward/positive-competence-feedback (i.e., a performance contingency) group with a no-reward/positive-competence-feedback group. There was no difference between them in terms of subsequent intrinsic motivation. There was a peculiarity in this study, however, that makes it not directly comparable to the Karniol and Ross study. The competence feedback was based on performance during a practice period rather than during the actual puzzle-solving period. Therefore, it is difficult to interpret their results with respect to the question at hand. Parenthetically, they did report the interesting finding that when rewards were made performance contingent, larger rewards tended to result in greater intrinsic motivation than smaller rewards. Finally, Harackiewicz (1979) reported that performance-contingent-rewards subjects displayed less intrinsic motivation than the no-reward/positive-feedback subjects. It appears, then, that the issue of the effects of performance-contingent rewards relative to the effects of no rewards that are accompanied by positive feedback, which is comparable to the positive feedback conveyed by the performance-contingent rewards, remains unresolved. We return to this later, as it is one of the main points addressed by the present study.

The relation between a performance-contingent-rewards condition and a no-reward/no-feedback control group was also addressed in the Harackiewicz study; however, in her study there were two performance-contingency groups and they yielded different results relative to the no-reward/no-feedback group. We will also return to this issue below as it is quite germane to the present study.

PERFORMANCE-CONTINGENT VERSUS TASK-CONTINGENT REWARDS

As with no rewards, task-contingent rewards can occur in a context either with or without competence feedback. First, consider a comparison of performance-contingent rewards to task-contingent rewards with comparable feedback. From cognitive evaluation theory, one would predict that if the feedback accompanying the two groups is comparable (so the information is the same), then performance-contingent rewards are likely to be more undermining than task-contingent rewards because, as we said, the performance contingency highlights the controlling nature of the rewards. There is only one study that included both these groups. Harackiewicz's (1979) results showed that performance-contingent subjects were considerably less intrinsically motivated than task-contingent subjects who got positive feedback.

The more complex comparison is between performance-contingent rewards and task-contingent rewards administered without positive feedback, because, as we said, the performance contingency can increase both the informational and controlling aspects, and if the task contingency is not accompanied by comparable information, there is no clear basis for making a prediction. As might be expected, the results are somewhat unclear.

Greene and Lepper (1974) reported no difference between a task-contingent group not receiving feedback and a performance-contingent group. Luyten and Lens (1981) reported a tendency for the performance-contingent rewards to lead to higher intrinsic motivation than task-contingent rewards, although the differences were not significant. Finally, Boggiano and Ruble (1979) found a significant difference between children who received task-contingent rewards without feedback versus performance-contingent rewards, and Enzle and Ross (1978) also reported that a performance-contingent group of college students was significantly more intrinsically interested than a task-contingent/no-feedback group. In the Enzle and Ross article, the authors used atypical terminology, which is important to recognize in interpreting their results. They referred to the group that we call performance contingent as 'criterion contingent' because their rewards depended on a specified performance criterion. Further, the group that we call task-contingent they referred to interchangeably as task contingent, task-performance contingent, and just performance contingent. None the less, the results show clearly that (using the present terminology) the performance-contingent group was more intrinsically interested than the task-contingent group.

In sum, although the results are mixed, there is the suggestion that performance-contingent rewards enhance intrinsic motivation relative to task-contingent rewards without feedback; however, a clear replication seems warranted. The present study includes such a comparison.

PERFORMANCE CONTINGENCY: INFORMATION AND CONTROL

Making rewards contingent upon skilled performance so that their receipt signifies competence has been interpreted by some authors (e.g., Enzle & Ross, 1978; Karniol & Ross, 1977) as a way of making the rewards more informational. As shown above, however, performance contingency can increase both the informational and the controlling aspect of rewards. We now suggest that performance-contingent rewards can be perceived as either informational or controlling, depending on how they are administered, and that if they are administered controllingly, they will decrease intrinsic motivation relative to comparable rewards administered informationally. This assertion derives in part from the earlier work by Ryan (1982) in which positive competence feedback was itself administered either informationally or controllingly. The feedback was made controlling by use of the concept 'should'. For example, controlling-feedback subjects were told, 'Good, you're doing as you *should*.' Ryan found that subjects who received positive competence feedback that was controlling were significantly less intrinsically motivated than those who received feedback informationally. This result occurred when the two types of feedback were self-administered just as it did when they were verbally administered by the experimenter.

Returning to the issue of performance contingency, it seems quite possible that performance-contingent rewards could be made quite controlling or quite informational and that they would have markedly different effects if administered in the two ways. The present study tested this hypothesis explicitly. Performance-contingent rewards were administered both informationally and controllingly. Further, there was a no-reward group that received informational feedback and one that received controlling feedback. This allowed for a comparison of performance-contingent reward groups (one of each kind) with no-reward control groups that received comparable feedback (one group receiving each kind of feedback).

COMPETITIVELY CONTINGENT REWARDS

Finally, we briefly review the effects of competitively administered rewards. Pritchard, Campbell, and Campbell (1977) reported that when a $5 reward was made contingent upon doing better than the other people in one's group (about six people), the rewards decreased intrinsic motivation relative to a no-payment group. This type of contingency is really a competitive contingency. Only one person can win the reward, so the other people in the group must lose. This type of contingency is likely to be quite controlling, for a winning performance is itself instrumental to attaining a reward. In fact, Deci, Betley, Kahle, Abrams, and Porac (1981) reported that this type of direct, face-to-face competition decreased subjects' intrinsic motivation even when there were no rewards involved. It seems clear that competitively contingent rewards decrease intrinsic motivation relative to no rewards.

It is interesting to reconsider the Greene and Lepper (1974) study in light of the competitive effects. They compared a kind of performance-contingent reward with task-contingent (no-feedback) rewards and found no difference, whereas Boggiano and Ruble (1979) found the performance-contingent rewards to be superior to the task-contingent rewards without feedback. In the Greene and Lepper study, the pre-school children in the so-called performance-contingent group were told that only a very few of the children in their class – those who drew the very best pictures – would get a good-player award. Thus, the performance feedback inherent in the reward really meant not only that they did well but also that they beat out their fellow classmates. According to cognitive evaluation theory, this competitive element would have made the performance-contingent (i.e., competitively contingent) reward quite controlling and would therefore explain why it did not yield higher intrinsic motivation than the task-contingent, no-feedback group.

THE PRESENT STUDY: HYPOTHESES

The present study was designed in an attempt to clear up some unanswered questions in this rather complex literature.

First, we considered the relation between performance-contingent rewards that were informationally versus controllingly administered. Further, we included two comparable no-reward groups, one that got the same informational feedback as the informational performance-contingency group and one that got the same controlling feedback as the controlling performance-contingency group.

We hypothesized that performance-contingent rewards would undermine intrinsic motivation relative to no-reward groups that get comparable feedback. We also hypothesized that the controlling administration of rewards and feedback would undermine intrinsic motivation relative to the informational administration.

Finally, the design included a no-reward/no-feedback control group and a no-feedback, task-contingent reward group. We hypothesized that the task-contingent reward group would display significantly less intrinsic motivation than the informationally administered, performance-contingent reward group but that the task-contingent reward group would not differ from the controllingly administered, performance-contingent reward group.

RESULTS AND DISCUSSION

To test the first hypothesis, the two no-reward/feedback groups were compared to the performance-contingent-reward groups. This contrast produced a significant main effect, $F(1, 89) = 4.34$, $p < .05$. Thus, the first hypothesis was supported; performance-contingent rewards undermined intrinsic motivation relative to comparable feedback without rewards.

The second hypotheses was tested by comparing the two informational feedback cells with the two controlling feedback cells. This contrast yielded a significant main effect, $F(1, 89) = 6.11$, $p < .02$. Thus, the second hypothesis was also supported; controlling feedback and controllingly administered performance-contingent rewards undermined intrinsic motivation relative to informational feedback and informationally administered performance-contingent rewards.

Finally, the third major hypothesis compared the two types of performance-contingent rewards (with feedback inherent in them) to task-contingent rewards (without feedback). Controllingly administered performance-contingent rewards did not differ from task-contingent rewards (without feedback). On the other hand, the informationally administered performance-contingent reward group was considerably higher in intrinsic motivation than the other two. A comparison of the two performance-contingent reward groups yielded a significant difference, $F(1, 89) = 4.25$, $p < .05$, as did a comparison of the informational, performance-contingent group with the task-contingent group, $F(1, 89) = 4.58$, $p < .04$. These contrasts confirm the third hypothesis, namely, that informationally administered performance-contingent rewards enhance intrinsic motivation relative to task-contingent rewards (without feedback), whereas controllingly administered, performance-contingent rewards do not.

CONCLUSIONS

The present article attempted to review and integrate the available literature on reward-contingency effects on intrinsic motivation and to test empirically some of the emergent formulations. The results of the review suggest that there is considerable coherence and convergence in the findings across various laboratories that become apparent once a common terminology is applied.

We have used the information–control distinction (Deci & Ryan, 1980) to clarify the important dimensions of context or psychological meaning. Briefly, that distinction suggests that rewards, even with the same contingency structure, can have varied impact depending on their functional significance.

Rewards in general appear to have a controlling significance to some extent and thus in general run the risk of undermining intrinsic motivation. Task-contingent rewards, because they convey control but generally hold little information value, predictably undermine intrinsic motivation, whereas task-non-contingent rewards, because they are not tied to the target activity, run less risk of negative effects.

The most interesting problem of interpretation, and the one most directly addressed by the present study and review, is that of performance-contingent reward effects. The information–control distinction suggests that performance-contingent rewards vary greatly in their impact because they can highlight either the informational aspects or the controlling aspects of the situation. That is, they can convey competency as well as pressure to different degrees depending on the interpersonal context of administration. As was suggested both by the present study and by Harackiewicz (1979), performance-contingent rewards can thus either increase intrinsic motivation with respect to no-feedback/no-reward controls when informationally administered or decrease intrinsic motivation when administered controllingly. In either case performance-contingent rewards, like all other rewards, tend to lower intrinsic motivation relative to no rewards if there is identical feedback within the same interpersonal context.

REFERENCES

Boggiano, A. K., & Ruble, D. M. (1979), 'Competence and the overjustification effect: A developmental study', *Journal of Personality and Social Psychology*, *37*, 1462–8.

Calder, B. J., & Staw, B. M. (1975), 'Self-perception of intrinsic and extrinsic motivation', *Journal of Personality and Social Psychology*, *31*, 599–605.

Condry, J. (1977), 'Enemies of exploration: Self-initiated versus other-initiated learning', *Journal of Personality and Social Psychology*, *35*, 459–77.

Daniel, T. L., & Esser, J. K. (1980), 'Intrinsic motivation as influenced by rewards, task interest, and task structure', *Journal of Applied Psychology*, *65*, 566–73.

Danner, F. W., & Lonky, E. (1981), 'A cognitive-developmental approach to the effects of rewards on intrinsic motivation', *Child Development*, *52*, 1043–52.

Deci, E. L. (1971), 'Effects of externally mediated rewards on intrinsic motivation', *Journal of Personality and Social Psychology*, *18*, 105–15.

Deci, E. L. (1972a), 'The effects of contingent and non-contingent rewards and controls on intrinsic motivation', *Organizational Behavior and Human Performance*, *8*, 217–29.

Deci, E. L. (1972b), 'Intrinsic motivation, extrinsic reinforcement, and inequity', *Journal of Personality and Social Psychology*, *22*, 113–20.

Deci, E. L. (1975), *Intrinsic Motivation*, New York: Plenum.

Deci, E. L., Betley, G., Kahle, J., Abrams, L., & Porac, J. (1981), 'When trying to win: Competition and intrinsic motivation', *Personality and Social Psychology Bulletin, 7,* 79–83.

Deci, E. L., & Ryan, R. M. (1980), 'The empirical exploration of intrinsic motivational processes', in L. Berkowitz (ed.), *Advances in Experimental Social Psychology* (Vol. 13), New York: Academic Press.

Deci, E. L., & Ryan, R. M. (1985), *Intrinsic Motivation and Self-Determination in Human Behavior*, New York: Plenum.

Dollinger, S. J., & Thelen, M. H. (1978), 'Overjustification and children's intrinsic motivation: Comparative effects of four rewards', *Journal of Personality and Social Psychology*, *36*, 1259–69.

Enzle, M. E., & Ross, J. M. (1978), 'Increasing and decreasing intrinsic interest with contingent rewards: A test of cognitive evaluation theory', *Journal of Experimental Social Psychology*, *14*, 588–97.

Farr, J. L. (1976), 'Task characteristics, reward contingency, and intrinsic motivation', *Organizational Behavior and Human Performance*, *16*, 294–307.

Farr, J. L., Vance R. J., & McIntyre, R. M. (1977), 'Further examination of the relationship between reward contingency and intrinsic motivation', *Organizational Behavior and Human Performance*, *20*, 31–53.

Fazio, R. H. (1981), 'On the self-perception explanation of the overjustification effect: The role of the salience of initial attitude', *Journal of Experimental Social Psychology*, 7, 417–26.

Fisher, C. D. (1978), 'The effects of personal control, competence, and extrinsic reward systems on intrinsic motivation', *Organizational Behavior and Human Performance*, 21, 273–88.

Greene, D., & Lepper, M. R. (1974), 'Effects of extrinsic rewards on children's subsequent intrinsic interest', *Child Development*, 45, 1141–5.

Harackiewicz, J. (1979), 'The effects of reward contingency and performance feedback on intrinsic motivation', *Journal of Personality and Social Psychology*, 37, 1352–63.

Karniol, R., & Ross, M. (1977), 'The effect of performance-relevant and performance-irrelevant rewards on children's intrinsic motivation', *Child Development, 48,* 482–7.

Kruglanski, et al. (1975), 'Can money enhance intrinsic motivation? A test of the content-consequence hypothesis', *Journal of Personality and Social Psychology*, 31, 744–50.

Lepper, M. R., Greene, D., & Nisbett, R. E. (1973), 'Undermining children's intrinsic interest with extrinsic rewards: A test of the "overjustification" hypothesis', *Journal of Personality and Social Psychology*, 28, 129–37.

Loveland, K. K., & Olley, J. G. (1979), 'The effect of external reward on interest and quality of task performance in children of high and low intrinsic motivation', *Child Development*, 50, 1207–10.

Luyten, H., & Lens, W. (1981), 'The effect of earlier experience and reward contingencies on intrinsic motivation', *Motivation and Emotion*, 5, 25–36.

McLoyd, V. C. (1979), 'The effects of extrinsic rewards of differential value on high and low intrinsic interest', *Child Development*, 50, 1010–19.

Morgan, M. (1981), 'The overjustification effect: A developmental test of self-perception interpretations', *Journal of Personality and Social Psychology*, 40, 809–21.

Phillips, J. S., & Lord, R. G. (1980), 'Determinants of intrinsic motivation: Locus of control and competence information as components of Deci's cognitive evaluation theory', *Journal of Applied Psychology*, 65, 211–18.

Pinder, C. C. (1976), 'Additivity versus nonadditivity of intrinsic and extrinsic incentives: Implications for work motivation, performance, and attitudes', *Journal of Applied Psychology*, 61, 693–700.

Pittman, T. S., Cooper, E. E., & Smith, T. W. (1977), 'Attribution of causality and the overjustification effect', *Personality and Social Psychology Bulletin*, 3, 280–83.

Pittman, T. S., Davey, M. E., Alafat, K. A., Wetherill, K. V., & Kramer, N. A. (1980), 'Informational versus controlling verbal rewards', *Personality and Social Psychology Bulletin*, 6, 228–33.

Pritchard, R. D., Campbell, K. M., & Campbell, D. J. (1977), 'Effects of extrinsic financial rewards on intrinsic motivation', *Journal of Applied Psychology*, 62, 9–15.

Rosenfield, D., Folger, R., & Adelman, H. (1980), 'When rewards reflect competence: A qualification of the overjustification effect', *Journal of Personality and Social Psychology*, 39, 368–76.

Ross, M. (1975), 'Salience of reward and intrinsic motivation', *Journal of Personality and Social Psychology*, 32, 245–54.

Ross, M., Karniol, R., & Rothstein, M. (1976), 'Reward contingency and intrinsic motivation in children: A test of the delay of gratification hypothesis', *Journal of Personality and Social Psychology*, 33, 442–7.

Ryan, R. M. (1982), 'Control and information in the intrapersonal sphere: An extension of cognitive evaluation theory', *Journal of Personality and Social Psychology*, 43, 450–61.

Seligman, M. E. P. (1975), *Helplessness: On Depression, Development and Death*, San Francisco: Freeman.

Smith, T. W., & Pittman, T. S. (1978), 'Reward, distraction, and the overjustification effect', *Journal of Personality and Social Psychology, 36*, 565–72.

Staw, B. M., Calder, B. J., Hess, R. K., & Sandelands, L. E. (1980), 'Intrinsic motivation and norms about payments', *Journal of Personality, 48*, 1–14.

Swann, W. B., & Pittman, T. S. (1977), 'Initiating play activity of children: The moderating influence of verbal cues on intrinsic motivation', *Child Development, 48*, 1128–32.

Weiner, M. J., & Mander, A. M. (1978), 'The effects of reward and perception of competency upon intrinsic motivation', *Motivation and Emotion, 2*, 67–73.

White, R. W. (1959), 'Motivation reconsidered: The concept of competence', *Psychological Review, 66*, 297–333.

Wilson, T. D., Hull, J. G., & Johnson, J. (1981), 'Awareness and self-perception: Verbal reports on internal states', *Journal of Personality and Social Psychology, 40*, 53–71.

28

FRED G. LESIEUR AND ELBRIDGE S. PUCKETT

The Scanlon Plan Has Proved Itself

Abridged from F. G. Lesieur and E. S. Puckett. 'The Scanlon Plan has
proved itself', *Harvard Business Review*, Vol. 47, 1969, pp. 109–18.

This is an excellent time to take a good look at the general principles of
employee participation in management – and probably the best time in
history to examine the Scanlon Plan in particular. Recent technological
advances involving the computer, numerically controlled machine tools,
and many other forms of automated processes have brought the activities of blue- and white-collar workers closer together than ever before.
The ability of these employees to work together and with management
has an enormous impact on a company's success in utilizing the new
technologies.

In contrast to other, more limited forms of incentive schemes, the
Scanlon Plan offers a flexible vehicle through which company, union,
and employees can meet changes in conditions, in technology, and in
corporate structure in a manner that is mutually rewarding for all.

In the first section of this article we will briefly outline the basic
philosophy and structure generally employed in a Scanlon-type plan.

Scanlon's first thoughts about employee participation in the workplace resulted from his experiences during the Depression, when citizens
worked together in a common endeavor to solve the very austere problems facing the community. The first application of his philosophy, in a
marginally profitable steel mill, contained no performance measurement
or bonus provisions, but represented a successful attempt to harness the
full efforts of management and the workforce in order to save an
organization that otherwise might very well have gone under (Lesieur,
1958).

Scanlon deeply believed that the typical company organization did
not elicit the full potential from employees, either as individuals or as a
group. He did not feel that the commonly held concept that 'the boss is
the boss and a worker works' was a proper basis for stimulating the
interest of employees in company problems; rather, he felt such a
concept reinforced employees' belief that there was an 'enemy' some-

where above them in the hierarchy and that a cautious suspicion should be maintained at all times. He felt that employee interest and contribution could best be stimulated by providing the employee with a maximum amount of information and data concerning company problems and successes, and by soliciting his contribution as to how he felt the problem might best be solved and the job best done.

Thus the Scanlon Plan is a common sharing between management and employees of problems, goals, and ideas. Scanlon felt that individual incentives worked against employee participation of this nature. He believed that individual incentives put the direct worker in business for himself, pitted him against the broader interests of the company, and produced inequities in the wage structure that in turn led to poor employee morale. His concept of a system of rewards that would stimulate employee interest and acceptance of technological change involved an appropriate wage structure reflecting (1) individual skills and (2) additional rewards, based on the success of the enterprise, to be shared by all employees and management.

In almost all the cases with which we are familiar, companies implement this philosophy of participation with a committee system made up of departmental production committees and an overall screening or steering committee. However, in very small plants one plantwide committee may be sufficient.

Production committees

Departmental production committees are made up of two or more employees, depending on the size of the department, and one or two management members. The management members are appointed by the company, and experience has shown that it is very important to have whoever is heading the department or area (such as a foreman, office manager, or chief engineer) take an active part as chairman of the committee. Employee members are usually elected by the employees in the department, in some cases they are appointed by the union leadership.

Committees meet regularly and discuss suggestions for improvements. The employee members must be allowed a certain amount of time to contact other employees to obtain new suggestions and to discuss the action taken on pending suggestions.

Is committee work time-consuming? Experience shows that the amount of time employee members lose from their regular jobs, either in attending meetings or in contacting employees, is surprisingly low. The production committee gets together formally once a month. At this meeting its members:

☐ Make sure that they have recorded each suggestion that has been submitted during the month and any action which has been taken.

☐ Process all suggestions, attend to previous suggestions on which action has not been completed, and then take up any other business considered important to the department's performance. (Such discussion may take many forms. Often a foreman or other member presents a departmental problem which he wants the committee to evaluate in the hope of achieving a solution. These problems range all the way from the layout of new equipment to cost factors on specific products.)

Although the majority of suggestions are approved by committees, the committees do not have the right to accept or reject ideas presented. That right is reserved by management. Moreover, there is one area of business that the production committee must not get into. This has to do with union business, grievances, wages, and so forth. The committee deals exclusively with operating improvements.

If the production committee has been functioning properly during the month and is doing its job thoroughly, the meetings described may take approximately one hour or slightly longer. If the production meeting is over in fifteen minutes, it is clear that the committee is functioning strictly as a suggestion committee and probably is not getting sufficient management leadership and direction.

Screening function

The minutes of the production committee are forwarded as quickly as possible to the screening committee, which meets once each month – as soon as the accounting department can make available the figures reporting the performance of the previous month. The chairman of this committee is usually a top executive who serves along with other top executives from the various departments of the company. The president, steward, or other officer of the local union or unions involved usually serves, too, and employee members represent various areas. In some cases the employee member may represent two or more production committee areas; in other cases there may be an employee member from each production committee area. As at the production committee level, the employee members are usually elected by their constituents, but in some cases they may be appointed by the union. The screening committee members proceed as follows:

1. Their first order of business is to go over the performance of the previous month and analyze the reasons why it was favorable or not so favorable, as the case might be. One of the most important functions of

each member is to understand fully the economic variables that affect the bonus result, so that he or she can impart such information to other employees. Employees must understand the results and have complete confidence in the method of measurement which is employed.

2. Their second function is to take up any company problems or matters of interest which management wants to communicate to all employees. For example, we have seen the sales department bring a competitor's product into the meeting, so that members could analyze the kind of competitive problems that they were facing. Again, samples of new products which the company has developed are often the topic of discussion, thus giving employees a chance to visualize the production problems they will eventually be facing.

3. They discuss and take care of any suggestions which have not been resolved at the production committee level. Hopefully, a vast majority of suggestions will have been handled at the lower level. However, there are certain areas (e.g., capital expenditures and new equipment) which involve the company as a whole, and problems in these areas must go to a higher level to be resolved. In a sense, the screening committee is also considered a kind of 'court of higher appeal' for suggestions which have not met with approval at the production committee level but which the suggestor would like to have considered further.

In all cases there is no voting by the committee on suggestions, but there is thorough discussion of all points of view when there is disagreement. After careful consideration, management makes the final decision.

Measurement of rewards

From the standpoint of employees, the payoff of a Scanlon Plan is in dollars and cents. How is the amount of reward determined?

Companies employing the Scanlon Plan follow widely differing methods of measuring the amounts of bonus payments to employees. In some of Scanlon's early work profit sharing was the basis of bonus rewards. In recent years the most commonly used type of measurement is what is loosely termed a sales value of production ratio, where the ratio of total payroll to sales value of production (net sales plus or minus the change in inventory) in a prior base period is compared with that ratio in the current period (Lesieur, 1958). Any improvement in this ratio provides a bonus pool. Part of this pool is set aside in a reserve against deficit months (months when the ratio goes above that of the base period). The amount set aside is determined by analysis of past fluctuations in the ratio.

After removing the reserved amount from the bonus pool each month, the remainder is divided. Usually 25 per cent is the company's share, and 75 per cent is paid out to all employees as that month's performance bonus. Participation usually encompasses everyone in the company up to and including the president, or, in the case of a very large, multi-plant company, everyone employed in the facility in which the plan is in effect. The bonus is distributed as a percentage of the employee's gross income during that accounting period, so that the bonus paid reflects differentials in wages or salaries paid for differences in job content.

At the end of a 'Scanlon Year' the reserve pool remaining after providing for any offsetting deficits is split up in the same manner as the monthly bonuses. The company retains its share, and the remainder is paid out as a year-end bonus (in the same proportions as the monthly bonuses).

Other types of measurements that have been used are for the most part similar to the one just described.

MAJOR FINDINGS

Why does the Scanlon approach lead to better results? Reasons like the following are important:

●Working under the Scanlon Plan, an employee finds it more natural to take a broader view of the company's problems.

●Management finds it easier to stress quality production, if that is important, in a Scanlon Plan environment than where the direct worker is paid according to his specific operation.

●Getting the cooperation and support of the indirect servicing groups – i.e., tool room, maintenance, and materials handling – is much easier when these groups receive incentive earnings.

●Through their committee activity, managers are able to discuss company objectives with employees and attain a response that is not possible under an individual incentive system. It is very important that the participants look on the success of the enterprise as being the basis for their own individual success. When this attitude is present, the entire organization responds to problems – such as quality problems, stepped up schedules, and customer delays – in a way calculated to get them solved as quickly as possible.

One of the most interesting aspects of the experience of these companies [using the Scanlon Plan] concerns employee attitudes toward technological change and new equipment. While there is a natural human reluctance to change, employees in [Scanlon Plan companies, often] push management to bring in new equipment and to get it operating properly for the benefit of all.

Management finds that discussing plans well in advance creates an interest in the organization and minimizes fears that might otherwise develop. Its experience has shown that thorough discussion of planned changes enables members of the organization (management as well as employees) to realize that the new technology is not going to bring with it all sorts of ills that cannot be solved satisfactorily.

One highly significant conclusion that emerges from corporate experience with the Scanlon Plan concerns the relationship between the kind of production process involved and the quality of employee participation. The nature of the production process may influence the *direction* that participation and suggestions take, but the general quality of participation can be equally high *regardless* of the type of operation.

In short, the success of the Scanlon Plan is measured by the ability of the organization to tackle and solve the problems posed by production.

Union reactions

How do unions react to the Scanlon Plan? In many union-management relationships the most difficult problem for the union leader is to get top management to sit down and discuss the various problems that are plaguing the union and its membership. A basic prerequisite for success with the Scanlon approach is that management be 'willing to listen'. Where the plan is in operation, therefore, it should not be surprising that the number of written grievances has dropped markedly. This does not imply that there are no longer any problems or that the unions play a lesser role in solving problems. The significance is that mutually satisfactory solutions were developed without going through four stages of grievance procedure and on to arbitration.

As every international union representative knows, the local which is most difficult to satisfy is the one which deals with a company that says no to everything. If the Scanlon approach eases such a relationship, it will surely result in a membership that is better satisfied with the efforts of the international union.

CONCLUSION

The message of the Scanlon Plan is simple: operations improvement is an area where management, the union, and employees can get together without strife. Collaboration is part of the job. In applying a Scanlon Plan, a company in essence says to its employees, 'Look, we can run the company – we have run it for a number of years – we can run it well. But we think we can run it much better if you will help us. We're willing to listen.'

REFERENCE

Lesieur, F. G. (1958), *The Scanlon Plan: A Frontier in Labor Management Cooperation*, Cambridge, Mass.: MIT Press.

29

ROSABETH MOSS KANTER

The Attack on Pay

Abridged from R. M. Kanter, 'The attack on pay', *Harvard Business Review*, Vol. 65(2), 1987, pp. 60–67.

Status, not contribution, has traditionally been the basis for the numbers on employees' paychecks. Pay has reflected where jobs rank in the corporate hierarchy – not what comes out of them.

Today this system is under attack. More and more senior executives are trying to turn their employees into entrepreneurs – people who earn a direct return on the value they help create, often in exchange for putting their pay at risk. In the process, changes are coming into play that will have revolutionary consequences for companies and their employees.

In traditional compensation plans, each job comes with a pay level that stays about the same regardless of how well the job is performed or what the real organizational value of that performance is. Pay scales reflect such estimated characteristics as decision-making responsibility, importance to the organization, and number of subordinates. If there is a merit component, it is usually very small. The surest way – often the only way – to increase one's pay is to change employers or get promoted. A mountain of tradition and industrial relations practice has built up to support this way of calculating pay.

Proponents of this system customarily assert that the market ultimately determines pay, just as it determines the price of everything else that buyers wish to acquire. Compensation systems cannot be unfair or inappropriate, therefore, because they are incapable of causing anything. Actually, however, because it is so difficult to link people's compensation directly to their contributions, all the market really does is allow us to assume that people occupying equal positions tend to be paid equally and that people with similar experience and education tend to be worth about the same. So while the market works in macro-economic terms, the process at a micro-economic level is circular: we know what people are worth because that's what they cost in the job market; but we also know that what people cost in the market is just what they're worth.

Given logic like this, it's not hard to see why such strange bedfellows as feminist activists and entrepreneurially minded managers both attack this traditional system as a manifestation of the paternalistic benefits offered across the board by Father Corporation. 'We've got corporate socialism, not corporate capitalism,' charged the manager of new ventures for a large industrial company. 'We're so focused on consistent treatment internally that we destroy enterprise in the process.'

These old arrangements are no longer supportable. For economic, social, and organizational reasons, the fundamental bases for determining pay are under attack. And while popular attention has focused on comparable worth – equalizing pay for those doing comparable work – the most important trend has been the loosening relationship between job assignment and pay level.

If pay practices continue to move toward contribution as the basis for earnings, as I believe they will, the change will unleash a set of forces that could transform work relationships as we know them now. To illustrate, let's look at what happens when organizations take modest steps to make pay more entrepreneurial.

In 1981, the city of Long Beach, California, established a pay-for-performance system for its management as part of a new budgeting process designed to upgrade the city government's performance against quantifiable fiscal and service delivery targets. Under the new system, managers can gain or lose up to 20 per cent of their base salaries, so the pay of two managers at the same level can vary by up to $40,000. Job category and position in the hierarchy are far weaker determinants of earnings. In fact, at least two people are now paid more than the city manager.

While the impact of a system like this on productivity and entre-preneurship is noticeable, its effect on work relationships is more subtle. People don't wear their paychecks over their name badges in the office, after all. But word does get around, and some organizations are having to face the problem of envy head-on. In two different companies with new-venture units that offer equity participation, the units are being attacked as unfair and poorly conceived. The attackers are aggrieved that venture participants can earn so much money for seemingly modest or even trivial contributions to the corporation overall, while those who keep the mainstream businesses going must accept salary ceilings and insignificant bonuses.

In companies that establish new-enterprise units, this clash between two different systems is self-inflicted. But sometimes the conflict comes as an unwelcome by-product of a company's efforts to expand into new businesses via acquisition. On buying a brokerage firm, a leading bank found that it had also acquired a very different compensation system: a generous commission arrangement means that employees often earn twice their salary in bonuses and, once in a while, five times. In 1985, six people made as much in salary and commissions as the chairman did in his base salary, or roughly $500,000 each. These people all made much more than their managers and their managers' managers and virtually everyone else in the corporation except the top three or four officers, a situation that would have been impossible a few years ago.

Now such discrepancies cannot be prevented or kept quiet. 'People in the trade know perfectly well what's happening,' the bank's senior administration executive told me. 'They know the formula, they see the proxy statements, and they are busy checking out the systems by which we and everybody else compensate these people.'

To avoid the equivalent of an employee run on the bank – with everyone trying to transfer to the brokerage operation – the corporation has felt forced to establish performance bonuses for branch managers and some piece-rate systems for clerical workers, though these are not nearly as generous as the managers' extra earning opportunities.

This system, though it solves some problems, creates others. The executive responsible recognizes that though these new income-earning opportunities are pegged to individual performance, people do not work in isolation. Branch managers' results really depend on how well their employees perform, and so do the results of nearly everyone else except those in sales (and even there a team effort can make a difference). Yet instead of teamwork, the bank's practices may encourage competition, the hoarding of good leads, and the withholding of good ideas until one person can claim the credit. 'We talk about teamwork at training sessions,' this executive said, 'and then we destroy it in the compensation system.'

Team-based pay raises its own questions, however, and generates its own set of prickly issues. There is the 'free rider' problem, in which a few non-performing members of the group benefit from the actions of the productive members. And problems can arise when people resent being dependent on team members, especially those with very different organizational status.

There are also pressure problems. Gain-sharing plans, in particular, can create very high peer pressure to do well, since the pay of all depends on everyone's efforts. Theodore Cohn, a compensation expert, likes to talk about the Dutch company, Philips, in which twice-yearly bonuses can run up to 40 per cent of base pay. 'Managers say that a paper clip never hits the floor – a hand will be there to catch it,' Cohn recounts. 'If a husband dies, the wake is at night so that no one misses work. If someone goes on vacation, somebody else is shown how to do the job. There is practically no turnover.'

Similarly, Cohn claims that at Lincoln Electric, where performance-related pay is twice the average factory wage, peer pressure can be so high that the first two years of employment are called purgatory (Cohn, 1984).

Another kind of pressure also emerges from equity-ownership and profit-sharing systems – the pressure to open the books, to disclose managerial salaries, and to justify pay differentials. Concerns like these bubble up when employees who may never have thought much about other people's pay suddenly realize that 'their' money is at stake.

These concerns and questions of distributional equity are all part of making the system more fair as well as more effective. Perhaps the biggest issue, and the one most disturbing to traditionalists, is what happens to the chain of command when it does not match the progression of pay. If subordinates can out-earn their bosses, hierarchy begins to crumble.

Social psychologists have shown that authority relationships depend on a degree of inequality. If the distance between boss and subordinate declines, so do automatic deference and respect. The key word here is *automatic*. Superiors can still gain respect through their competence and fair treatment of subordinates. But power shifts as relationships become more equal.

Once the measures of good performance are both clearly established and clearly achieved, a subordinate no longer needs the goodwill of the boss quite so much. Proven achievement reflected in earnings higher than the boss's produces security, which produces risk taking, which produces speaking up and pushing back. As a result, the relationship between boss and subordinate changes from one based on authority to one based on mutual respect.

This change has positive implications for superiors as well as subordinates. For example, if a subordinate can earn more than the boss and still stay in place, then one of the incentives to compete for the boss's job is removed. Gone, too, is the tension that can build when an ambitious subordinate covets the boss's job and will do anything to get it. In short, if some of the *authority* of hierarchy is eliminated, so is some of the *hostility*.

In most traditional organizations, however, the idea of earning more than the boss seems insupportable and, to some people, clearly inequitable. There are, of course, organizational precedents for situations in which people in lower-ranked jobs are paid more than those above. Field sales personnel paid on commission can often earn more than their managers; star scientists in R&D laboratories may earn more than the administrators nominally placed over them; and hourly workers can make more than their supervisors through overtime pay or union-negotiated wage settlements. But these situations are usually uncommon, or they're accepted because they're part of a dual-career ladder or the price of moving up in rank into management.

To get a feeling for the kinds of difficulties pay imbalances can create in hierarchical organizations, let's look at a less extreme case in which the gap between adjacent pay levels diminishes but does not disappear. This is called pay compression, and it bothers executives who believe in maintaining hierarchy.

In response to an American Management Association survey of 613 organizations, of which 134 were corporations with more than $1 billion in sales, 76 per cent reported problems with compression (Steele, 1982). Yet only a few percentage points divide the organizations expressing concern from those that do not. For example, the average earnings difference between first-line production supervisors and the highest-paid production workers was 15.5 per cent for organizations reporting compression problems, and only a little higher, 20 per cent, for those not reporting such problems. In the maintenance area, the difference was even less – a 15.1 per cent average earnings difference for those who said they had a problem versus 18.2 per cent for those who said they did not. Furthermore, for a large number of companies claiming a compression problem, the difference between levels is actually greater than their official guidelines stipulate.

What is most striking to me, however, is how great the gap between adjacent levels still is – at least 15 per cent difference in pay. Indeed, it is hard to avoid the conclusion that the executives concerned about compression are responding not to actual problems but to a perceived threat and the fear that hierarchy will crumble because of new pay practices.

What organizations say they will and won't do to solve compression problems supports this interpretation. While 67.4 per cent of those concerned agree that an instant-bonus program would help, 70.1 per cent say their companies would never institute one. And while 47.9 per cent say that profit sharing for all salaried supervisors would help, 64.7 per cent say that their companies would never do that either. In fact, the solutions least likely to be acceptable were precisely those that would change the hierarchy most – for example, reducing the number of job classifications, establishing fewer wage levels, and granting overtime compensation for supervisors (in effect, equalizing their status with that of hourly workers). On the other hand, the most favored solutions involved aids to upward mobility like training and rapid advancement that would keep the *structure* of the hierarchy intact while helping individuals move within it.

INNOVATIVE THOUGHTS

The attacks on pay I've identified all push in the same direction. Indeed, they overlap and reinforce each other as, for example, a decision to reward individual contributors makes otherwise latent concerns about equity much more visible and live. Without options, private concerns can look like utopian dreams. Once those dreams begin to appear plausible, however, what was 'the way things have to be' becomes instead a deliberate withholding of fair treatment.

By creating new forms for identifying, recognizing, and ultimately permitting contributions, the attack on pay goes beyond pay to color relationships throughout an organization. In the process, the iron cage of bureaucracy is being rattled in ways that will eventually change the nature, and the meaning, of hierarchy in ways we cannot yet imagine.

Wise executives, however, can prepare themselves and their companies for the revolutionary changes ahead. The shift toward contribution-based pay makes sense on grounds of equity, cost, productivity, and enterprise. And there are ways to manage that shift effectively. Here are some options to consider.

☐ Think strategically and systematically about the organizational implications of every change in compensation practices. If a venture unit offers an equity stake to participants, should a performance-based bonus with similar earning potential be offered to managers of mainstream business? If gain sharing is implemented on the shop floor, should it be extended to white-collar groups?

☐ Move toward reducing the fixed portion of pay and increasing the variable portion. Give business unit managers more discretion in distributing the variable pool, and make it a larger, more meaningful amount. Or allow more people to invest a portion of their salary in return for a greater share of the proceeds attributed to their own efforts later on.

☐ Manage the jealousy and conflict inherent in the more widely variable pay of nominal peers by making standards clear, giving everyone similar opportunities for growth in earnings, and reserving a portion of the earnings of stars or star sectors for distribution to others who have played a role in the success. Balance individual and group incentives in ways appropriate to the work unit and its tasks.

☐ Analyze – and, if necessary, rethink – the relationship between pay and value to the organization. Keep in mind that organizational levels defined for purposes of coordination do not necessarily reflect contributions to performance goals, and decouple pay from status or rank. And finally, be prepared to justify pay decisions in terms of clear contributions – and to offer these justifications more often, to more stake-holder groups.

REFERENCES

Cohn, T. H. (1984), 'Incentive compensation in smaller companies', *Proceedings of the Annual Conference of the American Compensation Association* (pp. 1–7), Scottsdale, Ariz.: ACA.

Steele, J. W. (1982), *Paying for Performance and Position*, New York: AMA Membership Publishing Division.

Understanding Management and Motivation

VICTOR H. VROOM

Management Theories and Their Motivational Bases

Management has been described as an ancient practice but a new academic discipline. Six thousand years ago the Egyptians faced a monumental management task with the construction of the pyramids. The leadership and organizational accomplishments represented by such a feat are impressive even by today's standards. Yet it has been only in the last century that serious scholars have sought to understand and codify the principles of effective management. Many would still question whether there is such a thing as an academic discipline called 'management', as there is no shared paradigm for generating new knowledge, let alone agreement on the existing facts. But few would quarrel with the idea that there are legitimate problems with substantial intellectual substance that can be clarified, if not solved, by such disciplines as psychology and sociology, by the management sciences such as operations research, and by the field of economics.

It is not the purpose of this essay to review systematically scholarly treatments of management. Instead, the primary concern is with the way in which various theoretical approaches to management have regarded people. Thus, the discussion will highlight the assumptions about human motivation that are either implicit or explicit in several approaches to management. In particular, four types of management theories and their motivational bases will be addressed: scientific management, participative management, management science, and visionary leadership.

SCIENTIFIC MANAGEMENT

Most early management theorists adopted a rather mechanistic view of human behavior. People were assumed to be alike and interchangeable, and, within the limits set by their shared perceptual, cognitive, and motoric capacities, they were assumed to be completely programmable. Their behavior could, and should, be programmed by their managers. This movement in the study and practice of management has come to be called Scientific Management, a term coined by Taylor (1911). To be accurate, the 'workers' in Taylor's theory were assumed to operate in their own self-interest, which included a natural disposition to 'take it easy' on the job – to display what psychologists have termed the 'principle of least effort'. This might, for example, be evinced as a conscious effort by workers to restrict output in accordance with group norms or standards.

The core of Taylor's approach was to replace workers' discretion over how they do their jobs with a management that formulates the plans, makes the decisions, gives the orders, directs the work, and monitors the results. These prescriptions, along with Taylor's motivation strategy, are described in Reading 30, which is an excerpt from his book. For our purposes, it is sufficient to say that the operation of Taylor's system reaffirmed Adam Smith's (1789) principle of the division of labor. Tasks were simplified, and managers decided on the one best way of doing each task, using data collected with objective 'scientific' methods by time-and-motion specialists. In effect, the use of brain power was removed from the shop floor as all problem solving, decision making, and thinking became the responsibility of managers. The job of workers was to do the work, not to decide how it was to be done.

To combat the laziness and loafing that he believed to be characteristic of workers, Taylor introduced a piece-work compensation system whereby employees' pay would depend directly on their output. These economic 'carrots' were the motivational element in Taylor's system as well as in those of his many descendants – people like Gantt (1919) and Gilbreth (1914).

Scientific management, with its two key ingredients of separating the planning and doing of a job and using economic incentives to motivate workers, had become highly influential in shaping the practices of American industry by the mid-1920s. It was particularly widespread in manufacturing operations at the rank-and-file level where operations were repetitive and could be easily standardized. Some scholars have suggested that many of the competitive problems currently being confronted by American and European manufacturing industries stem from clinging to outmoded motivational methods embodied in scientific management that were of questionable utility in the earlier part of the century and are highly dysfunctional now. For example, Drucker (1974) argued that knowledge work, as distinct from manual operations, cannot be designed *for* the worker but only *by* the worker.

In Taylor's system, the two key ingredients are inextricably intertwined. As some observers have described it, Taylor made work demeaning and devoid of any intrinsic interest, and then he relied on economic incentives to overcome people's lack of concern for what they were doing. Given the former, the latter was essential and unavoidable. However, it is possible to use the latter – namely economic incentives – without necessarily oversimplifying the work and compromising the use of discretion and judgement.

The reliance on economic incentives can be justified by various psychological theories and is widely advocated by economists. In psychology, for example, the use of contingent pay is consistent with the Law of Effect or the principle of reinforcement central to operant theory (Skinner, 1953; see Reading 1). Succinctly, the idea is that if a person does a behavior and it is rewarded, the probability that the behavior will be repeated is increased. On the other hand, if the behavior is ignored or punished, its probability of recurrence will decrease. The use of direct economic incentives can also be supported by the expectancy–valence theories of motivation proposed by Georgopoulos, Mahoney, and Jones (1957), Vroom (1964), and Porter and Lawler (1968), which were discussed in Reading 6 by Pinder, Reading 15 by Schwab and Cummings, and Reading 20 by Lawler. Simply stated, these theories suggest that people will be motivated to do actions that are instrumental for receiving desired outcomes such as economic incentives.

In economics, the most recent approach to treating the incentive problem is called 'agency theory' (Holmstrom & Tirole, 1989). The firm is treated as a complex network of persons acting at times as agents for their superiors or principals and at times in the service of their own interests. For the economist, the problem is one of designing contractual arrangements between principals and agents in such a way as to maximize the likelihood that the work of the agents will maximize the profit goals of the principals. This resolution of the incentive problem is not unlike that of Taylor, although, at least in its intent, it is as applicable to the motivation of salespersons, managers, and corporation presidents as it is to hourly workers.

HUMAN RELATIONS AND THE PARTICIPATIVE APPROACHES

By the 1930s, evidence was beginning to accumulate that spectacular increases in productivity could be achieved by motivational methods that were not only different from those advocated by Taylor but in many respects fundamentally opposed. Brown (1954, Reading 31) discussed the early phases of the experiments conducted in the relay assembly room at the Hawthorne works of the Western Electric Company. Those experiments began with a Tayloristic question: What are the effects of illumination on worker productivity? While there are continuing debates among scholars about what really did happen in these experiments, all would agree that there were continued and consistent increases in productivity that persisted as the illumination was either increased or decreased and that they were independent of the frequency and duration of rest pauses.

One continuing dispute is the source of the increases in productivity. Social scientists have coined a term for what happened, 'The Hawthorne Effect', though the term merely begs the question of what caused that effect. One possibility derives from the fact that the workers knew they were being experimented upon. Orne (1962) has proposed and demonstrated that effects can occur in psychological experiments because subjects know they are being experimented upon, have their own hypotheses about the purposes of the experiment, and then (depending on their relationship with the experimenter) behave in ways that they believe will either confirm or disconfirm the hypothesis. Perhaps the workers in the relay assembly room demonstrated enhanced productivity because of their beliefs about what the managers and experimenters hoped to see.

To this writer, a more plausible explanation for the spectacular productivity increases resides in the fact that workers were consulted about their feelings and reactions and actually had a voice in determining the conditions under which they would work in the experiment. Workers were accorded importance by the managers and social scientists conducting the experiment, and they had an opportunity to participate in decisions that affected them. It is quite possible that being taken seriously and being able to influence policies enhanced their commitment and motivation to perform well.

The Hawthorne experiments are typically viewed as the origins of what has been called the Human Relations Movement in industry, a term that has fallen into disfavor. Because the movement advocated concern for the needs of workers, it became associated with the oversimplified assumption discussed earlier in this volume that satisfying workers' needs will lead to high productivity (see the introductory essay for Part B by Deci). The assumption that satisfaction causes effective performance has been shown to be motivationally erroneous, but the interpretation of the productivity increases at the Hawthorne plant as resulting from workers' participation in decision making would make the relay assembly room the birthplace of modern-day participative management.

McGregor (1957, Reading 32) articulated the assumptions of the participative approach which he termed 'Theory Y Management'. People enjoy, not avoid, the expenditure of physical and mental effort in work, he said, particularly when they can exercise self-direction and self-control in the service of objectives to which they are committed. They seek responsibility and typically have considerably more capacity to exercise imagination, ingenuity, and creativity in the solution of organizational problems than they are given an opportunity to utilize in their jobs.

McGregor linked his assumptions to Maslow's (1943, Reading 2) motivation theory which emphasizes the higher-order needs for esteem and self-actualization. More broadly, the participative approaches focus on intrinsic motivation (e.g., Deci, 1975) and assume that it is possible to design jobs and to create the contextual conditions that will promote workers' motivating themselves. Section V of this book presented four readings that treat this issue in depth.

The differences between the assumptions about motivation that form the basis for the participative approaches and those that underlie Scientific Management (which McGregor called Theory X) are, of course, readily apparent. Taylorism means extrinsic control over performance, whereas participative management emphasizes self-regulation and, in McGregor's words, the integration of organizational and individual goals. Equally different are the organization practices to which these different motivational assumptions gave rise. Taylorism represents standardized, simplified work practices being planned by managers and carried out by workers. In contrast, participative management connotes broadly designed jobs with varied opportunities for the exercise of individual judgement by the employees – practices that are also advocated in what Drucker (1954) referred to as Management by Objectives (Tosi & Carroll, 1970, Reading 34).

Scientific and participative management represented two conflicting ideologies that became locked in a struggle that both could not win. One forum for this battle has been an extensive series of experiments and field studies conducted by behavioral scientists over the past forty years. Their results, as summarized by Locke and Schweiger (1979), Yukl (1981), and Schweiger and Leana (1986), provide little to cheer about for either the advocates of top-down autocratic management or the proponents of participation. There is tremendous variability in results from one investigation to another, leading Schweiger and Leana

(1986) to conclude that essentially no single approach, whether auto-cractic, consultative, or totally participative, can be effectively employed with all subordinates for all types of activities.

While researchers were seeking to provide an objective foundation for theories of management, organizational and managerial life continued. And as Drucker put it, 'the manager cannot wait till the scientists and scholars have done their work ... The manager has to manage today' (1974, p. 181). Managers did manage and in a variety of different ways, some more successful than others.

Leavitt (1958) argued that both scientific and participative management have had an important influence but at different levels of the organizational hierarchy. Taylorism became the dominant organizational philosophy at the lowest levels. The jobs of assembly-line workers, clerk-typists, and bank tellers were often subjected to time-and-motion studies, and these employees have had only limited opportunities for self-expression or discretion. Several levels higher, however, the managerial positions that were somehow less 'programmable' were being managed by objectives, and frequently their incumbents were involved in such participative vehicles as team building and consensus decision making. This bifurcation in managerial philosophy is reflected in different views of the motivation problem at lower and higher organizational levels. Managers typically asked how they could motivate people to work harder when those people were doing jobs that were essentially demotivating. They seldom raised such questions about researchers, new young MBAs, or themselves.

One consequence of these two different employee worlds was a change in typical career patterns. Whereas once people could start in the mailroom and move progressively upwards to become executives, increasingly, hourly workers have stayed hourly workers and managers have begun their careers in white-collar jobs.

The typical limiting of participative management practices to higher levels has been seriously questioned in the last decade. Hurt by foreign competition, American management methods, only a quarter of a century earlier held up as a model for the world (Servan-Schrieber, 1968), are now seen as inadequate. Cries for change come from many, not just from a few social scientists like McGregor (1957) and Likert (1967, Reading 33). They even come from top executives who are desperately trying to retain market share in the face of lower-cost and often higher-quality foreign products. The message from these executive voices is remarkably consistent with that heard earlier from the behavioral scientists. It refers to commitment rather than compliance and participation rather than control.

The newest approaches in the participative management tradition have taken varied forms. For example, the influence of Japanese management (Marsland & Beer, 1983, Reading 35), with its central ideas of trust and autonomy, is at the core of Ouchi's (1981) addendum to McGregor's lexicon – namely Theory Z Management. And the importance of managing groups for enhancing commitment and involvement of employees has been highlighted by Hackman and Walton in Reading 36. Lawler's (1986, Reading 37) general approach to management, referred to as High Involvement Management, is built around the idea of participation, with the intent of stimulating intrinsic motivation for work. This approach includes broad-ranging prescriptions for problem-solving groups, leadership styles, performance appraisals, incentive systems, and so on.

Increasingly during the past two decades, theorists who understand the advantages of participation when properly managed have asserted that the use of participative methods should be made contingent upon the situation. There are circumstances, they suggest, where consultative or group decision-making processes would be clearly useful and others where they would not.

Referred to as contingency theories of management, recent formulations have gone beyond vacuous statements about situational dependency to specify the important dimensions of the situation and the nature of this dependency. Reading 38 by Vroom and Jago (1988) gives an example of a contingency theory that is precise about the degree and form of participation in decision making that is appropriate in different situations.

MANAGEMENT SCIENCE

An account of the evolution of management simply in terms of the tensions between scientific and participative management would be far from complete. By the late 1950s, a third set of managerial ideas had also begun to take shape. After the Second World War, a new set of technologies consisting of powerful mathematical methods that have proven useful in solving war-related problems became available to industry. These new technologies, which are frequently referred to as management science, were aided by the concurrent development of the computer, which became their primary tool.

Management science, a term that is mildly reminiscent of Taylor's scientific management, shares many of the characteristics of that earlier approach to management. Both were concerned with the optimal way of doing tasks and both involved programming or standardizing activities that had previously been matters of judgement. The two fields differ in the kinds of tasks they address, however. Management science is devoted to cognitive tasks involving information-processing activities that were becoming more and more important in the knowledge-based work in organizations. Accordingly, the principal tool was no longer the stopwatch of time-and-motion study but rather the high-speed computer which made programmable decisions that had previously been left to human judgement and discretion. Both scientific management and management science represented analytical ways to decompose complex problems into component parts and then reconstitute them in an orderly fashion. Both were singularly focused on making analytically sound decisions, and pursuing this goal took decisions away from those who historically had both made and implemented them. In fact, Simon (1965) asserted that 'within the very near future, much less than twenty-five years, we shall have technical capability of substituting machines for any and all human functions in organizations' (p. 30).

While it is clear that there is still much room for human judgement in organizations, their shape and the roles of their members have been drastically changed as a result of the new information technology. To cite an extreme example, Rogers (1984) described a German full-service bank with 40,000 customers that employs only a president, secretary, thirty-nine staff members, and thirty-seven computer programmers. The bank has no building or tellers, only a mainframe computer with a videotext service linking the bank to its customers via telephone lines, computer terminals, and monitors.

Management science and its derivative technologies was not intended as a means of motivating people, so we have not included readings in this volume to describe this approach. As an approach, it was intended as a means of designing and performing decision-making tasks. The aim is to maximize the 'quality of decisions', relative to the goals of the organization, using the relevant information that is available. Management scientists typically ignored the commitment and motivation of people to execute decisions, whereas participative-management specialists had focused explicitly on commitment and motivation. In participative management, decision quality, when addressed at all, was said to result from the fact that more inputs were made by people who faced (and therefore better understood) the problems that were being solved.

The job consequences of management science methods seemed to have varied with organizational level. At upper levels, the methods have served primarily as a decision support system providing decision makers with information that could not have been obtained without the computer. At middle levels, the method may actually have 'taken over' jobs, an occurrence that was predicted by Leavitt and Whisler (1958) more than three decades ago. Finally, at lower levels, there is substantial evidence (Fountain, 1990) that the methods have de-skilled jobs much as the methods of scientific management did in an earlier era. The ongoing problems that formed the occasions for the exercise of human judgement are being solved by algorithms imbedded in a 'black box'. Operators are thus required to observe dials or gauges and to push buttons, often with little conceptual understanding of the automated routines. The benefits of the new methods, in terms of speed and quality of output, are clear when compared to what was attainable from the earlier, less systematic methods. However, when the systems malfunction, operators may lack the necessary conceptual understanding of the system to remedy the problem or even to distinguish the significance of errant readings that point to future serious problems. What's more, the automation of their jobs, with the accompanying removal of their discretion and flexibility, may also have dampened their motivation to anticipate and remedy malfunctions.

The foregoing points have been made with respect to the overheated Three Mile Island nuclear reactor in Pennsylvania. A more mundane example may be found in people's experience of operating their automobiles. Those of you over fifty will remember a time when you yourself could conceivably have made most minor repairs to your cars. It was commonplace to see cars with their bonnets propped up and their operators changing sparkplugs or points, adjusting timing, or replacing broken fan belts. Today the complexity of the modern automobile, with its myriad of interfacing computer systems, has outstripped the capabilities of virtually all but the mechanics who are specifically trained in the intricacies of that particular brand. Today's cars are faster, more roadworthy, and less likely to break than their predecessors, but the consequences of failures are usually more serious and their remedies are usually outside the capabilities of their operators.

THE 'LEADERSHIP' APPROACH

A fourth set of managerial ideas, ideas that are taking their place alongside scientific management, participative management, and management science, have begun to emerge in recent years. Spawned by the winds of global competition and the relative decline in the efficiency of our manufacturing sector, a new set of concepts to guide the effective management of organizations is gradually taking shape. These ideas emphasize that organizations need *leadership*, not just management. The basic premise is that businesses need to make fundamental changes in order to stay competitive in a rapidly changing economic environment. Leadership involves a sense of vision or mission and a capacity to inspire others to commit to its attainment. Tichy and Devanna (1986), for example, have stressed the need for transformational leadership, borrowing a term from Burns (1978). Reading 39 by Tichy and Devanna outlines this general approach.

Leavitt (1986) has used the term 'pathfinders' in a similar way to refer to executives with imagination, creativity, the ability to envision new kinds of organizations and new directions for existing ones. He drew a sharp contrast between the educational and organizational conditions that spawn pathfinding and those that give rise to the 'left-brained' analytic methodologies of scientific management and management science. The cognitive style associated with pathfinding, he suggested, is often undervalued and underrepresented in organizations, handicapping their ability to survive in a rapidly changing world. Along with leadership goes 'loosening up' the organization, eliminating layers of hierarchy, pushing power and responsibility down, and developing a strong organizational culture.

Leavitt pointed to a potential creative synthesis between the ideas of pathfinding and those of participative management. Organizations need both qualities – the sparkle and vitality of individualistic pathfinding styles and the coordination and teamwork that characterize participative organizations. A shared vision or mission within the organization may, in fact, facilitate the empowerment of individuals and groups in determining how to implement the vision. Part of this creative synthesis involves structural change – eliminating entire organizational layers. Along with flatter organizations goes the development of organizational cultures that define the uniqueness of the organization to its members and reinforce the twin values of innovation and collaboration.

COMPARING THE APPROACHES

The four sets of ideas about management that have been discussed in this chapter are by no means exhaustive. And in the next decade or two we will undoubtedly see the emergence of still different ideas, each resting on different motivational premises. To some extent, the sets of ideas discussed are complementary, but there are also fundamental inconsistencies among at least some of these concepts. To move toward participative management, for example, is to move away from tenets of scientific management like separating the planning and doing of a job.

Still, each of the four sets of ideas has performed an important historical function by helping organizations adapt to a particular set of environmental conditions. And it is likely that within each set of ideas are principles with utility for contemporary management, though different principles may be most relevant in different organizations, for different sub-systems within organizations, or for different classes of organizational decisions or actions. This proposition is consistent with the idea that there are no universal truths about management and that the effective use of each set of ideas is contingent on its congruence with situational demands. That, of course, is the central premise of contingency theories such as that of Vroom and Jago discussed earlier and summarized in Reading 38.

ORGANIZATION CHANGE AND DEVELOPMENT

The final section of the volume addresses the issue of organization change and development. The approach to change that managers operate with will undoubtedly be closely linked to their philosophy of management. Leavitt (1964, Reading 40) discussed four different foci for change – task, technology, structure, and people – and one can see that different approaches to management would stress different ones of these avenues for change. Whereas participative and transformational leadership approaches would likely attend more to structure and people, scientific management and management science approaches are likely to begin with tasks and technologies.

Argyris (1983, Reading 41) stresses the human development aspect of organization change and discusses psychological dynamics that interfere with what he terms double-loop learning by organizational members. Finally, Walton (1985, Reading 42) describes the quiet revolution in management practices that has moved progressive organizations toward commitment-oriented strategies represented by participative and leadership approaches.

REFERENCES

Argyris, C. (1983), 'Action science and intervention', *Journal of Applied Behavioral Science*, *19*, 115–40.

Brown, J. A. C. (1954), *The Social Psychology of Industry*, Harmondsworth, England: Penguin.

Burns, J. M. (1978), *Leadership*, New York: Harper & Row.

Deci, E. L. (1975), *Intrinsic Motivation*, New York: Plenum.

Drucker, P. F. (1954), *The Practice of Management*, New York: Harper.

Drucker, P. F. (1974), *Management: Tasks, Responsibilities, Practices*, New York: Harper & Row.

Fountain, J. E. (1990), 'Enacting technology: The effect of organizational logics on information technology use in government organizations', unpublished doctoral dissertation, Yale University.

Gantt, H. L. (1919), *Organizing for Work*, New York: Harcourt, Brace, & Howe.

Gilbreth, F. B. (1914), *Primer of Scientific Management*, New York: Van Nostrand.

Georgopoulos, B. S., Mahoney, G. M., & Jones, N. W. (1957), 'A path-goal approach to productivity', *Journal of Applied Psychology*, *41*, 345–53.

Hackman, J. R., & Walton, R. E. (1986), 'Leading groups in organizations', in P. S. Goodman (ed.), *Designing Effective Work Groups*, San Francisco: Jossey-Bass.

Holmstrom, B. R., & Tirole, J. (1989), 'The theory of the firm', in R. Schmalensee & R. D. Willig (eds.), *Handbook of Industrial Organization* (Vol. 1, pp. 63–133), New York: Elsevier Science Publishers, B. V.

Lawler, E. E., III (1986), *High-Involvement Management*, San Francisco: Jossey-Bass.

Leavitt, H. J. (1958), *Managerial Psychology*, Chicago: University of Chicago Press.

Leavitt, H. J. (1964), 'Applied organization change in industry: Structural, technical, and human approaches', in W. W. Cooper, H. J. Leavitt, & M. W. Shelly, II (eds.), *New Perspectives in Organizational Research*, New York: Wiley.

Leavitt, H. J., (1986), *Corporate Pathfinders*, Homewood, Ill.: Dow Jones-Irwin

Leavitt, H. J., & Whisler, T. L. (1958), 'Management in the 1980s', *Harvard Business Review*, *36*(6), 41–8.

Likert, R. (1967), *The Human Organization*, New York: McGraw-Hill.

Locke, E. A., & Schweiger, D. N. (1979), 'Participation in decision-making: One more look', in B. M. Staw (ed.), *Research in Organizational Behavior* (Vol. 1), Greenwich, Conn.: JAI Press.

McGregor, D.M. (1957), 'The human side of enterprise', in *Adventures in Thought and Action*, Proceedings of the Fifth Anniversary Convocation of the School of Industrial Management (pp. 23–30), Massachusetts Institute of Technology.

Marsland, S., & Beer, M. (1983), 'The evolution of Japanese management: Lessons for US managers', *Organizational Dynamics*, *11*(3), 49–67.

Maslow, A. H. (1943), 'A theory of human motivation', *Psychological Review*, *50*, 370–96.

Orne, M. T. (1962), 'On the social psychology of the psychological experiment', *American Psychologist*, *17*, 776–83.

Ouchi, W. G. (1981), *Theory Z*, Reading, Mass.: Addison-Wesley.

Porter, L. W., & Lawler, E. E., III (1968), *Managerial Attitudes and Performance*, Homewood, Ill.: Irwin-Dorsey.

Rogers, E. M. (1984), 'A sociological research perspective', in F. W. McFarlan (ed.), *The Information Systems Research Challenge: Proceedings*, Boston, Mass.: Harvard Business School Press.

Schweiger, D. M., & Leana, C. R. (1986), 'Participation in decision making', in E. Locke (ed.), *Generalizing from Laboratory to Field Settings: Findings from Research in Industrial/Organizational Psychology, Organizational Behavior, and Human Resources Management* (pp. 147–66), Lexington, Mass.: Lexington Books.

Servan-Schrieber, J. J. (1968), *The American Challenge*, New York: Atheneum.

Simon, H. A. (1965), *The Shape of Automation for Men and Management*, New York: Harper & Row.

Skinner, B. F. (1953), *Science and Human Behavior*, New York: Macmillan.

Smith, A. (1789), *An Inquiry into the Nature and Causes of the Wealth of Nations*, London: Strahan & Cadell.

Taylor, F. W. (1911), *Principles of Scientific Management*, New York: Harper.

Tichy, N. M., & Devanna, M. A. (1986), *The Transformational Leader*, New York: Wiley.

Tosi, H. L., & Carroll, S. (1970), 'Management by objectives', *Personnel Administration*, 33(3), 44–8.

Vroom, V. H. (1964), *Work and Motivation*, New York: Wiley.

Vroom, V. H., & Jago, A. (1988), 'Managing participation: A critical dimension of leadership', *Journal of Management Development*, 7(5), 32–42.

Walton, R. E. (1985), 'From control to commitment in the workplace', *Harvard Business Review*, 63(2), 77–84.

Yukl, G. (1981), *Leadership in Organizations*, Englewood Cliffs, NJ: Prentice Hall.

A Historical Perspective: Theories of Management

SECTION VII

A Historical Perspective:
Theories of Management

30

FREDERICK W. TAYLOR

The Principles of Scientific Management

Excerpts from Frederick W. Taylor, 'The principles of scientific management', in *Scientific Management*, Harper, 1947, pp. 36–9, 100–101, 117–22. (First published 1911.)

Under the old type of management, success depends almost entirely upon getting the 'initiative' of the workmen, and it is indeed a rare case in which this initiative is really attained. Under scientific management the 'initiative' of the workmen (that is, their hard work, their goodwill and their ingenuity) is obtained with absolute uniformity and to a greater extent than is possible under the old system; and in addition to this improvement on the part of the men, the managers assume new burdens, new duties and responsibilities never dreamed of in the past. The managers assume, for instance, the burden of gathering together all of the traditional knowledge which in the past has been possessed by the workmen and then of classifying, tabulating and reducing this knowledge to rules, laws and formulae which are immensely helpful to the workmen in doing their daily work. In addition to developing a *science* in this way, the management take on three other types of duties which involve new and heavy burdens for themselves.

These new duties are grouped under four heads:

1. They develop a science for each element of a man's work, which replaces the old rule-of-thumb method.

2. They scientifically select and then train, teach and develop the workman, whereas in the past he chose his own work and trained himself as best he could.

3. They heartily cooperate with the men so as to insure all of the work being done in accordance with the principles of the science which has been developed.

4. There is an almost equal division of the work and the responsibility between the management and the workmen. The management take over all work for which they are better fitted than the workmen, while in the past almost all of the work and the greater part of the responsibility were thrown upon the men.

It is this combination of the initiative of the workmen, coupled with the new types of work done by the management, that makes scientific management so much more efficient than the old plan.

Three of these elements exist in many cases in a small and rudimentary way, under the management of 'initiative and incentive', but they are then of minor importance, whereas under scientific management they form the very essence of the whole system.

The fourth of these elements, 'an almost equal division of the responsibility between the management and the workmen', requires further explanation. The philosophy of the management of 'initiative and incentive' makes it necessary for each workman to bear almost the entire responsibility for the general plan as well as for each detail of his work, and in many cases for his implements as well. In addition to this he must do all of the actual physical labor. The development of a science, on the other hand, involves the establishment of many rules, laws and formulae which replace the judgement of the individual workman and which can be effectively used only after having been systematically recorded, indexed, etc. The practical use of scientific data also calls for a room in which to keep the books, records,[1] etc., and a desk for the planner to work at. Thus all of the planning which under the old system was done by the workman, as a result of his personal experience, must of necessity under the new system be done by the management in accordance with the laws of the science; because even if the workman was well suited to the development and use of scientific data, it would be physically impossible for him to work at his machine and at a desk at the same time. It is also clear that in most cases one type of man is needed to plan ahead and an entirely different type to execute the work.

The man in the planning room, whose speciality under scientific management is planning ahead, invariably finds that the work can be done better and more economically by a subdivision of the labor; each act of each mechanic, for example, should be preceded by various preparatory acts done by other men. And all of this involves, as we have said, 'an almost equal division of the responsibility and the work between the management and the workman'.

To summarize: under the management of 'initiative and incentive' practically the whole problem is 'up to the workman', while under scientific management fully one-half of the problem is 'up to the management'.

Perhaps the most prominent single element in modern scientific man-

[1]For example, the records containing the data used under scientific management in an ordinary machine-shop fill thousands of pages.

agement is the task idea. The work of every workman is fully planned out by the management at least one day in advance, and each man receives in most cases complete written instructions, describing in detail the task which he is to accomplish, as well as the means to be used in doing the work. And the work planned in advance in this way constitutes a task which is to be solved, as explained above, not by the workman alone, but in almost all cases by the joint effort of the workman and the management. This task specifies not only what is to be done but how it is to be done and the exact time allowed for doing it. And whenever the workman succeeds in doing his task right, and within the time limit specified, he receives an addition of from 30 per cent to 100 per cent to his ordinary wages. These tasks are carefully planned, so that both good and careful work are called for in their performance, but it should be distinctly understood that in no case is the workman called upon to work at a pace which would be injurious to his health. The task is always so regulated that the man who is well suited to his job will thrive while working at this rate during a long term of years and grow happier and more prosperous, instead of being overworked. Scientific management consists very largely in preparing for and carrying out these tasks.

The change from rule-of-thumb management to scientific management involves not only a study of what is the proper speed for doing the work and a remodeling of the tools and the implements in the shop, but also a complete change in the mental attitude of all the men in the shop toward their work and toward their employers. The physical improvements in the machines necessary to insure large gains, and the motion study followed by minute study with a stopwatch of the time in which each workman should do his work, can be made comparatively quickly. But the change in the mental attitude and in the habits of the 300 or more workmen can be brought about only slowly and through a long series of object-lessons, which finally demonstrates to each man the great advantage which he will gain by heartily cooperating in his everyday work with the men in the management.

In most trades, the science is developed through a comparatively simple analysis and time study of the movements required by the workman to do some small part of his work, and this study is usually made by a man equipped merely with a stop-watch and a properly ruled notebook. Hundreds of these 'time-study men' are now engaged in developing elementary scientific knowledge where before existed only rule of thumb. Even the motion study of Mr Gilbreth in bricklaying involves a much more elaborate investigation than that which occurs in most cases. The general steps to be taken in developing a simple law of this class are as follows:

1. Find, say, ten to fifteen different men (preferably in as many separate establishments and different parts of the country) who are especially skilful in doing the particular work to be analyzed.

2. Study the exact series of elementary operations or motions which each of these men uses in doing the work which is being investigated, as well as the implements each man uses.

3. Study with a stopwatch the time required to make each of these elementary movements and then select the quickest way of doing each element of the work.

4. Eliminate all false movements, slow movements and useless movements.

5. After doing away with all unnecessary movements, collect into one series the quickest and best movements as well as the best implements.

This one new method, involving that series of motions which can be made quickest and best, is then substituted in place of the ten or fifteen inferior series which were formerly in use. This best method becomes standard, and remains standard, to be taught first to the teachers (or functional foremen) and by them to every workman in the establishment until it is superseded by a quicker and better series of movements. In this simple way one element after another of the science is developed.

In the same way each type of implement used in a trade is studied. Under the philosophy of the management of 'initiative and incentive' each workman is called upon to use his own best judgement, so as to do the work in the quickest time, and from this results in all cases a large variety in the shapes and types of implements which are used for any specific purpose. Scientific management requires, first, a careful investigation of each of the many modifications of the same implement, developed under rule of thumb; and second, after a time study has been made of the speed attainable with each of these implements, that the good points of several of them shall be united in a single standard implement, which will enable the workman to work faster and with greater ease than he could before. This one implement, then, is adopted as standard in place of the many different kinds before in use, and it remains standard for all workmen to use until superseded by an implement which has been shown, through motion-and-time study, to be still better.

With this explanation it will be seen that the development of a science to replace rule of thumb is in most cases by no means a formidable undertaking, and that it can be accomplished by ordinary, everyday men without any elaborate scientific training; but that, on the other hand, the successful use of even the simplest improvement of this kind calls for records, system and cooperation where in the past existed only individual effort.

There is another type of scientific investigation which should receive special attention, namely, the accurate study of the motives which influence men. At first it may appear that this is a matter for individual observation and judgement and is not a proper subject for exact scientific experiments. It is true that the laws which result from experiments of this class, owing to the fact that the very complex organism – the human being – is being experimented with, are subject to a larger number of exceptions than is the case with laws relating to material things. And yet laws of this kind, which apply to a large majority of men, unquestionably exist, and when clearly defined are of great value as a guide in dealing with men. In developing these laws, accurate, carefully planned and executed experiments, extending through a term of years, have been made, similar in a general way to the experiments upon various other elements which have been referred to in this paper.

Perhaps the most important law belonging to this class, in its relation to scientific management, is the effect which the task idea has upon the efficiency of the workman. This, in fact, has become such an important element of the mechanism of scientific management that, by a great number of people, scientific management has come to be known as 'task management'.

There is absolutely nothing new in the task idea. Each one of us will remember that in his own case this idea was applied with good results in his schoolboy days. No efficient teacher would think of giving a class of students an indefinite lesson to learn. Each day a definite, clear-cut task is set by the teacher before each scholar, stating that he must learn just so much of the subject; and it is only by this means that proper, systematic progress can be made by the students. The average boy would go very slowly if, instead of being given a task, he were told to do as much as he could. All of us are grown-up children, and it is equally true that the average workman will work with the greatest satisfaction, both to himself and to his employer, when he is given each day a definite task which he is to perform in a given time, and which constitutes a proper day's work for a good workman. This furnishes the workman with a clear-cut standard, by which he can throughout the day measure his own progress, and the accomplishment of which affords him the greatest satisfaction.

The writer had described in other papers a series of experiments made upon workmen, which have resulted in demonstrating the fact that it is impossible, through any long period of time, to get workmen to work much harder than the average men around them, unless they are assured a large and permanent increase in their pay. This series of experiments, however, also proved that plenty of workmen can be found who are willing to work at their best speed, provided they are given this liberal increase in wages. The workman must, however, be fully assured that this increase beyond the average is to be permanent. Our experiments have shown that the exact percentage of increase required to make a workman work at his highest speed depends upon the kind of work which the man is doing.

It is absolutely necessary, then, when workmen are daily given a task which calls for a high rate of speed on their part, that they should also be insured the necessary high rate of pay whenever they are successful. This involves not only fixing for each man his daily task, but also paying him a large bonus, or premium, each time that he succeeds in doing his task in the given time. It is difficult to appreciate in full measure the help which the proper use of these two elements is to the workman in elevating him to the highest standard of efficiency and speed in his trade, and then keeping him there, unless one has seen first the old plan and afterwards the new tried upon the same man. And, in fact, until one has seen similar accurate experiments made upon various grades of workmen engaged in doing widely different types of work. The remarkable and almost uniformly good results from the *correct* application of the task and the bonus must be seen to be appreciated.

31

J. A. C. BROWN

The Social Psychology of Industry

Abridged from J.A.C. Brown, *The Social Psychology of Industry*,
Chapter 3, Harmondsworth: Penguin Books, 1954.

But there was another side to the F. W. Taylor success story. Taylor, who stood with his stopwatch over the workers, timing their rest-pauses and their every movement, altering the layout of the plant and changing the traditional ways of doing things, was not very popular. Years later he wrote of this period of his life: 'I was a young man in years but I give you my word I was a great deal older than I am now, what with the worry, meanness and contemptibleness of the whole damn thing. It's a horrid life for any man to live not being able to look any workman in the face without seeing hostility there, and a feeling that every man around you is your virtual enemy.' The movement which, as it now appears, Taylor had hoped would increase not only industrial efficiency but also the standard of living and the health of the worker was to appear to many workers as a form of exploitation, a means of increasing output for the benefit of the owners. Since the success of his work was measured in part by the number of workers who could be discarded when the new methods were applied, and Taylor himself took the view that 'all employees should bear in mind that each shop exists first, last and all the time, for the purpose of paying dividends to its owners', the attitude of the workers is hardly surprising. The researches of Taylor and his successor Frank B. Gilbreth came to form the basis of what is now known as time-and-motion study, while the professional psychologists studied for the most part such problems as fatigue and conditions of work or the devising of selection tests for vocational guidance.

What, to the modern student, is most striking about this early work is not so much its specific content as the assumptions upon which it is based. It is clear that the psychologists and efficiency experts of this period had accepted the attitudes of management which arose during the early stages of the Industrial Revolution and these tended to form the background to all their investigations. Behind each experiment there lies the tacit implication that human nature is possessed of certain fixed properties which decree that most men find work distasteful, are naturally lazy, solely motivated by fear or greed (a motive now described as 'the carrot and the stick'), and always do as little work as possible for the largest possible wage.

In this view of mankind, every detail is completely fallacious. There is no such thing as a fixed human nature, either good or bad, which determines minutely how people shall behave. There is no evidence that men are naturally competitive or self-interested and there are many things which are more important to the worker than his wages. Human beings are not machines in any significant sense of the word, nor does a good physical environment, in itself, make them happy.

THE WORK OF ELTON MAYO

The inadequacy of the assumptions on which most of the early work in industrial psychology had been based was first shown by George Elton Mayo, professor of Industrial Research at the Harvard Graduate School of Business. It is interesting to follow the development of Mayo's thought from his first researches in 1923 to the Hawthorne researches which influence all his later works.

Mayo began this early piece of research with the introduction of rest periods which amounted to two ten-minute breaks in the morning and two in the afternoon. The workers were encouraged to sleep for these periods, which initially were made available to only one-third of the men in the department. The results were impressive, since labour turnover decreased and output went up. It was further noted that morale had improved and the men were more friendly in their attitude. But what was at that time quite inexplicable to Mayo was that there was an almost equivalent rise in production and decrease in labour turnover among the two-thirds of the men who had been excluded from the experiment although they worked in the same department. By the end of the first month, production efficiency had reached nearly 80 per cent and the workers received their first bonus. Within four months the level of production was 82 per cent.

At this point, certain difficulties began to arise. The supervisors of the department had never liked the new system and, it seems probable, shared with many other supervisors a dislike of what they considered to be pampering the workers in the name of science. They believed that the rest pauses should be earned (that is to say that the men should be expected to complete certain jobs before being authorized to rest), and, when a special rush order was received, they abandoned the rest pauses completely. (The assumption that, the longer the hours of work, the more goods should be produced, dies hard.) Within five days, conditions were back to what they had been when the experiment started, production was the lowest for months, absenteeism went up and morale went down. The supervisors were, not unnaturally, upset, and brought back the rest periods once more, but this time strictly on an earned basis. Again the workers failed to respond, and production was back at 70 per cent. The position was a desperate one for the firm, since it looked as if the rush order would never be completed. But, at this moment, the President of the company, in consultation with Mayo, took charge. He ordered that during the rest pauses the machines should be shut down so that everyone in the department would be compelled to rest whether he was worker or supervisor. The supervisors were still more alarmed, for it seemed impossible that the time lost on the job could ever be recovered. But once more absenteeism diminished, morale went up, and production increased to $77\frac{1}{2}$ per cent. Subsequent changes permitted the men to select their own rest pauses which alternated with each other, so that the machines could be kept running continuously. This was the final phase of the experiment. Production reached $86\frac{1}{2}$ per cent, and several years later the President of the company was able to report that labour turnover had never since exceeded 5 to 6 per cent – that is, it was the same in the spinning department as in the rest of the factory. The problem had been solved.

Mayo gives an explanation of the results, in view of his later work.

He pointed out that, firstly, the mere fact of the research being carried out demonstrated to the workers that their problems were not being ignored. That, secondly, the President of the company had always been popular with his employees, and was never more so than when he took the side of the workers against the supervisors who had put a stop to the rest pauses. But, finally, and most important of all, a crowd of solitary workers had been transformed into a group with a sense of social responsibility when they had themselves been given control over their rest periods.

Miller and Form in their *Industrial Sociology* (Harper, 1951) summarize in detail some conclusions to be drawn from this and other of Mayo's research.

1. Work is a group activity.

2. The social world of the adult is primarily patterned about work activity.

3. The need for recognition, security and sense of belonging is more important in determining workers' morale and productivity than the physical conditions under which he works.

4. A complaint is not necessarily an objective recital of facts; it is commonly a *symptom* manifesting disturbance of an individual's status position.

5. The worker is a person whose attitudes and effectiveness are conditioned by social demands from both inside and outside the work plant.

6. Informal groups within the work plant exercise strong social controls over the work habits and attitudes of the individual worker.

7. The change from an established to an adaptive society (i.e. from the older type of community life to the atomistic society of isolated individuals, from eotechnic to paleotechnic society) tends continually to disrupt the social organization of a work plant and industry generally.

8. Group collaboration does not occur by accident; it must be planned for and developed. If group collaboration is achieved, the work relations within a work plant may reach a cohesion which resists the disrupting effects of adaptive society.

32

DOUGLAS M. McGREGOR

The Human Side of Enterprise

Douglas M. McGregor, 'The human side of enterprise', in *Adventures in Thought and Action*, Proceedings of the Fifth Anniversary Convocation of the School of Industrial Management, Massachusetts Institute of Technology, 1957, pp.23–30.

It has become trite to say that the most significant developments of the next quarter century will take place not in the physical but in the social sciences, that industry – the economic organ of society – has the fundamental know-how to utilize physical science and technology for the material benefit of mankind, and that we must now learn how to utilize the social sciences to make our human organizations truly effective.

Many people agree in principle with such statements; but so far they represent a pious hope – and little else. Consider with me, if you will, something of what may be involved when we attempt to transform the hope into reality.

I

Let me begin with an analogy. A quarter century ago basic conceptions of the nature of matter and energy had changed profoundly from what they had been since Newton's time. The physical scientists were persuaded that under proper conditions new and hitherto unimagined sources of energy could be made available to mankind.

We know what has happened since then. First came the bomb. Then, during the past decade, have come many other attempts to exploit these scientific discoveries – some successful, some not.

The point of my analogy, however, is that the application of theory in this field is a slow and costly matter. We expect it always to be thus. No one is impatient with the scientist because he cannot tell industry how to build a simple, cheap, all-purpose source of atomic energy today. That it will take at least another decade and the investment of billions of dollars to achieve results which are economically competitive with present sources of power is understood and accepted.

It is transparently pretentious to suggest any *direct similarity* between the developments in the physical sciences leading to the harnessing of atomic energy and potential developments in the social sciences. Nevertheless, the analogy is not as absurd as it might appear to be at first glance.

To a lesser degree, and in a much more tentative fashion, we are in a position in the social sciences today like that of the physical sciences with respect to atomic energy in the thirties. We know the past conceptions of the nature of man are inadequate and in many ways incorrect. We are becoming quite certain that, under proper conditions, unimagined resources of creative human energy could become available within the organizational setting.

We cannot tell industrial management how to apply this new knowledge in simple, economic ways. We know it will require years of exploration, much costly development research and a substantial amount of creative imagination on the part of management to discover how to apply this growing knowledge to the organization of human effort in industry.

May I ask that you keep this analogy in mind – overdrawn and pretentious though it may be – as a framework for what I have to say.

Management's task: conventional view

The conventional conception of management's task in harnessing human energy to organizational requirements can be stated broadly in terms of three propositions. In order to avoid the complications introduced by a label, I shall call this set of propositions 'Theory X':

1. Management is responsible for organizing the elements of productive enterprise – money, materials, equipment, people – in the interest of economic ends.

2. With respect to people, this is a process of directing their efforts, motivating them, controlling their actions, modifying their behavior to fit the needs of the organization.

3. Without this active intervention by management, people would be passive – even resistant – to organizational needs. They must therefore be persuaded, rewarded, punished, controlled – their activities must be directed. This is management's task – in managing subordinate managers or workers. We often sum it up by saying that management consists of getting things done through other people.

Behind this conventional theory there are several additional beliefs – less explicit, but widespread:

4. The average man is by nature indolent – he works as little as possible.

5. He lacks ambition, dislikes responsibility, prefers to be led.

6. He is inherently self-centered, indifferent to organizational needs.

7. He is by nature resistant to change.

8. He is gullible, not very bright, the ready dupe of the charlatan and the demagogue.

The human side of economic enterprise today is fashioned from propositions and beliefs such as these. Conventional organization structures, managerial policies, practices and programs reflect these assumptions.

In accomplishing its task – with these assumptions as guides – management has conceived of a range of possibilities between two extremes.

The hard or the soft approach?

At one extreme, management can be 'hard' or 'strong'. The methods for directing behavior involve coercion and threat (usually disguised), close supervision, tight controls over behavior. At the other extreme management can be 'soft' or 'weak'. The methods for directing behavior involve being permissive, satisfying people's demands, achieving harmony. Then they will be tractable and accept direction.

This range has been fairly completely explored during the past half century, and management has learned some things from the exploration. There are difficulties in the 'hard' approach. Force breeds counter-forces: restriction of output, antagonism, militant unionism, subtle but effective sabotage of management objectives. This approach is especially difficult during times of full employment.

There are also difficulties in the 'soft' approach. It leads frequently to the abdication of management – to harmony, perhaps, but to indifferent performance. People take advantage of the soft approach. They continually expect more, but they give less and less.

Currently, the popular theme is 'firm but fair'. This is an attempt to gain the advantages of both the hard and the soft approaches. It is reminiscent of Teddy Roosevelt's 'speak softly and carry a big stick'.

Is the conventional view correct?

The findings which are beginning to emerge from the social sciences challenge this whole set of beliefs about man and human nature and about the task of management. The evidence is far from conclusive, certainly, but it is suggestive. It comes from the laboratory, the clinic, the schoolroom, the home and even to a limited extent from industry itself.

The social scientist does not deny that human behavior in industrial organization today is approximately what management perceives it to be. He has, in fact, observed it and studied it fairly extensively. But he is pretty sure that this behavior is *not* a consequence of man's inherent nature. It is a consequence rather of the nature of industrial organizations, of management philosophy, policy and practice. The conventional approach of Theory X is based on mistaken notions of what is cause and what is effect.

'Well,' you ask, 'what then is the *true* nature of man? What evidence leads the social scientist to deny what is obvious?' And, if I am not mistaken, you are also thinking, 'Tell me – simply, and without a lot of scientific verbiage – what you think you know that is so unusual. Give me – without a lot of intellectual claptrap and theoretical nonsense – some practical ideas which will enable me to improve the situation in my organization. And remember, I'm faced with increasing costs and narrowing profit margins. I want proof that such ideas won't result simply in new and costly human relations frills. I want practical results, and I want them now.'

If these are your wishes, you are going to be disappointed. Such requests can no more be met by the social scientist today than could comparable ones with respect to atomic energy be met by the physicist fifteen years ago. I can, however, indicate a few of the reasons for asserting that conventional assumptions about the human side of enterprise are inadequate. And I can suggest – tentatively – some of the propositions that will comprise a more adequate theory of the management of people. The magnitude of the task that confronts us will then, I think, be apparent.

II

Perhaps the best way to indicate why the conventional approach of management is inadequate is to consider the subject of motivation. In discussing this subject I will draw heavily on the work of my colleague, Abraham Maslow of Brandeis University. His is the most fruitful approach I know. Naturally, what I have to say will be over-generalized and will ignore important qualifications. In the time at our disposal, this is inevitable.

Physiological and safety needs
Man is a wanting animal – as soon as one of his needs is satisfied, another appears in its place. This process is unending. It continues from birth to death.

Man's needs are organized in a series of levels – a hierarchy of importance. At the lowest level, but pre-eminent in importance when they are thwarted, are his physiological needs. Man lives by bread alone, when there is no bread. Unless the circumstances are unusual, his needs for love, for status, for recognition are inoperative when his stomach has been empty for a while. But when he eats regularly and adequately, hunger ceases to be an important need. The sated man has hunger only in the sense that a full bottle has emptiness. The same is true of the other physiological needs of man – for rest, exercise, shelter, protection from the elements.

A satisfied need is not a motivator of behavior! This is a fact of profound significance. It is a fact which is regularly ignored in the conventional approach to the management of people. I shall return to it later. For the moment, one example will make my point. Consider your own need for air. Except as you are deprived of it, it has no appreciable motivating effect upon your behavior.

When the physiological needs are reasonably satisfied, needs at the next higher level begin to dominate man's behavior – to motivate him. These are called safety needs. They are needs for protection against danger, threat, deprivation. Some people mistakenly refer to these as needs for security. However, unless man is in a dependent relationship where he fears arbitrary deprivation, he does not demand security. The need is for the 'fairest possible break'. When he is confident of this, he is more than willing to take risks. But when he feels threatened or dependent, his greatest need is for guarantees, for protection, for security.

The fact needs little emphasis that since every industrial employee is in a dependent relationship, safety needs may assume considerable importance. Arbitrary management actions, behavior which arouses uncertainty with respect to continued employment or which reflects favoritism or discrimination, unpredictable administration of policy – these can be powerful motivators of the safety needs in the employment relationship *at every level* from worker to vice-president.

Social needs

When man's physiological needs are satisfied and he is no longer fearful about his physical welfare, his social needs become important motivators of his behavior – for belonging, for association, for acceptance by his fellows, for giving and receiving friendship and love.

Management knows today of the existence of these needs, but it often assumes quite wrongly that they represent a threat to the organization. Many studies have demonstrated that the tightly knit, cohesive work group may, under proper conditions, be far more effective than an equal number of separate individuals in achieving organizational goals.

Yet management, fearing group hostility to its own objectives, often goes to considerable lengths to control and direct human efforts in ways that are inimical to the natural 'groupiness' of human beings. When man's social needs – and perhaps his safety needs, too – are thus thwarted, he behaves in ways which tend to defeat organizational objectives. He becomes resistant, antagonistic, uncooperative. But this behavior is a consequence, not a cause.

Ego needs

Above the social needs – in the sense that they do not become motivators until lower needs are reasonably satisfied – are the needs of greatest significance to management and to man himself. They are the egoistic needs, and they are of two kinds:

1. Those needs that relate to one's self-esteem – needs for self-confidence, for independence, for achievement, for competence, for knowledge.

2. Those needs that relate to one's reputation – needs for status, for recognition, for appreciation, for the deserved respect of one's fellows.

Unlike the lower needs, these are rarely satisfied; man seeks indefinitely for more satisfaction of these needs once they have become important to him. But they do not appear in any significant way until physiological, safety and social needs are all reasonably satisfied.

The typical industrial organization offers few opportunities for the satisfaction of these egoistic needs to people at lower levels in the hierarchy. The conventional methods of organizing work, particularly in mass-production industries, give little heed to these aspects of human motivation. If the practices of scientific management were deliberately calculated to thwart these needs – which, of course, they are not – they could hardly accomplish this purpose better than they do.

Self-fulfillment needs

Finally – a capstone, as it were, on the hierarchy of man's needs – there are what we may call the needs for self-fulfillment. These are the needs for realizing one's own potentialities, for continued self-development, for being creative in the broadest sense of that term.

It is clear that the conditions of modern life give only limited opportunity for these relatively weak needs to obtain expression. The deprivation most people experience with respect to other lower-level needs diverts their energies into the struggle to satisfy *those* needs, and the needs for self-fulfillment remain dormant.

III

Now, briefly, a few general comments about motivation. We recognize readily enough that a man suffering from a severe dietary deficiency is sick. The deprivation of physiological needs has behavioral consequences. The same is true – although less well recognized – of deprivation of higher-level needs. The man whose needs for safety, association, independence, or status are thwarted is sick just as surely as is he who has rickets. And his sickness will have behavioral consequences. We will be mistaken if we attribute his resultant passivity, his hostility, his refusal to accept responsibility to his inherent 'human nature'. These forms of behavior are *symptoms* of illness – of deprivation of his social and egoistic needs.

The man whose lower-level needs are satisfied is not motivated to satisfy those needs any longer. For practical purposes they exist no longer. (Remember my point about your need for air.) Management often asks, 'Why aren't people more productive? We pay good wages, provide good working conditions, have excellent fringe benefits and steady employment. Yet people do not seem to be willing to put forth more than minimum effort.'

The fact that management has provided for these physiological and safety needs has shifted the motivational emphasis to the egoistic needs. Unless there are opportunities at *work* to satisfy these higher-level needs, people will be deprived; and their behavior will reflect this deprivation. Under such conditions, if management continues to focus its attention on physiological needs, its efforts are bound to be ineffective.

People *will* make insistent demands for more money under these conditions. It becomes more important than ever to buy the material goods and services which can provide limited satisfaction of the thwarted needs. Although money has only limited value in satisfying many higher-level needs, it can become the focus of interest if it is the *only* means available.

The carrot and stick approach
The carrot and stick theory of motivation (like Newtonian physical theory) works reasonably well under certain circumstances. The *means*

for satisfying man's physiological and (within limits) his safety needs can be provided or withheld by management. Employment itself is such a means, and so are wages, working conditions and benefits. By these means the individual can be controlled so long as he is struggling for subsistence. Man lives for bread alone when there is no bread.

But the carrot and stick theory does not work at all once man has reached an adequate subsistence level and is motivated primarily by higher needs. Management cannot provide a man with self-respect, or with the respect of his fellows, or with the satisfaction of needs for self-fulfillment. It can create conditions such that he is encouraged and enabled to seek such satisfactions *for himself*, or it can thwart him by failing to create those conditions.

But this creation of conditions is not 'control'. It is not a good device for directing behavior. And so management finds itself in an odd position. The high standard of living created by our modern technological know-how provides quite adequately for the satisfaction of physiological and safety needs. The only significant exception is where management practices have not created confidence in a 'fair break' – and thus where safety needs are thwarted. But by making possible the satisfaction of low-level needs, management has deprived itself of the ability to use as motivators the devices on which conventional theory has taught it to rely – rewards, promises, incentives, or threats and other coercive devices.

Neither hard nor soft

The philosophy of management by direction and control – *regardless of whether it is hard or soft* – is inadequate to motivate because the human needs on which this approach relies are today unimportant motivators of behavior. Direction and control are essentially useless in motivating people whose important needs are social and egoistic. Both the hard and the soft approach fail today because they are simply irrelevant to the situation.

People, deprived of opportunities to satisfy at work the needs which are now important to them, behave exactly as we might predict – with indolence, passivity, resistance to change, lack of responsibility, willingness to follow the demagogue, unreasonable demands for economic benefits. It would seem that we are caught in a web of our own weaving.

In summary, then, of these comments about motivation: management by direction and control – whether implemented with the hard, the soft, or the firm but fair approach – fails under today's conditions to provide effective motivation of human effort towards organizational objectives. It fails because direction and control are useless methods of motivating people whose physiological and safety needs are reasonably satisfied and whose social, egoistic and self-fulfillment needs are predominant.

IV

For these and many other reasons, we require a different theory of the task of managing people based on more adequate assumptions about human nature and human motivation. I am going to be so bold as to suggest the broad dimensions of such a theory. Call it 'Theory Y', if you will.

1. Management is responsible for organizing the elements of productive enterprise – money, materials, equipment, people – in the interest of economic ends.

2. People are *not* by nature passive or resistant to organizational needs. They have become so as a result of experience in organizations.

3. The motivation, the potential for development, the capacity for assuming responsibility, the readiness to direct behavior toward organizational goals are all present in people. Management does not put them there. It is a responsibility of management to make it possible for people to recognize and develop these human characteristics for themselves.

4. The essential task of management is to arrange organizational conditions and methods of operation so that people can achieve their own goals *best* by directing *their own* efforts toward organizational objectives.

This is a process primarily of creating opportunities, releasing potential, removing obstacles, encouraging growth, providing guidance. It is what Peter Drucker has called 'management by objectives' in contrast to 'management by control'.

And I hasten to add that it does *not* involve the abdication of management, the absence of leadership, the lowering of standards or the other characteristics usually associated with the 'soft' approach under Theory X. Much on the contrary: it is no more possible to create an organization today which will be a fully effective application of this theory than it was to build an atomic power plant in 1945. There are many formidable obstacles to overcome.

Some difficulties

The conditions imposed by conventional organization theory and by the approach of scientific management for the past half century have tied men to limited jobs which do not utilize their capabilities, have discouraged the acceptance of responsibility, have encouraged passivity, have eliminated meaning from work. Man's habits, attitudes, expectations – his whole conception of membership in an industrial organization – have been conditioned by his experience under these circumstances. Change in the direction of Theory Y will be slow, and it will require extensive modification of the attitudes of management and workers alike.

People today are accustomed to being directed, manipulated, controlled in industrial organizations and to finding satisfaction for their social, egoistic and self-fulfillment needs away from the job. This is true of much of management as well as of workers. Genuine 'industrial citizenship' – to borrow again a term from Drucker – is a remote and unrealistic idea, the meaning of which has not even been considered by most members of industrial organizations.

Another way of saying this is that Theory X places exclusive reliance upon external control of human behavior, while Theory Y relies heavily on self-control and self-direction. It is worth noting that this difference is the difference between treating people as children and treating them as mature adults. After generations of the former, we cannot expect to shift to the latter overnight.

V

Before we are overwhelmed by the obstacles, let us remember that the application of theory is always slow. Progress is usually achieved in small steps.

Consider with me a few innovative ideas which are entirely consistent with Theory Y and which are today being applied with some success.

Decentralization and delegation

These are ways of freeing people from the too-close control of conventional organization, giving them a degree of freedom to direct their own activities, to assume responsibility and, importantly, to satisfy their egoistic needs. In this connection, the flat organization of Sears, Roebuck and Company provides an interesting example. It forces 'management by objectives' since it enlarges the number of people reporting to a manager until he cannot direct and control them in the conventional manner.

Job enlargement

This concept, pioneered by IBM and Detroit Edison, is quite consistent with Theory Y. It encourages the acceptance of responsibility at the bottom of the organization; it provides opportunities for satisfying social and egoistic needs. In fact, the reorganization of work at the factory level offers one of the more challenging opportunities for innovation consistent with Theory Y. The studies by A. T. M. Wilson and his associates of British coal mining and Indian textile manufacture have added appreciably to our understanding of work organization. Moreover, the economic and psychological results achieved by this work have been substantial.

Participation and consultative management

Under proper conditions these results provide encouragement to people to direct their creative energies toward organizational objectives, give them some voice in decisions that affect them, provide significant opportunities for the satisfaction of social and egoistic needs. I need only mention the Scanlon Plan as the outstanding embodiment of these ideas in practice.

The not infrequent failure of such ideas as these to work as well as expected is often attributable to the fact that a management has 'bought the idea' but applies it within the framework of Theory X and its assumptions.

Delegation is not an effective way of exercising management by control. Participation becomes a farce when it is applied as a sales gimmick or a device for kidding people into thinking they are important. Only the management that has confidence in human capacities and is itself directed toward organizational objectives rather than toward the preservation of personal power can grasp the implications of this emerging theory. Such management will find and apply successfully other innovative ideas as we move slowly toward the full implementation of a theory like Y.

Performance appraisal

Before I stop, let me mention one other practical application of Theory Y which – while still highly tentative – may well have important consequences. This has to do with performance appraisal within the ranks of management. Even a cursory examination of conventional programs of performance appraisal will reveal how completely consistent they are with Theory X. In fact, most such programs tend to treat the individual as though he were a product under inspection on the assembly line.

Take the typical plan: substitute 'product' for 'subordinate being appraised', substitute 'inspector' for 'superior making the appraisal', substitute 'rework' for 'training or development', and except for the attributes being judged, the human appraisal process will be virtually indistinguishable from the product inspection process.

A few companies – among them General Mills, Ansul Chemical and General Electric – have been experimenting with approaches which involve the individual in setting 'targets' or objectives *for himself* and in a *self*-evaluation of performance semi-annually or annually. Of course, the superior plays an important leadership role in this process – one, in fact, which demands substantially more competence than the conventional approach. The role is, however, considerably more congenial to many managers than the role of 'judge' or 'inspector' which is forced upon them by conventional performance. Above all, the individual is encouraged to take a greater responsibility for planning and appraising his own contribution to organizational objectives; and the accompanying effects on egoistic and self-fulfillment needs are substantial. This approach to performance appraisal represents one more innovative idea being explored by a few managements who are moving toward the implementation of Theory Y.

VI

And now I am back where I began. I share the belief that we could realize substantial improvements in the effectiveness of industrial organizations during the next decade or two. Moreover, I believe the social sciences can contribute much to such developments. We are only beginning to grasp the implications of the growing body of knowledge in these fields. But if this conviction is to become a reality instead of a pious hope, we will need to view the process much as we view the process of releasing the energy of the atom for constructive human ends – as a slow, costly, sometimes discouraging approach toward a goal which would seem to many to be quite unrealistic.

The ingenuity and the perseverance of industrial management in the pursuit of economic ends have changed many scientific and technological dreams into commonplace realities. It is now becoming clear that the application of these same talents to the human side of enterprise will not only enhance substantially these materialistic achievements but will bring us one step closer to 'the good society'. Shall we get on with the job?

33

RENSIS LIKERT

A Look at Management Systems

Abridged from R. Likert, *The Human Organization*, Chapter 2, New
York: McGraw-Hill, 1967.

This will be more interesting and more readily understood if a few
minutes are taken now to complete the following form in accordance
with these directions:

'Please think of the *most* productive department, division, or organization you have known well. Then place the letter *h* on the line under
each organizational variable in the following table to show where this
organization would fall. Treat each item as a continuous variable from
the left extreme of System 1 to the right extreme of System 4.'

Now that you have completed the form (Table 1) to describe the
highest-producing department or unit you know well, please think of the
least productive department, division, or organization you know well.
Preferably it should be about the same size as your most productive
unit and engaged in the same general kind of work. Then put the letter
l on the line under each organizational variable on Table 1 to show
where, in the light of your observations, you feel this least-productive
organization falls on that item. As before, treat each item as a continuous variable from the left extreme of System 1 to the right extreme
of System 4.

After you have completed Table 1 to describe both the most and the
least productive departments you know well, compare the relative position of your two answers on each item. You are very likely to discover
that on all items, or virtually all, your *l*'s are to the left of your *h*'s, i.e.,
that your high-producing department has a management system more
to the right in the table and your low-producing department is characterized by having a management system more to the left.

Many different groups of managers, totaling several hundred persons,
have completed Table 1 describing both the highest- and lowest-
producing departments which they knew well. They have varied in their
descriptions of the most productive departments; some are quite far to
the right, the *h*'s being largely under System 4. For others, the most

Table 1. Table of organizational and performance characteristics of different management systems

Organizational variable	System 1	System 2	System 3	System 4
1. Leadership processes used				
Extent to which superiors have confidence and trust in subordinates	Have no confidence and trust in subordinates	Have condescending confidence and trust, such as master has to servant	Substantial but not complete confidence and trust; still wishes to keep control of decisions	Complete confidence and trust in all matters
Extent to which superiors behave so that subordinates feel free to discuss important things about their jobs with their immediate superior	Subordinates do not feel at all free to discuss things about the job with their superior	Subordinates do not feel very free to discuss things about the job with their superior	Subordinates feel rather free to discuss things about the job with their superior	Subordinates feel completely free to discuss things about the job with their superior
Extent to which immediate superior in solving job problems generally tries to get subordinates' ideas and opinions and make constructive use of them	Seldom gets ideas and opinions of subordinates in solving job problems	Sometimes gets ideas and opinions of subordinates in solving job problems	Usually gets ideas and opinions and usually tries to make constructive use of them	Always gets ideas and opinions and always tries to make constructive use of them

Rensis Likert / 381

2. Character of motivational forces

	System 1	System 2	System 3	System 4
Manner in which motives are used	Fear, threats, punishment, and occasional rewards	Rewards and some actual or potential punishment	Rewards, occasional punishment, and some involvement	Economic rewards based on compensation system developed through participation; group participation and involvement in setting goals, improving methods, appraising progress toward goals, etc.
Amount of responsibility felt by each member of organization for achieving organization's goals	High levels of management feel responsibility; lower levels feel less; rank and file feel little and often welcome opportunity to behave in ways to defeat organization's goals	Managerial personnel usually feel responsibility; rank and file usually feel relatively little responsibility for achieving organization's goals	Substantial proportion of personnel, especially at high levels, feel responsibility and generally behave in ways to achieve the organization's goals	Personnel at all levels feel real responsibility for organization's goals and behave in ways to implement them

3. Character of communication process

	System 1	System 2	System 3	System 4
Amount of interaction and communication aimed at achieving organization's objectives	Very little	Little	Quite a bit	Much with both individuals and groups

3. Character of communication process (cont.)

	Downward	Mostly downward	Down and up	Down, up, and with peers
Direction of information flow	Downward	Mostly downward	Down and up	Down, up, and with peers
Extent to which downward communications are accepted by subordinates	Viewed with great suspicion	May or may not be viewed with suspicion	Often accepted but at times viewed with suspicion; may or may not be openly questioned	Generally accepted, but if not, openly and candidly questioned
Accuracy of upward communication via line	Tends to be inaccurate	Information that boss wants to hear flows; other information is restricted and filtered	Information that boss wants to hear flows; other information may be limited or cautiously given	Accurate
Psychological closeness of superiors to subordinates (i.e., how well does superior know and understand problems faced by subordinates?)	Has no knowledge or understanding of problems of subordinates	Has some knowledge and understanding of problems of subordinates	Knows and understands problems of subordinates quite well	Knows and understands problems of subordinates very well

	System 1	System 2	System 3	System 4
4. Character of interaction–influence process				
Amount and character of interaction	Little interaction and always with fear and distrust	Little interaction and usually with some condescension by superiors; fear and caution by subordinates	Moderate interaction, often with fair amount of confidence and trust	Extensive, friendly interaction with high degree of confidence and trust
Amount of cooperative teamwork present	None	Relatively little	A moderate amount	Very substantial amount throughout the organization
5. Character of decision-making process				
At what level in organization are decisions formally made?	Bulk of decisions at top of organization	Policy at top, many decisions within prescribed framework made at lower levels	Broad policy and general decisions at top, more specific decisions at lower levels	Decision making widely done throughout organization, although well integrated through linking process provided by overlapping groups
To what extent are decision makers aware of problems, particularly those at lower levels in the organization?	Often are unaware or only partially aware	Aware of some, unaware of others	Moderately aware of problems	Generally quite well aware of problems

5. Character of decision-making process (cont.)

Extent to which technical and professional knowledge is used in decision making	Used only if possessed at higher levels	Much of what is available in higher and middle levels is used	Much of what is available in higher, middle, and lower levels is used	Most of what is available anywhere within the organization is used
To what extent are subordinates involved in decisions related to their work?	Not at all	Never involved in decisions; occasionally consulted	Usually are consulted but ordinarily not involved in the decision making	Are involved fully in all decisions related to their work
Are decisions made at the best level in the organization so far as the motivational consequences go (i.e., does the decision-making process help to create the necessary motivations in those persons who have to carry out the decisions?)	Decision making contributes little or nothing to the motivation to implement the decision, usually yields adverse motivation	Decision making contributes relatively little motivation	Some contribution by decision making to motivation to implement	Substantial contribution by decision-making processes to motivation to implement

6. Character of goal setting or ordering				
Manner in which usually done	Orders issued	Orders issued, opportunity to comment may or may not exist	Goals are set or orders issued after discussion with subordinate(s) of problems and planned action	Except in emergencies, goals are usually established by means of group participation
Are there forces to accept, resist, or reject goals?	Goals are overtly accepted but are covertly resisted strongly	Goals are overtly accepted but often covertly resisted to at least a moderate degree	Goals are overtly accepted but at times with some covert resistance	Goals are fully accepted both overtly and covertly
7. Character of control processes				
Extent to which the review and control functions are concentrated	Highly concentrated in top management	Relatively highly concentrated, with some delegated control to middle and lower levels	Moderate downward delegation of review and control processes; lower as well as higher levels feel responsible	Quite widespread responsibility for review and control, with lower units at times imposing more rigorous reviews and tighter controls than top management

7. Character of control process (cont.)

Extent to which there is an informal organization present and supporting or opposing goals of formal organization	Informal organization present and opposing goals of formal organization	Informal organization usually present and partially resisting goals	Informal organization may be present and may either support or partially resist goals of formal organization	Informal and formal organization are one and the same; hence all social forces support efforts to achieve organization's goals
Extent to which control data (e.g., accounting, productivity, cost, etc.) are used for self-guidance or group problem solving by managers and non-supervisory employees; or used by superiors in a punitive, policing manner	Used for policing and in punitive manner	Used for policing coupled with reward and punishment, sometimes punitively; used somewhat for guidance but in accord with orders	Largely used for policing with emphasis usually on reward but with some punishment; used for guidance in accord with orders; some use also for self-guidance	Used for self-guidance and for coordinated problem solving and guidance; not used punitively

productive unit was largely under System 3. The striking fact, however, is that irrespective of where the *h*'s describing the high-producing unit fall in the table, the *l*'s for the low-producing department fall to the left. Quite consistently, the high-producing department is seen as toward the right end of the table.

For the vast majority of managers, this has been the pattern for every item in the table irrespective of the field of experience of the manager – production, sales, financial, office, etc. – and regardless of whether he occupies a staff or a line position. In about one case in twenty, a manager will place the low-producing unit to the right of the high on one or two items. But with very few exceptions, high-producing departments are seen as using management systems more to the right (toward System 4) and low-producing units as more to the left (toward System 1).

One would expect that such extraordinary consensus would lead managers to manage in ways consistent with it. When managers or non-supervisory employees are asked, however, to use Table 1 to describe their own organization as they experience it, the answers obtained show that most organizations are being managed with systems appreciably more to the left than that which managers quite generally report is used by the highest-producing departments.

Parenthetically, some low-producing managers, although they display the same pattern of answers as other managers, believe that a manager should move toward System 4 *after* he has achieved high levels of productivity (Miles, 1966). They feel that the way to move from low to high productivity is to use a management system well toward the left (e.g., System 1 or 2) and move toward System 4 only after high productivity is achieved. Their view is essentially that of the supervisor of a low-producing unit who said: 'This interest-in-people approach is all right, but it is a luxury. I've got to keep pressure on for production, and when I get production up, then I can afford to take time to show an interest in my employees and their problems.' Research results show that managers who hold this view are not likely to achieve high productivity in their units (Likert, 1961, Chapter 2).

REFERENCES

Miles, R. E. (1966), 'The affluent organization', *Harvard Business Review*, *44*(3), 106–14.
Likert, R. (1961), *New Patterns of Management*, New York: McGraw-Hill.

34

HENRY L. TOSI AND STEPHEN CARROLL

Management by Objectives

H. L. Tosi and S. Carroll, 'Management by objectives', *Personnel Administration*, Vol. 33(3), 1970, pp. 44–8.

Since Drucker (1954) and McGregor (1960) made statements about management by objectives, organizations of all types have made increasing use of this method. While most of the early discussions of MBO emphasized its use as a tool for the development of more objective criteria for performance evaluation, it has become apparent that subordinate participation in goal setting has resulted in greater levels of ego involvement, increased motivation and increased planning behavior, all of which have an effect upon performance.

These advantages stemmed from the process of setting goals and using them, in place of personality traits and characteristics for evaluation of performance. Management by objectives has been described as a general process in which '. . . The superior and the subordinate manager of an organization jointly define its common goals, define each individual's major areas of responsibility in terms of the results expected of him and use these measures as guides for operating the unit and assessing the contribution of each of its members' (Odiorne, 1965).

The logic of MBO is, indeed, attractive. There is an intrinsic desirability to a method which motivates performance and enhances measurement while at the same time increasing the participation and involvement of subordinates.

THE ELEMENTS OF MBO

There are three basic aspects of MBO which will affect its success: goals and goal setting; participation and involvement of subordinates; and feedback and performance evaluation.

Goals and goal setting
A number of studies have clearly demonstrated that when an individual

or group has a specific goal, there is higher performance than when the goals are general, or have not been set.[1] Generally, high performance can be associated with higher individual or group goals. A number of studies[2] also suggest that performance improvement occurs when an individual is successful in achieving past goals. When there is previous goal success, the individual is more likely to set higher goals in future periods, and he is more likely to attain them.

Participation

There have been a number of diverse findings about the relationship of participation in decision making and productivity. These apparently contradictory findings have been resolved by concluding that if the subordinate perceives the participation to be legitimate, it will have positive effects on productivity. In addition, participation does seem to have an effect on the degree of acceptance of decisions reached mutually. There is also evidence[3] that involvement and participation are positively correlated with the level of job satisfaction.

Feedback

Both laboratory and field research have demonstrated that relatively clear, unambiguous feedback increases problem-solving capacities of groups and improves the performance of individuals.[4] Positive attitudes, increased confidence in decisions, and greater certainties of superior's expectations were found to be related to communications

[1] See for instance J. F. Bryan and E. A. Locke, 'Goal setting as a means of increasing motivation', *Journal of Applied Psychology*, 1967, *51*, 274–7; E. A. Locke, 'Motivational effects of knowledge of results: knowledge or goal setting?' *Journal of Applied Psychology*, 1967, *51*, 324–9.

[2] See R. R. Lockette, 'The effect of level of aspiration upon the learning of skills', unpublished doctoral dissertation, University of Illinois, 1956; G. K. Yacorzynski, 'Degree of effort III. Relationship to the level of aspiration', *Journal of Experimental Psychology*, 1941, *30*, 407–13; M. Horowitz et al., *Motivational Effects of Alternative Decision Making Processes in Groups*, Bureau of Education Research, University of Illinois, 1953.

[3] Victor Vroom, *Some Personality Determinants of the Effects of Participation*, Englewood Cliffs, N. J.: Prentice Hall; Henry Tosi, 'A reexamination of personality as a determinant of the effects of participation', *Personnel Psychology* (forthcoming).

[4] See J. A. Wertz, Antoinetti, and S. R. Wallace, 'The effect of home office contact on sales performance', *Personnel Psychology*, 1954, *7*, 381–4; E. E. Smith, 'The effects of clear and unclear role expectations on group productivity and effectiveness', *Journal of Abnormal and Social Psychology*, 1957, *55*, 213–17; and H. Leavitt and A. Mueller, 'Some effects of feedback on communication', *Human Relations*, 1951, *4*, 401–10.

which clarified roles and role expectancies with more and better information.

Feedback, in the form of formal appraisal in a work setting, when based on relatively objective performance standards, tends to be related to a more positive orientation by subordinates of the amount of supervision their boss exercises. Positive actions are more likely to be taken by subordinates when feedback is viewed as supportive and is objectively based.

MBO AND EMPLOYEE MOTIVATION

Studies of the MBO process in organizations strongly suggest that changes in performance and attitude, which seem positive and desirable, appear to be associated with how it is formally implemented. The implementation of MBO alters the expectations of organization members about performance appraisal and evaluation. These expectations, if not met, may affect the degree of acceptance of the MBO approach. (See Raia, 1965; Tosi & Carroll, 1968.)

This problem may be resolved, to some degree, through proper setting of objectives and use of the MBO process. We believe certain minimal conditions must prevail if MBO is to have its motivational effect:

Goal clarity and relevance
Few managers would quarrel with the notion that organizational goals should be made known to the members. Individual perceptions of the goals are important here. Tosi and Carroll (1968) have suggested some dimensions of goals which need to be communicated to members. First, goals should represent the unit's needs. The members must be aware of the importance of the goals. The development of relatively objective criteria increases the perception of goal clarity. If goals have these properties, they are more likely to have effects upon the individual working towards them.

Managerial use and support
'Top-management support' is important for the success of any program. The best evidence of support is the use of the technique by the manager himself. Formulating goals, discussing them with subordinates, and providing feedback based on these goals will have substantially greater

effect on a subordinate than simply saying 'this has the support of top management'.

Many managers mistakenly feel the verbalization of support for a policy is adequate enough. They send a memo to subordinates stating that top management wishes a program to be implemented. This, obviously, does not insure compliance. 'Do as I say, not as I do' will not work. Verbalized policy support must be reinforced by the individual's perception of the superior's action and behavior in using an objective approach. It is of little or no use to support MBO philosophy orally and not use it!

The need for feedback

While a number of studies have concluded that goals have a greater impact on performance than just feedback alone we do not believe it to be an either/or situation. Feedback about well-developed goals seems a fundamental requirement for behavior change. It may be that the subordinate's perception of the specificity, objectivity and frequency of feedback is interpreted as a measure of the superior's support of an objectives approach.

Some other cautions

There are other significant points that cut across those made above: there are personal as well as organization constraints which must be taken into consideration in the development of goals. The organizational unit and the organization level affect the nature of the goals which can, and will, be set. Goals at lower levels may be more precise and probably more objectively measured. The goals of one functional area, engineering for instance, may be much more general than those of another, say the marketing department.

MBO AND THE COMPENSATION PROCESS

If, as McClelland (1961) suggests, individuals high in need achievement will expend more effort in reaching challenging goals irrespective of external rewards associated with goal accomplishment, MBO may supplement or complement standard compensations procedures. Tying MBO into the financial reward system could have a handsome payoff. It is for this reason that we suggest how information obtained from MBO can be used in making improved compensation decisions.

Internal wage administration

MBO can be of assistance in developing salary differentials within a particular job class. By assessing the level of difficulty and contribution of the goals for a particular job and comparing them with similar jobs, better determination of the appropriateness of basic compensation differentials may be made.

MBO may be useful in providing information about changes in job requirements which may necessitate re-evaluation and adjustment of compensation levels for different positions. By observing changes in objectives over time, changes in job requirements may be detected which could lead to revisions in compensation schedules.

The objectives approach can aid in determining supplementary compensation levels such as stock options, bonus plans, and administration of profit-sharing plans. This type of compensation is usually given when performance exceeds the normal position requirements. A properly developed objectives approach will take into account both normal job duties as well as goals and activities which extend beyond them. The extent to which an incumbent is able to achieve these non-routine objectives should be one, but perhaps not the only, factor in ranking unit members in order of their additional contribution to group effectiveness. It will provide a sound basis for determining what the level of supplemental compensation should be. Needless to say, goals which extend beyond normal job requirements should contribute importantly to organizational success.

A possible problem needs to be noted here. When goals go substantially beyond the current job requirements it may be due to the individual's initiative and aggressiveness. If this happens, it may be more appropriate strategy to change the position of the individual, not to redefine his job and change his compensation levels. A method must be developed which takes this possibility into consideration, as well as the fact that different managers will have different goals. This does not seem to be the appropriate place to detail such a device. A weighing approach which considers the capability of the manager, the difficulty of the goal, and its importance to the unit might resolve this problem.

Performance-linked rewards

If goals are developed properly, their achievement may be more readily associated with an individual so that appropriate individual rewards may be given. The *goal statement* is the heart of the 'objectives approach'. It is a description of the boss's expectancies which will be used in the feedback and evaluation process. It is a communicative artifact which spells out, for both the boss and the subordinate, the objectives *and* the manner in which they will be obtained. It should *contain two elements*, the *desired goal level* and the *activities* required to achieve that level of performance. This permits not only a comparison of performance against some criterion, but also allows determination of whether or not events, which are presumed to lead to goal achievement, have taken place if appropriate criteria are not available.

This has important implications for the problems of assessment, evaluation, and compensation. Some goals may be neither measurable nor adequately verifiable. Yet, intuitively we know what must be done to achieve them. If this is the case, and we have distinguished between goals and activities, we can at least determine whether activities which are presumed to lead to desired ends have taken place.

It is important to recognize the distinction between measuring the achievement of a goal level and determining whether or not an event presumed to lead to goal achievement has taken place. If we are unable to quantify or specify a goal level in a meaningful way, then we must simply assume that the desired level will be achieved if a particular event, or set of activities, has taken place. For example, it is very difficult to find measurable criteria to assess a manager's capability in developing subordinates, yet we can determine if he has provided them with development opportunities. If they have participated in seminars, attended meetings or gone to school it may be *assumed* that the development activities are properly conducted.

PROMISES AND PROBLEMS

By its very nature, MBO seems to be a promising vehicle for linking performance to the evaluation process and the reward system in order to encourage both job satisfaction and productivity. It appears that higher performance and motivation is most likely when there is a link between performance and the reward systems (Tosi & Carroll, 1968; Porter & Lawler, 1968). It may be that this link can be achieved through the process of feedback regarding goal achievement and the association of rewards and sanctions with achievement. Goal attainment should be organizationally reinforced, and the reinforcement should be different for individuals, as a function of their own attainment. The use of an 'objectives' approach in conjunction with a compensation program may also result in less dissatisfaction with the allocation of compensation increases made. Certainly there is virtually universal agreement among managers that rewards should go for actual accomplishments rather than for irrelevant personal characteristics and political or social standing.

There may be problems arising from the use of MBO and its emphasis on goals and goal achievement. Many organizations have adopted the objectives approach because it seems to be a better appraisal device, and they have used it primarily in this manner. But, an appraisal system should furnish information needed to make other personnel decisions, such as promotion and transfer. Information furnished by the objectives approach may not be adequate for these purposes. Accomplishment of goals at a lower-level job may be a good indicator of capability in the current job and/or level of motivation, but not of the individual's abilities to perform at higher levels of responsibility, especially if the requirements on the higher-level job are much different from the current position.

Conversely, goals accomplished at a lower level may be indicative of promotability to a particular high-level job if there is high goal congruence between the two positions. At any rate, there is certainly no reason to rely strictly upon the objectives approach for these decisions. It can be used along with other criteria, such as assessment of traits, when this is deemed an important dimension by the decision makers. Another potential difficulty should be pointed out. If the objectives approach becomes the basic vehicle for the determination of compensation increases, then managers may quickly learn to 'beat the system'. Unless higher-level managers are skilled in the use of MBO, subordinates may set objectives which have high probabilities of achievement, refraining from setting high-risk goals. When any system becomes too formalized, managers learn how to beat it, and those using it become more concerned with simply meeting the formal [requirements of the system].

The 'objectives approach' seems to be a practical way of motivating organization members, but it is not an easy path to follow. It requires a considerable amount of time and energy of *all managers*, in addition to extensive organization support to make it work. MBO may lose some of its mystique, value, importance, and significance when it must be translated into a formal policy requirement. It is too easy to consider a formal MBO program as merely another thorn in the manager's side, with no positive gains for implementing it. To succeed, an MBO program must be relevant, applicable, helpful, and receive organization support and reinforcement. One way in which this can be done is to link it to other elements of the structural system which reinforce behavior, such as compensation and reward programs.

REFERENCES

Drucker, P. (1954), *The Practice of Management*, New York: Harper.

McClelland, D. C. (1961), *The Achieving Society*, Princeton, NJ: Van Nostrand

McGregor, D. (1960), *The Human Side of Enterprise*, New York: McGraw-Hill.

Odiorne, G. (1965), *Management by Objectives*, New York: Pitman.

Porter, L., & Lawler E. E., III (1968), *Managerial Attitudes and Performance*, Homewood, Ill.: Irwin-Dorsey.

Raia, Anthony (1965), 'Goal Setting and Self Control', *Journal of Management Studies*, II-I, February, 34–5.

Tosi, H. & Carroll, S. (1968), 'Managerial reactions to management by objectives', *Academy of Management Journal*, December, 415–26.

Contemporary Behavioral Approaches to Management

35

STEPHEN MARSLAND AND MICHAEL BEER

Japanese Management

Abridged from S. Marsland and M. Beer, 'The evolution of Japanese management: Lessons for US managers', *Organizational Dynamics*, Vol. 11 (3), 1983, pp. 49–67.

In the last several years US executives have shown increasing interest in the Japanese approach to management. This interest has been stimulated by the emergence of Japanese companies as a major competitive force in world markets. In the United States, for example, Japanese automobiles, televisions, and other consumer electronic products are competing very successfully with US manufacturers' products on the basis of both price and quality. As the productivity of US firms leveled off in the 1970s, US executives looked to the Japanese 'model' of management for potential answers.

In Japan, Western managers found increasing productivity and rapid economic growth, of course. But they found more – Japanese male turnover was far lower than that of the United States: 4.7 per cent versus 9.9 per cent. Japanese unemployment rates were extremely low – although they had climbed from 1.1 per cent in 1970, they had plateaued at 2 per cent after 1976. Industrial strife was rare – the Japanese economy lost, on average, .13 workdays per work year because of strike action in the period from 1974 to 1976. This was much better than the record in the United States (.45 workdays per work year), about the same as France's record (.20 workdays per work year) and worse than West Germany's (.02 workdays per work year).

The more executives and scholars try to understand the basis of Japan's success, the clearer it becomes that the Japanese approach to human resources management is different from that of the United States. Contrary to common concepts, however, management and employment systems in Japan are post-Second World War creations. Although Japanese human-resources policies and practices are consistent with Japan's unique societal values and culture, they are neither an inevitable nor a natural outcome of them. Far from it – poor economic conditions and severe labor-management conflict following the Second

World War, together with the American Occupation, prompted Japanese management to find new human-resources management approaches. While these approaches were frequently based on American ideas, they were applied in a manner consistent with traditional values regarding groups and hierarchy.

To facilitate understanding of the 'Japanese' approach to management, Japanese management systems themselves will be discussed. These management systems, to be successful, require employees to be highly motivated and committed to the firm. The Japanese have developed a unique mix of human-resources management policies that result in these outcomes. These policies are slow promotion, frequent transfer of employees, intensive training, support for and promotion of cooperation at all levels, and 'lifetime' employment.

Of necessity, the description of Japanese management systems that follows is sketchy and over-generalized. It applies most accurately to the large Japanese companies (300 or more employees), which accounted for about 30 per cent of the workforce in 1979. Even within these large companies, managerial patterns of management can and do differ. Similarly caution should be taken against over-generalizing about Japanese employment systems. For example, day laborers, temporary employees, and regular female employees (three groups that make up an average one-third of the workforce in a Japanese firm) enjoy neither the benefits nor the status of regular, male employees.

With an understanding of the Japanese management experience, managers can ask themselves which Japanese management practices and human-resource policies are critical to obtaining high employee commitment and what shape these might take in companies [that] have quite a different social, political, and historical context.

JAPANESE MANAGEMENT SYSTEMS

Japanese management systems are based on three principles: (1) emphasis on information flows, (2) 'bottom-up' decision making, and (3) division of managerial labor – lower-level managers implement, middle managers develop their subordinates, and top managers deal with outside groups.

Japanese companies process and circulate a vast amount of information at all times. Proposals being considered are sent to all levels, information-gathering on the market-place and competitors is constantly underway, and statistics are always being compiled. The lifetime-employment system and frequent transfers and training mean that Japanese managers always have networks of friends in other departments who keep them posted on developments in their areas. Japanese managers nearly always know who in the organization has the information they need – and can locate the answers to their questions in minutes. Exchange of information throughout the organization goes on after hours at night when the elite go out drinking together. Information exchange creates involvement for managers, stimulates creativity, enhances teamwork, and makes sure all parts of the organization act in concert. Conflict is resolved by gathering more and more information until the proper course of action becomes clear to all concerned.

'Bottom-up' decision making characterizes many management decisions. When a problem is identified by the organization, a low-level manager or task force is assigned the job of developing solutions. These managers develop their proposal and present it to successively higher levels of the organization for suggestions and approvals. This wide circulation of memoranda is known as the *ringi* system. At each level, refinements are made in the proposal. When the plan has been approved at all levels in that department, it is circulated to all concerned managers in other departments for their perusal and routine approval. Only when the plan has been approved at all levels will it be implemented. Under this system, getting a decision approved takes a long time – but once it is approved, it is quickly implemented. This is the reverse of the US system, where decisions are quickly made but take a long time to implement, because those who must implement them must be fully briefed on the plan and persuaded that it is a good idea.

Another aspect of Japanese bottom-up management is the evolution of worker groups that seek to develop safer work methods, improve processes, and achieve better quality control. Known by various names – quality circle (QC) groups, zero defect (ZD) groups, or JK (Jishu Kanri – 'self-management') activities – the concept involves tapping the skills and knowledge of blue-collar workers to improve operations, quality, safety, and profitability. Originally based on a US concept of zero defects (workmanship with no errors), these groups sought quality. By 1980 they had branched out into safety and process improvements. Each group of blue-collar workers meets after hours to work on its current project – a project developed from a group member's idea. The group can call on white-collar staff for help, but the group is responsible for investigating, documenting, and presenting its own proposal. Proposals deemed feasible by management are implemented, and token cash prizes are awarded to the best proposals.

The final aspect of Japanese management is division of labor between management levels. Implementation and development of plans is left to low-level managers, who are *not* responsible for evaluating or developing their immediate subordinates (section staff). Middle managers are concerned with reviewing their subordinates' plans and their implementation and with developing all their subordinates for several levels down. Top managers are responsible for maintaining consensus within the firm, developing the firm's policies, and maintaining good relations with the public, allied firms, banks, trading companies, and the government. Top managers merely review decisions by lower levels and do not directly concern themselves with company operations. This pattern of delegation tends to encourage decision making at the lowest level consistent with available information and knowledge – a pattern too seldom found in American firms.

Japanese management systems are, therefore, information intensive; rely on people at all levels to take responsibility for the firm's goals; and require teamwork. To gain superior information flow, managers must have a network of relationships and contacts built up over time – thus the need for managers to remain with the firm for a long time to build those information networks and thus the need for permanent employment. To allow bottom-up decision making, lower-level managers and blue-collar workers alike must be experienced in their jobs and in the organization's ways – another argument for long tenure and slow promotion. Moreover, a heavy investment in selection, training, and development – which extends to blue-collar workers as well as white-collar staff – further develops the competencies required in bottom-up decision making. Teamwork among managers and implementation of bottom-up plans is enhanced by a spirit of cooperation and commitment to the firm – thus lifetime employment, company housing, company vacations, company cafeteria, and company-sponsored club activities. These create a 'closed society' that reinforces cooperation within management and between management and labor.

At the root of successful Japanese management, therefore, are a number of internally consistent human-resources management policies and practices that enable employee development and commitment.

The evolution of Japanese human-resources management has spurred rapid economic growth and impressive productivity gains in the postwar years. As the Japanese have realized, the human resource is the ultimate resource – and management by trust and collaboration yields high commitment and superior performance.

36

J. RICHARD HACKMAN AND RICHARD E. WALTON

Leading Groups in Organizations

Abridged from J. R. Hackman and R. E. Walton, 'Leading groups in organizations', in P. S. Goodman (ed.), *Designing Effective Work Groups*. San Francisco: Jossey-Bass, 1986, pp. 72–119.

What are the critical functions that need to be fulfilled if a *work group in an organization* is to perform effectively? To answer that question requires that we know something about those aspects of the group and the situation that are particularly potent in determining how well organizational teams perform – those matters about which something may 'need to be done' by group leaders.

GROUP EFFECTIVENESS

There are several factors that determine whether or not a team is an appropriate device for performing some piece of work. Rather than delve into [that] matter here, we will assume that a team *is* the performing unit of choice and proceed to explore what is required to foster its effectiveness.

Group Effectiveness Defined. The overall effectiveness of a group, in our view, depends on its standing on the following three dimensions:

1. *The degree to which the group's productive output (that is, its product or service) meets the standards of quantity, quality, and timeliness of the people who receive, review, and/or use that output.*

2. *The degree to which the process of carrying out the work enhances the capability of members to work together interdependently in the future.*

3. *The degree to which the group experience contributes to the growth and personal well-being of team members.*

INGREDIENTS OF WORK GROUP EFFECTIVENESS

In this section, we will identify and discuss three general ingredients of team effectiveness.

Clear, Engaging Direction. In work organizations, we have repeatedly observed a group formed and given a task to perform without any briefing about the purpose of the work or how it fits into overall organizational aspirations. Although ambiguity about direction is common in organizations, it is a mistake.

It is, of course, possible to have direction that is both crystal clear and alienating (rather than engaging). What will engage a given team depends in part on members' personal interests and aspirations, and on the degree of motivational alignment between the team and the organization. Engagement also is enhanced when objectives have the following attributes:

- Room for the team to 'tailor' the objectives to fit with the members' own inclinations.
- Substantial effects on the psychological or physical well-being of other people.
- Stretch team members and provide them with opportunities for personal learning and growth.
- Success or failure will be directly consequential for the team and its members.

An engaging, authoritative statement of purpose orients and empowers teams (Walton, 1985). Having a clear sense of what is expected, and why it is important, appears to be a prerequisite condition for team effectiveness. Direction is not, however, the whole story: How the group's performance situation is structured can either undermine good direction or exploit its positive potential.

An Enabling Performance Situation. Groups that know where they are supposed to be going have three hurdles to surmount in order to get there. They must (1) exert sufficient *effort* to get the task accomplished at acceptable levels of performance, (2) bring adequate levels of *knowledge and skill* to bear on their task work, and (3) employ *task performance strategies* that are appropriate to the work and to the setting in which it is being performed (Hackman, 1987).

We refer to these hurdles as the *process criteria of effectiveness*. They are not the ultimate test of how well a group has done, but they turn out to be of great use both in assessing how a group is doing as it proceeds with its work and in diagnosing the nature of the problem if things are not going well.

Although a high standing on the process criteria suggests that a group is performing well, it is not possible to achieve that by merely issuing an exhortation or ultimatum. Instead, we must probe a bit further and identify conditions that do increase the likelihood that a group's work will be characterized by sufficient effort, ample task-relevant knowledge and skill, and task-appropriate performance strategies. As we do that, we will identify three additional points of leverage for promoting team effectiveness.

1. *A group structure that promotes competent work on the task*. Some groups have difficulty getting anything done because they were not set up right in the first place. Our research suggests that particularly important structural features include the following:

- *Task structure*. The task should be clear, consistent with the direction of the group, and high on what Hackman and Oldham (1980) call motivating potential – that is, the team task is a meaningful piece of work, for which members share responsibility and accountability and which provides many opportunities for the team to learn how well it is doing.
- *Group composition*. There should be as few members as possible given the work that needs to be done, they should have among them the talents required by the task, and they should be balanced on homogeneity/heterogeneity (that is, members should be neither functional replicas of one another nor so different that they cannot learn from one another).
- *Core norms that regulate member behavior*. To foster effective task performance, norms should, at minimum, provide for the efficient regulation of member behavior, thereby making coordinated action possible, and promote active scanning of the task and situation and pro-active planning of group performance strategies.

2. *An organizational context that supports and reinforces excellence*. Specific features of the organizational context that are significant in creating conditions for team effectiveness include the following:

- The reward system. It should provide recognition and other positive consequences for excellent *team* performance. Rewards to individuals should never provide disincentives for task-oriented collaboration.
- The educational system. It should provide the group with technical assistance regarding any aspect of the task work for which members do not presently have adequate knowledge, skill, or experience.
- The information system. It should make available to group members the data and projections they need to invent or select a task- and situation-appropriate strategy for proceeding with the work.

3. *Available, expert coaching and process assistance*. A leader or consultant can do much to promote team effectiveness by helping team members learn *how* to work interdependently – although this is probably

a hopeless task if the group has an unsupportive organizational context or was poorly structured in the first place.

The role of the help provider is not, of course to dictate to group members the 'one right way' to go about their collaborative work. It is, instead, to help members learn how to minimize the 'process losses' that invariably occur in groups (Steiner, 1972) and how they might work together in ways that generate synergistic process *gains*. Specific kinds of help that might be provided can be divided into three areas and may include the following:

1. Regarding *effort*: Helping members minimize coordination and motivation decrements (process losses that can waste effort) and helping members build commitment to the group and its task (a process gain that can build effort).

2. Regarding *knowledge and skill*: Helping members avoid inappropriate 'weighting' of members' ideas and contributions (a process loss) and helping members share expertise and learn from one another (a process gain).

3. Regarding *performance strategies*: Avoiding flawed implementation of performance plans (a process loss) and developing inventive, creative ways of proceeding with the work (a process gain).

Adequate Material Resources. The third generic condition required for effectiveness is having the wherewithal needed to do what needs to be done – such as money, space, staff time, tools, and so on. This condition is not terribly interesting conceptually, but it turns out to be a major roadblock to team effectiveness in many organizations we have studied. Even groups that have a clear and engaging direction, and who are ready to sail over the process hurdles, eventually will fail if they do not have (and cannot get) the resources they need to do their work. Indeed, among the saddest kinds of failures are those experienced by well-designed and well-supported groups with a clear sense of direction but who cannot obtain the resources they need to fulfill their promise.

We have explored three generic ingredients that support team effectiveness and have broken the second one down into three components. The result is a list of five conditions that we believe to be key to the effectiveness of task-performing teams in organizations:

1. Clear, engaging direction
2. An enabling performance situation
   - A group structure that fosters competent task work
   - An organizational context that supports and reinforces excellence
   - Available, expert coaching and process assistance

3. Adequate material resources

CRITICAL LEADERSHIP FUNCTIONS

How do we put a functional approach to leadership together with the conditions for team effectiveness just discussed? The answer, we hope, is obvious: The critical leadership functions for a task-performing team in an organization are *those activities that contribute to the establishment and maintenance of favorable performance conditions.* Following McGrath's (1962) framework, this involves two types of behavior: *monitoring* – obtaining and interpreting data about performance conditions and events that might affect them – and *taking action* to create or maintain favorable performance conditions.

Monitoring. The team effectiveness model prompts a number of diagnostic questions. Does the team have clear and engaging direction? Is the team well structured? Does it have a supportive organizational context? Are ample coaching and process assistance available to the team? Does it have adequate material resources? While these questions are posed here in the present tense, the monitoring function includes not only assessments of the present state of affairs (diagnosis) but also projections about how things are changing and what deleterious or fortunate events may be about to occur (forecasting).

Taking Action. On the basis of assessments of the group and the situation, action can be taken to improve the present state of affairs, to exploit existing opportunities, or to head off impending problems. Again, the content of the actions will be to clarify direction, to strengthen the design of the group or its contextual supports, to provide coaching or process assistance to the group, or to ensure it has adequate material resources.

Sometimes the focus of such actions will be within the group (as when the leader works with members to help them understand the significance of their task or learn better ways of coordinating their activities). Other times external action will be required (as when the leader negotiates a change in the organization's compensation system to provide rewards for excellent team performance, or when he or she helps establish a relationship between the group and a consultant or trainer from elsewhere in the organization).

So far we have defined what we mean by group effectiveness, identified the conditions we believe to be most potent in promoting it, and specified a set of critical leadership functions based on that material.

Now, continuing to work backwards, we turn to the behavior of group leaders. What is it, we ask, that a leader actually *does* to help a group perform as effectively as possible?

Leading a group that is having problems. Let us consider now a typical leadership situation. A group is performing a piece of work in a business organization, its leader has some concern that all may not be well with the group and its performance, and he or she wants to figure out whether that is in fact a problem – and if so what might be done to remedy it.

Our overall approach suggests that remedial action would be initiated by a leader when he or she observes that a team is falling short on one or more of the three criteria of team effectiveness. It might be that the clients of the team's work are becoming increasingly less satisfied with its products. Or that the capability of team members to work inter-dependently is slipping. Or that individual members are finding their experiences in the team frustrating or alienating.

In such circumstances, the leader would begin by collecting diagnostic data and then take action to remedy problems revealed in the diagnosis. For clarity of presentation, we will discuss the leader's behavior in terms of an ordered set of questions, recognizing that in practice they may not be dealt with in this order. Indeed, some of them will be quickly dismissed as of little consequence for a given group, and attention will turn immediately to other issues that have greater significance for that team's effectiveness.

1. *Does the group have clear direction?* Are there signs that members have oriented their work activities toward inappropriate ends, that there is disagreement among them about what they are actually supposed to be doing and why, or that members do not understand the significance of their work?

If direction is a problem, then the leader must do further diagnostic work to determine *why* it is a problem. It may be that direction has always been unclear, that the people who created the group were unsure just what it actually was supposed to accomplish. Or it may be that organizational representatives were clear about the direction of the group, but the word never got to the group (or was never understood by them). Or it may be that direction was communicated but not *accepted* by group members – that is, they redefined the task to fit better with their own interests and aspirations without much concern for organizational needs.

Obviously, the behaviors of a leader to solve a 'direction problem' would depend significantly upon the answers to these diagnostic questions. In one case, the appropriate behavior might be to exercise influence outward or upward to get senior managers to be clearer about what they seek from the group. In another, it might be to spend time with group members, communicating and teaching the direction and its implications. In yet another, it might require the leader to exercise his or her *own* authority to articulate organizational expectations of the group insistently.

2. *Are performance conditions satisfactory?* To deal with this question, the leader would first examine how the group is doing on the three process criteria of effectiveness.

First, effort. Is sufficient effort being applied to the task? If this is a problem, then diagnostic questions continue. Is the group task unmotivating? Does the organization fail to provide positive consequences for *team* excellence (or, worse, are members competing for scarce rewards given out for individual performance)? Are members interacting in ways that result in coordination or motivation decrements, or in the alienation and withdrawal of individuals?

Second, knowledge and skill. Is sufficient talent being brought to bear on the work? If not, is the main difficulty with members' knowledge (that is, they do not know what they need to know to do the task) or with their skills (that is, they know what needs to be done, but they are not able to pull it off)? If there is a problem with knowledge or skill, what are its roots? Is it a composition issue (too many people, the wrong people, or the wrong mix of people)? Is it an organizational support problem (for example, the unavailability of task-related training or consultation needed by the group)? Is it a group dynamics problem (members weighting each other's contributions in accord with some task-irrelevant criterion, such as demographic attributes rather than task expertise, or failing to recognize and use non-obvious talents of individual members)?

And finally, performance strategies. Are the performance strategies being used by the group appropriate to the task and the situation? Or are members going about the work in a way that does not quite fit with what is required for effectiveness? Again, if this is a problem, the questions continue. Do norms discourage rather than encourage active scanning of the performance situation and planning of alternative ways for proceeding with the work? Does the group not have access to information that members need to develop performance strategies that fit with the realities of the task and situation? Are members interacting in ways that introduce 'slippage' in the implementation of their performance strategies?

Obviously, the actions of a leader should depend on the answers to these diagnostic questions. Although one cannot state ahead of time what specific behaviors will be particularly useful in aiding team effectiveness, there is a preferred order to actions that might be taken. In general, one would attempt first to get the structure of the group in shape; that would be followed by attention to organizational supports, and attention to group dynamics issues would come last.

3. *Does the group have adequate resources?* As noted earlier, even a well-designed and well-supported group in which members are interacting competently will fail if the resources needed to accomplish the work are unavailable. Generally, inadequate resources are easy to discern and difficult to remedy: a search committee that discovers late in the game that it has no candidates to consider, for example, may be genuinely stuck. The same is true for a production team that cannot get the raw materials it needs because there is a worldwide scarcity of those materials. So the *forecasting* part of the diagnostic work is of special importance here – so that action can be taken before a resource crisis occurs to head it off or to redirect the work of the group when it hits. And, once again, the actions taken by a leader to remedy the problem may focus much more on exercising influence external to the group than on attempts to alter members' behaviors in relation to one another.

SUMMARY

A summary of our approach, from the perspective of the leader, is provided in Figure 1. The figure reviews the performance-enhancing conditions we have been discussing; its main purpose, however, is to highlight the monitoring function of team leaders. It shows that a leader's first priority is to keep track of changes in a team's standing on the effectiveness dimensions. 'How is the group doing?' the effective leader asks. 'Are there signs of problems in the task work, in members' ability to work together interdependently, or in the quality of individuals' group experiences?' When problems, unexploited opportunities, or negative trends are noted, he or she would examine the process indicators in the center of the figure to learn more about what may be going on.

Then, guided by the answers to the diagnostic questions, a leader's attention would turn to the group and organizational conditions at the left of the figure. 'Which performance conditions most need strengthen-

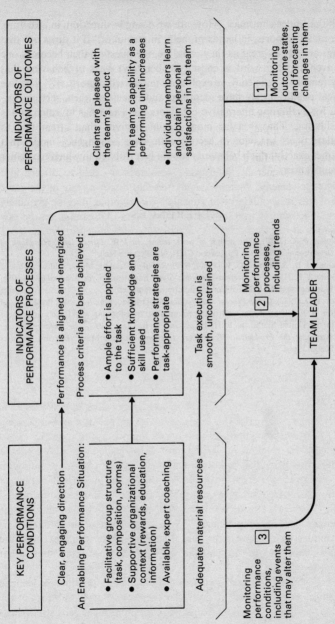

Figure 1. Summary of the team leader's monitoring function.

ing?' the leader continues. 'How are we doing in direction, in structure, in context supports, in hands-on help, in resources?' If it turns out that things are not as great as they could be, the question then becomes one of inventing (the word is chosen deliberately) ways of behaving that may remedy a deficiency or exploit an unrealized opportunity. The five critical conditions we have identified and discussed, then, serve as criteria for evaluating alternative behaviors the leader has invented and is considering. That is a far more feasible activity than attempting to regulate one's behavior in accord with some contingency model that specifies exactly which behaviors should be exhibited in which particular circumstances.

REFERENCES

Hackman, J. R. (1987), 'The design of work teams', in J. W. Lorsch (ed.), *Handbook of Organizational Behavior*, Englewood Cliffs, N J: Prentice Hall.

Hackman, J. R., & Oldham, G. R. (1980), *Work Redesign*, Reading, Mass.: Addison-Wesley.

McGrath J. E. (1962), *Leadership Behavior: Some Requirements for Leadership Training*, Washington, DC: US Civil Commission (mimeographed).

Steiner, I. D. (1972), *Group Process and Productivity*, Orlando, Fla.: Academic Press.

Walton, R. E. (1985), 'From control to commitment: transforming workforce management in the United States', in R. H. Hayes and K. B. Clark (eds.), *The Uneasy Alliance: Managing the Productivity–Technology Dilemma*, Boston, Mass.: Harvard Business School Press.

37

EDWARD E. LAWLER, III

How High-Involvement Management Works

Excerpt from E. E. Lawler, III, *High-Involvement Management*, Chapter 11, San Francisco: Jossey-Bass, 1986.

High-involvement management starts with beliefs about people that support their being involved. Douglas McGregor (1960) was the first to articulate the importance of the assumptions we make about people. They turn out to be the basis for the design of many organizational features.

A high-involvement organization's core values and principles must be congruent with the idea of employee involvement and responsibility for decision making. Examples of assumptions are listed below.

●People can be trusted to make important decisions about their work activities.

●People can develop the knowledge to make important decisions about the management of their work activities.

●When people make decisions about the management of their work, the result is greater organizational effectiveness.

ORGANIZATIONAL STRUCTURE

High-involvement management requires an organizational structure that [has] few levels of management and light staffing, especially in the area of staff support. Many of the staff-support activities should be accomplished by the production people. The remaining staff groups should be largely in a consulting and training role. An important objective for them is the transfer of their expertise to other employees.

The reason for having a flat structure should be obvious. The best way to assure that decisions are made at lower levels is to have very few levels of management, so that managers cannot make all the decisions. The struggle that occurs in traditional organizations – to hoard decisions because there are so few per person – is best eliminated by eliminating levels of management.

The fundamental grouping approach in a high-involvement organization should be toward organizational units that feel responsible for a particular product or customer. The alternative of structuring around function (such as engineering or accounting) is incongruent with high-involvement management because it creates a situation where individuals are performing their own particular specialty; they have no identification with the product or contact with the customer. This creates the need for hierarchy and extensive control systems to assure that the different functions work together to deliver the product or service that the customer wants. It also limits the degree to which they understand the business and are motivated to produce a high-quality product or service.

In large corporations, high-involvement management almost inevitably means a decentralized organization that is structured around businesses. It does not mean large, highly specialized corporate staffs and organizing around such functions as manufacturing, finance, sales, and marketing.

In high-involvement organizations, many mini-enterprises need to be created so that employees are part of a business they can relate to. These mini-enterprises should sell products and services either to each other, if this is appropriate, or to outside customers. This is the best way to break down large plants into areas small enough for people to identify with, and where they have a line of sight to overall performance. It is crucial to create a situation where people face a customer who can give them feedback and react to their particular product or service, whether this customer is a member of the same organization or not. Each part of the organization should have customer responsibility of some type. Only then can people get a sense of motivation and satisfaction from serving a customer.

It is particularly important in larger high-involvement organizations to have a representative council or committee to deal with important organization-wide matters.

These groups deal with varying issues, including hours of work, personnel policies, scheduling production work, communication, and planning major introductions of new products and new equipment.

JOB DESIGN

The type of job design follows directly from the organizational structure and the technology. It should involve individually enriched jobs or teams. The choice between individual enrichment and teams should be based on technology and the degree to which an individual can be given responsibility for a whole task or a whole piece of work. If an individual can be given a whole task, then individual enrichment is usually the best choice because it avoids the complexities and training that are involved in developing effective teams. Often, however, there is no choice: teams are needed because an individual cannot personally produce a product or service and relate to a customer.

One other consideration is relevant – the psychological needs of the employees. If teams are used, it is important to staff the organization with people who like social contact, so that the interaction involved in team work will be pleasurable to them and not a source of discontent.

PROBLEM-SOLVING GROUPS

Task forces are needed, at times, to deal with key issues. Production, service, or quality problems that involve several areas are good candidates for task-force solutions. These task forces should get the problem-solving and group-process training that are common in quality circles, but there is no need for an elaborate quality-circle structure in most high-involvement organizations. The normal functions of quality circles can be done by the teams or by the participative-council structure. What remains are certain special issues that need to be addressed by a cross-section of people from the plant. This can best be done by temporary task forces that make recommendations to the existing structure.

INFORMATION SYSTEM

The information system is the key to effective coordination and feedback in any organization but is particularly crucial in a high-involvement system. Since many of the levels of hierarchy and staff support are gone, the information system must provide the capability for people to coordinate and manage themselves. Even with the best of intentions, in the absence of an effective information system, employees cannot become self-regulating.

The availability of inexpensive computing and the capability to create networks among computers makes it much easier to structure a high-involvement organization these days. Computers provide the potential of putting large amounts of information in the hands of individuals or groups throughout the organization. They can directly communicate with each other in order to coordinate their activities.

The information system needs to be open to all members of the organization, so that they can get the kind of financial, production, and other information that they need. Mini-enterprises or teams need to get information about how effectively they are performing and how their performance compares to standards and to their competitors. It also needs to tell them how they are servicing their customers.

The information system should not only include data about financial operating results; it should also include information on the human system. In particular, survey data should be regularly collected and fed back to individuals in the organizations.

PHYSICAL AND TECHNICAL DESIGN

High-involvement organizations need a particular physical layout. First, they need to be egalitarian and to meet people's needs for a safe, pleasant work environment. Perhaps the most controversial point here is the issue of egalitarian surroundings. This is done to reinforce the classless structure of the organization and to impress upon people that decisions are based on expertise, not hierarchy. Thus, such status symbols as reserved parking spaces, separate entrances, executive dining rooms, and special offices are not acceptable.

In general, high-involvement organizations should have small locations. A basic principle of involvement is to create small units that can be self-managing and that people can identify with. The large multi-thousand-person plant or office structure is the exact opposite of the kind of physical structure that supports a high-involvement work model. Sometimes these are necessary because of the advantages that they offer. If this is the case, then they should be broken down into mini-enterprises and everything possible should be done to avoid the depersonalization, communication problems, and powerlessness that people feel when working in such large structures.

REWARD SYSTEM

A high-involvement organization needs a different reward system than traditional organizations. Specifically, it calls for skill-based pay, gainsharing, profit sharing, employee ownership, flexible benefits, an all-salary workforce, and open, participative decision processes.

Skill-based pay is a critical element in developing knowledge and in communicating one of the high-involvement core values: personal growth. It has been shown to be effective in new plants (Lawler & Ledford, 1985). In high-involvement organizations, it needs to be expanded to pay for economic-knowledge skills as well as normal production skills. It also needs to include managers.

The reward system also needs to include some form or forms of gainsharing. It offers a vehicle for pushing rewards throughout the organization. This can increase the motivation level and help everyone relate to the larger unit of which they are part. It provides people with ongoing excitement about the business that is absent when their economic fate is not tied to the success of their organization.

The reward system should also allow individuals to choose their fringe benefits (Lawler, 1981). With flexible benefit plans, individuals choose a package of fringe benefits, cash, and other rewards. This particular approach reinforces the fact that people differ in their needs and that the organization considers them to be mature and capable of making important decisions.

LEADERSHIP STYLE

Leadership in a high-involvement work organization is a different activity from that in a traditional workplace. Here I am using the term *leader* to apply to someone who inspires loyalty, commitment, and motivation through his or her personal style and behavior. High-involvement management requires leaders who energize people in ways that support self-motivation (Bennis & Nanus, 1985); leaders who help people move in positive directions, where questioning and debate is acceptable and part of the organization's search for the best answer (Burns, 1978); leaders who help the organization know the right things to do rather than helping it do things right.

In high-involvement organizations, the key positions need to be staffed by leaders. Traditional managerial behaviors are not needed because of the self-regulatory nature of the design. Leadership, however, is needed to provide a sense of purpose and direction as well as to shape the organization's culture and decision processes.

Overall, managers in high-involvement organizations need a particular set of leadership skills that will allow them to do four critical

things for the organization.
1. Build trust and openness.
2. Provide a vision and communicate it.
3. Move decisions to the proper location.
4. Empower others.

PUTTING IT ALL TOGETHER

The key to success for high-involvement organizations is the same as for any organization: consistency and congruence. Individual practices must fit together and must affect everyone in the same way. The features discussed in this chapter all contribute to building an organization in which power, information, knowledge, and rewards are moved downward. They meet the twin criteria of affecting the total organization and of being consistent in their approach to dealing with people. The reward system encourages employees to develop their skills; the information system gives them the foundation they need to use their skills; the training and selection system helps them develop their skills; and the work design gives them the power and tasks that utilize their skills.

When all these features are combined, they produce a congruent high-involvement organization that is distinctly different from existing organizations. In this sense, it may seem like an idealistic model that involves considerable risk. Quite the contrary is true. It is merely a complete development of the idea of moving power, rewards, knowledge, and information to the lowest levels of the organization. It may appear to be a high-risk approach, but in many respects it is low-risk because it is congruent and covers the entire organization. It is much riskier to move only some of these features downward, thereby creating an incongruent organization. It is even riskier to continue to practice traditional management in a changing environment.

High-involvement management is the best way to make many American organizations competitive in an international arena where some countries have a competitive advantage through raw materials, others through low labor cost, and still others through geographic position. High-involvement management is the competitive advantage available to countries with educated, achievement-oriented workforces who want to perform effectively, whose core values support participative decision making, and who can engage in substantial amounts of self-regulation. At this point, it is more of a concept than a reality, but many of the practices have been proven in the sense that they have worked in new plants and in plants with gainsharing. The key question at this point is not whether high-involvement organizations will work. It is how to create such organizations.

REFERENCES

Bennis, W., & Nanus, B. (1985), *Leaders*, New York: Harper & Row.

Burns, J. M. (1978), *Leadership*, New York: Harper & Row.

Lawler, E. E., III (1981), *Pay and Organization Development*, Reading, Mass.: Addison-Wesley.

Lawler, E. E., III, & Ledford, G. E. (1985), 'Skill-based pay', *Personnel*, *62* (9), 30–37.

McGregor, D. (1960), *The Human Side of Enterprise*, New York: McGraw-Hill.

38

VICTOR H. VROOM AND ARTHUR G. JAGO

Managing Participation: A Critical Dimension of Leadership

Abridged from V. H. Vroom and A. G. Jago, 'Managing participation: A critical dimension of leadership', *Journal of Management Development*, Vol. 7 (5), 1988, pp. 32–42.

It is now almost a truism that managers must adapt their leadership styles to fit the demands of the situations they face. One of the necessary manifestations of this situational view of leadership is the need to adapt the form and degree of participation in decision-making by subordinates to the personalities of the subordinates, the decisions to be made, and the general organizational circumstances.

In a classic *Harvard Business Review* article written in 1958, Tannenbaum and Schmidt first laid out the problem and sketched some of the factors that should be included in an attempt to solve it. Fifteen years later, Vroom and Yetton (1973) introduced a normative model which tried to specify which of a set of alternative decision-making processes, varying in opportunity for subordinate participation, should be used in different situations. The processes used by Vroom and Yetton are shown in Table I.

Selection among these processes for a particular problem or decision is based on four criteria: (1) the quality of decisions produced, (2) the acceptance or commitment to decisions by subordinates, (3) the time required to make the decision, and (4) the opportunities for subordinate development.

The Vroom–Yetton model is, in fact, quite simple. Those processes thought to risk either decision quality or acceptance are eliminated by seven 'rules'. For example, if the quality of the decision is important and if the leader lacks the necessary information, AI is eliminated from consideration. When all seven rules have been applied, a feasible set consisting of at least one or as many as five alternatives is generated. The last two criteria, time and development, are then used to select within the feasible set.

Table I. Types of management decision methods – group problems

Symbol	Definition
AI	You solve the problem or make the decision yourself using the information available to you at the present time.
AII	You obtain any necessary information from subordinates, then decide on a solution to the problem yourself. You may or may not tell subordinates the purpose of your questions or give information about the problem or decision on which you are working. The input provided by them is clearly in response to your request for specific information. They do not play a role in the definition of the problem or in generating or evaluating alternative solutions.
CI	You share the problem with the relevant subordinates individually, getting their ideas and suggestions without bringing them together as a group. Then you make the decision. This decision may or may not reflect your subordinates' influence.
CII	You share the problem with your subordinates in a group meeting. In this meeting you obtain their ideas and suggestions. Then you make the decision, which may or may not reflect your subordinates' influence.
GII	You share the problem with your subordinates as a group. Together you generate and evaluate alternatives and attempt to reach agreement (consensus) on a solution. Your role is much like that of chairperson, coordinating the discussion, keeping it focused on the problem, and making sure that the critical issues are discussed. You can provide the group with information or ideas that you have, but you do not try to 'press' them to adopt 'your' solution, and you are willing to accept and implement any solution that has the support of the entire group.

Reprinted from *Leadership and Decision-Making* by Victor H. Vroom and Philip W. Yetton by permission of the University of Pittsburgh Press, © 1973 by University of Pittsburgh Press.

During the fifteen years since its introduction, the Vroom–Yetton Model has become the principal technology for informing choices about the appropriateness of different degrees of participation in different situations. Literally hundreds of management textbooks have incorporated the decision trees or the rules on which they are based. In addition, the number of managers who have received training in the model can conservatively be placed in six figures.

While the Vroom–Yetton model is both popular and useful, it is not without faults. The most frequent shortcomings noted by ourselves or by others can be summarized as follows.

Model fails to differentiate among feasible and among non-feasible processes. The structure of the decision rules is such that the rules tell you what not to do, not what to do. After the rules are applied, a feasible set remains that sometimes contains a single decision strategy but more often contains a variety of strategies from which to choose.

The average feasible set contains between two and three alternatives. While time pressures and developmental concerns can be used to select among these alternatives, it is apparent that the quality and acceptance rules do too little of the work of the model and that too much of a role is left for the subsidiary criteria of time and development.

The concept of decision rule which prevents the model from differentiating among leader behaviors within the feasible set also prevents it from differentiating among behaviors outside that set. The former are deemed equally effective, the latter are deemed equally ineffective. Our own research (1978) directly challenges this assumption showing that choices that violate more than one rule are even less effective than those which violate only one rule.

Model requires yes/no responses. Perhaps the most frequent reaction that experienced managers have to the Vroom–Yetton model is that it does not permit an answer of 'probably yes, maybe, or probably no to any of the seven questions measuring the problem attributes'. The model makes the assumption that situations are black or white while managers tell us that the most difficult ones that they encounter come in varying shades of grey.

Important aspects of the situations are ignored. The Vroom–Yetton model utilizes seven features of the situation to decide which process to use. While these variables are important, they are not an exhaustive list of the relevant factors. Our research evidence as well as our experience in teaching the model to managers has suggested a number of specific factors to be added in the interest of enhancing model validity.

A NEW MODEL

For the last three years, the authors have been working on an improved model. Our revisions have been basic – addressing all three of the criticisms that we have outlined. A recent book entitled *The New Leadership: Managing Participation in Organizations* (Vroom & Jago, 1988) describes the model in detail. Here we will touch on the highlights.

The concepts of rules and of the feasible set were integral to the Vroom–Yetton model, but proved to be cumbersome and restrictive of efforts to improve the model. For example, the addition of another attribute or another rule might be necessary to improve the validity of its prescriptions but would render the feasible set empty under some circumstances. As a result, our first step was to replace the existing rules with equations which expressed our beliefs about the manner in which each of the four criteria – quality, commitment, time and development – were likely to be affected by both the decision process used and by the problem attributes. When we began formulating mathematical equations to express the rules, we felt at times as if we were replacing a candle with a laser beam. The medium enabled us as model builders to do far greater justice to the cause/effect relationships implied in the original rules and to the accumulating wisdom both from research and from experiences in using the model.

The equations operate on problem attributes which served to moderate the effects of participation on one or more of the criteria. To the seven problem attributes of the Vroom–Yetton model have been added five new attributes for a total of twelve. Table II lists the entire set of problem attributes along with acceptable responses.

As shown in Table II, most of the problem attributes permit five levels of response. The four questions pertaining to the importance of criteria require estimates ranging from no importance to critical importance. Six other attributes lending themselves to probability estimates permit five levels ranging from No through Maybe to Yes. Finally, the remaining two attributes, time constraints and geographical dispersion, permit only dichotomous responses of No and Yes.

The reader has undoubtedly realized that the new model is substantially more complex than the old. The key question is the benefit realized from this added complexity. Is the new model more valid than its predecessor? Jago, Ettling and Vroom (1985) conducted an experiment designed to answer that question. The results of this comparison, reported in Figure 1, are very encouraging. The structural changes introduced to remedy the problems previously noted appear to have resulted in a model far more predictive of both decision quality and decision commitment.

While the new model would seem to be a distinct improvement over its predecessor, it remains to be seen whether it is as usable as its simpler predecessor. Managers accustomed to the simple decision trees of the Vroom–Yetton model are not likely to view complex equations in the same 'user friendly' spirit!

In spite of its complexity, three ways have been found to put the new model within reach of most managers. The first method is a set of 'rules of thumb', which social scientists interested in complex decision making have termed 'heuristics'. There are four sets of heuristics corresponding to the four criteria of decision effectiveness. Each set parallels the equation for a single criterion with words replacing the mathematical symbols. Table III shows the heuristics pertaining to decision quality.

The reader familiar with the Vroom–Yetton model will note the

Table II. Problem attributes in the revised model (Vroom & Jago, 1988).

QR: Quality Requirement
How important is the technical quality of this decision?

1	2	3	4	5
No import	Low import	Average import	High import	Critical import

CR: Commitment Requirement
How important is subordinate commitment to the decision?

1	2	3	4	5
No import	Low import	Average import	High import	Critical import

LI: Leader Information
Do you have sufficient information to make a high-quality decision?

1	2	3	4	5
No	Probably no	Maybe	Probably yes	Yes

ST: Problem Structure
Is the problem well structured?

1	2	3	4	5
No	Probably no	Maybe	Probably yes	Yes

CP: Commitment Probability
If you were to make the decision by yourself, is it reasonably certain that your subordinates would be committed to the decision?

1	2	3	4	5
No	Probably no	Maybe	Probably yes	Yes

GC: Goal Congruence
Do subordinates share the organizational goals to be attained in solving this problem?

1	2	3	4	5
No	Probably No	Maybe	Probably yes	Yes

CO: Subordinate Conflict
Is conflict among subordinates over preferred solutions likely?

1	2	3	4	5
No	Probably no	Maybe	Probably yes	Yes

SI: Subordinate Information
*Do subordinates have sufficient information to make a high-quality decision?

1	2	3	4	5
No	Probably no	Maybe	Probably yes	Yes

TC: Time Constraint
*Does a critically severe time constraint limit your ability to involve subordinates?

1		5
No		Yes

GD: Geographical Dispersion
*Are the costs involved in bringing together geographically dispersed subordinates prohibitive?

1		5
No		Yes

MT: Motivation-Time
*How important is it to you to minimize the time it takes to make the decision?

1	2	3	4	5
No import	Low import	Average import	High import	Critical import

MD: Motivation-Development
*How important is it to you to maximize the opportunities for subordinate development?

1	2	3	4	5
No import	Low import	Average import	High import	Critical import

*New attributes

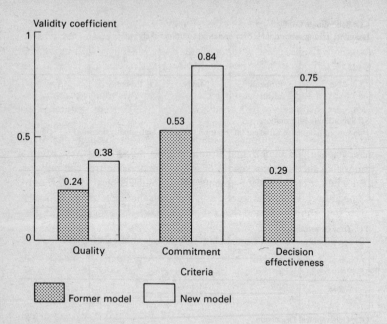

Figure 1. A Comparison of Model Validity (Vroom & Jago, 1988)

similarity in form and substance of these heuristics to the quality rules in the earlier model. The heuristics are useful in explaining the component mechanisms of the model. They fall short, however, in enabling managers to put together these components to figure out the optimal method to use in particular circumstances.

This purpose is best achieved by a computer program which makes the computations called for in the equations. In their new book, Vroom and Jago (1988) describe an expert system which enables a manager to analyse a decision problem extremely quickly and to determine the model's advice. Each of the diagnostic questions shown in Table II appears on the screen along with the range of possible responses to that question. Upon request, help screens are available that explain the meaning of the question and the types of situations for which each response is appropriate. When all questions have been answered, the screen indicates the model's choice of a decision process considering all four criteria weighted in the manner indicated by the manager's answers. In addition one can see the optimal choice for each of the four criteria considered alone.

Additional output is available after the model's choice is displayed.

A complete definition of the recommended process and bar graphs showing the relative effectiveness of the five processes are but two of about a dozen available options for the user. Managers with just a few hours of training with the new model or its predecessor can learn to use the software quickly and easily.

The third method of making the complex new model accessible to managers involves a return to the decision tree concept of the earlier model. A decision tree representation of the new model is possible if two simplified assumptions are made. Both of these assumptions were made explicitly in the original Vroom–Yetton model. The first assumption is that there are no 'shades of grey'. The decision tree can only be used when the presence or absence of attributes is clear cut and only yes/no answers exist. The second assumption is that there are no critically severe time constraints and that subordinates are not geographically dispersed.

Decision trees have been created for a Time-Driven model (Time is critically important and Development is unimportant) and for a Development-Driven model (Development is critically important and Time is unimportant). The former is shown in Figure 2.

Training in managing participation. These three mechanisms (heuristics, a computer-based expert system and decision tree) make the more complex, newer, model at least as accessible as its predecessor. We continue to view the models, both new and old, as a useful ingredient in management training programs intended to help managers to adapt their style to situational demands.

Over the last fifteen years, thousands of managers have taken part in residential training programs on the Vroom–Yetton model. A common ingredient in virtually all programs has been the use of a problem set as a basis for helping participants to view similarities and differences between their style, and both other managers and the model. A typical problem set is made up of thirty cases, each describing a leader faced with a specific decision to make. Managers work on these cases in advance of the training program and decide which of the alternative decision processes shown in Table I they would employ if they were in that situation. These choices then become the basis for an individualized analysis of each manager's style. In four pages, a manager can view the similarities and differences between his/her use of participation and that of other managers as well as similarities and differences with the time-driven and development-driven models. The expected consequences of the manager's choices on decision quality, commitment, time and development are computed and cases flagged for restudy where the

Table III. Heuristics for decision quality (1988).

For group problems, to improve decision quality:

---

   (1)   *Avoid* the use of AI when:
       a. the leader lacks the necessary information.
   (2)   *Avoid* the use of G11 when:
       a. subordinates do not share the organizational goals, and/or
       b. subordinates do not have the necessary information.
   (3)   *Avoid* the use of A11 and C1 when:
       a. the leader lacks the necessary information, and
       b. the problem is unstructured.
   (4)   *Move* toward G11 when:
       a. the leader lacks the necessary information.
       b. subordinates share the organizational goals, and
       c. there is conflict among subordinates over preferred solutions.

---

choice is deemed to be less than optimal. Finally managers can see the problem attributes which affect their behavior.

This powerful and effective training method has been shown to cause managers to be more participative in this management style, to be more cognizant of the need to adapt their style to situational demands, and pay more attention to development of subordinates. These effects have been shown for time periods between six months and three years after the original training.

The essential features of the training are unchanged with the new model. The concepts of the feasible set and rules are replaced by heuristics, and new decision trees replace those of the old model. In addition, new problem sets have been developed to reflect the larger number of problem attributes and new computer programs written to take advantage of the greater analytical possibilities of the new model.

So far more than a thousand managers have received training in the new model. On the basis of results with this training, we have become convinced that it is a significant advance over its much publicized predecessor. Managers faced with the task of solving the enormous challenges of today's organizations should find its prescriptions much more specific and of greater value than those of its older brother. While the computer version undoubtedly provides the most information and is of greatest value, the decision trees provide potentially useful guidance on how effectively to match one's behavior with situational demands.

The greater precision of the new model should also be of benefit to the many hundreds of trainers who have tried to make the old model 'come alive' to the managers they train. In fact, we have found the new

QR **Quality requirement:**
How important is the technical quality of this decision?

CR **Commitment requirement:**
How important is subordinate commitment to the decision?

LI **Leaders information:**
Do you have sufficient information to make a high-quality decision?

ST **Problem structure:**
Is the problem well-structured?

CP **Commitment probability:**
If you were to make the decision by yourself, is it reasonably certain that your subordinate(s) would be committed to the decision?

GC **Goal congruence:**
Do subordinates share the organizational goals to be attained in solving this problem?

CO **Subordinate conflict:**
Is conflict among subordinates over preferred solutions likely?

SI **Subordinate information:**
Do subordinates have sufficient information to make a high-quality decision?

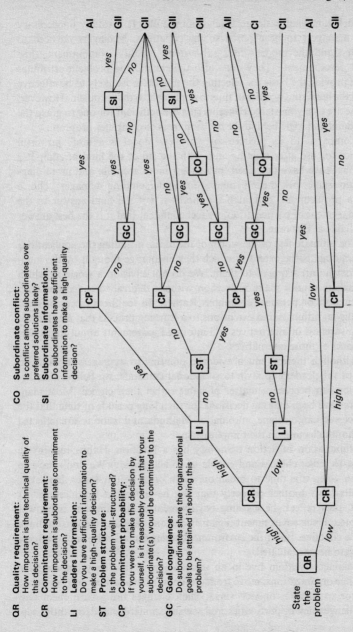

Figure 2. Time-Driven Decision Tree – Group Problems

model somewhat easier to teach than the old. It is totally unnecessary for managers to be exposed to the equations. Managers *do* need to understand the model's four sub-criteria (quality, commitment, time and development). They must also understand the problem attributes that provide the basis for selecting the process most likely to be effective and the heuristics or rules of thumb applicable to that problem. However, these are easily mastered concepts that are sufficient for one to grasp the fundamental logic behind the decision trees or computer program.

Compared to its predecessor, the new model is a more powerful device for use after training and, with the aid of the kind of computer feedback we have described, provides a more accurate and more diagnostic framework during training for understanding managers' choice on a problem set. Although the model is not the final answer to the management of participation, we feel confident that it is the best answer available at this time.

The ultimate test of the worth of the ideas, including the applications to training, is the extent to which they encourage thought by the managers who are exposed to them. We do not envision a world in which managers cannot make a decision without referral to a decision tree, calculator, or personal computer. Rather, we see these pieces of technology as adjuncts and extensions to a learning process that emphasizes an awareness of alternatives and informed judgements about the consequences of those alternatives.

Although there is much evidence pointing to managers' abilities to adapt this leadership style to situational demands, we believe that behavior can become a matter of habit rather than choice. Most managers have been making decisions for such long periods of time that the processes can become automatic. Methods and actions are selected without reflecting on their implications.

Habituation of action obviously has a function. Habits reduce the need to make choices and enable us to act quickly. We don't have to think when it is time to brush our teeth or to tie our shoes. However, habits have another property that can be somewhat troublesome. At best, they reflect the learning environment at the time the habit was formed. If the environment remains constant, they are likely to continue to be effective. But if the environment changes markedly, habit patterns have to be re-evaluated.

Managers seldom live in an unchanging world. They change jobs, change organizations, move from one country to another, or from public sector to private, or vice versa. Such changes bring with them new challenges, new opportunities, and new situational demands on leadership.

Old approaches need to be re-thought and new habits substituted for old.

While mobility requires change, it is by no means its only cause. Deregulation, foreign competition and new tax laws have brought with them massive changes in the way in which corporations have to be structured and managed. Managerial leadership is no longer maintaining the *status quo*. Old habits must be discarded if one is to respond to today's challenges and opportunities.

To meet these challenges, managers must have the capabilities of being both participative and autocratic and of knowing when to employ each. They must be capable of identifying situational demands, of selecting or designing appropriate methods of dealing with them, and they must have the skills necessary to implement their choices. Our experience in working with managers over the last fifteen years suggests that training focused on analytical models of participation contributes to these critical components of effective leadership.

REFERENCES

Vroom, V. H., & Yetton, P. W. (1973), *Leadership and Decision-Making*, Pittsburgh: University of Pittsburgh Press.

Vroom, V. H., & Jago, A. G. (1978), 'On the validity of the Vroom/Yetton model', *Journal of Applied Psychology*, *63*, 151–62.

Vroom, V. H., & Jago, A. G. (1988), *The New Leadership: Managing Participation in Organizations*, Englewood Cliffs, NJ: Prentice Hall.

Jago. A. G., Ettling, J. T., & Vroom, V. H. (1985), 'Validating a revision to the Vroom/ Yetton model: first evidence', Proceedings of the 45th Annual Meeting of the Academy of Management, pp. 220–23.

39

NOEL M. TICHY AND MARY ANNE DEVANNA

The Transformational Leader

Abridged from N. M. Tichy and M. A. Devanna, 'The transformational leader', *Training and Developmental Journal*, 1986, Vol. 40 (7), pp. 27–32.

Corporate leadership is America's scarcest natural resource!

At a time when our economy, as well as that of the entire industrialized world, is in the midst of major upheaval and transformation, a new type of leadership at the middle and senior levels of our corporations is desperately needed. From undisputed leadership we have at best become *primus inter pares*. Many are concerned that we may fall further behind. The Japanese have certainly led the way in product excellence. The Koreans and other former third world nations are trying hard. A resurgent Europe is gaining fast.

The time has come to talk about how corporations, our wealth-producing institutions, can develop leadership with the courage and imagination to change our corporate lifestyles. What's needed, in historian James MacGregor Burn's terms, is not the old style of transactional leadership, but a new *transformational* leadership. Transactional leaders were fine for an era of expanding markets and non-existent competition. In return for compliance they issued rewards. These managers changed little; they managed what they found and left things pretty much as they found them when they moved on.

Transformational leadership is about change, innovation, and entrepreneurship. We agree with Peter Drucker that these are not the provinces of lonely, half-mad individuals with flashes of genius. Rather, this brand of leadership is a behavioral process quite capable of being learned and managed. It's a leadership process that is systematic, consisting of purposeful and organized searches for changes, systematic analysis, and the capacity to move resources from areas of lesser to greater productivity.

The strategic transformation of organizations is a discipline with a set of predictable steps. Though complex, transformation can be thought about and acted on with a framework that's easy to understand.

We see corporate transformation as a drama that can be thought about in terms of a three-act play.

This three-act play is portrayed in Figure 1. It has a set of dynamics which the organization goes through, as well as a set of individual dynamics associated with each act. In *The Transformational Leader* (Tichy & Devanna, 1986) we trace the drama of a group of protagonists as they struggle to revitalize their companies. The protagonists were chosen from dramas that we have had the opportunity to observe. Some have received a great deal of attention while others have played to smaller houses. Although most of these leaders were senior-level managers when their plays began, the lessons they have learned are applicable and useful for middle managers as well as policy-makers. The purpose of our book is not to present actions for managers to imitate, but to spread a new way of thinking about corporate transformation as an everyday way of acting.

THE DRAMA: LEADERSHIP AND PARADOX

Leaders must deal with the tensions of the middle managers whose organization is about to embark on a major transformation. Many of the tensions involve the paradox of changing what has been successful.

Our transformational leaders deal with these feelings by creating organizations that embrace paradox, that are characterized by the ability to manage uncertainty.

Paradoxes create the dramatic tensions in our transformational drama. They include:

● *A struggle between the forces of stability and forces of change*. Successful organizations must find ways to balance the need for adaptation with the need for stability.

● *A struggle between denial and acceptance of reality*. Potential revitalization dramas become tragedies when key protagonists attempt to deny reality and hide from its implications.

● *A struggle between fear and hope*. Organizations can regenerate themselves. The process, however, necessitates that the aging and increasingly impotent form be destroyed before a new form can emerge. The faith that destruction will result in rebirth is tied to the tension between stability and change and countered by the denial that change is necessary.

● *A struggle between the manager and the leader*. Managers are dedicated to the maintenance of the existing organization, whereas leaders

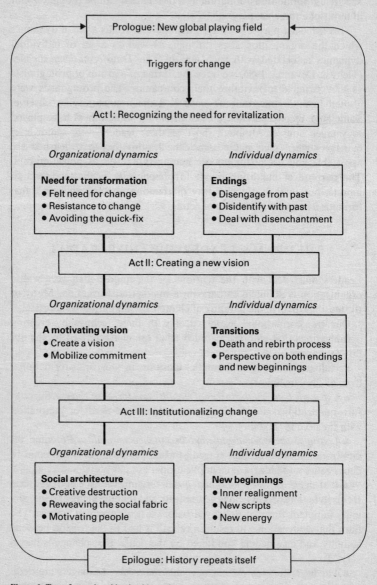

Figure 1. Transformational leadership: a three-act drama

often are committed to its change. A tension arises between doing things right and doing the right things.

THE ORGANIZATION DURING ACT I

● *Trigger events*. Environmental pressures trigger the need for change, though not all organizations respond to such signals. The failure of leadership to respond litters our economic landscape with bankruptcies.

● *Felt need for change*. Once leaders accept the fact that their business environment is changing, key decision makers in the organization must be made to feel dissatisfaction with the *status quo*. Feeling the need for change provides the impetus for transition, and this process requires able leadership.

THE ORGANIZATION DURING ACT II

● *Creating a vision*. In organizational transformation, leaders need to create a vision of change that a critical mass of employees will accept as desirable for the organization. The vision and its communication must match the leader's philosophy and style.

● *Mobilizing commitment*. When the organization, or at least some critical mass within it, accepts the new vision and makes it happen, the leader must tap into a deeper sense of meaning for the followers.

THE ORGANIZATION DURING ACT III

● *Institutionalizing change*. Revitalization becomes reality when the new way of thinking becomes day-to-day practice. At a deeper level, this requires shaping and reinforcing a new culture that fits the revitalized organization. It requires a new architecture for the organization's human resource systems, structure, and management.

THE INDIVIDUAL DURING ACT I

● *Endings*. All individual transitions start with endings. Employees who cling to old ways of doing things will be unable to adjust to new demands. They must follow a process that includes disengagement from the past, disidentification with its demands, disenchantment with its implications, and disorientation while learning new behaviors.

THE INDIVIDUAL DURING ACT II

● *Transition state.* Employees need time to disconnect from the past and commit emotionally to the future. This neutral zone causes the most trouble in action-oriented cultures, for it tends to be viewed as non-productive. Yet it can mean the difference between success and failure in organizational transformations.

THE INDIVIDUAL DURING ACT III

● *New beginnings.* Once employees are ready to deal with a new order, they must be prepared for the frustration that accompanies failure as they replace thoroughly mastered routines with a new act.

What follows are excerpts from *The Transformational Leader*.

In them, the authors play out the three-act drama they have developed throughout the book.

The excerpts also discuss the unique characteristics of the transformational leader: the traits enabling these individuals to continually renew themselves and their organization.

THE PARADOX OF RENEWAL

Paradox involves contradictory, mutually exclusive elements that are present and operate at the same time. Renewal is paradoxical for both organizations and individuals.

Renewal involves creative destruction and disintegration. Fundamental change for people and organizations requires exchange. People have to unlearn and relearn, exchange power and status, and exchange old norms and values for new norms and values. These changes are often frightening and threatening, while at the same time potentially stimulating and provocative of new hope.

One must recognize the nature of exchanges; there are costs and benefits which ultimately must be balanced in favor of the benefits side.

Transformational leaders are able to empower others to endure the costs of change and be renewed with the new beginnings.

The paradox of renewal is captured in the cliché 'no pain no gain'. There is a price paid in the short run to realize the longer term gain. The delicate balance in a transformation hinges on the need to see progress before people's psychological reserves are depleted. This is one of the major challenges facing several of the transformational leaders in our book.

At GE, where [chairman] Jack Welch has been driving the organization hard, there have been five years of cutting costs, rationalizing businesses, divestitures, and downsizing (more than 85,000 people in a workforce of 400,000 have left). Managers and employees are wondering when all this will ease. One part of Welch's answer is that if they think it is tough now, it will only be tougher in the future – that is the painful side of renewal. On the other hand, Welch answers that they are part of what is to become the most exciting, vibrant, challenging organization in the world, and that they will be winners.

Welch argues that there are two types of organizational issues. They are the hard issues: budget, manufacturing, marketing, distribution, head count; and the soft issues: values, culture, vision, leadership style, innovation. There are also two types of leadership, weak and strong. He believes that for several decades following the Second World War we were soft on both hard and soft issues.

Since the early 1980s, corporate leaders have been getting stronger on the hard issues. They have rationalized businesses, downsized their employee populations, and reduced the levels of management. GE, Welch claims, has been in the forefront here. These activities tend to take the fun out of the organization, and they are not enough to renew the organization. The new frontier will be to provide strong leadership on the soft issues. Failure to do so leaves the organization drained, lacking the will to renew itself, and unable to adapt effectively to a changing environment.

The entrepreneurial organization is one that values change as healthy. In this environment, entrepreneurial behavior seeks change, responds to it and exploits it as an opportunity and is rewarded.

CHARACTERISTICS OF SELF-RENEWING
ORGANIZATIONS

In self-renewing organizations, control is primarily self-control. There's less constraint; the emphasis is on learning with as few rules as possible. Errors are embraced. People admit mistakes, examine the causes, and learn from them. There's an emphasis on risk taking and innovation, and responsibility is realistically accepted and shared. Goals are set and constantly revised. Decision-making processes value intuition and creativity, and there is less emphasis on purely analytic approaches. People perceive power as a non-zero-sum game; there is expansion in sharing. Uncertainty is confronted, not denied. Interpersonal relationships are open, and there are high levels of trust.

Self-renewing organizations embrace paradox. They possess many attributes that are simultaneously contradictory – even mutually exclusive. It is these paradoxical attributes which provide the capacity for successfully surviving multiple unpredictable blows from the environment.

Kim Cameron has identified a set of paradoxical attributes of organic organizations which are further developed below.

● *Loose/tight couplings.* To enhance creativity and innovation, transformational leaders need to give people throughout the organization power to initiate and sustain efforts based on faith in an idea. Loose coupling fosters wide search and a creative perspective, and allows individual units a fair degree of latitude. This autonomy must be coupled with sustained financial support and with tight coupling for quick execution of the innovation. This is the antithesis of the mechanistic system that drives many organizations which require multi-level approval for new projects which must show quick returns.

At GE, one response to the loose–tight coupling paradox has been the creation of internal boards to govern a number of the businesses. These boards provide both latitude and control: loose–tight coupling.

● *High specialization and generalization of roles.* Innovation depends on professionals with a depth of expertise in their technical specialties. This frequently means they have been narrowly trained. At the same time, they need to be flexible, broad-minded, and capable of working well with other professionals. They must blend the talents of technical experts and business leaders. Mechanistic systems produce specialists and generalists, but rarely do they nurture these qualities in the same person.

● *Continuity/discontinuity of leadership.* New leadership brings a fresh perspective to organizational problems, while old leadership enhances organizational stability and institutional memory. Both are needed. Change efforts require the sustained attention of a fairly stable group of highly committed leaders. Mechanistic organizations tend to miss this point and transfer managers in and out of units without regard to their commitment to a change mission.

●*Productive conflict.* Conflict is a dual-edged sword. Unchecked, it can bring out the worst in human nature, resulting in violence and destruction. Properly channeled, it is the source of energy for challenging people and renewing organizations. Organizations need processes that encourage contention, as well as processes that foster consensus.

IBM has both elements. Its homogeneous culture provides the major support for consensus while its institutionalized contention system provides the major support for productive conflict.

●*Expanded and restricted search for information.* Organizations need to expand their ability to collect relevant information to enhance their problem-solving capacity. At the same time, they must find a way to buffer decision makers from information overload. Analytic frameworks enable decision makers to reduce information and eliminate irrelevant data.

●*The paradox of participation.* Democratic organizations are designed for long-term survival, not short-term gains. During Chrysler's period of crisis, [CEO Lee] Iacocca centralized power so that decisions could be made rapidly. However, Chrysler's ability to ensure its future survival depends on cooperation through involvement of its varied constituencies. Thus, the current decentralization of power is meant to prepare the company for the next decade, not the next year.

Through planning, the self-renewing organization can initiate the creative/destructive forces of change. This means taking on the paradox of the need for continuity and discontinuity in people. To deal with the rapid transformation of the economy into a more competitive arena, an organization must develop a routine for waking up the organization, focusing it on a vision, institutionalizing the change, and remaining alert to the next call for transformation.

LEADERS WHO CAN INITIATE SELF-RENEWAL

An interesting question to ponder is the capacity of any individual to lead an organization through multiple transformations. It may be that the way in which this epilogue is played out in most organizations is by changing the leaders when an era comes to an end and quantum change is required.

For example, Reginald Jones led General Electric for a decade. Perhaps his most significant leadership act was the recognition that GE's future success demanded a leader with quite different qualities and skills from his own.

CHARACTERISTICS OF TRANSFORMATIONAL LEADERS

Transformational leaders share a number of common characteristics that differentiate them from transactional managers.

● *They identify themselves as change agents*. These leaders' professional and personal image was to make a difference and transform the organization for which they had assumed responsibility. None is a professional turnaround artist – someone who comes in, takes a mess, cleans it up, and leaves.

● *It is an interesting self-concept*. It is not that of an entrepreneur trying to make a mark on the world by building a better mousetrap, and therefore building an organization to build the mousetrap. This is a group of people who have both the mousetrap and the organization. Like athletic coaches who take over troubled teams with the goal of turning them into national champions, these leaders must find a way to inspire the team while they rebuild the franchise. These are professional managers who have had to grow into transformational leaders.

● *They are courageous individuals*. Courage is not stupidity. These are prudent risk-takers, individuals who take a stand.

What does it mean to be courageous? In Harvey Hornstein's terms, it means being able to take a stand, being able to take risks, being able to stand against the *status quo* in the larger interest of the organization.

There is both an intellectual and an emotional component to courageous behavior. Intellectually, one must gain a perspective in which it is possible to confront reality even if it is painful. Emotionally, one must be able then to reveal the truth to others who may not want to hear it. Social psychology and organization theory tell us that this is not an easy challenge. The pressures for conformity are great. Thus, to be courageous means being willing to risk the ridicule and the social pressures of being a deviant. What makes our protagonists able to do this? These people had healthy egos. They knew who they were and did not need constant reinforcement in difficult situations.

●*They believe in people.* These transformational leaders are not dictators. They are powerful yet sensitive of other people, and ultimately work toward the empowerment of others.

One of the most articulate about the whole notion of empowerment is John Harvey-Jones, Chairman of Imperial Chemical.

'I suppose my belief in managing through motivating people is what we're talking about, rather than through organizational controls ... Industrial success is a matter of getting commitment from people, and the art is to get them involved. Then you can sort of ratchet people up by continuously setting them or getting them to set themselves aims which are a little more achievable to them. Then every time they achieve, you can ratchet them a bit further, and after a little while you can get a team which really believes it's a leading team ...

'That corresponds very much to my service experience where I learned over many years that there are really no bad troops, only bad officers.'

The leaders in this book all had a keen understanding and set of principles for dealing with motivation, emotion, pain, trust, loyalty. Every one of them could articulate a set of principles that guided their actions as transformational leaders. In every case they dealt with the emotional side through use of humor, symbolism, rewards, and punishment. Ultimately each was a cheerleader, coach, counselor, and leader attempting to meld the team. Even those with the strongest and most visible power were clearly working towards empowerment of the organization.

●*They are value-driven.* Each one of our transformational leaders was able to articulate a set of core values and exhibited behavior that was quite congruent with their value positions.

Jim Renier, vice-chairman of Honeywell, sums up the importance of values and being value-driven as follows:

'A leader is more than a technician to me. If there's a need to separate the two, then I say leave the definition of leader to the person who knows how to deal with the value system of the organization and paint a picture of where we're going. The managers can take what the leader has done for a while, as long as the value system stays constant and the vision is valid. But if the value system changes or the vision is no longer valid, the manager, the technical managers, will take you right into oblivion.'

●*They are life-long learners.* All the transformational leaders were able to talk about mistakes they had made. But, as with Warren Bennis's leaders, they did not view these as failures, but as learning experiences. As a group, our protagonists show an amazing appetite for continuous self-learning and development.

Bob Stempel and Lloyd Reuss at General Motors are going through a learning process. Stempel talks about his learning in the following terms:

'Sometimes it's like a cold shower, but after you are in it for a while, it gets warmer. One realization is that when you really use the team process, you buy a group of people who are going to make it run, to reach that consensus decision, and reach the idea that this is the way we want to do it. It might not be my first choice, but I'm far better off to accept the fact that the team bought into it, took responsibility for it, and will go ahead and execute it. I think the lesson for me has been that it's a very powerful process and can be a very effective one in developing a strong organization'.

Perhaps one of the most intriguing aspects of these protagonists is their continuous commitment to learning. Their heads have not become hard-wired. Their attitudes, behaviors, and approaches to managing and leading have been very adaptable. They spend time being self-reflective and many of them have made some rather dramatic shifts in their styles and approaches to management. Perhaps this is the basic condition necessary for their own self-renewal that makes them able to play a self-renewal leadership role

● *They have the ability to deal with complexity, ambiguity, and uncertainty.* Each transformational leader was able to cope with and frame problems in a complex, changing world.

All of these protagonists were not only capable of dealing with the cultural and political side of the organization, but they were very sophisticated in dealing with the technical side. They don't argue for seat-of-the-pants management, or for a non-conceptual approach to running the business. They are entranced by the world of ideas.

All of them believe the disciplined thinking that went with formal education helped them to deal with complex problems that needed to be structured. These are individuals who build theory, articulate principles, examine assumptions. And this fits with the demands of an increasingly complex world which demands complex problem-solving ability on the part of leaders. It is this balance of the emotional and the cognitive that is striking when we examine our transformational leaders.

● *They are visionaries.* Our transformational leaders were able to dream, able to translate those dreams and images so that other people could share them: Mary Ann Lawlor, CEO of Drake Business Schools, describes her thought processes when she's in the midst of difficult problems as follows:

'When we're in any kind of problem, I always meditate and then I write and then I think some more, and in the end I have a feeling in my gut and I trust it. I trust my instincts, my intuition. And eventually I just know what I have to do. I think of the organization as a kind of mystical body – you know the religious concept where the actions of each member of the body affect every other member. You need the ability to empathize if you want to lead ... you need the ability to understand how your actions are going to affect others.'

THE REMAINING CHALLENGES

The transformational leaders in this book '... are in the race right now'. Who will win and who will lose is unknown, but these people have a very good chance of making it. They are all keenly aware that the race is not over. The runners are passing various milestones with some challenges already met and some surprises waiting for them.

The United States and many Western European companies have yet to recognize the need for revitalization. They continue to bury their heads in the sand because they are not willing to face the truth: that there is no place to hide. Individuals can insulate themselves from the consequences of continuing economic decline only if they are willing to mortgage their children's future. We have not yet come to grips with the reality: what has been can no longer be. We must deal with the endings so we can move on and create a vision consistent with the current reality and mobilize commitment to it. Each of us must approach this issue on three levels: our personal dreams and aspirations, the organizations we work in, and the society we live in.

History contains powerful lessons and no minority – whether one of class, race, or privilege – has been able to hold the aspirations of a majority at bay forever. Our founding fathers understood this lesson well and they created a society able to deal with the aspirations of all people: one of sharing and sacrifice as well as ambition.

Our challenge is to adapt what we have learned to a world where the frontier is closed and opportunity is more limited. Our challenge is to transform ourselves and our institutions to meet the challenge of the new reality without losing the things that we value the most. We hope you will join our protagonists in this quest.

REFERENCE

Tichy, N. M., & Devanna, M. A. (1986), *The Transformational Leader*, New York: Wiley.

Organization Change and Development

40

HAROLD J. LEAVITT

Applied Organization Change in Industry: Structural, Technical and Human Approaches

Abridged from Harold J. Leavitt, 'Applied organization change in industry: structural, technical and human approaches', in W. W. Cooper, H. J. Leavitt and M. W. Shelly, II (eds.), *New Perspectives in Organizational Research*, New York: Wiley, 1964, pp. 55–71.

This is a mapping chapter. It is part of a search for perspective on complex organizations, in this instance, through consideration of several classes of efforts to change ongoing organizations. Approaches to change provide a kind of sharp caricature of underlying beliefs and prejudices about the important dimensions of organizations. Thereby, perhaps, they provide some insights into areas of real or apparent difference among perspectives on organization theory.

To classify several major approaches to change, I have found it useful, first, to view organizations as multivariate systems, in which at least four interacting variables loom especially large: the variables of task, structure, technology and actors (usually people) (Figure 1).

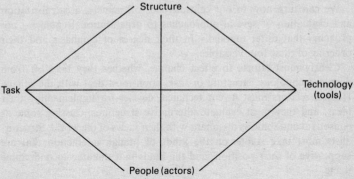

Figure 1

Roughly speaking, task refers to organizational *raisons d'être* – manufacturing, servicing, etc., including the large numbers of different, but operationally meaningful, sub-tasks which may exist in complex organizations.

By actors I mean mostly people, but with the qualification that acts usually executed by people need not remain exclusively in the human domain.

By technology I mean technical tools – problem-solving inventions like work measurement, computers or drill presses. Note that I include both machines and programs in this category, but with some uncertainty about the line between structure and technology.

Finally, by structure I mean systems of communication, systems of authority (or other roles) and systems of work flow.

These four are highly interdependent, so that change in any one will most probably result in compensatory (or retaliatory) change in others. In discussing organizational change, therefore, I shall assume that it is one or more of these variables that we seek to change. Sometimes we may aim to change one of these as an end in itself, sometimes as a mechanism for effecting some changes in one or more of the others.

Thus, for example, structural change toward, say, decentralization should change the performance of certain organizational tasks (indeed, even the selection of tasks), the technology that is brought to bear (e.g. changes in accounting procedures), and the nature, numbers, and/or motivation and attitudes of people in the organization. Any of these changes could presumably be conscientiously intended; or they could occur as unforeseen and often troublesome outcomes of efforts to change only one or two of the variables.

We can turn now to our central focus of, namely, a categorization and evaluation of several approaches to organizational change – approaches that differ markedly in their degree of emphasis and their ordering of these four variables.

Clearly most efforts to effect change, whether they take off from people, technology, structure or task, soon must deal with the others. Human relators must invent technical devices for implementing their ideas, and they must evaluate alternative structures, classing some as consonant and some as dissonant with their views of the world. Structuralists must take stands on the kinds of human interaction that are supportive of their position, and the kinds that threaten to undermine it, etc.

Although I differentiate structural from technical from human approaches to organizational tasks, the differentiation is in points of origin, relative weightings and underlying conceptions and values, not in the exclusion of all other variables.

This categorization must be further complicated by the fact that the objectives of the several approaches to organizational change are not uniform. All of them do share a considerable interest in improved solutions to tasks. But while some of the technical approaches focus almost exclusively on task solutions, that is, on the *quality* of decisions, some of the people approaches are at least as interested in performance of task subsequent to decisions. Although improved task solution serves as a common goal for all of these approaches, several carry other associated objectives that weigh almost as heavily in the eyes of their proponents. Thus some of the early structural approaches were almost as concerned with maintaining a power *status quo* as with improving task performance, and some of the current people approaches are at least as interested in providing organizations that fulfill human needs as they are in efficacious performance of tasks.

The several approaches are still further complicated by variations in the causal chains by which they are supposed to bring about their intended changes. Some of the structural approaches, for example, are not aimed directly at task but at people as mediating intervening variables. In these approaches, one changes structure to change people to improve task performance. Similarly, some of the people approaches seek to change people in order to change structure and tools, to change task performance, and also to make life more fulfilling for people. We can turn now to the several varieties of efforts themselves.

THE STRUCTURAL APPROACHES

Applied efforts to change organizations by changing structure seem to fall into four classes. First, structural change has been the major mechanism of the 'classical' organization theorist. Out of the deductive, logical, largely military-based thinking of early non-empirical organization theory, there evolved the whole set of now familiar 'principles' for optimizing organizational performance by optimizing structure. These are deductive approaches carrying out their analyses from task backward to appropriate divisions of labor and appropriate systems of authority. These early structural approaches almost always mediated their activities through people to task. One improves task performance by clarifying and defining the jobs of people and setting up appropriate relationships among these jobs.

In retrospect, most of us think of these early approaches as abstractions, formal and legalistic, and poorly anchored in empirical data. They were also almost incrediby naïve in their assumptions about human behavior. In fact, almost the only assumptions that were made were legalistic and moralistic ones: that people, having contracted to work, would then carry out the terms of their contract; that people assigned responsibility would necessarily accept that responsibility; that people when informed of the organization's goals would strive wholeheartedly to achieve those goals.

In one variation or another, such structural approaches are still widely applied. It is still commonplace for consultants or organization planning departments to try to solve organizational problems by redefining areas of responsibility and authority, enforcing the chain of command, and so on.

A second widespread approach to structural change, allied to the first, somewhat more modern and sophisticated and somewhat narrower, too, is the idea of decentralization. The idea of changing organizations by decentralizing their structure was probably more an invention of the accounting profession than anyone else, though it has been widely endorsed by structuralists and by human relators too. Almost nobody is against it.

Decentralization affects the performance of tasks partially through its intervening effects on people. By creating profit centers one presumably increases the motivation and goal-oriented behavior of local managers. One also adds flexibility so that variations in technology appropriate to the different tasks of different decentralized units now become more possible; so do sub-variations in structure and local variations in the use of people. Decentralization can be thought of as a mechanism for changing organizations at a meta level, providing local autonomy for further change. Thus, within limits, decentralization units may further change themselves through the use of any one of the many alternatives available, and perhaps for this reason no group has questioned it, at least until the last couple of years.

Recently, two other structural approaches have shown up, but they have not yet reached a widespread level of application. One of them is best represented by Chappel and Sayles (1961). Theirs is a form of social engineering aimed at task, but via people. They seek to modify the behavior of people in order to improve task performance, but they do it by modifying structure, in this case, the flow of work. Out of the tradition of applied anthropology, they argue that planning of work flows and groupings of specialties will directly affect the morale, behavior and output of employees. One of the failings of earlier structural models, in their view, is that the design of work was almost entirely determined by task and technical variables, and failed to take account of human social variables. They provide illustrative cases to show that appropriate redesigning of work, in a social engineering sense, affects both human attitudes and output.

I cannot overlook in this discussion of structure the implications of a second approach – the research on communication networks (Glanzer & Glaser, 1961). I know of no *direct* applications of this laboratory research to the real world, though it has had some indirect influence on structural planning. In that research, variations in communication nets affect both routine and novel task performance rather significantly. The results suggest that appropriate communication structures might vary considerably within a complex organization, depending upon the type of task that any sub-unit of the organization undertakes. Thus for highly programmed repetitive tasks, highly centralized communication structures seem to operate most efficiently, but with some human costs. For more novel, ill-structured tasks, more wide-open communication nets with larger numbers of channels and less differentiation among members seem to work more effectively.

TECHNOLOGICAL APPROACHES TO ORGANIZATIONAL CHANGE

My first entry in this technological category is Taylor's *Scientific Management* (1947). Its birth date was around 1910, its father, Frederick W. Taylor [see Reading 30 – *Editors*].

Like the early structural approaches, scientific management was to a great extent ahuman, perhaps even inhuman. For in creating the separate planning specialist, it removed planning from its old location – the head of the doer of work. Many observers, both contemporary and subsequent, saw this phase of scientific management as downright demeaning of mankind.

But despite the flurry of congressional investigations and active counter-attack by Taylor's contemporaries, scientific management grew and prospered, and radically changed structure, people and the ways jobs got done.

Scientific management receded into a relatively stable and undramatic background in the late 1930s and 1940s and has never made a real comeback in its original form. But the technological approaches were by no means dead. The development of operations research and the more or less contemporaneous invention and exploitation of computers have more than revived them.

I submit that operational operations-research methods for organizational problem solving can be reasonably placed in the same category with scientific management. They have both developed a body of technical methods for solving work problems. They both are usually *external* in their approach, essentially separating the planning of problem-solving programs from the routine acting-out of solutions. Operations research, too, is quickly developing in its operational form a new class of hot-shot staff specialists, in many ways analogous to the earlier staff efficiency man. What is *clearly* different, of course, is the nature of the techniques, although there may be larger differences that are not yet so clear.

The operations-research and information-processing techniques are turning out to be, if not more general, at least applicable to large classes of tasks that scientific management could not touch (Schultz & Whisler, 1960). Now armed with linear programming methods, one can approach a task like media selection in an advertising agency, though it would have been nonsense to time-study it.

But note the over-all similarity: change the setting of the movie from Bethlehem, Pa., to Madison Avenue, the time from 1910 to 1962; the costuming from overalls to gray-flannel suits; and the tasks from simple muscular labor to complex judgemental decisions. Turn worried laborer Schmidt into worried media executive Jones. Then replace Taylor with Charnes and Cooper and supplant the stop-watch with the computer. It is the same old theme either way – the conflict between technology and humanity.

A distinction needs to be drawn, of course, between operational operations-research and other computer-based, information-processing approaches, although they are often closely allied. 'Management Science' hopefully will mean more than highly operational applications of specific techniques, and organizations are also being changed by simulation techniques and by heuristic, problem-solving methods. Their impact has not yet been felt in anything like full force; but tasks, people and structures are already being rather radically modified by them.

Without delving further into the substance of these more recent technological approaches, it may be worth pointing up one other characteristic that they share with many of their predecessors – a kind of faith in the ultimate victory of *better* problem solutions over less good ones. This faith is often perceived by people-oriented practitioners of change as sheer naïveté about the nature of man. They ascribe it to a pre-

Freudian fixation on rationality; to a failure to realize that human acceptance of ideas is the real carrier of change; and that emotional human resistance is the real road block. They can point, in evidence, to a monotonously long list of cases in which technological innovations, methods changes or operations-research techniques have fallen short because they ignored the human side of the enterprise. It is not the logically better solutions that get adopted, this argument runs, but the more humanly acceptable, more feasible ones. Unless the new technologist wises up, he may end up a miserable social isolate, like his predecessor, the unhappy industrial engineer.

Often this argument fits the facts. Operations-research people can be incredibly naïve in their insensitivity to human feelings. But in another, more gracious sense, one can say that the technological approaches have simply taken a more macroscopic, longer view of the world than the people approaches.

The technological approaches seem not only to predict the victory of cleaner, more logical, and more parsimonious solutions but also to *value* them. Failure of human beings to search for or use more efficient solutions is a sign, from this perspective, of human weakness and inadequacy. People must be teased or educated into greater logic, greater rationality. Resistance to better solutions is proof only of the poverty of our educational system; certainly it is not in any way an indication that 'optimal' solutions are less than optimal.

THE PEOPLE APPROACHES

The people approaches try to change the organizational world by changing the behavior of actors in the organization. By changing people, it is argued, one can cause the creative invention of new tools, or one can cause modifications in structure (especially power structure). By one or another of these means, changing people will cause changes in solutions to tasks and performance of tasks as well as changes in human growth and fulfillment.

In surveying the people approaches, one is immediately struck by the fact that the literature dealing directly with organizational change is almost all people-oriented. Just in the last four or five years, for example, several volumes specifically concerned with organizational change have been published. All of them are people-type books (see Bennis, et al., 1961; Ginsberg & Reilly, 1957; Guest, 1962; Lawrence, 1958; Lippitt, et al., 1958).

This tendency to focus on the process of change itself constitutes one of the major distinguishing features of the people approaches. The technological and structural approaches tend to focus on problem solving, sliding past the micro-processes by which new problem-solving techniques are generated and adopted.

Historically, the people approaches have moved through at least two phases: the first was essentially manipulative, responsive to the primitive and seductive question, 'How can we get people to do what we want them to do?'

Carnegie's *How to Win Friends and Influence People* was first published in 1936, a few years ahead of most of what we now regard as psychological work in the same area. Like the social scientists that followed, Carnegie's model for change focused on the relationship between changer and changee, pointing out that changes in feelings and attitudes were prerequisites to voluntary changes in overt behavior.

Though social scientists have tended to reject it out of hand, current research on influence processes suggests that the Carnegie model is not technically foolish at all, although we have disavowed it as manipulative, slick and of questionable honesty.

However, Carnegie-like interest in face-to-face influence has finally become a respectable area of social scientific research. Several works of Hovland, et al. (1953) on influence and persuasion provide experimental support for the efficacy of certain behavioral techniques of influence over others.

But if we move over into the traditionally more 'legitimate' sphere of social science, we find that much of the work after the Second World War on 'overcoming resistance to change' was still responsive to the same manipulative question. Consider, for example, the now classic work by Kurt Lewin (1952) and his associates on changing food habits, or the later industrial work by Coch and French (1948). In both cases, A sets out to bring about a predetermined change in the behavior of B. Lewin sets out to cause housewives to purchase and consume more variety meats – a selling problem. Coch and French set out to gain acceptance of a preplanned methods change by hourly workers in a factory. In both cases the methodology included large elements of indirection with less than full information available to the changees.

But whereas Dale Carnegie built warm personal relationships and then bargained with them, neither Lewin nor Coch and French are centrally concerned about intimate relationships between changer and changee. Their concern is much more with warming up the interrelationships among changees.

Thus 32 per cent of Lewin's test housewives exposed to a group-decision method served new variety meats, as against only 3 per cent of the women exposed to lectures. Lewin accounts for these results by calling upon two concepts: 'involvement' and 'group pressure'. Lectures leave their audiences passive and unpressed by the group, whereas discussions are both active and pressing. Similarly, Coch and French, causing the girls in a pajama factory to accept a methods change, emphasize *group* methods, seeing resistance to change as a function partially of individual frustration and partially of strong group-generated forces. Their methodology, therefore, is to provide opportunities for need satisfaction and quietly to corner the group forces and redirect them toward the desired change.

One might say that these early studies wrestled rather effectively with questions of affect and involvement, but ducked a key variable – power.

It was to be expected, then, that the next moves in the development of people approaches would be toward working out the power variable. It was obvious, too, that the direction would be toward power equalization rather than toward power differentiation. The theoretical underpinnings, the prevalent values and the initial research results all pointed that way.

But though this is what happened, it happened in a complicated and mostly implicit way. Most of the push has come from work on individuals and small groups, and has then been largely extrapolated to organizations. Client-centered therapy (Rogers, 1942) and applied group dynamics (Miles, 1959) have been prime movers. In both of those cases, theory and technique explicit aimed at allocating at least equal power to the changee(s), a fact of considerable importance in later development of dicta for organizational changes.

At the group level, a comparable development was occurring, namely, the development of the T- (for training) group (or sensitivity training or development group). The T-group is the core tool of programs aimed at teaching people how to lead and change groups. It has also become a core tool for effecting organizational change. T-group leaders try to bring about changes in their groups by taking extremely permissive, extremely non-authoritarian, sometimes utterly non-participative roles, thus encouraging group members not only to solve their own problems but also to define them. The T-group leader becomes, in the language of the profession, a 'resource person', not consciously trying to cause a substantive set of changes but only changes in group processes, which would then, in turn, generate substantive changes.

Though the T-group is a tool, a piece of technology, an invention, I include it in the people rather than the tool approaches, for it evolved out of those approaches as a mechanism specifically designed for effecting change in people.

In contrast to earlier group-discussion tools the T-group deals with the power variable directly. Its objective is to transfer more power to the client or the group.

But these are both non-organizational situations. For the therapist, the relationship with the individual client bounds the world. For the T-group trainer, the group is the world. They can both deal more easily with the power variable than change agents working in a time-constrained and work-flow-constrained organizational setting.

At the organizational level, things therefore are a little more vague. The direction is there, in the form of movement towards power equalization, but road blocks are many and maps are somewhat sketchy and undetailed. McGregor's (1960) development of participative Theory Y to replace authoritarian Theory X is a case in point. McGregor's whole conception of Theory Y very clearly implies a shift from an all-powerful superior dealing with impotent subordinates to something much more like a balance of power.

Bennis, Benne and Chin (1961) specifically set out power equalization (PE) as one of the distinguishing features of the deliberate collaborative process they define as planned change: 'A power distribution in which the client and change agent have equal, or almost equal, opportunities to influence' is part of their definition.

In any case, power equalization has become a key idea in the prevalent people approaches, a first step in the theoretical causal chain leading toward organizational change. It has served as an initial sub-goal, a necessary predecessor to creative change in structure, technology, task solving and task implementation. Although the distances are not marked, there is no unclarity about direction – a more egalitarian power distribution is better.

It is worth pointing out that the techniques for causing redistribution of power in these models are themselves power-equalization techniques – like counseling and T-group training. Thus both Lippitt, Watson and Westley (1958) and Bennis, Benne and Chin (1961) lay great emphasis on the need for collaboration between changer and changee in order for change to take place. But it is understandable that neither those writers nor most other workers in power equalization seriously investigate the possibility that power may be redistributed unilaterally or authoritatively (e.g. by the creation of profit centers in a large business firm or by coercion).

If we examine some of the major variables of organizational behavior, we will see rather quickly that the power-equalization approaches yield outcomes that are very different from those produced by the structural or technological approaches.

Thus in the PE models, *communication* is something to be maximized. The more channels the better, the less filtering the better, the more feedback the better. All these because power will be more equally distributed, validity of information greater, and commitment to organizational goals more intense.

Contrast these views with the earlier structural models which argued for clear but limited communication lines, never to be circumvented, and which disallowed the transmission of affective and therefore task-irrelevant information. They stand in sharp contrast, too, to some current technical views which search for optimal information flows that may be far less than maximum flows.

The PE models also focus much of their attention on issues of *group pressure*, *cohesiveness*, and *conformity*. The more cohesiveness the better, for cohesiveness causes commitment. The broader the group standards, the better. The more supportive the group, the freer the individual to express his individuality.

Consider next the *decision-making* variable. Decision making, from the perspective of power equalization, is viewed not from a cognitive perspective, nor substantively, but as a problem in achieving committed agreement. The much discussed issues are commitment and consensual validation, and means for lowering and spreading decision-making opportunities.

Contrast this with the technical emphasis on working out optimal decision rules, and with the structuralist's emphasis on locating precise decision points and assigning decision-making responsibility always to individuals.

REFERENCES

Asch, S. E. (1952), *Social Psychology*, Englewood Cliffs, NJ: Prentice Hall.

Bendix, R. (1956), *Work and Authority in Industry*, New York: Wiley.

Bennis, W. G., Benne, K. D., & Chin, R. (eds.) (1961), *The Planning of Change*, New York: Holt, Rinehart & Winston.

Carnegie, D. (1936), *How to Win Friends and Influence People*, New York: Simon & Schuster.

Chappel, E. D., & Sayles, L. R. (1961), *The Measure of Management*, New York: Macmillan.

Coch, L., & French, J. R. P., (1948), 'Overcoming resistance to change', *Human Relations*, *1*, 512–32.

Ginsberg, E., & Reilly, E. (1957), *Effecting Change in Large Organizations*, New York: Columbia University Press.

Glanzer, M., & Glaser, R. (1961), 'Techniques for the study of group structure and behavior', *Psychological Bulletin*, *58*, 1–27.

Guest, R. H. (1962), *Organizational Change: The Effect of Successful Leadership*, Homewood, Ill.: Dorsey.

Hovland, C., Janis, I., & Kelley, H. (1953), *Communication and Persuasion: Psychological Studies of Opinion Change*, New Haven, Conn.: Yale University Press.

Lawrence, P. R. (1958), *The Changing of Organizational Behavior Patterns*, Harvard University Business School, Division of Research.

Lewin, K. (1952), 'Group decision and social change', in G. E. Swanson, T. Newcomb and E. Hartley (eds.), *Readings in Social Psychology*, New York: Holt, 2nd edn.

Lippitt, R., Watson, J., & Westley, B. (1958), *The Dynamics of Planned Change*, New York: Harcourt, Brace.

McGregor, D. (1960), *The Human Side of Enterprise*, New York: McGraw-Hill.

Miles, M. B. (1959), *Learning to Work in Groups*, Bureau of Publications, Teachers College, Columbia University.

Rogers, C. R. (1942), *Counselling and Psychotherapy*, Boston, Mass.: Houghton Mifflin.

Schultz, G. P., & Whisler, T. L. (1960) (eds.), *Management Organization and the Computer*, New York: Free Press.

Taylor, F. W. (1947), *Scientific Management*, New York: Harper.

41

CHRIS ARGYRIS

Action Science and Intervention

Abridged from C. Argyris, 'Action Science and Intervention', *Journal of Applied Behavioral Science*, Vol. 19, 1983, pp. 115–40.

The intellectual beginnings of intervention and action science can be traced to Kurt Lewin's early concepts of action research. In his work during the Second World War, Lewin's action research was characterized by six features: (1) it was problem-driven, (2) it was client-centered, (3) it challenged the *status quo* and was simultaneously concerned with (4) producing empirically disconfirmable propositions that (5) could be systematically interrelated into a theory designed to be (6) usable in everyday life (Lewin, 1946; Marrow, 1969).

As action research became more popular, Lewin's plea to keep these six features together went unheeded. Practice-oriented scholars became so client-centered that they failed to question how clients themselves defined their problems and they ignored the building and testing of propositions and theories embedded in their own practice. On the theoretical side, these scholars conducted research that met normal science criteria in its rigor and precision but which became disconnected from and distanced from everyday life (Argyris, 1980).

Action science represents an attempt to restore to primacy the six features of Lewin's early action research. Action scientists assume that learning is the first and overarching objective for the researcher, the clients, and the system in which they are embedded. The second major objective is that any knowledge produced should be formulated into empirically disconfirmable propositions that in turn will be organized into a theory.

In order to achieve these objectives, we must take into account the way individuals and systems learn and the way research is conducted and theory is created.

ACTION SCIENCE AND LEARNING

Learning may be defined as occurring whenever a match exists between intentions and outcomes and/or one detects and corrects an error – a mismatch – between intention and outcome. Producing matches and detecting and correcting mismatches is performed by individuals. In groups, intergroups, and organizations, individuals act as agents for the social unit.

It is useful to differentiate two types of learning. One type involves the production of matches, or the detection and correction of mismatches, without change in the underlying governing policies or values. This is called *single-loop learning*. A second type, *double-loop learning*, does require re-examination and change of the governing values. Single-loop learning is usually related to the routine, immediate task. Double-loop learning is related to the non-routine, the long-range outcome.

INDIVIDUAL LEARNING AND ACTION

Human beings can be viewed as designers and implementers of their actions. One approach to how they accomplish these tasks is represented by a theory-of-action perspective (Argyris & Schön, 1978, 1974; Argyris, 1976, 1980, 1982). The major ideas may be summarized briefly as follows:

1. Human beings design their diagnoses of reality as well as their actions. It is unlikely that under everyday time constraints individuals can be totally informed about a situation or have unlimited time to design and implement their actions. To operate within these everyday constraints, people have a master program showing how to design and implement effective action. This master program contains two components. The first is the *espoused theory*, made up of (1) the beliefs, values, and attitudes that an individual can state in the form of an 'if–then' proposition that defines effective action in a given context, and (2) the operating assumptions that define effective action regardless of the context (Smith, 1982). An example of an espoused theory that takes the context into account is 'When trying to help individuals learn, minimize actions that may make them defensive.' An example of an operating assumption is 'Don't trust people who have power.' Although individuals hold dear their espoused theories and operating assumptions, they rarely behave consistently with them when they attempt double-loop learning. The second component of the master program is

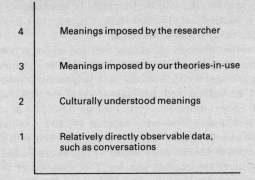

Figure 1. Ladder of inference.

the *theory-in-use*. This is the set of 'if–then' propositions that an individual uses when he or she acts.

Individuals may or may not be aware of the discrepancies between their espoused theories and their actions. They are rarely aware, however, of the discrepancies between espoused theories, actions, and their theories-in-use. Indeed, it can be shown that propositions in their theories-in-use keep them unaware of these discrepancies. Their ignorance is a programmed one.

2. Whether designing to understand or to act, individuals must reason. When they reason, they create premises and draw conclusions. In the world of action, this reasoning often has embedded in it causal theories of effectiveness. For example,

If Y acts insensitively and punitively [premise], then [given a tacit theory of human defenses] X, as the recipient of Y's action, will probably act defensively [conclusion].

X's defenses now become a premise for further reasoning about action.

The inferences made may be conceptualized as closer to, or further from, the relatively directly observable data. When Y says to X, 'Your performance has consistently missed the targets set. It has been below standard,' their conversation may be described as relatively directly observable data – the first rung on the ladder of inference (Figure 1).

Strictly speaking the identification of the conversation as a conversation is also an inference. Hence, we call it relatively directly observable behavior. Also embedded in Y's sentence is a culturally understood meaning, namely, 'X, your performance is unacceptable.' Since the meaning is inferred from the first rung, it is assigned a position on the second rung of the ladder of inference.

People make inferences about their own and others' actions to understand them, to judge others' effectiveness, and to determine whether they have achieved their intentions. Such judgements consist of attributions and evaluations and are inferred from the first two rungs of inference. They constitute the third rung on the ladder of inference. In research with a case involving a superior (Y) and a subordinate (X), most respondents evaluate Y as insensitive and blunt with the subordinate, though a few additionally see her or him as candid and forthright. The majority of respondents also see Y in violation of the espoused theory that one should not make people defensive and in violation of the operating assumption that negative evaluations will produce negative consequences. A minority believe that Y is consistent with the operating assumption that it is important to be candid, but most see Y as violating their espoused theory that other people should not be made defensive.

When designing ways to tell Y their evaluations, most respondents demonstrate theory-in-use propositions that may be defined as 'easing in'. The easing-in approach goes something like this: Ask questions that will cause the other person (Y) to come to the same diagnosis you have made if he or she answers the questions correctly – namely, that her or his performance is below par and probably because of her or his own actions.

A minority of respondents act in a straightforward manner. For example, they may tell Y that her or his actions were blunt and insensitive. In doing so, they of course utilize the same theory-in-use they are telling Y not to use. The easing-in approach is just as likely to produce defensiveness as this direct approach because the recipient feels prejudged. The easing-in questions include 'hints' of Y's errors, hints purportedly given to enlighten Y.

3. At the fourth rung on the ladder of inference, the researchers impose their own meanings. These imposed meanings can be organized in the form of a model entitled Model I theory-in-use. To date, most subjects (i.e. 99 per cent of nearly 2,000 cases) appear to hold only the theory-in-use called Model I (Figure 2).

The very existence of Model I theory-in-use makes life more manageable and predictable. It enables people to have a good idea of the theory-in-use that they and others will use to make sense of, or to act in, a situation. This does not mean that people can predict the precise

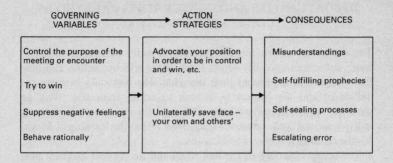

Figure 2. Model I theory-in-use.

behavior (rung one), but it does mean that they can become increasingly better predictors of the meanings at rungs two and three.

4. Two difficulties that complicate real life are (a) empirically speaking, most people appear to be unaware of their theory-in-use, and (b) Model I theories-in-use are counter-productive for double-loop learning. Hence, a paradox exists: The theories-in-use most people learn to design and implement their actions lead to productive *and* counter-productive consequences when they deal with double-loop issues.

Individuals are unaware of their theories-in-use because they have been learned early in life. The actions people produce are consistent with their theories-in-use and are highly skilled. The three core features of skillful action are that it achieves the intended objectives, that it appears automatic and effortless, and that it is performed with little conscious attention; indeed, conscious attention may inhibit skillful action.

The reason that Model I theories-in-use are counter-productive for double-loop learning is that they turn the actors' attention away from their governing variables. Simultaneously, Model I theories-in-use escalate the error and defensiveness that focus the actors' attention on self-protection and false inquiry.

The implication for action science is that we must go beyond beliefs, values, and attitudes (that is, beyond espoused theories) to collect relatively directly observable data from which to infer the theories-in-use. We must focus on the reasoning processes that individuals use to design and implement their actions.

OPPORTUNITIES AND CONSTRAINTS CREATED BY CONTEXTUAL FACTORS

The context or environment is the second major element that significantly influences how individuals think about effective action and how they design and implement their thoughts. The boundary between the individual and the context is difficult to define accurately. Why do most individuals appear to have a Model I theory-in-use when clearly individuals and contexts vary? One answer is that the learning of Model I is the result of extensive socialization.

The interpenetration of the individual and the context makes it possible to predict that individuals programmed with Model I theories-in-use will necessarily create Model O-I (O for organizational) learning systems, whether they act in a school, family, business, government agency, union, or other group. For example, when people programmed with Model I deal with double-loop issues, they create defensiveness, self-fulfilling prophecies, self-sealing processes, and escalating error.

These conditions tend to create win–lose situations and intergroup dynamics in which competitiveness dominates cooperation, mistrust overcomes trust, unquestioned obedience replaces informed dissent, and coalition groups arise. The organizational politicking has been described by Graham T. Allison (1971), Bacharach & Lawler (1980), Baldridge (1971), Cyert & March (1963), and Pettigrew (1973).

Under these conditions, structural and policy changes alone should not lead to double-loop learning. For this to occur, individuals must be able to alter their theories-in-use and to change the O-I learning system. But unless they learn a new theory-in-use, individuals will continue to use their highly skilled, automatic Model I responses. This may explain why people who want to learn theories-in-use that facilitate double-loop learning are unable to do so during the early phases of learning, even if economically autonomous and powerful, even if in an environment that is designed to bring about such learning (Argyris, 1976, 1982).

These findings imply that structural changes will not bring about organizational double-loop learning until they become part of an individual's theory-in-use. This is one reason why interventions should begin at the highest level of the organization. If the top people do not implement the new actions and learning systems, it is doubtful that those below can do so.

The automatic reasoning processes that lead to inconsistency and escalating error will be triggered, no matter whether the subject is long-range investments, internal resource allocation, or marketing strategy, and no matter whether the unit involved is a small group, a division, or the whole corporation organization. The required conditions are that (1) individuals be programmed only with Model I, (2) they be embedded in an O-I learning system, and (3) that the subject matter be individually or organizationally threatening. These predictions do not hold if the error in question is easily and objectively indentifiable, and/or the cost of hiding the error is greater than the cost of violating the Model I values and behavioural strategies, or if the error is easily illustrated and the illustration is difficult to disprove. Indeed, one reason management information systems (in the broadest sense) are becoming popular may be that management hopes these systems will make it easier to surface error and more difficult to hide it, that this will lower the cost to individuals for surfacing it and raise the cost for not doing so. The predictions are broad in scope, yet they are easily falsified. One need only present a case in which individuals with Model I theories-in-use, and who are embedded in O-I learning systems, dealt with a double-loop threatening issue (excluding the exceptions noted above) in such a way that errors did not escalate.

To summarize, individuals appear to be programmed with theories-in-use that lead them to deal with double-loop issues in ways that produce self-fulfilling prophecies, self-sealing processes, and error escalation. Moreover, the same theories-in-use lead them to become unaware of their own contribution to these counter-productive consequences and to become unaware of the program that keeps them unaware. Organizations and contexts are structured in ways to reinforce this situation and may in turn be reinforced by cultural and societal norms. An extensive set of layered factors appears to inhibit double-loop learning.

The action scientists are therefore faced with clients who may genuinely wish to cooperate in double-loop learning, yet who are programmed with highly skilled, automatic social reactions that, reinforced by context, inhibit such learning. The action scientists are also faced with 'subjects' who may unknowingly distort data. The distortions may go undetected because the context and the cultural sanctions reinforce them as if they were not distortions. How can action scientists, under these conditions, conduct research where disconfirmability is possible while simultaneously helping individuals and organizations solve double-loop problems?

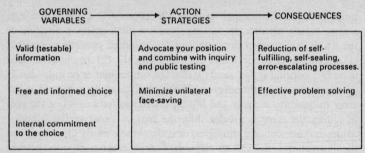

Figure 3. Model II theory-in-use

OVERCOMING THE COUNTER-PRODUCTIVE CONSEQUENCES OF MODEL I THEORIES-IN-USE AND THEIR ORGANIZATIONAL COUNTERPARTS, O-I LEARNING SYSTEMS

It is possible to change the counter-productive features of Models I and O-I by first educating individuals in another theory-in-use, namely Model II. The basic features of Model II are described in Figure 3. Model II governing variables are not the opposite of Model I, as may be the case for the theories-in-use embedded in many T Group activities (Argyris, 1980). Nor is Model II a substitute for Model I under any conditions. For example, Model I may be relevant for the more routine single-loop issues that do not threaten individuals, groups, intergroups, or organizations.

We believe that a useful way for individuals to learn is first to produce data that they consider valid and not created by external sources (e.g., by the interventionist or his methods). They must feel personally causally responsible so that when we identify their causal theories, they cannot reject them by saying that they are not personally causally responsible for the data from which we made the inferences.

Second, we believe that feeding back the analysis of their reasoning and actions in the form of the ladder of inference provides them an important tool for analysing and organizing their actions as well as the consequences they have for the organization. The development of such a map will help clients understand the problem. Being able to identify and manage the problem is a key step to changing it.

Third, if individuals can identify the causes of a problem, and if they can manage them, they can then make changes and/or consultants can help them develop the skills and organizational features to do so. For example, if the team members lack the skill to be candid and to invite the same candor from others, we can help them to learn that skill. If the organizational culture contains norms against trust and risk-taking, we can help individuals alter these norms by the very processes we used to teach them the skills. If organizational policies exist that inhibit the new skills and values, we can help alter them by bringing them to the attention of the managing officers in the form of solutions that have been developed by officers and managers.

CONCLUSION

Five important features can be identified from empirical research about every intervention intended to generate double-loop learning (see Table 1).

Table 1

From the finding that	The implication about
Many individuals value Model II theory-in-use and O-II learning systems but doubt their own or others' ability to produce them as well as the organization's ability to accept them.	*Commitment:* The underlying attitude of most people to individual and organizational double-loop learning will be ambivalent. Those that support it may have as much difficulty as those who are completely against it.
Many individuals are unaware that they cannot produce Model II simply by wanting to do so and intellectually understanding it. They are also unaware of the assumptions that make them unaware.	*Level of threat:* Double-loop learning activities will lead people to question their sense of competence and and confidence, as well as their capacity to create the kind of justice they value.
Most individuals use reasoning processes that decrease their ability to detect and correct double-loop errors. Most are unaware of their reasoning processes; they remain sane because they deal with this root problem by distancing themselves from the consequences (all of us tend to do this).	*Key role of reasoning, disconnection, and distancing:* Individuals will come to learn that the suppression of feelings, or the unawareness of one's feelings, is important, but it is not as basic an issue as the disconnection from one's reasoning processes and the flaws in those reasoning processes. Individuals will also learn that the distancing they use to make their everyday life manageable leads to a social pollution that in the long run may make them feel that they are society's prisoners, leading impossible lives.

Table 1 *continued*

From the finding that	The implication about
Organizations contain learning systems that reinforce the organizational entropy in any given situation.	*Key targets:* Organizational activities that focus on altering individual theories-in-use must also focus on altering the learning systems (which include such features as the politics, the win/lose dynamics of coalition, the norms against risk-taking, the hiding of error, and the concealment that error is being hidden). Alteration of organizations so that they can double-loop learn will be genuine (and will not bypass or be limited) if individuals learn to produce actions in congruence with Model II theories-in-use. Such learning will lead to Model O-II learning systems in organizations.
Model I theories-in-use are probably one of the most powerful consequences of the socialization process. They are at the core of the society and culture in which we are embedded.	All organizational development programs necessarily impinge on the larger social and cultural milieu in which individuals and organizations are embedded. Strictly speaking, there is no organizational development of the kind we are referring to without societal and cultural changes.
Individuals learn at different rates, and the pace may vary for the same person under different conditions. This implies that the pace at which organizational factors change will vary also.	*Pace of learning:* Although the processes used, and the objectives, can be defined relatively clearly, the pace of achievement cannot be accurately predicted. A slow pace is not necessarily a sign of resistance, nor is a fast pace necessarily a sign of genuine acceptance. Nor is a fast pace followed by a slow one necessarily a sign of difficulty. It may mean that the person is dealing with an especially threatening issue. Organizational development activities should test continually and publicly to determine whether the learning is genuine and lasting.

REFERENCES

Allison, G. T. (1971), *Essence of Decision: Explaining the Cuban Missile Crisis*, Boston, Mass.: Little, Brown.

Argyris, C. (1976), *Increasing Leadership Effectiveness*, New York: Wiley.

Argyris, C. (1980), *Inner Contradictions of Vigorous Research*, New York: Academic Press.

Argyris, C. (1982), *Reasoning, Learning, and Action: Individual and Organizational*, San Francisco, Calif.: Jossey-Bass.

Argyris, C., & Schön, D. A. (1974), *Theory in Practice*, San Francisco, Calif.: Jossey-Bass.

Argyris, C., & Schön, D. A. (1978), *Organizational Learning*, Reading, Mass.: Addison-Wesley.

Bacharach, S. B., & Lawler, E. J. (1980), *Power in Politics in Organizations*, San Francisco, Calif.: Jossey-Bass.

Baldridge, J. V. (1971), *Power and Conflict in the University: Research in the Sociology of Organizations*, New York: Wiley.

Cyert, R. M., & March, J. G. (1963), *A Behavioral Theory of the Firm*, Englewood Cliffs, NJ: Prentice Hall.

Lewin, K. (1946), 'Action research and minority problems', *Journal of Social Issues*, 2(4), 34–46.

Marrow, A. J. (1969), *The Practical Theorist: The Life and Work of Kurt Lewin*, New York: Basic Books.

Pettigrew, A. M. (1973), *The Politics of Organizational Decision Making*, London: Tavistock Publications.

Smith, D. M. (1982), *Maintaining the Status Quo*, Cambridge, Mass.: Harvard University.

42

RICHARD E. WALTON

From Control to Commitment in the Workplace

Abridged from R. E. Walton, 'From control to commitment in the workplace', *Harvard Business Review*, Vol. 63 (2), 1985, pp. 77–84.

The larger shape of institutional change is always difficult to recognize when one stands right in the middle of it. Today, throughout American industry, a significant change is under way in long-established approaches to the organization and management of work.

The 'control' strategy

The traditional – or control-oriented – approach to workforce management took shape during the early part of this century in response to the division of work into small, fixed jobs for which individuals could be held accountable. The actual definition of jobs, as of acceptable standards of performance, rested on 'lowest common denominator' assumptions about workers' skill and motivation. To monitor and control effort of this assumed caliber, management organized its own responsibilities into a hierarchy of specialized roles buttressed by a top-down allocation of authority and by status symbols attached to positions in the hierarchy.

For workers, compensation followed the rubric of 'a fair day's pay for a fair day's work' because precise evaluations were possible when individual job requirements were so carefully prescribed. Most managers had little doubt that labor was best thought of as a variable cost, although some exceptional companies guaranteed job security to head off unionization attempts.

In the traditional approach, there was generally little policy definition with regard to employee voice unless the workforce was unionized, in which case damage control strategies predominated. With no union, management relied on an open-door policy, attitude surveys, and similar devices to learn about employees' concerns. If the workforce was unionized, then management bargained terms of employment and established an appeal mechanism. These activities fell to labor relations specialists, who operated independently from line management and whose very existence assumed the inevitability and even the appropriateness of an adversarial relationship between workers and managers. Indeed, to those who saw management's exclusive obligation to be to a company's shareowners and the ownership of property to be the ultimate source of both obligation and prerogative, the claims of employees were constraints, nothing more.

At the heart of this traditional model is the wish to establish order, exercise control, and achieve efficiency in the application of the workforce. Although it has distant antecedents in the bureaucracies of both church and military, the model's real father is Frederick W. Taylor, the turn-of-the-century 'father of scientific management', whose views about the proper organization of work have long influenced management practice as well as the reactive policies of the US labor movement [see Reading 30].

Recently, however, changing expectations among workers have prompted a growing disillusionment with the apparatus of control. At the same time, of course, an intensified challenge from abroad has made the competitive obsolescence of this strategy clear. A model that assumes low employee commitment and that is designed to produce reliable if not outstanding performance simply cannot match the standards of excellence set by world-class competitors. Especially in a high-wage country like the United States, market success depends on a superior level of performance, a level that, in turn, requires the deep commitment, not merely the obedience – if you could obtain it – of workers. And as painful experience shows, this commitment cannot flourish in a workplace dominated by the familiar model of control.

The 'commitment' strategy

Since the early 1970s, companies have experimented at the plant level with a radically different workforce strategy. The more visible pioneers have begun to show how great and productive the contribution of a truly committed workforce can be. For a time, all new plants of this sort were non-union, but by 1980 the success of efforts undertaken jointly with unions was impressive enough to encourage managers of both new and existing facilities to rethink their approach to the workforce.

Stimulated in part by the dramatic turnaround at GM's Tarrytown assembly plant in the mid-1970s, local managers and union officials are increasingly talking about common interests, working to develop mutual trust, and agreeing to sponsor quality-of-work-life (QWL) or employee involvement (EI) activities.

A growing number of manufacturing companies has begun to remove levels of plant hierarchy, increase managers' spans of control, integrate quality and production activities at lower organizational levels, combine production and maintenance operations, and open up new career possibilities for workers. Some corporations have even begun to chart organizational renewal for the entire company.

In this new commitment-based approach to the workforce, jobs are designed to be broader than before, to combine planning and implementation, and to include efforts to upgrade operations, not just maintain them. Individual responsibilities are expected to change as conditions change, and teams, not individuals, often are the organizational units accountable for performance. With management hierarchies relatively flat and differences in status minimized, control and lateral coordination depend on shared goals, and expertise rather than formal position determines influence.

Under the commitment strategy, performance expectations are high and serve not to define minimum standards but to provide 'stretch objectives', emphasize continuous improvement, and reflect the requirements of the market-place. Accordingly, compensation policies reflect less the old formulas of job evaluation than the heightened importance of group achievement, the expanded scope of individual contribution, and the growing concern of such questions of 'equity' as gainsharing, stock ownership, and profit sharing.

Equally important to the commitment strategy is the challenge of giving employees some assurance of security, perhaps by offering them priority in training and retraining as old jobs are eliminated and new ones created. Guaranteeing employees access to due process and providing them the means to be heard on such issues as production methods, problem solving, and human-resource policies and practices is also a challenge. In unionized settings, the additional tasks include making relations less adversarial, broadening the agenda for joint problem solving and planning, and facilitating employee consultation.

Underlying all these policies is a management philosophy, often embodied in a published statement, that acknowledges the legitimate claims of a company's multiple stakeholders – owners, employees, customers, and the public. At the center of this philosophy is a belief that eliciting employee commitment will lead to enhanced performance. The evidence shows this belief to be well-grounded. In the absence of genuine commitment, however, new management policies designed for a committed workforce may well leave a company distinctly more vulnerable than would older policies based on the control approach. The advantages – and risks – are considerable.

THE COSTS OF COMMITMENT

Because the potential leverage of a commitment-oriented strategy on performance is so great, the natural temptation is to assume the universal applicability of that strategy. Some environments, however, especially those requiring intricate teamwork, problem solving, organizational learning, and self-monitoring, are better suited than others to the commitment model. Indeed, the pioneers of the deep commitment strategy – a fertilizer plant in Norway, a refinery in the United Kingdom, a paper mill in Pennsylvania, a pet-food processing plant in Kansas – were all based on continuous-process technologies and were all capital and raw-material intensive. All provided high economic leverage to improvements in workers' skills and attitudes, and all could offer considerable job challenge.

Is the converse true? Is the control strategy appropriate whenever – as with convicts breaking rocks with sledgehammers in a prison yard – work can be completely prescribed, remains static, and calls for individual, not group, effort? In practice, managers have long answered yes. Mass production, epitomized by the assembly line, has for years been thought suitable for old-fashioned control.

But not any longer. Many mass producers, not least the automakers, have recently been trying to reconceive the structure of work and to give employees a significant role in solving problems and improving methods. Why? For many reasons, including to boost in-plant quality, lower warranty costs, cut waste, raise machine utilization and total capacity with the same plant and equipment, reduce operating and support personnel, reduce turnover and absenteeism, and speed up implementation of change. In addition, some managers place direct value on the fact that the commitment policies promote the development of human skills and individual self-esteem.

The benefits, economic and human, of worker commitment extend not only to continuous-process industries but to traditional manufacturing industries as well. What, though, are the costs? To achieve these gains, managers have had to invest extra effort, develop new skills and relationships, cope with higher levels of ambiguity and uncertainty, and experience the pain and discomfort associated with changing habits and attitudes. Some of their skills have become obsolete, and some of their careers have been casualties of change. Union officials, too, have had to face the dislocation and discomfort that inevitably follow any upheaval in attitudes and skills. For their part, workers have inherited more responsibility and, along with it, greater uncertainty and a more open-ended possibility of failure.

Part of the difficulty in assessing these costs is the fact that so many of the following problems inherent to the commitment strategy remain to be solved.

Employment assurances

As managers in heavy industry confront economic realities that make such assurances less feasible and as their counterparts in fiercely competitive high-technology areas are forced to rethink early guarantees of employment security, pointed questions await.

Will managers give lifetime assurances to the few, those who reach, say, fifteen years' seniority, or will they adopt a general no-layoff policy? Will they demonstrate by policies and practices that employment security, though by no means absolute, is a higher priority item than it was under the control approach? Will they accept greater responsibility for outplacement?

Compensation

In one sense, the more productive employees under the commitment approach deserve to receive better pay for their better efforts, but how can managers balance this claim on resources with the harsh reality that domestic pay rates have risen to levels that render many of our industries uncompetitive internationally? Already, in such industries as trucking and airlines, new domestic competitors have placed companies that maintain prevailing wage rates at a significant disadvantage. Experience shows, however, that wage freezes and concession bargaining create obstacles to commitment, and new approaches to compensation are difficult to develop at a time when management cannot raise the overall level of pay.

Which approach is really suitable to the commitment model is unclear. Traditional job classifications place limits on the discretion of supervisors and encourage workers' sense of job ownership. Can pay systems based on employees' skill levels, which have long been used in engineering and skilled crafts, prove widely effective? Can these systems make up in greater mastery, positive motivation, and workforce flexibility what they give away in higher average wages?

In capital-intensive business, where total payroll accounts for a small percentage of costs, economics favor the move toward pay progression based on deeper and broader mastery. Still, conceptual problems remain with measuring skills, achieving consistency in pay decisions, allocating opportunities for learning new skills, trading off breadth and flexibility against depth, and handling the effects of 'topping out' in a system that rewards and encourages personal growth.

There are also practical difficulties. Existing plants cannot, for example, convert to a skill-based structure overnight because of the vested interests of employees in the higher classifications. Similarly, formal profit- or gainsharing plans like the Scanlon Plan (which shares gains in productivity as measured by improvements in the ratio of payroll to the sales value of production) cannot always operate. At the plant level, formulas that are responsive to what employees can influence, that are not unduly influenced by factors beyond their control, and that are readily understood are not easy to devise. Small stand-alone businesses with a mature technology and stable markets tend to find the task least troublesome, but they are not the only ones trying to implement the commitment approach.

Yet another problem is the relationship between compensation decisions affecting salaried managers and professionals, on the one hand, and hourly workers, on the other. A manager's ability to elicit and preserve commitment, however, is sensitive to issues of equity.

Technology

Computer-based technology can reinforce the control model or facilitate movement to the commitment model. Applications can narrow the scope of jobs or broaden them, emphasize the individual nature of tasks or promote the work of groups, centralize or decentralize the making of decisions, and create performance measures that emphasize learning or hierarchical control.

To date, the effects of this technology on control and commitment have been largely unintentional and unexpected. Even in organizations otherwise pursuing a commitment strategy, managers have rarely appreciated that the side-effects of technology are not somehow 'given' in the nature of things or that they can be actively managed. In fact, computer-based technology may be the least deterministic, most flexible technology to enter the workplace since the industrial revolution. As it becomes less hardware-dependent and more software-intensive and as the cost of computer power declines, the variety of ways to meet business requirements expands, each with a different set of human implications. Management has yet to identify the potential role of technology policy in the commitment strategy, and it has yet to invent concepts and methods to realize that potential.

Supervisors

The commitment model requires first-line supervisors to facilitate rather than direct the workforce, to impart rather than merely practice their technical and administrative expertise, and to help workers develop the ability to manage themselves. In practice, supervisors are to delegate away most of their traditional functions – often without having received adequate training and support for their new team-building tasks or having their own needs for voice, dignity, and fulfillment recognized.

These dilemmas are even visible in the new titles many supervisors carry – 'team advisers' or 'team consultants', for example – most of which imply that supervisors are not in the chain of command, although they are expected to be directive if necessary and assume functions delegated to the workforce if they are not being performed. Part of the confusion here is the failure to distinguish the behavioral style required of supervisors from the basic responsibilities assigned them. Their ideal style may be advisory, but their responsibilities are to achieve certain human and economic outcomes. With experience, however, as first-line managers become more comfortable with the notion of delegating what subordinates are ready and able to perform, the problem will diminish.

Other difficulties are less tractable. The new breed of supervisors must have a level of interpersonal skill and conceptual ability often lacking in the present supervisory workforce. Some companies have tried to address this lack by using the position as an entry point to management for college graduates. This approach may succeed where the workforce has already acquired the necessary technical expertise, but it blocks a route of advancement for workers and sharpens the dividing line between management and other employees. Moreover, unless the company intends to open up higher-level positions for these college-educated supervisors, they may well grow impatient with the shift work of first-line supervision.

Even when new supervisory roles are filled – and filled successfully – from the ranks, dilemmas remain. With teams developed and functions delegated, to what new challenges do they turn to utilize fully their own capabilities? Do those capabilities match the demands of the other managerial work they might take on? If fewer and fewer supervisors are required as their individual span of control extends to a second and a third work team, what promotional opportunities exist for the rest? Where do they go?

Union–management relations

Some companies, as they move from control to commitment, seek to decertify their unions and, at the same time, strengthen their employees' bond to the company. Others pursue cooperation with their unions, believing that they need their active support. Management's interest in cooperation intensified in the late 1970s, as improved workforce effectiveness could not by itself close the competitive gap in many industries and wage concessions became necessary. On the basis of their own analysis of competitive conditions, unions sometimes agreed to these concessions but expanded their influence over matters previously subject to management control.

These developments open up new questions. Where companies are trying to preserve the non-union status of some plants and yet promote collaborative union relations in others, will unions increasingly force the company to choose? If forced to choose, what will other managements do? Further, where union and management have collaborated in promoting QWL, how can the union prevent management from using the program to appeal directly to the workers about issues, such as wage concessions, that are subject to collective bargaining?

And if, in the spirit of mutuality, both sides agree to expand their joint agenda, what new risks will they face? Do union officials have the expertise to deal effectively with new agenda items like investment, pricing, and technology? To support QWL activities, they already have had to expand their skills and commit substantial resources at a time when shrinking employment has reduced their membership and thus their finances.

THE TRANSITIONAL STAGE

Although some organizations have adopted a comprehensive version of the commitment approach, most initially take on a more limited set of changes, which I refer to as a 'transitional' stage or approach. The challenge here is to modify expectations, to make credible the leaders' stated intentions for further movement, and to support the initial changes in behavior. These transitional efforts can achieve a temporary equilibrium, provided they are viewed as part of a movement toward a comprehensive commitment strategy.

The cornerstone of the transitional stage is the voluntary participation of employees in problem-solving groups like quality circles. In unionized organizations, union–management dialogue leading to a jointly sponsored program is a condition for this type of employee involvement, which must then be supported by additional training and communication and by a shift in management style. Managers must also seek ways to consult employees about changes that affect them and to assure them that management will make every effort to avoid, defer, or minimize layoffs from higher productivity. When volume-related layoffs or concessions on pay are unavoidable, the principle of 'equality of sacrifice' must apply to all employee groups, not just the hourly workforce.

As a rule, during the early stages of transformation, few immediate changes can occur in the basic design of jobs, the compensation system, or the management system itself. It is easy, of course, to attempt to change too much too soon. A more common error, especially in established organizations, is to make only 'token' changes that never reach a critical mass. All too often managers try a succession of technique-oriented changes one by one: job enrichment, sensitivity training, management by objectives, group brainstorming, quality circles, and so on. Whatever the benefits of these techniques, their value to the organization will rapidly decay if the management philosophy – and practice – does not shift accordingly.

A different type of error – 'over-reaching' – may occur in newly established organizations based on commitment principles. In one new plant, managers allowed too much peer influence in pay decisions; in another, they underplayed the role of first-line supervisors as a link in the chain of command; in a third, they overemphasized learning of new skills and flexibility at the expense of mastery in critical operations. These design errors by themselves are not fatal, but the organization must be able to make mid-course corrections.

RATE OF TRANSFORMATION

How rapidly is the transformation in workforce strategy occurring? Hard data are difficult to come by, but certain trends are clear. In 1970, only a few plants in the United States were systematically revising their approach to the workforce. By 1975, hundreds of plants were involved. Today, I estimate that at least a thousand plants are in the process of making a comprehensive change and that many times that number are somewhere in the transitional stage.

In the early 1970s, plant managers tended to sponsor what efforts there were. Today, company presidents are formulating the plans. Not long ago, the initiatives were experimental; now they are policy. Early change focused on the blue-collar workforce and on those clerical operations that most closely resemble the factory. Although clerical change has lagged somewhat – because the control model has not produced such overt employee disaffection, and because management has been slow to recognize the importance of quality and productivity improvement – there are signs of a quickened pace of change in clerical operations.

Only a small fraction of US workplaces today can boast of a comprehensive commitment strategy, but the rate of transformation continues to accelerate, and the move toward commitment via some explicit transitional stage extends to a still larger number of plants and offices. This transformation may be fueled by economic necessity, but other factors are shaping and pacing it – individual leadership in management and labor, philosophical choices, organizational competence in managing change, and cumulative learning from change itself.

Further Readings

PART A: UNDERSTANDING HUMAN MOTIVATION

Section I: Basic Needs and Human Nature: The Content of Motivation

Deci, E. L., & Ryan, R. M. (1985), *Intrinsic Motivation and Self-Determination in Human Behavior*, New York: Plenum.

Maslow, A. H. (1970), *Motivation and Personality* (2nd edn), New York: Harper & Row.

Murray, H. A. (1938), *Explorations in Personality*, New York: Oxford University Press.

Skinner, B. F. (1953), *Science and Human Behavior*, New York: Macmillan.

Section II: Reinforcements and Goals: The Process of Motivation

Bandura, A. (1986), *Social Foundations of Thought and Action: A Social Cognitive Theory*, Englewood Cliffs, NJ: Prentice Hall.

House, R. J. (1971), 'A path–goal theory of leader effectiveness', *Administrative Science Quarterly*, *16*, 321–38.

Porter, L. W., & Lawler, E. E., III (1968), *Managerial Attitudes and Performance*, Homewood, Ill.: Irwin-Dorsey.

Vroom, V. H. (1964), *Work and Motivation*, New York: Wiley.

Section III: Social and Group Influences on Motivation

Aronson, E. (1988), *The Social Animal* (5th edn), San Francisco: Freeman.

Asch, S. E. (1958), 'The effects of group pressure upon the modification and distortion of judgments', in E. E. Maccoby, T. E. Newcomb, & E. L. Hartley (eds.), *Readings in Social Psychology* (pp. 174–83), New York: Holt.

Milgram, S. (1974), *Obedience to Authority*, New York: Harper & Row.

Shaw, M. E. (1976), *Group Dynamics: The Psychology of Small Group Behavior*, New York: McGraw-Hill.

PART B: MOTIVATION IN WORK SETTINGS

Section IV: Motivation, Satisfaction, and Performance: Persons and Contexts

Brayfield, A. H., & Crockett, W. H. (1955), 'Employee attitudes and employee performance', *Psychological Bulletin*, *52*, 396–424.

Latham, G. P., Cummings, L. L., & Mitchell, T. R. (1981), 'Behavioral strategies to improve productivity', *Organizational Dynamics*, *8* (3), 5–23.

Locke, E. A., & Latham, G. P. (1990), *A Theory of Goal Setting and Task Performance*, Englewood Cliffs, NJ: Prentice Hall.

McClelland, D. C. (1985), *Human Motivation*, Glenview, Ill.: Scott, Foresman.

Section V: Making the Job More Motivating

Gyllenhammar, P. G. (1977), 'How Volvo adapts work to people', *Harvard Business Review*, *54* (4), 102–13.

Hackman, J. R., & Oldham, G. R. (1980), *Work Redesign*, Reading, Mass.: Addison-Wesley.

Herzberg, F. (1966), *Work and the Nature of Man*, New York: World.

Myers, M. S. (1970), *Every Employee a Manager*, New York: McGraw-Hill.

Section VI: Performance Evaluations and Reward Structures

Kerr, S. (1975), 'On the fallacy of rewarding A, while hoping for B', *Academy of Management Journal*, *18*, 769–83.

Lawler, E. E., III (1981), *Pay and Organization Development*, Reading, Mass.: Addison-Wesley.

Myers, H. H. (1975, Winter), 'The pay for performance dilemma', *Organizational Dynamics*, 39–49.

Zander, A. F. (ed.) (1963), *Performance Appraisals: Effects on Employees and Their Performance*, Ann Arbor, Mich.: Foundation for Research on Human Behavior.

PART C: UNDERSTANDING MANAGEMENT AND MOTIVATION

Section VII: An Historical Perspective: Theories of Management

Drucker, P. F. (1974), *Management: Tasks, Responsibilities, Practices*, New York: Harper & Row.

McGregor, D. (1960), *The Human Side of Enterprise*, New York: McGraw-Hill.

Marrow, A. J., Bowers, D. G., & Seashore, S. E. (1967), *Management by Participation*, New York: Harper & Row.

Roethlisberger, F.J., & Dickson, W. J. (1939), *Management and the Worker*, Cambridge, Mass.: Harvard University Press.

Section VIII: Contemporary Behavioral Approaches to Management

Leavitt, H. J. (1986), *Corporate Pathfinders*, Homewood, Ill.: Dow Jones-Irwin.

Ouchi, W. G. (1981), *Theory Z*, Reading, Mass.: Addison-Wesley.

Peters, T. J., & Waterman, R. H. (1982), *In Search of Excellence*, New York: Harper & Row.

Vroom, V. H., & Jago, A. G. (1988), *The New Leadership: Managing Participation in Organizations*, Englewood Cliffs, NJ: Prentice Hall.

Section IX: Organization Change and Development

Argyris, C. (1970), *Intervention Theory and Method*, Reading, Mass.: Addison-Wesley.

Bennis, W., & Nanus, B. (1985), *Leaders*, New York: Harper & Row.

Coch, L., & French, J. R. P. (1948), 'Overcoming resistance to change', *Human Relations*, *1* (4), 512–33.

French, W. L., & Bell, C. H. (1973), *Organization Development*, Englewood Cliffs, NJ: Prentice Hall.

Acknowledgements

Permission to reproduce the readings in this volume is acknowledged from the following sources:

Reading 1   Random House, Inc., and Jonathan Cape Ltd.
Reading 4   W. C. Hamner
Reading 5   American Psychological Association and A. Bandura
Reading 6   Harper Collins Publishers
Reading 7   American Psychological Association
Reading 8   American Psychological Association and P. E. Spector
Reading 9   Brooks/Cole Publishing Company
Reading 10   Academic Press, Inc., and J. S. Adams
Reading 11   American Association for the Advancement of Science and R. B. Zajonc
Reading 12   American Psychological Association and M. Deutsch
Reading 13   Institute for Social Research, University of Michigan
Reading 14   John Wiley & Sons, Inc.
Reading 15   Institute of Industrial Relations, University of California at Berkeley
Reading 16   American Management Association
Reading 17   Johnson Graduate School of Management, Cornell University
Reading 18   American Psychological Association, B. M. Staw and J. Ross
Reading 19   *Harvard Business Review*
Reading 20   Personnel Psychology, Inc., and Edward E. Lawler, III
Reading 21   *Harvard Business Review*
Reading 22   Addison-Wesley Publishing Co., Inc.
Reading 23   American Psychological Association and Edward L. Deci
Reading 24   *Harvard Business Review*
Reading 25   *Harvard Business Review*
Reading 26   American Psychological Association, R. L. Opsahl and M. D. Dunnette
Reading 27   American Psychological Association
Reading 28   *Harvard Business Review*

Reading 29   *Harvard Business Review*
Reading 31   Penguin Books Ltd.
Reading 32   MIT Press
Reading 33   McGraw-Hill Publishing Company
Reading 34   Society for Human Resource Management
Reading 35   American Management Association
Reading 36   Jossey-Bass, Inc.
Reading 37   Jossey-Bass, Inc.
Reading 38   MCB University Press
Reading 39   John Wiley & Sons, Inc.
Reading 40   John Wiley & Sons, Inc.
Reading 41   JAI Press, Inc.
Reading 42   *Harvard Business Review*

The publishers would be pleased to hear from any copyright holders not here acknowledged. Readings 2, 3 and 30 are in the public domain.

Author Index

Subject Index

Discover more about our forthcoming books through Penguin's FREE newspaper...

READ MORE IN PENGUIN

In every corner of the world, on every subject under the sun, Penguin represents quality and variety – the very best in publishing today.

For complete information about books available from Penguin – including Puffins, Penguin Classics and Arkana – and how to order them, write to us at the appropriate address below. Please note that for copyright reasons the selection of books varies from country to country.

In the United Kingdom: Please write to *Dept. EP, Penguin Books Ltd, Bath Road, Harmondsworth, West Drayton, Middlesex UB7 ODA*

In the United States: Please write to *Consumer Sales, Penguin USA, P.O. Box 999, Dept. 17109, Bergenfield, New Jersey 07621-0120*. VISA and MasterCard holders call 1-800-253-6476 to order Penguin titles

In Canada: Please write to *Penguin Books Canada Ltd, 10 Alcorn Avenue, Suite 300, Toronto, Ontario M4V 3B2*

In Australia: Please write to *Penguin Books Australia Ltd, P.O. Box 257, Ringwood, Victoria 3134*

In New Zealand: Please write to *Penguin Books (NZ) Ltd, Private Bag 102902, North Shore Mail Centre, Auckland 10*

In India: Please write to *Penguin Books India Pvt Ltd, 706 Eros Apartments, 56 Nehru Place, New Delhi 110 019*

In the Netherlands: Please write to *Penguin Books Netherlands bv, Postbus 3507, NL-1001 AH Amsterdam*

In Germany: Please write to *Penguin Books Deutschland GmbH, Metzlerstrasse 26, 60594 Frankfurt am Main*

In Spain: Please write to *Penguin Books S. A., Bravo Murillo 19, 1º B, 28015 Madrid*

In Italy: Please write to *Penguin Italia s.r.l., Via Felice Casati 20, I–20124 Milano*

In France: Please write to *Penguin France S. A., 17 rue Lejeune, F–31000 Toulouse*

In Japan: Please write to *Penguin Books Japan, Ishikiribashi Building, 2–5–4, Suido, Bunkyo-ku, Tokyo 112*

In Greece: Please write to *Penguin Hellas Ltd, Dimocritou 3, GR–106 71 Athens*

In South Africa: Please write to *Longman Penguin Southern Africa (Pty) Ltd, Private Bag X08, Bertsham 2013*

READ MORE IN PENGUIN

POLITICS AND SOCIAL SCIENCES

National Identity Anthony D. Smith

In this stimulating new book, Anthony D. Smith asks why the first modern nation states developed in the West. He considers how ethnic origins, religion, language and shared symbols can provide a sense of nation and illuminates his argument with a wealth of detailed examples.

The Feminine Mystique Betty Friedan

'A brilliantly researched, passionately argued book – a time-bomb flung into the Mom-and-Apple-Pie image . . . Out of the debris of that shattered ideal, the Women's Liberation Movement was born' – Ann Leslie

Faith and Credit Susan George and Fabrizio Sabelli

In its fifty years of existence, the World Bank has influenced more lives in the Third World than any other institution yet remains largely unknown, even enigmatic. This richly illuminating and lively overview examines the policies of the Bank, its internal culture and the interests it serves.

Political Ideas Edited by David Thomson

From Machiavelli to Marx – a stimulating and informative introduction to the last 500 years of European political thinkers and political thought.

Structural Anthropology Volumes 1–2 Claude Lévi-Strauss

'That the complex ensemble of Lévi-Strauss's achievement . . . is one of the most original and intellectually exciting of the present age seems undeniable. No one seriously interested in language or literature, in sociology or psychology, can afford to ignore it' – George Steiner

Invitation to Sociology Peter L. Berger

Sociology is defined as 'the science of the development and nature and laws of human society'. But what is its purpose? Without belittling its scientific procedures Professor Berger stresses the humanistic affinity of sociology with history and philosophy. It is a discipline which encourages a fuller awareness of the human world . . . with the purpose of bettering it.

READ MORE IN PENGUIN

POLITICS AND SOCIAL SCIENCES

Conservatism   Ted Honderich

'It offers a powerful critique of the major beliefs of modern conservatism, and shows how much a rigorous philosopher can contribute to understanding the fashionable but deeply ruinous absurdities of his times' – *New Statesman & Society*

The Battle for Scotland   Andrew Marr

A nation without a parliament of its own, Scotland has been wrestling with its identity and status for a century. In this excellent and up-to-date account of the distinctive history of Scottish politics, Andrew Marr uses party and individual records, pamphlets, learned works, interviews and literature to tell a colourful and often surprising account.

Bricks of Shame: Britain's Prisons   Vivien Stern

'Her well-researched book presents a chillingly realistic picture of the British sytstem and lucid argument for changes which could and should be made before a degrading and explosive situation deteriorates still further' – *Sunday Times*

Inside the Third World   Paul Harrison

This comprehensive book brings home a wealth of facts and analysis on the often tragic realities of life for the poor people and communities of Asia, Africa and Latin America.

'Just like a Girl'   Sue Sharpe
How Girls Learn to be Women

Sue Sharpe's unprecedented research and analysis of the attitudes and hopes of teenage girls from four London schools has become a classic of its kind. This new edition focuses on girls in the nineties – some of whom could even be the daughters of the teenagers she interviewed in the seventies – and represents their views and ideas on education, work, marriage, gender roles, feminism and women's rights.

READ MORE IN PENGUIN

A CHOICE OF NON-FICTION

Citizens   Simon Schama

'The most marvellous book I have read about the French Revolution in the last fifty years' – *The Times*. 'He has chronicled the vicissitudes of that world with matchless understanding, wisdom, pity and truth, in the pages of this huge and marvellous book' – *Sunday Times*

Heisenberg's War   Thomas Powers

'Heisenberg was one of the few distinguished German scientists who, rather than accepting the chance to emigrate to the US, elected to stay and work for Hitler. How concertedly he helped the Nazi war effort is the subject of Thomas Powers's brilliantly researched and compellingly narrated *Heisenberg's War*' – *Independent on Sunday*

A Short Walk from Harrods   Dirk Bogarde

In this volume of memoirs, Dirk Bogarde pays tribute to the corner of Provence that was his home for over two decades, and to Forwood, his manager and friend of fifty years, whose long and wretched illness brought an end to a paradise. 'A brave and moving book' – *Daily Telegraph*

Murder in the Heart   Alexandra Artley
Winner of the CWA Gold Dagger Award for Non-Fiction

'A terrible and moving account of domestic violence leading to murder . . . a profound indictment of the world we live in' – Beryl Bainbridge. 'A grim account of human savagery, but it enlightens as much as it horrifies' – *The Times Literary Supplement*

Water Logic   Edward de Bono

Edward de Bono has always sought to provide practical thinking tools that are simple to use but powerful in action. In this book he turns his attention to providing a simple way of thinking about practical problems based on a visual 'flowscape'.

READ MORE IN PENGUIN

A CHOICE OF NON-FICTION

Stones of Empire   Jan Morris

There is no corner of India that does not contain some relic of the British presence, whether it is as grand as a palace or as modest as a pillar box. Jan Morris's study of the buildings of British India is as entertaining and enlightening on the nature of imperialism as it is on architecture.

Bitter Fame   Anne Stevenson

'A sobering and salutary attempt to estimate what Plath was, what she achieved and what it cost her ... This is the only portrait which answers Ted Hughes's image of the poet as Ariel, not the ethereal bright pure roving sprite, but Ariel trapped in Prospero's pine and raging to be free' – *Sunday Telegraph*

Here We Go   Harry Ritchie

From Fuengirola to Calahonda, *Here We Go* is an hilarious tour of the Costa del Sol ... with a difference! 'Simmering with self-mocking humour, it offers a glorious celebration of the traditions of the English tourist, reveals a Spain that Pedro Almodovar couldn't have conjured up in his worst nightmare, and character-assassinates every snob and pseud' – *Time Out*

Children First   Penelope Leach

Challenging the simplistic nostalgia of the 'family values' lobby, Leach argues that society today leaves little time for children and no easy way for adults – especially women – to be both solvent, self-respecting citizens and caring parents.

Young Men and Fire   Norman Maclean

On 5 August 1949, a crew of fifteen airborne firefighters, the Smokejumpers, stepped into the sky above a remote forest fire in the Montana wilderness. Less than an hour after their jump, all but three were dead or fatally burned. From their tragedy, Norman Maclean builds an unforgettable story of courage, hope and redemption.

READ MORE IN PENGUIN

BUSINESS AND ECONOMICS

North and South   David Smith

'This authoritative study ... gives a very effective account of the incredible centralization of decision-making in London, not just in government and administration, but in the press, communications and the management of every major company' – *New Statesman & Society*

I am Right – You are Wrong   Edward de Bono

Edward de Bono expects his ideas to outrage conventional thinkers, yet time has been on his side, and the ideas that he first put forward twenty years ago are now accepted mainstream thinking. Here, in this brilliantly argued assault on outmoded thought patterns, he calls for nothing less than a New Renaissance.

Lloyds Bank Small Business Guide   Sara Williams

This long-running guide to making a success of your small business deals with real issues in a practical way. 'As comprehensive an introduction to setting up a business as anyone could need' – *Daily Telegraph*

The *Economist* Economics   Rupert Pennant-Rea and Clive Crook

Based on a series of 'briefs' published in the *Economist* , this is a clear and accessible guide to the key issues of today's economics for the general reader.

The Rise and Fall of Monetarism   David Smith

Now that even Conservatives have consigned monetarism to the scrap heap of history, David Smith draws out the unhappy lessons of a fundamentally flawed economic experiment, driven by a doctrine that for years had been regarded as outmoded and irrelevant.

Understanding Organizations   Charles B. Handy

Of practical as well as theoretical interest, this book shows how general concepts can help solve specific organizational problems.

READ MORE IN PENGUIN

BUSINESS AND ECONOMICS

The Affluent Society   John Kenneth Galbraith

Classical economics was born in a harsh world of mass poverty, and it has left us with a set of preoccupations hard to adapt to the realities of our own richer age. Our unfamiliar problems need a new approach, and the reception given to this famous book has shown the value of its fresh, lively ideas.

Lloyds Bank Tax Guide   Sara Williams and John Willman

An average employee tax bill is over £4,000 a year. But how much time do you spend checking it? Four out of ten never check the bill – and most spend less than an hour. Mistakes happen. This guide can save YOU money. 'An unstuffy read, packed with sound information' – *Observer*

Trouble Shooter II   John Harvey-Jones

The former chairman of ICI and Britain's best-known businessman resumes his role as consultant to six British companies facing a variety of problems – and sharing a new one: the recession.

Managing on the Edge   Richard Pascale

Nothing fails like success: companies flourish, then lose their edge through a process that is both relentless and largely invisible. 'Pascale's analysis and prescription for "managing on the edge" are unusually subtle for such a readable business book' – *Financial Times*

The Money Machine: How the City Works   Philip Coggan

How are the big deals made? Which are the institutions that really matter? What causes the pound to rise or interest rates to fall? This book provides clear and concise answers to a huge variety of money-related questions.

READ MORE IN PENGUIN

BUSINESS